Alamo Traces

New Evidence and New Conclusions

Thomas Ricks Lindley

REPUBLIC OF TEXAS PRESS

Lanham • New York • Toronto • Oxford

Published by Republic of Texas Press
A Member of the Rowman & Littlefield Publishing Group
4501 Forbes Boulevard, Suite 200
Lanham, Maryland 20706

Distributed by NATIONAL BOOK NETWORK

Library of Congress Cataloging-in-Publication Data

Lindley, Thomas Ricks.
    Alamo traces : new evidence and new conclusions / Thomas Ricks Lindley.
        p. cm.
    Includes index.
    ISBN 1-55622-983-6 (alk. paper)
    1. Alamo (San Antonio, Tex.)—Siege, 1836. I. Title.

F390 .L54 2003
976.4'03—dc21   2002152692

⊖™ The paper used in this publication meets the minimum requirements of
American National Standard for Information Sciences—Permanence of
Paper for Printed Library Materials, ANSI/NISO Z39.48–1992.
Manufactured in the United States of America.

For
Alvy and Ethel Pullin

Contents

Foreword

If there is such a thing as a dispassionate Alamo scholar, I've never met one. Even the soberest and tweediest of academic historians seem to have been infatuated, at an impressionable age, by the mysterious blend of annihilation and redemption that is at the core of the Alamo myth.

From time to time Thomas Ricks Lindley has tried to sell me on the idea that he is an exception to this rule, that his own interest in the subject is purely a matter of rational historical inquiry. But I know Alamo obsession when I see it. All the signs are there: the Alamo baseball cap on Tom's head, the framed photograph of the cast of John Wayne's *The Alamo* on his wall, the dog buried in the backyard whose name had been—what else?—Alamo.

But the quality that distinguishes Tom Lindley from garden-variety Alamoheads like myself, and that sometimes contentiously sets him apart from eminent historians working the same ground, is his grinding focus. I first met him about ten years ago in the Texas State Archives when I was beginning the research on my novel *The Gates of the Alamo*, and that is where he is still likely to be found today, still reading through old letters and muster rolls and military claims in musty old files that have never before been examined with such relentless scrutiny, if they have even been examined at all.

People who make their livings writing or teaching history tend to be, at least to some degree, generalists. Their goal is not just to discover facts but to interpret those facts within a broader context of thesis or theory or narrative. Tom Lindley is not a professional historian in that way, but neither is he what is sometimes condescendingly described as an "avocational" or "recreational" historian. He is a dead-serious specialist, a relentless researcher who for a decade and a half has been on the trail of one single thing: the unambiguous truth of the events of the siege and storming of the Alamo in 1836.

Lindley's training for this work comes not from university instruction in historical methodology but from his early experience in the United

States Army as a criminal investigator, from which he developed habits and attitudes that are perhaps more characteristic of the pursuit of justice than of conventional scholarship. For instance, Lindley's innate skepticism is famous in the tight little world of Alamo researchers. Historians, of course, must routinely assay the relative credibility of their research material, but Lindley has a way of raising the stakes when it comes to considering whether or not a particular document is to be trusted. He seems to retain, from his days as an investigator, a visceral understanding that any source is apt to be lying. As a result, his tireless questioning of the authenticity or veracity of certain primary documents—from John Sutherland's 1860 personal account of the first day of the Alamo siege to, most notoriously, the narrative of Mexican captain Jose Enrique de la Pena—has helped to hold Alamo research to a higher standard of credibility, even if it does occasionally annoy other historians who complain that Lindley has never met a document he likes.

His days as a criminal investigator might help to explain another quality in his work, the sense of an urgent and personal quest. Talking to Tom about his discoveries, sometimes arguing with him about his conclusions, I've often come away with the conviction that he is trying to solve not just a historical puzzle but an actual crime. In the case of the Alamo, the crime in question is what has been allowed to pass for the historical record.

In *Alamo Traces,* he attacks this record with such authority and doggedness that it is hard to imagine anyone writing about the Alamo in the future who would not have to seriously wrangle with his reassessments and reinterpretations. As Lindley himself admits, his book is not a popular history. It is, instead, a methodical, piece-by-piece dismantling of what we thought we knew, combined with convincing speculation about what might have really happened.

People will argue with some of Lindley's conclusions. No doubt there will be a howl of outrage among Sam Houston's many partisans after they have read the first chapter, in which the once-unassailable hero of the Texas revolution is indicted for what Lindley regards as his duplicitous inaction during the siege of the Alamo. And there will certainly be readers who will continue to cling to the image of Colonel William B. Travis drawing a line in the sand, despite Lindley's definitive discrediting of that beloved story. But *Alamo Traces* is the farthest thing from a revisionist manifesto. It may take on a cherished historical chestnut or two, but it does so with the intention of casting a clear light rather than a dark shadow. At the same time it also offers an abundance of new information, particularly in its groundbreaking chapters on the hitherto-unknown attempts to reinforce the Alamo.

Alamo Traces is a book that must and will be reckoned with. It burrows deep into the historical record, shovels away deposits of myth and folklore and faulty assumptions that are generations deep, and never wavers in its search for a bedrock level of fact. It is a book that showcases a lifetime of fervent research and marks an audacious new direction for Alamo scholarship.

Stephen Harrigan

Acknowledgments

I owe a debt of thanks to many individuals who helped me in researching and writing this book. Foremost, *Alamo Traces: New Evidence and New Conclusions* would not have been written without the encouragement and support of former state Supreme Court justice Jack Hightower. Writer Steve Harrigan read the manuscript and offered advice on how to improve the writing and organization of the book. Steve also wrote a foreword for the work. Artist and historian Jack Jackson read some of the chapters and offered suggestions for improvement. Moreover, Jack shared some of his research on the Mexican army and drew me a map. Historian William C. "Jack" Davis also shared a number of Mexican documents he had found in researching *Three Roads to the Alamo* and furnished a back cover promotional blurb. He also read the manuscript and offered his help in locating a publisher. Historian Stephen Hardin furnished support and often acted as a sounding board for my arguments and interpretations. Dr. Jim Lutzweiler read the Moses/Louis Rose chapters and made a number of criticisms. Historian and researcher Dorcas Baumgarter, who probably knows more about Gonzales County than any other person, shared an unknown Susanna Dickinson interview with me. Lee Spencer-White of Freer, Texas, furnished me with names and evidence for two new Alamo defenders. Rod Timanus made some useful observations concerning the Jose Enrique de la Pena memoir manuscript. Bill Groneman allowed me the use of his research on forgery detection. Also, Bill was an important sounding board in regard to my Pena analysis. Dr. David B. Gracy II always answered my questions in regard to his point of view on the authenticity of the Pena manuscripts. Historian Jesus F. (Frank) de la Teja read an early draft of the manuscript. He made a number of important suggestions on how to improve the work. Dr. "Red" Duke of the University of Texas Medical School at Houston helped with information about wounds. Elias J. Dugie and Doyle Colwell were very generous in allowing me on their farm and ranch land in my search for the old road bed of the Gonzales to San Antonio road. Historian Paul A. Hutton has always been supportive and interested in my research. Historian David J. Weber read an early draft of the Houston chapter and furnished a back cover blurb. His comments were generous, gracious, and helpful.

Then there were certain individuals employed at the various libraries and archives who helped a great deal. The Texas General Land Office operates one of three state archives in Austin. The division was well managed before David Dewhurst took over as Land Commissioner. Today, the Land Office archives are, bar none, including the University of Texas, the best archives operation in the state of Texas. Fortunately, Dewhurst had the ability to listen to the improvement ideas of his archival staff. Susan Smith-Dorsey, Carol Finney, John Molleston, Kevin Klaus, Jerry C. Drake, Bobby Santiesteban, and Galen Greaser were always friendly, professional, and knowledgeable in the assistance they gave me. Whatever the subject: land, oil, history, cartography, or genealogy, the Land Office "information specialists" can generally find the answer or point one in the right direction. John Molleston and Jerry Drake made me aware of an untapped collection of land grant applications that contained new Alamo data.

The Texas State Library also has a pretty good archives operation, second only to the Land Office. Eddie Williams, the former copy person, was extremely helpful to me. She made thousands of copies for me and I never had reason to complain. When she retired she left some big shoes to fill. Former reference archivist Michael R. Green alerted me to Alamo documents that I would never have found on my own. Donaly E. Brice and Jean Carefoot were always able to answer my questions or tell me where to look for an answer. John Anderson helped me locate the pictures I needed and took the photos of the Jose Enrique de la Pena handwriting samples.

The Daughters of the Republic of Texas Library on the Alamo grounds had a few documents that proved useful. Alamo historian and curator Dr. Richard B. Winders has been supportive of my work. Dora Guerra, Martha Utterback, and Rusty Gamez always bent over backwards to help me. Dora was most helpful when she was director of the Special Collections at the University of Texas at San Antonio. She made copies of pages from the Pena manuscripts that later proved to be very helpful after the collection was broken up and sold. The late Bernice Strong was also very helpful in the last few months she worked at the DRT Library.

Ralph Elder and John Wheat at the Center for American History, the former Eugene C. Barker Texas History Center, at the University of Texas at Austin helped immensely. Ned Brierley made numerous copies and a number of excellent Spanish translations. Kathryn Kenefick has been extremely helpful in recent days. Her friendly smile and professional attitude are a welcome addition to that operation. Upstairs at the Texas State Historical Association, Ron Tyler and George B. Ward have always welcomed me and have been willing to let me bounce my research and ideas off their reflecting minds.

The staff at Nacogdoches County Courthouse archives and the East Texas Research Center at Stephen F. Austin University in Nacogdoches helped me locate what was left of the original Louis Rose land grant documents. Cassey Edward Greene at the Rosenberg Library at Galveston did the same in regard to a James Bowie document.

Special thanks to Brian Huberman and Cynthia Wolf for their support and inclusion in their film work. They have been good company in the long debate over the reality of the Pena memoir.

Fellow members and friends in the Alamo Society include William R. (Bill) Chemerka and Joseph Musso. Chemerka, publisher of *The Alamo Journal*, has always published my work without question. Musso, the expert on James Bowie and Bowie knives, shared research and a passion for the Alamo with me. The friendship of individuals like Chemerka, Musso, Groneman, and other members of the Alamo Society is one of the unexpected rewards of this work. A large thanks to the men and women of the Alamo Society. It is a group probably more like the men and women of the Alamo than any other Alamo organization. Just being a member of this group has been a big encouragement for me.

Many other individuals, members of the Southwest Vaqueros, have been supportive: Dorothy Black, Charlie Eckhardt, Frank W. Jennings, Al and Darlyne Lowman, Wayne Cox, Anne Fox, Sharon Crutchfield, and Wes Williams. At a former job, coworkers Marti Granger, Helen Durrett, and Leon Ashbrook always showed a sincere interest in my research and writing.

In my hometown of Nixon, thanks for the support of Donald and Patricia Hoffman, Richard and Kathleen Faulkner, Nathan and Dixell Wheat, Wendle and Carolyn Scott, Don and Gladyne Finch, Calvin Ray Pullin, Billy Steubing, Phyllis Stone, Sam Nixon, Gary Davis, and historian Sylvan Dunn. Also, Mike and Phyllis Mahan of Dermott, Arkansas.

Thanks to Dianne Stultz, Ginnie Bivona, and the rest of the staff at Republic of Texas Press. Their work made this book a reality.

Many thanks to "little mom" Ethel Sears, Daryl and Fran Pullin, Larry and Cyndi Pullin, Bill and Sue Shelton, and the rest of the Deason clan for their love and support over the years. I would never have gotten here without all of you.

If I forgot anyone, please forgive me. It was not intentional. It has just been a long journey with many, many human encounters.

Introduction

Any person who takes up this book expecting a work like Lon Tinkle's *13 Days to Glory*, Walter Lord's *A Time To Stand*, Stephen L. Hardin's *Texian Iliad*, or Jeff Long's *Duel of Eagles* will be disappointed. The aforementioned histories are similar in one way. They are highly readable narrative histories. *Alamo Traces* is not a narrative history that presents the Alamo story in a manner that reads like an adventure tale. The work's concept, source material, and purpose dictated a different organizational structure.

This work critically examines selected features from the supposed body of historical truth that reports the story of the Battle of the Alamo, the most famous event in Texas history. As separate pieces, each of the subjects I have tackled would usually be submitted as an article for a scholarly journal devoted to the military history or the history of the southwestern United States. Such expression does offer the opportunity of critical acceptance by the academic community. That acceptance, however, can have a high cost. In my opinion, journal editors often place restrictions on an investigator that are very close to censorship. That is especially true when a subject goes against the grain of prevailing historical trends of the day. Therefore, because this book is different, I traveled a different road.

The book's chapters are linked together in two ways. Each chapter has, as a subject or subjects, a piece or pieces of the evidentiary puzzle that makes up the story of the Alamo. The underlying topic of each chapter is the method that the original historian, writer, or researcher used in researching and writing about the Alamo. My writing style and the book's organizational structure are aimed at one goal—clarity—so that the reader will understand the evidence, the arguments, the speculative interpretations, and the conclusions.

Some readers may see certain elements of this work as ax grinding. For example, many individuals will find the chapter on Sam Houston's role in the fall of the Alamo hard to take. Today, Houston is considered the greatest Texas hero of all time. Military historian Michael Lee

Lanning, in *The Military 100: A Ranking of the Most Influential Military Leaders of All Time,* rated Houston as the fifty-seventh best general of all time, ahead of such combat geniuses as Richard I (the Lion-Hearted), Robert E. Lee, Chester W. Nimitz, Bernard L. Montgomery, Erwin Rommel, and George S. Patton.

Clearly, my analysis shows that Houston would make any list of the top one hundred Machiavellian politicians of all time. Historian Jack Jackson, on reading chapter one, told me that I had "stacked the deck" against Houston by using only sources that portray him in a negative light. My answer to Jackson was: Show me some primary sources of the period that support Houston's version of events, and I will use them. I have searched for contemporary sources that speak well of Houston's behavior during the revolution, but in regard to Houston's role in the fall of the Alamo, I found no such sources. Still, I want to make it clear that my intent in writing about Houston was not malicious. In my conclusions, I feel I have only gone to those places of the past where the evidence took me.

Also, as with all the book's chapters, the falsehoods, misconceptions, and misinterpretations investigated in this study have long been entrenched in the various Alamo histories as the truth. I felt they had to be hit hard to get the evidence and my arguments across to the reader.

The work contains many long quotations that are out of fashion with historians. I presented the data in such an extended manner so that it would be almost impossible for a reader to misunderstand the evidence's context or misunderstand the information's relationship to my arguments, interpretations, and conclusions.

My training and investigative philosophy comes from my experience as a U.S. Army military policeman and criminal investigator. It might not be obvious to a professional historian, but if one views a historian's job as a search for the truth, then a detective or criminal investigator is a historian in the truest sense. Granted, crimes have generally taken place in the very recent past and the scope of the subject is limited. Nevertheless, the crime investigator, like any *competent* historian, must determine the objective and unbiased truth of the "who, what, when, where, how, and why" of the criminal incident under investigation. In other words, the policeman's truth must be the one that is supported by definitive and creditable evidence because the consequences for the accused are severe. Thus, a police detective must always be concerned with the authenticity of the evidence used to build a case against a suspect. Such was the nature of the "historical truth" in the real world in which I learned my investigative skills. Does that make me a good historian? That is for others to decide.

Also, I do not take the sociological values of today and apply them to the people of Mexico, Texas, and the United States who lived in the first third of the nineteenth century, and then judge those long dead people as morally deficient because the two sets of values are in conflict over how people should have treated each other. As best-selling author Louis L'Amour said in *Education of a Wandering Man:* "A mistake constantly made by those who should know better is to judge people of the past by our standards rather than their own. The only way men and women can be judged is against the canvas of their own time."

Thus, *Alamo Traces* is a "nuts and bolts" study aimed at readers who have a serious interest in the Battle of the Alamo and the Texas Revolution. At times, I had to speculate in order to tie certain pieces of evidence together in a way that made sense. I attempted to make such interpretations reasonable so that they are not essentially fiction, a common characteristic of some narrative histories.

If I have learned one thing from the experience of researching and writing this book, it is a lesson that serves as a conclusion for this work. The historical Alamo must be reassembled almost from scratch. A lot of what we believe about the Texian Alamo today appears to be true, but a great deal of what is currently believed to be the truth about the event appears to be wrong. In the end, the new "truth" as I have presented it may not be totally correct (of course, it never can be) or politically correct, but perhaps the new evidence, arguments, interpretations, and conclusions in this book will bring us closer to the real thing—that is knowledge based on valid sources and reasonable interpretation.

Thomas Ricks Lindley
Nixon, Texas

Chapter One

Sam Houston and the Alamo: "Drawing Truthful Deductions"

No man is more completely master of the art of appropriating to himself the merit of others' good acts, and shifting on to others the odium of his bad ones, than Gen. Houston.

Dr. Anson Jones[1]

In 1990 the Book-of-the-Month Club of New York issued a fine press reprint of *The Raven*, Marquis James's Pulitzer Prize-winning biography of Sam Houston.[2] Robert M. Utley, former chief historian and assistant director of the National Park Service, wrote the introduction for the reprint. He observed:

Like some great giant of fable, Sam Houston bestrode America's historical landscape for nearly half a century. In physique and character he was a giant, and on the stage of American history he played the part of a giant combining all the ingredients of gripping fiction—a dramatic, adventurous, suspenseful life and a powerful, complex, enigmatic personality—he seems more the subject for a creative novelist than a historian....

Even though scholars still debate his true significance, Sam Houston has always been popularly regarded as the George Washington of Texas. As Henry Steele Commager observed in introducing an earlier edition of *The Raven*, Houston served Texas as Charlemagne, Alfred the Great, and other nation builders served their realms—as inspirational folk hero as well as shaper of great events. "In a sense," wrote Commager, "if he had not existed we should have had to create him."[3]

The Imperial Sam Houston, ca. 1850
Photo courtesy Texas State Library & Archives Commission

Clearly, there is no question about Houston's personal bravery and skill as a politician and statesman. While historians, in off-handed ways, have acknowledged that Houston was not perfect, they have ignored a great deal of evidence that indicates that the Sam Houston of "giant character" and military genius belongs to the realm of folklore, rather than in the evidence-driven pages of a history book. Although modern Texans will find it hard to accept that Houston was not a great general, the men who fought beside him at San Jacinto did not see him as the Washington of their blood-won republic.[4]

In early 1837 the first published attack on Houston's military role in the Texas revolution appeared in the form of an unofficial account of the San Jacinto campaign, a pamphlet titled *Houston Displayed Or, Who Won the Battle of San Jacinto? By a Farmer in the Army.* The "Farmer" was Robert M. Coleman, an aide-de-camp to Houston during the campaign, who had also participated in the Battle of Gonzales and the siege of Bexar in 1835. Coleman had been a member of the Consultation of 1835 and a signer of the Texas Declaration of Independence. After the revolution he served his country as a Texas Ranger colonel.[5]

John H. Jenkins, Texas historian and rare book dealer, described the Coleman account with these words:

> The volume was issued, without doubt, as a political maneuver, but it must be remembered that Sam Houston himself seldom wrote a word that was not [political]. Scurrilous and biased as it is, there is truth to at least some of the accusations, and it was undoubtedly believed to be literal truth by scores of veterans of the campaign. Many of its accusations were substantiated by some of Texas's most highly revered heroes of that era. One finds, in fact, that a considerable majority of the officers in Houston's army were severely critical of Houston's actions in the campaign. These men sincerely felt that his laurels were too easily won and too lightly granted by thousands of post-revolution immigrants who, fed by a pro-Houston press in the United States, came to Texas thinking of Houston as Texas's savior. General Edward Burleson, second in command, despised Houston till the day he died because of the campaign, as did Col. Sidney Sherman, third in command. David G. Burnet, President of Texas, was even more fanatical than Coleman in his denunciation of Houston's part. Gen. Thomas J. Rusk, Adj. Gen. John A. Wharton, Lt. Col. J. C. Neill, Lt. Col. Mirabeau B. Lamar, Lt. Col. John Forbes, Maj. J. H. Perry, Maj. James Collinsworth, Maj. Lysander Wells, Captains Turner, Moreland, Billingsley, Baker, Calder, Heard, Kuykendall, Ben Smith, Karnes, Fisher, Gillespie, and Surgeons Anson Jones and William Labadie all criticized some of Houston's actions in the campaign. Only three officers—Henry Millard, Alexander Somervell, and J. L. Bennett—appear to have unceasingly supported Houston.[6]

Texas historians and Houston biographers are familiar with the debate over Houston's command competency during the San Jacinto campaign. However, Houston's role in the rebellion previous to the 1836 retreat and the April victory, especially the Alamo, is another question. No historian has ever objectively examined Houston's activities in regard to the defense of that frontier outpost. The possibility that blame, big or small, for the fall of the Alamo can be placed on Houston's shoulders may seem implausible. Still, there is ample evidence to show that Houston was not an innocent bystander when the Alamo garrison fell to defeat. Also, the record shows that Houston was well aware of his culpability and thereafter misrepresented his Alamo-related activities to protect his reputation.

The story started on the afternoon of March 11, 1836, at about 4:00 p.m., when Houston, commander of the Texian military forces, arrived at Gonzales to take control of the troops at that location and to reinforce the Alamo. What Houston did not know at that time was that the Alamo had fallen five days earlier. When Houston finally realized that William B. Travis, David Crockett, James Bowie, and the other Alamo defenders were all dead and that the Mexican victory could seriously damage him politically, he began a campaign to separate himself from any blame for the tragic event.[7]

Houston commenced his defensive offense a week after the Mexican victory in a missive to James Collinsworth, chairman of the government's military committee. Houston wrote: "The enclosed order to Colonel Fannin will indicate to you my convictions, that, with our small, unorganized force, we can not maintain sieges in fortresses, in the country of the enemy. Troops pent up in forts are rendered useless; nor is it possible that we can ever maintain our cause by such a policy.... I am informed that Colonel Fannin had about seven hundred men under his command; and, at one time, had taken up the line of march for the Alamo, but the breaking down of a wagon induced him to fall back, and abandon the idea of marching to the relief of our last hope in Bexar.... The projected expedition to Matamoros, under the agency of the council has already cost us over two hundred and thirty-seven lives; and where the effects are to end, none can foresee." The spin that Houston put on the fall of the Alamo was subtle, but the message was clear. Colonel James W. Fannin Jr. was to blame for the Alamo defeat.[8]

The same day Houston dispatched a letter to Henry Raguet, a close friend at Nacogdoches. This time Houston was direct: "Colonel Fannin should have relieved our Brave men in the Alamo. He had 430 men with artillery under his command, and had taken up the line of march with a full knowledge of the situation of those in the Alamo, and owing to the breaking down of a wagon abandoned the march, returning to Goliad and left our Spartans to their fate!"[9]

On March 15 Houston reported to Collinsworth: "Our forces must not be shut up in forts, where they can neither be supplied with men nor provisions. Long aware of this fact, I directed, on the 16th of January last, that the artillery should be removed, and the Alamo blown up; but it was prevented by the expedition upon Matamoros, the author of all our misfortunes."[10]

By 1859 Houston had added Alamo commander William B. Travis to his scapegoat recipe and boiled the story down to a single dish of disobedience. In a speech to the United States Senate, Houston claimed his political life was at an end and declared: "How that service has been performed I leave it to posterity to determine. My only desire is, that truth shall be vindicated, and that I may stand upon that foundation, so far as posterity may be concerned with my action, that they may have an opportunity of drawing truthful deductions."[11]

Houston then continued with a speech defending his military leadership in the revolution. Speaking to the Alamo, Houston detailed how he had ordered Lt. Colonel James C. Neill, the Alamo commander, to blow up the fortress and fall back to the Guadalupe River to establish a new defensive position.[12] He said that the enemy would advance no farther than Gonzales and continued: "That order was secretly superseded by the council; and Colonel Travis, having relieved Colonel Neill, did not blow up the Alamo, and retreat with such articles as were necessary for the defense of the country; but remained in possession from the 17th of January until the last of February, when the Alamo was invested by the force of Santa Anna. Surrounded there, and cut off from all succor, the victims to the ruthless feelings of Santa Anna, by the contrivance of the council, and in violation of the plans of the Major-General for the defense of the country."[13]

The construction took many years, but Houston had set a solid foundation for the story he wanted historians to write. If there was to be any blame for the fall of the Alamo, his story went, it should fall on the provisional government and the victims because of insubordination by the Alamo commanders, Neill, Bowie, and Travis.

Today that false impression persists. In November 1993, at a rededication of Fort Sam Houston in honor of Houston's bicentennial birthday, Madge Roberts, Houston's great-great granddaughter, claimed that the Alamo defenders failed to follow Houston's instructions to destroy the Alamo. She said, "He [Houston] knew that [defense of the Alamo] was a hopeless cause. He knew that the Texians could not defend the Alamo against a siege."[14]

Marshall De Bruhl, author of *Sword of San Jacinto: A Life of Sam Houston,* expressed the same sentiment this way: "Travis and Bowie's disobedience of Houston's direct orders to abandon and then blow up the Alamo not only cost them their lives. Another 187 brave men were lost with them. But the gallant band's defense against the superior Mexican force that besieged them for thirteen days has become America's greatest example of military bravado. It was rash and foolish, yes, but it was grandly heroic."[15]

In August 1994 De Bruhl stated his position with more precision when he complained: "There are two transcendent moments in the war for Texas independence, at Washington on the Brazos, on March 2, 1836, and the Battle of San Jacinto, at Buffalo Bayou on April 21, 1836, which guaranteed that independence.... It is these two events attending the birth of the republic that should be celebrated—not the bitter defeats of the Alamo and Goliad. Those baleful failures were caused by the rash acts of disobedient men and resulted in the unnecessary loss of half the manpower and much of the weaponry available to fight the invader."[16]

Elizabeth Crook, in her work of fiction *Promised Lands,* wrote: "Eccentric and verbose but surefooted as a marching band, Sam Houston spoke with a drumbeat. He had told the volunteers not to go to Matamoros: those who had ignored him were now dead. He had told them to blow up the Alamo and abandon San Antonio de Bexar: those who had disobeyed were now trapped like a nest of rabbits with the hole plugged up."[17]

Jeff Long, in his novel of the Texas Revolution *Empire of Bones* (promoted as historically accurate), contributed this: "If they [Travis and Bowie] had survived their battle at the Alamo and he could ever get his hands on them, Houston thought it might be most fitting to just shoot them out of hand. Goddamn them for not blowing up their pile of mud and falling back. Bowie and the young maniac Travis had deliberately disobeyed his orders. They had stayed in their forts showboating with their own command. As a direct consequence of their hubris they had sailed off the edge of the world with some hundred and eighty men in that worthless mission corral."[18]

Most recently, James L. Haley, an independent scholar and Houston apologist, wrote: "... so now Houston sent Jim Bowie with orders to the commander there [San Antonio] to remove the artillery from the Alamo, blow the fortress up and retire to Gonzales."[19]

Such is the historical record today: a resoundingly pro-Houston slant in both history and fiction that has been accepted by historians and writers without a single challenge to the tale's veracity. There are, however, other documents that speak to the defense of the Alamo—evidence that gives objective readers the "opportunity of drawing truthful deductions" about Houston's alleged order to destroy the Alamo and abandon Bexar. However, before an examination of the other documents is presented, a detailed analysis of the one document that seems to support Houston's version of the events is necessary.[20]

In mid-January 1836 Houston was in Goliad, attempting to bring the various factions of the Texian military machine together for an invasion of Matamoros. While at that location, he received a missive from Lt. Colonel James C. Neill, the commander at San Antonio. Neill wrote: "There are at Laredo now 3,000 men under the command of General Ramirez [y Sesma], and two other generals, and, as it appears from a letter received here last night, 1,000 of them are destined for this place, and two thousand for Matamoros. We are in a torpid, defenseless condition, and have not and cannot get from the citizens here horses enough to send out a patrol or spy company.... I hope we will be reinforced in eight days, or we will be overrun by the enemy."[21]

Neill also wrote Governor Henry Smith and the Council about the situation at San Antonio, stressing that he needed horses and men to form a spy unit to scout the area between Bexar and the Rio Grande. Neill believed the enemy was nearer to his command than the rumors indicated, and he did not want to be caught unaware of their approach.[22]

The exact nature of Houston's response to Neill's call for help is ambiguous because we have no copy of the orders that Houston sent to Neill. A letter to Governor Smith, however, details some of Houston's actions in response to the anticipated attack on San Antonio. This is the document that is often cited as proof that Houston ordered the Alamo destroyed and the garrison abandoned.[23] The letter reads:

Sir: I have the honor to enclose for your information a communication from Lt. Col. J. C. Neill, under the date of [January] the 14th inst. Colonel Bowie will leave here in a few hours for Bexar with a detachment of from thirty to fifty men. Capt. [William H.] Patton's [Columbia] Company, it is believed, are now there. I have ordered the fortifications in the town of Bexar to be demolished, and, *if you should think well of it, I will remove all the cannon and other munitions of war to Gonzales and Copano, blow up the Alamo and abandon the place, as it will be impossible to keep up the Station with volunteers, the sooner I can be authorized the better it will be for the Country* [italics added]. In an hour I will take up the line of march for Refugio Mission with about 209 efficient men, where I will await orders from your Excellency, believing that the army should not advance with a small force upon Matamoros with the hope or belief that the Mexicans will cooperate with us. I have no confidence in them and the disaster at Tampico should teach us a lesson to be noted in future operations. I have learned that Colonel Gonzales is somewhere on the Nueces with one hundred and seventy men, but accounts vary as to the actual number. They are to cooperate in the eastern Confederacy, I am told.

I will leave Captain [Peyton S.] Wyatt in command at this point [with his Huntsville Volunteers] until I can relieve him with thirty-five regulars now at Refugio. I pray that your Excellency will cause all the regulars now enlisted to be formed into companies, and march to headquarters [Copano]. It will be impossible to keep up a garrison with the volunteers. Do forward the regulars. Capt. [Benjamin Fort] Smith had been relieved, and I met him on his way home today. Captain Patton will return to Lavaca County and bring on a company as soon as possible. I have sent Captain [Philip] Dimmitt to raise one hundred more men and march to Bexar forthwith, if it be invested; and if not to repair to headquarters with his company. Captain Patton will do likewise. I would myself have marched to Bexar but the Matamoros rage is up so high that I must see Colonel [William] Ward's men. You have no idea of the difficulties I have encountered. Patton has told me of the *men* that make the trouble. Better materials never were in ranks. The government and all its offices have been misrepresented to the army.

I pray you send me copies of Austin's letters, or rather extracts. If the Council is in session I do wish they would say something about the Confederacy. Please send me frequent expresses and advise me of your pleasure.[24]

On the surface, the January 17 letter appears to support Houston's claim that he ordered the Alamo demolished and the city abandoned because manning forts such as the Alamo was not good military policy. A careful and complete analysis of the document, however, reveals the error of such an interpretation.

The missive shows Houston did order the "fortifications in the town" destroyed, but those barricades were in the streets west of the San Antonio River. The Alamo was a separate structure and garrison on the east side of the river. In regard to the defense of the Alamo, the letter shows *Houston did not order* the fortress destroyed and the town abandoned.[25] Houston appealed to Governor Smith: "...if you should think well of it, I will remove all the cannon and other munitions of war to Gonzales and Copano, blow up the Alamo and abandon the place, as it will be impossible to keep up the Station with volunteers, the sooner I can be authorized the better it will be for the country."[26]

Thus Houston only requested Smith's approval to demolish the Alamo and abandon the post. Also, the document shows Houston did not request authority to execute the two measures because as he later said, "Troops pent up in forts are useless," but rather he wanted to take the actions because it was impossible "to keep up the Station with volunteers."[27]

In his 1859 Senate speech, Houston claimed his orders to blow up the Alamo and abandon the city were "superseded by the Council." In that allegation, the old general was half right. He failed to mention that Governor Smith, his political comrade and civilian superior, also ignored his recommendations regarding the evacuation of Bexar and the destruction of the Alamo.[28]

At that point in the Texas rebellion the provisional government of Texas was in disarray, split into two political factions. Governor Smith,

Houston, and the Bexar troops were in favor of independence and total separation from Mexico. Lt. Governor James W. Robinson and the General Council, with the backing of Stephen F. Austin, supported the federal constitution of 1824 and continued participation in the Mexican nation as a state. The political fray was finally resolved with the arrival of Santa Anna's army and the March 1 convention that selected independence and separation. Regardless, in mid-January 1836, the one issue on which the two political camps agreed was that the Alamo must not be destroyed and that San Antonio must not be abandoned.[29]

On or about January 21, Governor Smith ordered Lt. Colonel William B. Travis, a Smith and Houston supporter, to reinforce the Bexar garrison with one hundred men. Travis, however, was only able to muster about thirty soldiers for the assignment. Ironically, the unit arrived at Bexar on February 5, the date that Smith wrote: "Owing to their base management, much confusion prevails among our volunteer troops on the frontier, but, by using much vigilance, I have now got Bexar secure."[30]

On January 31 the Council, having been informed of Houston's advice to Smith, ordered that an "express be sent immediately to Bejar, with orders from the acting Governor [James W. Robinson] countermanding the orders of Genl. Houston, and that the Commandant be required to put the place in the best possible state for defense, with assurances that every possible effort is making to strengthen, supply and provision the Garrison, and in no case to abandon or surrender the place unless in the last extremity." Truly, if there was an edict that Travis and Bowie did not obey, it was the last dictate that gave them the authority to "abandon or surrender the place" in the "last extremity"—death. Even in that situation, the commanders did not abandon the Alamo.[31]

Several questions, however, remain. On January 23, 1836, Colonel Neill notified Governor Smith: "If teams could be obtained here by any means to remove the Cannon and Public property I would immediately destroy the fortifications and abandon the place, taking the men I have under my command here, to join the Commander in chief at Copano...." Historians and popular writers have offered Neill's statement as evidence that he attempted to obey Houston's alleged order to blow up the Alamo and abandon the city, but was prevented from doing so because of the lack of draft animals. An objective reading of the document, however, reveals that Neill did not want to leave Bexar because Houston had ordered him to do so. Neill had just received reliable intelligence that indicated Santa Anna was going to direct his forces against Goliad and Copano, not Bexar. Therefore, if the means had been available to move the cannon, Neill would have destroyed the Alamo and abandoned San Antonio in order to reinforce the troops at Goliad and Copano, not to fall back to Gonzales as Houston later claimed he had ordered.[32]

Additionally, other than ordering the destruction of the fortifications west of the San Antonio River, what other orders did Houston issue in response to Neill's letter of alarm? Houston's January 17 letter to Smith furnishes a partial answer.

Despite nearly two hundred and forty volunteers in the Goliad-Refugio area, Houston looked to the colonies east of the Guadalupe River to reinforce San Antonio. He sent orders to Captain Philip Dimmitt, who resided on the east side of Lavaca Bay, about forty miles east of Goliad, instructing him "to raise one hundred more men and march to Bexar forthwith, if it be invested; and if not to repair to headquarters with his company."[33]

Also, according to the letter, Houston believed Captain William H. Patton was already at San Antonio with his mounted infantry company. Houston informed Smith that Patton was to "return to Lavaca county and bring on a company as soon as possible." If the enemy was not at Bexar, Patton was ordered to join Houston at Copano.[34]

Many historians and writers insist that Houston dispatched James Bowie to the relief of Bexar with a quickly organized company of volunteers. While Bowie did hurry to San Antonio with a small volunteer company, the evidence suggests it was on his own initiative, not Houston's order.

In writing Smith, Houston simply said, "Colonel Bowie will leave here in a few hours for Bexar with a detachment of from thirty to fifty men." On January 30, 1836, Houston detailed events at Goliad and Refugio: "I immediately requested Colonel James Bowie to march with a detachment of volunteers to his [Lt. Colonel James C. Neill] relief." Then on February 2 Bowie reported his version of the relief effort to Smith: "It was forthwith determined that I should go instantly to Bejar; accordingly I left Genl Houston and with a few very efficient volunteers came on to this place about 2 weeks since. I was received by Col. Neill with great cordiality, and the men under my command entered at once into active service."[35]

Years later William G. Cooke, who was at Goliad in January 1836, recalled: "Bowie's object appeared to be to induce our men to return to San Antonio—he used every means in his power to effect this object—They however at length determined to recognize the order of Genl Houston and marched to Refugio."[36]

The fact that Bowie and Houston were contending for the services of the same men at Goliad and the fact that Houston ordered the Alamo reinforced from the colonies suggest that the decision to support Bexar was made by Bowie and that Houston may not have truly supported the action. Thus the question remains: If Houston ordered the Alamo destroyed and the city abandoned, why did he allow Bowie to relieve the command? Also, if Houston ordered the Alamo destroyed, why did he make arrangements for other reinforcements to march to the city?

The totality of the evidence shows that Houston wanted to destroy all of the fortifications in Bexar and abandon the city. His reasons for wanting to take those actions, however, are clouded. Before the fall of the Alamo his reason for making the request to Governor Smith was that the location could not be manned with volunteers. After the tragic defeat, he alleged that he had actually issued orders for the actions because "with our small, unorganized force, we can not maintain sieges in fortresses, in the country of the enemy."[37]

Until Bowie and his volunteers, members of Captain John Chenoweth's United States Invincibles, arrived at Bexar, the town was for the most part garrisoned by Houston's regular army soldiers. Houston was Lt. Colonel Neill's commanding officer. Thus, Houston had the power to order all of the city's fortifications destroyed and the site abandoned. After all, he had made the decision to garrison the city following the fall of Bexar and the expulsion of the Mexican army in 1835. Instead, Houston "passed the buck" to Governor Henry Smith. Also, because Houston made no mention of abandoning Bexar in his January 30 report to Smith, it appears he had backed down from the proposal in the face of Smith's order for Travis and the Legion of Cavalry to join Neill at the Alamo. In regard to San Antonio, Houston only advised Smith: "Should Bexar remain a military post, Goliad must be maintained, or the former will be cut off from all supplies arriving by sea at the port of Copano." If Houston truly believed that the Alamo should be demolished and the city abandoned, he could have sent written orders to Neill by Bowie. Neill, an excellent soldier, would have obeyed them without question. Why did

Houston fail to send such orders to Neill? Bowie, because of his strong ties to the city and its citizens, probably voiced strong objections that stopped Houston from dispatching such orders to Neill.[38]

Houston appears to have been blind to the strategic importance of San Antonio. The town was the gateway to the Anglo-Celtic colonies of Texas. From Bexar, the Camino Real continued northeast to Nacogdoches. The road to Gonzales, Columbus, and San Felipe ran east from San Antonio to the heart of the colonies. Indeed, Bowie defined the significance: "The salvation of Texas depends in great measure in keeping Bejar out of the hands of the enemy. It serves as the frontier picquet guard and if it were in possession of Santa Anna there is no strong hold from which to repel him in his march towards the Sabine.... Col. Neill & myself have come to the solemn resolution that we will rather die in these ditches than give it up to the enemy. The citizens deserve our protection and the public safety demands our lives rather than to evacuate this post to the enemy."[39]

Travis, who did not even want to be stationed at San Antonio, once at the Alamo, came to feel the same as Bowie. On February 11 temporary command of the garrison was transferred to Travis when Neill had to return home to Mina (Bastrop) because of an illness in his family.[40] After taking command, Travis, echoing Bowie's earlier concern about Bexar, warned Governor Smith: "This being the Frontier Post nearest the Rio Grande, will be the first to be attacked. We are illy prepared for their reception, as we have not more than 150 men here and they in a very disorganized state – Yet we are determined to sustain it as long as there is a man left; because we consider death preferable to disgrace, which would be the result of giving up a Post which has been so dearly won, and thus opening the door for the Invaders to enter the sacred Territory of the colonies." Again, on February 16, Travis advised Smith: "I have nothing of interest to communicate that has transpired since my last. I must, however, again remind your Excellency that this [post] is the key to Texas and should not be neglected by the Govt."[41]

Marshall De Bruhl, a recent Houston biographer, argues that the Battle of the Alamo is not worth remembering today. He observed: "Texas Independence and San Jacinto Day can be celebrated with honor by all Texans, no matter what and recognize the Alamo, for what it is—a sad, heart-wrenching monument to the dead, not the storied battleground of song and legend."[42]

Mr. De Bruhl's opinion notwithstanding, had the Alamo been demolished and Bexar abandoned as Houston wished, there would have been no constitutional convention to declare Texas independent and probably no conclusive Texian victory, at least not at San Jacinto. The thirteen days that Travis, Bowie, Crockett, and their men, women, and children valiantly gave Texas and the world prevented the fast moving Mexican army from sweeping deep into the Texian colonies.

On the other hand, some individuals argue that the Alamo siege gave Houston time to organize and train the army that defeated Santa Anna on April 21, 1836. Nothing could be further from the truth. At probably the most critical point in the Texas rebellion, February 1, 1836, when chaos and confusion ruled within the temporary Texas government, Houston relinquished his command over Texas's military forces and went on furlough to adjust his private affairs and to smoke the peace pipe with his most loyal supporters, the friendly Indians of Texas.[43]

On February 23, 1836, as Mexican soldiers commenced their investment of the Alamo, Houston was safely ensconced in East Texas with his Cherokee friends, signing a needless peace treaty. On March 1, 1836, Houston, with full knowledge of the situation at San Antonio, took a seat at the convention as a delegate from Refugio, a settlement he had probably only visited once in his life, and ignored his military duties so he could play a political role at the birth of an independent Texas.[44]

Houston spent most of his free time at the convention in the local grog shops. Edwin Waller described delegate Houston with these words: "I found Genl. Houston drunk at the Consultation in Nov[ember] 1835 and left him in the same situation in Washington [on-the-Brazos] in [18]36. He had often to be picked up and put to bed by his friends."[45]

Even Houston acknowledged his binge drinking at the Convention. Interview notes from an 1844 encounter with Mary Austin Holley quote Houston as having said: "Travis sending for assistance – none to give – had to make a constitution on my birthday – had a grand spree – eggnog – everybody – two days – bad business – hated it."[46]

The previously mentioned Colonel Robert M. Coleman left this description of Houston's activities at the convention:

> Thus, while Col. Travis and his gallant companions were closely besieged by an overwhelming Mexican force, with Santa Anna at its head and letters were daily received from that brave officer imploring aid, and declaring that

without timely and efficient assistance he must perish. While Col. Fannin was daily calling for a force to enable him to meet the enemy in the vicinity of Goliad. While too, the citizens were abandoning their homes and fleeing to the Eastward to escape from their barbarous enemy, the Commander-in-Chief of the Army of Texas was spending his nights in the grog-shops of Washington, in company with the gamblers and dissipated multitude which the session of the Convention had collected at that place; and his days were devoted to sleep, except that portion of them which he spent in vain efforts to ally the fears of the people, and to account for his disgraceful inactivity.

With this view he declared that a fraud had been practiced upon the people by the officers of the frontier, for party purposes; that there was not an enemy on our borders; that one of the officers was endeavoring to wrest from him the command of the army, for which purpose he had caused these reports to be circulated, hoping the authorities, in the event of an invasion, and absence of the Commander-in-Chief, would confer that appointment upon another.[47]

One document that appears to repudiate Coleman's allegation that Houston did not believe the enemy was on the frontier is an entreaty to the public that was published under Houston's name, allegedly on March 2, 1836. It reads:

War is raging on the frontiers. Bexar is besieged by two thousand of the enemy under the command of General Sesma. Reinforcements are on the march to unite with the besieging army. By the last report, our force in Bexar was only one hundred and fifty men. The citizens of Texas must rally to aid of our army, or it will perish. Let the citizens of the east march to the combat. The enemy must be driven from our soil, or desolation will accompany their march upon us. *Independence is declared*; it must be maintained. Immediate action united with valor, can alone achieve the great work. The services of all are forthwith required in the field.

Sam Houston Commander-in-Chief of the Army.

P.S. It is rumored that the enemy are on their march to Gonzales, and that they have entered the colonies. The fate of Bexar is unknown. The country must and shall be defended. The patriots of Texas are *appealed to in behalf of their bleeding country.*[48]

Houston's words were the truth, but his previous actions, his subsequent behavior, and the ensuing actions of the convention suggest that if the proclamation was actually issued on March 2, 1836, it was an insincere political action to give the impression that Houston was doing something to answer Travis's call for assistance. Indeed, "the services of all" were required at the front, including the services of the "Commander-in-Chief of the Army." Other evidence indicates that the Coleman accusation is true, and that Houston was successful in convincing most of the delegates that the Alamo was not threatened.[49]

On February 25 Travis wrote Houston of the conditions at the Alamo. He detailed the events that had passed since the enemy's arrival and praised his troops: "I take great pleasure in stating that both officers and men conducted themselves with firmness and bravely." Then, he closed with: "Do hasten on aid to me as rapidly as possible, as from the superior number of the enemy, it will be impossible for us to keep them out much longer. If they overpower us, we fall a sacrifice at the shrine of our country, and we hope posterity and our country will do our memory justice. Give me help, oh my Country! Victory or Death!" The missive arrived at Washington-on-the-Brazos on the evening of March 2. The impact of Travis's call for immediate aid is recorded in the diary of a spectator at the convention. It reads: "It is believed the Alamo is safe."[50]

The following day the delegates, indicating they possessed a degree of skepticism about Travis's call for relief, passed the following resolution: "Believing it of vital importance that this convention know correctly the condition of our army, they would recommend the convention to accept the services of Major [Matthew] Caldwell, who purposes to start this day for the frontier." Caldwell, a Gonzales resident, had every reason (Gonzales was next in line after San Antonio) to believe that Travis's letters were the truth, even if Houston and the other delegates doubted the documents.[51]

The convention took no further action until the morning of Friday, March 4. Houston claimed that because of the actions of the General Council he was no longer the army's commander-in-chief. He argued that independence demanded a new appointment, as his "former oath of office was under the constitution of 1824, and in obedience thereto."[52] To satisfy Houston, the following preamble and resolution were introduced.

> Whereas we are now in a state of Revolution, and threatened by a large invading army, from the central government of Mexico; and whereas our present situation, and the emergency of the present crisis, renders it indispensably necessary that we should have an army in the field; and, whereas, it is also necessary that there should be one Supreme head or Commander in Chief, and due degrees of subordination defined, established and strictly observed, Therefore, be it Resolved, that General Samuel Houston be appointed Commander in Chief of all land forces of the Texian Army, both regulars, volunteers, and militia, while in actual service, and endowed with all the rights, privileges and powers due to a Commander in Chief in the United States of America, and that he forthwith proceed to take command, establish headquarters and organize the army accordingly.[53]

Apparently over lunch a number of the delegates decided the government needed to ensure its control over Houston. Thus, the preamble and resolution were passed with an addition:

"And that Samuel Houston retain such command until the election of a chief magistrate of this government, and to continue in such office unless, superseded by order of the government, subject, however, to the general orders of the government *de facto,* until the general organization agreeable to the constitution, and always amenable to the laws and civil authorities of this country."[54]

Another resolution was introduced that specified that if Houston did not "immediately set out for the army" he should resign. Houston said that he would depart the next morning and requested that the resolution be withdrawn. The proposed mandate was dropped by its sponsor. The body then adjourned for the weekend, agreeing to meet on Monday, March 7.[55]

In the late 1830s, Isaac W. Burton reported his opinion of Houston's behavior at the convention: "I thought him a man of uncommon natural abilities – But I *fancied* perhaps that his acquired ones were in a great measure superficial – I thought him in the main a man of an excellent heart but dissipated, eccentric, and vain – and on the whole I ranked him among the first men in Texas and was at that time his Political as well as warm personal friend – However, he delayed taking Command of the Volunteer Army and staid [*sic*] in the Convention employed in Legislative matters when I thought that his honor as a soldier was hourly getting dimmed."[56]

On Sunday morning, March 6, Houston still had not left for the Alamo. Travis's final dispatch, however, arrived at Washington-on-the-Brazos during the delegates' breakfast and, after some hesitation, brought the issue of Houston's departure to a head. Richard Ellis, president of the convention, called the delegates together and the secretary read the letter. Many members, apparently because of Houston's influence, continued to doubt that the Alamo was under siege.[57] Forty years later, Lancelot Abbotts remembered it this way:

> The veracity of the courier who carried it to Washington, and the authenticity of the signature of Travis, were questioned by some members of the Convention and by citizens. Two or three of the members were aware that I knew well the handwriting of Col. Travis, and a Committee of the Convention waited on me to ascertain my opinion on the matter. I unhesitatingly pronounced the despatch (brief as it was) to be the handwriting of the brave Travis.
>
> A public meeting was called for the purpose of enlisting volunteers for the relief of the Alamo. At this time there was living in Washington a doctor by the name of Biggs, or Briggs, who was a big, burly, brave Manifest Destiny man. He made a speech, in which he declared his unbelief in the despatch, and the utter impossibility of any number of Mexicans to take the Alamo, when defended by near 200 men.[58]

Finally, late that afternoon Houston left for Gonzales to take command of the forces that had mustered under the command of Lt. Colonel James C. Neill to reinforce the Alamo. Mrs. Angelina Eberly, a San Felipe resident, reported Houston's departure with these strong words: "it was Sunday – collecting his besotted faculties, he [Houston] said, with much levity, to the anxious spectators, [']You must throw a shoe at me for good luck.['] No one did so – why? 'I would have had my foot in it,' they cried. It was the 6th of March – the last express came from Fannin and Travis, with a letter from the latter to Miss Cummings to whom he was engaged.

They [Houston and staff] got off the same evening. That morning Travis fell!"[59]

The ride to Gonzales should have taken two and a half days at the most. Instead, Houston took five days to make the trip. He spent the night of the sixth at Dr. Asa Hoxey's plantation at Coles Settlement, northwest of Washington-on-the-Brazos. On the seventh he traveled to Burnam's Crossing on the Colorado River, south of present-day La Grange. At Burnam's, William W. Thompson, an old settler, confronted Houston about his obvious delay in moving to the relief of the Alamo. Thompson described the encounter with these words: "Houston swore that he believed it [Santa Anna at the Alamo] to be a damned lie, and that all those reports from Travis & Fannin were lies, for there were no Mexican forces there and that he believed that it was only electioneering schemes [by] Travis & Fannin to sustain their own popularity[.] And Genl Houston showed no disposition of being in a hurry to the army, much to the surprise of myself & others; for he remained at Capt. Burnums all night, & all that day, and all night again before he started for Gonzales. And this at a time, when anxiety for the relief of Colo. Travis & his heroic comrades, appeared to fill the minds of everybody."[60]

Whereas, in 1859, Houston reported his ride to Gonzales with these words: "The Alamo was known to be in siege. Fannin was known to be embarrassed. Ward, also, and Morris and Johnson, destroyed. All seemed to bespeak calamity of the most ireful character.... The general proceeded on his way and met many fugitives. The day on which he left Washington, the 6th of March, the Alamo had fallen. He anticipated it; and marching to Gonzales as soon as practicable, though his health was infirm, he arrived there on the 11th of March."[61] Thus, Houston did not hurry to Gonzales because he was sick and he believed the Alamo had already fallen.

Still others, besides Thompson, believed that Houston had traveled too slowly in riding to the sounds of war. San Jacinto captain Moseley Baker penned a private letter to Houston that detailed Baker's knowledge of Houston's participation in the revolution. In regard to the Alamo, Baker wrote:

> While the coming of Santa Anna was ... daily expected in the month of January, 1836, you [Houston] deliberately took your departure for Nacogdoches, on a plea of going to pacify the Indians, without having previously organized a single

19

company for the defense of the country. You remained absent, and was still so, when the Mexicans actually invaded the country and besieged the immortal Travis in the Alamo, and he in calling for assistance writes to the Convention, on account, as he himself says, "of the absence of the commander-in-chief." But sir he called in vain – you had left no organization, nothing on which the people could rally, and no one to whom to look for orders in your absence, and before the people could recover from their consternation, the Alamo had fallen, he [Travis] and his brave comrades shouting for Texas and her rights [paper torn] if we are to believe all contempt [torn] testimony you fell shouting [torn] your post should have [torn] [San Antonio] because it was one of danger and glory. You should have been there because the destinies of Texas were nominally resting on you. But you were in the East removed from danger, and in a condition that even your enemies, for the honor of Texas are loath to mention.

On learning the fact that Santa Anna had actually invaded the country, you hurried to Washington to meet the Convention. You there read the appeals of Travis for assistance, but you stirred not, you remained for days waiting a reappointment, and how far you restrained yourself from your accustomed habits, let those speak who had the mortification to see you. You finally reached Gonzales, but before you did so, Travis and his Texian band had shouted their last battle cry for Texas, and then slept the sleep of the Brave. Lamented Travis, so long as brave and generous deeds shall command the admiration of the free and the good – will you and your band – be immortal. Had [Ben] Milam lived or had [Edward] Burleson commanded, you [Travis] now would be among us, but friend of my early days rest in peace. When the name of Houston shall be forgotten, yours will be repeated as the more than successful rival of Leonidas.[62]

Today one can argue that the Coleman, Thompson, and Baker statements were nothing more than political attacks on Houston. While political considerations may have produced the statements, that does not mean the declarations are false. Moreover, a document from Houston's own quill verifies an important element of the Coleman and Thompson reports.

On March 7, 1836, before Houston left for Burnam's Crossing, he wrote James Collinsworth, chairman of the government's military committee. In this missive, Houston's own words prove he was telling people he did not believe that the men, women, and children of the Alamo were under attack by the Mexican army. Also, the letter reveals that Houston, the commanding general of all Texian land forces, was oblivious to the military situation that faced the newly formed country. Houston wrote:

> Before I proceed on my way this morning, you will allow me to call your attention, if you please, with that of the committee, to the subject of fortifying "Live Oak Point," on the bay of Copano. Troops coming from the U. States via New Orleans can sail for that point on armed vessels, with artillery and *lumber* sufficient for such fortifications as will be necessary for the present. The cannon there placed should be large pieces, 12 and 18 [pounders], and very few will suffice. Col. [James] Power can give you all the information that you may desire; I will only suggest that it will give us command of all supplies destined for Goliad and San Antonio, *if the enemy should even possess them* [italics added]. If a liberal appropriation of money should be made for the army, although we should not immediately receive it, it will keep down much discontent until it can be had. I pray you to have the Cherokee treaty ratified, and Major Washington Lewis, residing at Masters' on the road, appointed agent for the Cherokees to reside near Bowls'. This will be of importance to the safety of the frontier. – If any plan be devised by which the Comanches can be approached by the head waters of the Brazos, and they induced to fall down and range upon the Laredo route to Bexar and steal horses, it will be important. A Mr. Dillard, residing at the Falls of the Brazos will be a proper person to communicate with. Measures should be attended to if possible to prevent the Creek Indians from emigrating to the East of Texas. Col. [Thomas J.] Rusk can inform you of the fact of A. Hotchkiss' interest in inducing the Indians to emigrate to the country. The evidence is

conclusive. – It would be well that the steam packet "Wm. Brown," if purchased, should have such guns placed on her as would enable her to throw grape and canister into the enemy in close contact, as I am told she cannot carry large pieces. If Copano is occupied by us, the enemy will never advance into the Colonies. God bless you and may you long continue useful to Texas. I rode until late last night, and rose early this morning....

There is a Blount in Washington, who deserves a Captaincy in the cavalry, if you should think proper to advance him. I pray that all appointments in the army, since the 6th of January, made by the self-styled "Council," may be set aside, if the persons should be afterwards appointed. – Please see Doctor [Stephen H.] Everitt, and he can speak to you of a Mr. [Stephen W.] Blount of Jasper. He only received a Lieutenancy when he should have been advanced....

What say you of a resolution, that Texas is part of Louisiana, and the U. States by [the] treaty of 1803?[63]

On March 7, 1836, when Houston dictated the previously detailed letter, "the key to Texas" had been turned. In fact, the door to "the sacred Territory of the Colonies" had been blown off its hinges and was about to crash down on Gonzales. Thus, with all of the territory south of the San Antonio River under control or soon to be under the control of Santa Anna's centralist soldiers, what were Houston's plans for the defense of Texas?

Not much, as Houston's words, "if the enemy should even possess them [Bexar and Goliad]," coupled with the Coleman and Thompson statements, demonstrate an apparent denial of everything military that had occurred in Texas since February 1, 1836. Otherwise, he planned to defend the Republic of Texas with the following actions: (1) ratification of his Cherokee treaty and appointment of an Indian agent for the tribe, (2) arrange for the Comanche Indians to travel the Laredo road to steal horses from the Mexican army, which suggests that Houston did not believe the Mexican army was at the Alamo and was anticipating a future advance of the enemy on the Laredo road, (3) stop any Creek Indian immigration from the United States, (4) arm a steamboat with appropriate cannon, (5) void many of the military appointments of the previous

Texas government, which would have given him stronger control over the army forming at Gonzales, (6) fortify Copano, Texas's most remote and least used gulf port, which he saw as the "key to Texas," (7) request Collinsworth have the new Texas government pass a resolution that claimed Texas was included in the "Louisiana Purchase" of 1803, which would mean it was part of the United States.[64]

In the aggregate, the evidence supports a number of conclusions concerning Houston's role in the defense of Bexar and the fall of the Alamo. First, Houston did not order the Alamo demolished and San Antonio abandoned as he later claimed. He did, however, suggest those actions to Governor Henry Smith, who ignored the advice and reinforced San Antonio. Also, the General Council instructed the Alamo commander: "... in no case to abandon or surrender the place unless in the last extremity."

The Cherokee Sam Houston, ca. 1820s
Photo courtesy Texas State Library & Archives Commission

Second, between February 1, 1836, and February 23, 1836, a time when the San Antonio garrison and Texas most needed its commander-in-chief, Houston was on leave from his military responsibilities. He was taking care of private affairs and conducting peace talks with the Cherokee Indians of East Texas.[65]

Third, Houston, after learning of Santa Anna's arrival at Bexar, ignored his military duties so that he could play a political role at the convention. He appears to have acted the politician to protect his position as commander-in-chief and to obtain even greater authority in that role. Houston obviously understood that if the Texians defeated Santa Anna's army, the Texian general would be seen as hero, which would give that commander a political advantage after the revolution. He insisted that because of the General Council's former acts he was no longer the army's commander-in-chief, that the Declaration of Independence required a reappointment of the position. After being reaffirmed, he was threatened with dismissal if he did not depart immediately for the army. He promised to leave the next day. Then, after the threat of being fired was removed, he broke his pledge. Otherwise, he spent his free time in the grog shops, celebrating the declaration of independence, which he alleged had been passed on his birthday.[66]

Fourth, Houston, at the convention and on the long ride to Gonzales, protested that there was no need to hurry to the army because the enemy was not on the frontier, and that such claims by Travis and Fannin were political schemes. In the case of the convention, the evidence suggests that Houston was successful in convincing most of the delegates that the Bexar command was not threatened.

Fifth, Houston, when only days away from taking command of the troops at Gonzales, appears to have been totally out of touch with the military conditions that had existed on the frontier for over a month and the strategic reality he was about to encounter.

Sixth, Houston's suggesting the Texas government claim that Texas had been part of the Louisiana Purchase and was rightfully part of the United States appears to have been an attempt to give President Andrew Jackson and the United States an interest in Texas's struggle against Mexico.

The idea that Houston did not believe the enemy was at Bexar or Goliad is incomprehensible. Still, the evidence shows that Houston was telling people he did not believe the Mexican forces were at those locations. He even suggested the same to James Collinsworth, chairman of the government's military committee. Nevertheless, could Houston have really have been that out of touch or stupid? Who knows? Only time and new sources will tell.

In 1845 Houston responded to a critical letter from Anthony Butler, minister to Mexico at the time of the Revolution, with these words: "The sliding scale may do in politics, but it will not do in matters of character." Such may be the case with most politicians, but for Houston everything was politics. In the end, the Alamo defenders, whose loyalties were with Houston and Governor Smith, were just problems that Houston left to the "sliding scale." What would the men, women, and children of the Alamo have thought of Houston's actions? Given that Captain James B. Bonham, on the morning of March 3, brought in the news that Houston would not be riding to the rescue, the people of the Alamo probably saw Houston's behavior as pure and simple betrayal of the worst kind.[67]

Chapter One Notes

1   Dr. Anson Jones, *Memoranda and Official Correspondence Relating to the Republic of Texas, its History and Annexation* (New York: D. Appleton & Co., 1859), 35.

2   Marquis James, *The Raven: A Biography of Sam Houston*, Introduction by Robert M. Utley (1929; reprint, New York: Book-of-the-Month Club, Inc., 1990), ix-x.

3   Ibid.

4   Moseley Baker to Sam Houston, October (1842), Evergreen, Manuscript Collection, Archives Division, Texas State Library, Austin, Texas, hereafter cited as MC-TSL; D. G. Burnet, *Review of the Life of Gen. Sam Houston* (Galveston: News Power Press Print, 1852), entire publication; Sidney Sherman, *Defense of Gen. Sidney Sherman Against the Charges made by Gen. Sam Houston in His Speech Delivered in the United States Senate, February 28th, 1859* (Galveston: "News" Book and Job Office, 1859), entire publication. The year is not given in the Baker letter's date, but Baker referred to the invasion that had taken place the previous spring. This appears to have been the Mexican attack on San Antonio conducted by Rafael Vasquez that occurred in March 1842. The Baker missive and the two pamphlets detail many of the complaints made against Houston by his fellow soldiers. Baker wrote the letter in response to political attacks Houston made upon him.

 William C. Davis, in *Three Roads to the Alamo: The Lives and Fortunes of David Crockett, James Bowie, and William Barret Travis* (New York: Harper Collins Publishers, 1998), 547-548 and 568-569, was the first twentieth-century historian to objectively and accurately report on Houston's negative military behavior during the revolution. Davis, in making his case, used Thomas Ricks Lindley, "Drawing Truthful Deductions," *Journal of the Alamo Battlefield Association*, I (September 1994), 31-33.

5   Robert M. Coleman, *Houston Displayed, or Who Won the Battle of San Jacinto By a Farmer In the Army* (Velasco: [Press of the Velasco Herald], 1837), entire publication.

6   John H. Jenkins, *Basic Texas Books* (1983; revised, Austin: Texas State Historical Association, 1988), 81.

7   Sam Houston to James Collinsworth, March 13, 1836, Gonzales, in John H. Jenkins, ed., *The Papers of the Texas Revolution, 1835-1836* (10 vols.; Austin: Presidial Press, 1973), V: 69-70; hereafter cited as *Papers*.

8   Ibid.

9   Sam Houston to Henry Reguet, March 13, 1836, Gonzales, Jenkins, ed., *Papers*, V: 71-72.

10 Sam Houston to James Collinsworth, March 15, 1836, Camp on the Navadid [River], Jenkins, ed., *Papers*, V: 82-84. This letter conflicts with Houston's January 17, 1836, missive to Governor Henry Smith in which

Houston asked for Smith's approval to destroy the Alamo and abandon San Antonio.

Also, in writing Collinsworth, Houston alleged that he gave the order on January 16, 1836, which is at odds with the date of January 17, in the actual missive to Smith. It is of note that Houston, on March 13, damned Fannin for not reinforcing the Alamo. Then on March 15, Houston wrote Collinsworth that the *troops should not be garrisoned in forts where they could not be supplied with "men and provisions."* Could Houston have been worried that Collinsworth might order him to reinforce Fannin, who was at that time ensconced in Fort Defiance at Goliad?

11   Sam Houston, "A Refutation of Calumnies Produced and Circulated Against His Character as Commander-In-Chief of the Army of Texas, February 28, 1859," in Amelia W. Williams and Eugene C. Barker (eds.), *The Writings of Sam Houston, 1813-1863* (8 vols.; 1938-1943; reprint; Austin and New York: Pemberton Press, 1970), VII: 306-336; hereafter cited as *Writings*.

12   Ibid.

13   Ibid. This Houston statement contains several errors. Travis was not sent to Bexar to relieve Neill, but rather to reinforce him and furnish cavalry to scout the roads west of San Antonio. Travis arrived on February 5 and assumed temporary command on February 11, 1836. The Mexican army entered Bexar on February 23, not the "last of February."

In "A Lecture on Trials and Dangers of Frontier Life, January 28, 1851," in Williams and Barker, eds., *Writings*, V: 272, Houston claimed: "The commander-in-chief had expressly ordered the Alamo to be blown up, and everything that could be, brought off forty days before the enemy besieged it...." Santa Anna commenced the investment of the Alamo on February 23, thus "forty days before" would have been January 15, 1836, two days before Houston received Neill's letter that requested assistance.

Houston's blaming of Travis for not destroying the Alamo and abandoning San Antonio appears to be the foundation for the twentieth-century view of Travis as an insane young man who was consumed with ambition to command at the Alamo, regardless of the human cost. That interpretation of Travis and the Alamo, however, is false. For a more accurate picture of Travis see William C. Davis's *Three Roads to the Alamo*.

14   James Coburn, "Houston descendant to attend rededication of Fort Sam," *San Antonio Express-News*, November 12, 1993.

15   Marshall De Bruhl, *Sword of San Jacinto: A Life of Sam Houston* (New York: Random House, 1993), 186.

16   Marshall De Bruhl, "Letters to the Editor," *Austin-American Statesman*, August 21, 1994.

17   Elizabeth Crook, *Promised Lands: A Novel of the Texas Rebellion* (New York: Doubleday, 1994), 143.

18   Jeff Long, *Empire of Bones* (New York: William Morrow and Company, Inc., 1993), 54. Long, in his work of nonfiction, *Duel of Eagles* (New York:

William Morrow and Company, Inc., 1990), 119-121, does not claim that Houston ordered the Alamo destroyed and the city abandoned. Instead, he wrote: "Bowie's mission was to prepare the destruction of the Alamo."

Then, Long continues that Bowie, after talking with Lt. Colonel James C. Neill, decided: "And so, rather than ready the Alamo for demolition, Bowie added his voice to Neill's in calling for reinforcements, money, and food. One thing Bowie was not candid about was how a remote command, like the Alamo, meant both prestige and autonomy. Above all, the Alamo command meant limelight, for it positioned upon the bowhead of the Anglo-American warship. It stood clean and separate from the hurly-burly."

There is no evidence that suggests Bowie recommended that Bexar be defended because he wanted a "remote command" away from the "hurly-burly." Long's pen does not serve history but rather his thesis that United States imperialism was behind the Texas Revolution.

19 James L. Haley, *Sam Houston* (Norman: University of Oklahoma Press, 2002), 119.

20 Sam Houston to Henry Smith, January 17, 1836, Goliad, Jenkins, ed., *Papers,* IV: 46-47.

21 Sam Houston to Henry Smith, December 6, 1836, San Felipe, Jenkins, ed., *Papers,* III: 101; Henry Smith to Sam Houston, December 17, 1835, San Felipe, Jenkins, ed., *Papers,* III: 239; Sam Houston to James Bowie, December 17, 1836, San Felipe, Jenkins, ed., *Papers,* III: 222; James C. Neill to Sam Houston, January 6, 1836, Bexar, Jenkins, ed., *Papers,* III: 425; Sam Houston to Henry Smith, January 6, Washington-on-the-Brazos, Jenkins, ed., *Papers,* III: 426; Henry Smith to William Ward, January 6, 1836, San Felipe, Jenkins, ed., *Papers,* III: 428; James C. Neill to Sam Houston, January 14, 1836, Bexar, Jenkins, ed., *Papers,* IV: 14; Sam Houston to D. C. Barrett, December 15, 1835, San Felipe, Jenkins, ed., *Papers,* III: 201-202; Sam Houston to James C. Neill, December 21, 1835, Jenkins, ed., *Papers,* III: 278-279. On December 15 Houston wrote Barrett, a member of the General Council, that he was going to locate a "field officer in command of San Antonio de Bexar with a sufficient number of troops for the defense of the station, I also design, the employment of an Engineer, and [to] have the fortifications and defenses of the place improved." On December 21 Houston wrote Neill, "On receipt of this you will take command of the Post of Bexar and make such disposition of the troops there as you may deem proper for the security & protection of the place."

For those historians who believe that Henry Smith and Sam Houston did not support an attack on Matamoros, read this. Smith wrote William Ward: "...Every man that is not in favor of Texas becoming independent and free, distrust him! Every one that wishes to supercede the commander-in-chief, or not recognize him in his proper place, distrust him! I have anticipated them and ordered the commander-in-chief forthwith to proceed to the frontier, take charge of the army, establish his headquarters at the most eligible point, and to immediately concentrate his troops, at the different points, so as to be in readiness for active operations, at the earliest possible date. A descent will be made on Matamoros, as soon as it can possibly be fitted out.... Some men of whom I have cautioned you are making bold moves to become commander-in-chief of expeditions. I will rob them of the army and they will be flat."

22 James C. Neill to Governor [Smith] and Council, January 14, 1836, Bexar, Jenkins, ed., *Papers*, IV: 15-16.

23 Houston to Smith, January 17, 1836.

24 Ibid.

25 F. W. Johnson to General Council, January 3, 1836, San Felipe, Jenkins, ed., *Papers*, III: 412-413. Johnson, speaking to Bexar's defense, wrote: "I have ordered all the guns from the town into the Alamo and the fortifications in the town to be destroyed." Johnson was probably talking about the street barricades from the siege and storming of Bexar in 1835.

26 Houston to Smith, January 17, 1836.

27 Houston to Collinsworth, March 13, 1836.

28 Williams and Barker, eds., *Writings*, VII: 306-336.

29 D. C. Barrett, J. D. Clements, Alexander Thomson, and G. A. Pattillo to James W. Robinson, January 31, 1836, San Felipe, Jenkins, ed., *Papers,* IV: 206; Henry Smith to William Bryan, February 5, 1836, San Felipe, Jenkins, ed., *Papers,* IV: 268.

See Chapter Four for the data and sources on the three political movements that attempted to turn a defensive struggle into an offensive war by organizing an attack on the port of Matamoros, an act that split the Texas government into two factions. Governor Smith, Houston, James Bowie, and the Alamo garrison were in support of total independence from Mexico so that the region could be joined to the United States. Lt. Governor Robinson, James W. Fannin Jr., and the Council, with the support and influence of Stephen F. Austin, wished to continue the fight in the name of federalism and maintain Texas as a state in the Mexican nation.

30 William B. Travis to W. G. Hill, January 21, 1836, San Felipe, Jenkins, ed., *Papers*, IV: 109; Smith to Bryan, February 5, 1836; William B. Travis to Henry Smith, January 28, 1836, Burnam's Crossing on the Colorado River, Jenkins, ed., *Papers,* IV: 176-177.

Travis wrote Smith: "In obedience to my orders, I have done everything in my power to get ready to march to the relief of Bexar, but owing to the difficulty of getting horses and provisions, and owing to desertions, I shall march today with only about thirty men, all regulars except one."

William B. Travis to Henry Smith, January 29, 1836, Burnam's Crossing, Army Papers, TSL; hereafter cited as AP-TSL. Travis wrote: "I must beg that your Excellency will recall the order for me to go on to Bexar in command of so few men.... Therefore I hope Your Excellency will take my situation into consideration, & relieve me from the orders to command in person the men who are now on their way to Bexar – Otherwise I shall feel it due to myself to resign my commission. I would remark that I can be more useful at present, In Superintending the recruiting service."

Smith did not recall Travis. Travis, however, continued to complain to Smith. In William B. Travis to Smith, February 13, 1836, Bexar, Jenkins, ed., *Papers*, IV: 327-328, Travis wrote: "Dear Sir, I wrote you an official letter last night as Comdt of this Post in the absence of Col. Neill; & if you had taken the trouble to answer my letter from Burnam's I should not now have been under the necessity of troubling you.... I do not solicit the command of this post but as Col. Neill has applied to the Commander in Chief to be relieved [and] is anxious for me to take command, I will do it if it be your order for a time until an artillery officer can be sent here." So much for the allegation that Travis was consumed with a burning ambition to command at the Alamo.

31 D. C. Barrett, J. D. Clements, Alex Thomson, and G. A. Pattillo to James W. Robinson, January 31, 1836, San Felipe, Jenkins, ed., *Papers*, IV: 204-206.

32 James C. Neill to Governor and Council, January 23, 1836, Bexar, Jenkins, ed., *Papers*, IV: 204-206.

33 Houston to Smith, January 17, 1836; Walter Prescott Webb, H. Bailey Carroll, and Eldon Stephen Branda, eds., *The Handbook of Texas* (3 vols.; Austin: Texas State Historical Association, 1952, 1976), I: 503-504; hereafter cited as *Handbook;* James W. Robinson to Philip Dimmitt, February 16, 1836, San Felipe, Jenkins, ed., *Papers,* IV: 353. Robinson ordered Dimmitt to furnish the Alamo and Goliad supplies and provisions.

34 Houston to Smith, January 17, 1836; James Bowie to Henry Smith, February 2, 1836, Bexar, Jenkins, ed., *Papers*, IV: 236-238; William H. Patton file, Audited Military Claims collection, Archives Division, Texas State Library, Austin, Texas; said collection is hereafter cited as AMC-TSL; John Sutherland file, AMC-TSL.

Bowie wrote Smith: "Capt. Patton with 5 or 6 [men] has come in." Documents in the Patton and Sutherland AMC-TSL files that detail their trip to San Antonio place Patton's small company at Gonzales on January 27, 1836, and show the unit entered Bexar on February 1, 1836.

These documents also show that Sutherland and Patton departed San Antonio for Gonzales on February 19, 1836. Patton left a small detachment at Bexar. Then he appears to have returned to the colonies to recruit men and attend the March 1 convention at Washington-on-the-Brazos.

According to a petition in the John Sutherland file, January 1, 1854, Memorials and Petitions collection, TSL; hereafter cited as M & P-TSL, Sutherland claimed Travis had sent him to Gonzales on February 23, 1836, "with the express to urge the citizens to his relief." Sutherland failed to furnish any supporting evidence to prove his claim. The petition was forwarded to a legislative committee, where it was rejected for insufficient evidence.

Neill had informed Houston that if the Bexar garrison was not reinforced within eight days it would be overrun. On January 17 when Houston moved to arrange for relief for Neill from the colonies, three of the eight days had already passed. Thus, there was not enough time to raise a relief command outside of Goliad. Either Houston did not take Neill's concern seriously or he did not care about getting sufficient assistance to Neill.

35 Sam Houston to Henry Smith, January 30, 1836, Washington-on-the-Brazos, Jenkins, ed., *Papers*, IV: 187-196; Bowie to Smith, February 2, 1836.

36 William G. Cooke, "No. 2169 [1844 Feb. W. G. Cook, Washington, Texas]," in Lamar's *The Papers of Mirabeau Buonaparte Lamar*, Gulick, Elliot, Allen, and Smither, eds. (6 vols., reprint; Austin and New York: Pemberton Press, 1968), IV: Part I: 42-46.

37 Houston to Collinsworth, March 13, 1836; Houston to Collinsworth, March 15, 1836.

38 Houston to Smith, January 30, 1836.

39 Bowie to Smith, February 2, 1836.

40 G. B. Jameson to Henry Smith, February 11, 1836, Bexar, Jenkins, ed., *Papers*, IV: 303; William B. Travis to Henry Smith, February 12, 1836, Bexar, Jenkins, ed., *Papers*, IV: 317-318. See Chapter Ten for more information about Lt. Colonel Neill's departure from San Antonio.

41 Travis to Smith, February 12, 1836; William B. Travis to Henry Smith, February 16, 1836, Bexar, Jenkins, ed., *Papers,* IV: 317, and 368.

42 De Bruhl, "Letters to the Editor," August 21, 1994.

43 Henry Smith to Sam Houston, January 28, 1836, San Felipe, Jenkins, ed., *Papers*, IV: 176; Sam Houston to Chief Bowles, February 5, 1836, Nacogdoches, Jenkins, ed., *Papers*, IV: 260-261.

44 Houston et al. Treaty, February 23, 1836, Bowles's Village, Jenkins, ed., *Papers*, IV: 415-418; William B. Travis to Sam Houston, February 25, 1836, Bexar, Jenkins, ed., *Papers*, IV: 433-434; Houston to Public, March 2, 1836, Washington-on-the-Brazos, Jenkins, ed., *Papers*, IV: 490-491; De Bruhl, *Sword of San Jacinto*, 180.

According to De Bruhl, Houston also ran as a delegate for the convention in Nacogdoches, but in a field of seventeen candidates he finished next to last. De Bruhl believed the Refugio "army vote" elected Houston to the convention. Ira Westover, in Westover to Sam Houston, February 7, 1836, Refugio, Jenkins, ed., *Papers*, IV: 284, reported that Houston was elected by the municipality vote. In Volunteers to Convention [February 1836], Refugio, Jenkins, ed., *Papers*, IV: 473-474, we see that the soldiers elected David Thomas and Edward Conrad to represent them in the convention, not Sam Houston.

45 Edwin Waller affidavit, n.d., David Gouverneur Burnet Papers, Box 2B159, Center for American History, The University of Texas, Austin, Texas; hereafter cited as CAH.

According to Webb, Carroll, and Branda, eds., *Handbook*, II: 856-857, Waller represented Columbia in the 1835 Consultation and was elected to the General Council. At the March 1836 convention Waller represented Brazoria.

Houston's biographers, while recognizing his alcoholism before the Texas Revolution, have consistently failed to objectively consider that element of his character during the revolution.

Nevertheless, in Marquis James to Mr. Asbury, June 21, year not given, Pleasantville, N.Y., Box 2N488, Amelia W. Williams Papers, CAH, James, the author of *The Raven: A Biography of Sam Houston,* made the following observation about Houston's drinking problem: "Houston would have drunk himself to death but for her [his wife Margaret Moffette Lea]. Maybe Anna Raguet was a little better fixed to be the wife of a public man, as nearly as I can view it, but maybe not. Texas owes a lot to Margaret, who isn't the wife I'd have picked for Houston on the ground maybe, but that would have been my lack of good judgment. And even in the church business I think Margaret knew best, or did best whether she knew what she was doing or not. Houston was a serener man after he joined up."

46 Mary Austin Holley, *Notes Made by Mrs. Holley in Interviews with Prominent Texans of the Early Days,* April 7, 1844, Mary Austin Holley Papers, Box 2R40, CAH.

47 Coleman, *Houston Displayed,* 3. Coleman misrepresented Houston's attendance at the Convention. Houston did not spend his days totally in the activity of sleeping. According to the "Journals of the Convention," Jenkins, ed., *Papers,* IX: 289-314, Houston was in session with the convention from March 1 to March 6, conducting its business.

48 Houston to Public, March 2, 1836, Washington-on-the-Brazos, Jenkins, ed., *Papers,* IV: 490-491. The date of March 2, 1836, for this document comes from Henry Stuart Foote, *Texas and The Texians; or Advance of The Anglo-Americans to the Southwest* (2 vols.; Philadelphia: Thomas, Cowperthwait & Co., 1841), II: 265-266. The only other known version of the proclamation is in the form of a broadside that is only dated March 1836. Therefore, there is a possibility that Foote's date of March 2 is incorrect. A content comparison of the document with Travis's letter of February 25, 1836, shows that the March 2 declaration does not include any of the data found in Travis's missive of the twenty-fifth. Most likely the call for assistance was actually issued soon after March 6, the date that Houston departed for Gonzales.

49 In fact Houston appears to have ordered one company that was organized to relieve the Alamo to go no farther west than Gonzales. In the William G. Hall file, RV 1391, Texas General Land Office, the affidavit of Jackson Hall reports: "I Jackson Hall do hereby certify that William G. Hall did on or about the first day of February 1836 [William G. Hall said March 1], raise a part of a company of volunteers to [go to] Travis' relief at San Antonio. Said William G. Hall was elected Captain of said company. I have been creditable informed that said William Hall was ordered by General Houston to stop at Gonzales."

50 Travis to Houston, February 25, 1836; William Fairfax Gray, *From Virginia to Texas, 1835: Diary of Col. Wm. F. Gray, Giving Details of His Journey to Texas and Return in 1835-1836 and Second Journey to Texas in 1837* (1909; reprint, Houston: Fletcher Young Publishing Co., 1965), 124.

51 "Journals of the Convention," Jenkins, ed., *Papers*, IX: 305. It appears that Travis's famous "I shall never surrender or retreat" letter of February 24, 1836, made little impression on the convention members.

52 Henderson Yoakum, *History of Texas From its First Settlement in 1655 to its Annexation to the United States in 1846* (2 vols.; New York: Redfield, 1855), II: 74-75. Houston probably had another reason for his reappointment. He wanted total control over the Texian military forces, regular and volunteer, so that he would not have to answer to the soldiers as was the norm with a volunteer force. If volunteers did not like the way their commander operated, they elected a new commander. Houston wanted to avoid such a situation as the one he had found at the siege of Bexar and in Goliad in January 1836, with Fannin and Johnson.

53 "Journals of the Convention," Jenkins, ed., *Papers*, IX: 309-310.

54 Ibid.

55 Yoakum, *History*, II: 75. Yoakum wrote that this exchange took place on the "day before General Houston received his final instructions," which was March 6, 1836, thus the exchange would have occurred on March 5. The convention did not meet on that date, thus the incident could only have occurred on March 4 after the convention reappointed Houston commander-in-chief. James Collinsworth and Richard Ellis to Sam Houston, March 6, 1836, Washington-on-the-Brazos, Jenkins, ed., *Papers*, V: 6.

56 Gulick, et al., *Lamar Papers*, III: 278-295; Webb, Carroll, and Branda, eds., *Handbook*, I: 256-257. Burton, a former West Point student and Nacogdoches lawyer, commanded a Texas Ranger company in far East Texas in the winter of 1835-1836. He fought as a private in Henry W. Karnes's cavalry company at San Jacinto. In his account to Lamar, he also implied that Houston, at the convention was more interested in getting resolutions passed in favor of the "Cherokee & 12 other bands of Indians" than he was in reporting to the army at Gonzales.

57 Lancelot Abbotts to General [William Steele], January 26, 1876, Warwick, England, Adjutant General Correspondence, TSL, said collection hereafter cited as the AJC-TSL; C. B. Stewart affidavit, Lancelot Abbotts file, AMC-TSL; Lancelot Abbotts file, Republic of Texas Pension collection, TSL, said collection is hereafter cited as PC-TSL; Joseph D. Clements affidavit, Joseph D. Clements file, AMC-TSL; Webb, Carroll, and Branda, eds., *Handbook*, I: 709-710.

Abbotts served as an assistant secretary to Governor Henry Smith during December 1835. He served as a private in Moseley Baker's company of San Felipe volunteers from March 1836 to May 1836 and participated in the Battle of San Jacinto.

William Bull carried Travis's March 3, 1836 letter from Gonzales to the convention.

Doctor "Biggs or Briggs" appears to have been Benjamin Briggs Goodrich, a member of the convention from Washington-on-the-Brazos. His younger brother, John Calvin Goodrich, died at the fall of the Alamo.

58 Ibid.

59 Holley, *Interviews*, 20; Baker to Houston, October 1842, MC-TSL. Mrs. Peyton [Eberly was her second husband] was quite an individual. Years later Moseley Baker, who torched San Felipe on orders from Sam Houston, remembered her: "I remained on the western side until Mrs. Peyton, now Mrs. Eberly, whose firmness inspired many a family with confidence and whose spirits had you [Houston] possessed, no Mexican force would have reveled in San Felipe."

60 William W. Thompson affidavit, December 1, 1840, Austin, Folder 5, Box 2-9/6, Home Paper, TSL.

Houston had every reason to consider James W. Fannin Jr. as a political rival. Houston had given Fannin a regular army commission as a colonel (Houston to Fannin, November 13, 1835, Jenkins, *Papers*, II: 396), then Fannin sided with the General Council against Governor Henry Smith and Houston over the goal of the Matamoros Expedition. Houston had to have considered Fannin's actions a betrayal.

Reuben R. Brown, a member of the proposed Matamoros expedition, reported the following about Houston's feelings toward Fannin. Brown ("Reuben R. Brown's Account of His Part in the Texas Revolution," *Lamar Papers,* V: 368) wrote: "Genl Saml Houston joined us at this place [Goliad] and addicted himself to the most shameful dissipation carousing and drinking continually with the soldiers. He did not at first disapprove of the expedition until he learned that Fannin was the choice of the volunteers to command them – his jealous feelings towards Col. Fannin prompted him to put down the expedition if possible...."

Travis, however, was not a political threat to Houston. Travis's only involvement in the revolution was military. Had Travis lived, he would have been a potential rival for Houston.

Thompson's confrontation with Houston may have made an impact on the slow moving general. We find, in Hockley Memorandum, March 9, 1836, Burnam's Crossing, Jenkins, ed., *Papers*, V: 35, that Houston on that date sent orders to Lt. Colonel James C. Neill at Gonzales, instructing Neill that Fannin had been sent a missive which read: "Colonel Fannin to march immediately with all his effective force (except one hundred and twenty men, to be left for the protection of his post), to co-operate with the command of Colonel Neill, at some point to be designated by him, to the relief to Colonel Travis, now in the Alamo."

James L. Haley, Houston's most recent biographer, attacked the Thompson statement (Haley, *Houston,* 123) with these words: "The possibility of Houston indulging in either drink or drugs is out of the question; his sobriety on the campaign was admitted by even his worst enemies in attendance.

The Thompson affidavit was sworn to an official of Mirabeau Lamar's State Department at a time when government minions were always looking to swear in somebody to say something defamatory about Houston. Thompson also swore that Houston insisted of the siege of the Alamo, 'that he believed it to be a damn lie, & that all those reports from Travis and Fannin were lies, for there were no Mexican forces there and that he believed it was only electioneering schemes on [the part of] Travis & Fannin to sustain their own popularity.' The Thompson affidavit loses its little credibility there. Houston had predicted the arrival of Santa Anna within a week's accuracy since the first of December, had repeated it many times, and then published a broadside to the people announcing Santa Anna's arrival on March 2."

There are a number of problems with Haley's point of view on the Thompson document. First, Thompson made no accusations about Houston being drunk or drinking. Second, the statement was not given to a member of Lamar's State Department. Thompson testified before J. W. Smith, the Chief Justice of Travis County, who had been elected by the citizens of that county. Also, how about a valid source for the claim that "government minions were always looking to swear in somebody to say something defamatory about Houston."

Moreover, Thompson does not appear to have been too anti-Houston. In 1841, as an Austin alderman, he was one of the citizens who greeted Houston's return with an extremely pro-Houston declaration (Address of Austin Committees to Gen. Houston upon the occasion of his visiting that City to be inaugurated third President of the Republic, November 20, 1841, Washington D. Miller Papers, 1873/3-2, Archives, TSL), of which a part reads: "At this crisis, when our country is encompassed with difficulties and perils and through every range of her internal polity embarrassed and overcast with gloom and despondency, it is [a] matter of joyous graduation that our well tried chieftain and statesman has been again called, by the unbought and overwhelming voice of the people, to preside in the chair of state and give a new and salutary impulse to our destinies."

As for Haley's claim that Houston had, as early as December 1, 1835, predicted Santa Anna's arrival within a week accuracy and had repeated it a number of times, this investigator does not know what to make of the allegation. Haley did not cite any source or sources for the statement. This investigator was not able to locate any source that support Haley's claim. Haley's failure to cite a source for what he writes occurs far too often in this pro-Houston work. Historians need to be able to check Haley's sources to determine if his interpretation is a reasonable one or if it is just fiction to make Houston look good to the reader.

61 Williams and Barker, eds., *Writings*, VII: 306-336.

62 Baker to Houston, October 1842, MC-TSL.

63 Sam Houston to James Collinsworth, March 7, 1836, Coles Settlement, Jenkins, ed., *Papers*, V: 17-18.

64 Ibid.

65   The Convention, because of the arrival of the Mexican forces, failed to ratify Houston's treaty with the Indians. After the war, the first Texas Congress rejected the treaty.

66   Webb, Carroll, and Branda, eds., *Handbook*, II: 403-404; Louis Wiltz Kemp, *The Signers of the Texas Declaration of Independence* (Houston: Anson Jones Press, 1944), 178; Sam Houston to James Power, December 28, 1835, Jenkins, ed., *Papers*, III: 350.

   On December 28, 1835, as Houston set the stage for the invasion of Matamoros, he wrote James Power: "Colonel [Peyton S.] Wyatt will relieve Captain [J. M.] Allen [at Copano], who will repair to New Orleans, and return by the first of March. Say to our friends that, by the rise of grass [early March], we will be on the march." Who the "friends" were remains a mystery.

   Houston, even after learning the fate of the Alamo, continued to advise the government that fortifications should be constructed at Copano. Live Oak Point, the location on Copano Bay where Houston wished to construct the structures, was the site of James Power's home.

   History will probably never know the exact nature of the Houston and Power relationship, but historian Louis Wiltz Kemp wrote: "At Refugio, someone, probably James Power, influenced the voters to elect Houston a delegate from the thinly populated municipality. Were it not for this, Houston's subsequent career might have been materially different from the brilliant one now recorded."

67   Sam Houston to Anthony Butler, December 25, 1845, Houston, W. W. Fontaine Papers, Box 2D150, CAH. William B. Travis to the Convention, March 6, 1836, Jenkins, ed., *Papers*, IV: 502-504; Milledge L. Bonham Jr. "James Butler Bonham: A Consistent Rebel," *Southwestern Historical Quarterly*, XXXV: 129. The Houston quotation comes from a letter that was Houston's answer to a bitter and caustic missive from Butler, in which Butler accused Houston of almost every indiscretion under the sun and the moon.

Chapter Two

A Critical Study of a Critical Study: "Puzzling Questions"

As a researcher [Dr. Eugene C.] Barker's methods were characterized by exactness, although as a practical historian he realized the virtual impossibility of checking all the source material for any given project. Barker adhered, more or less, to the theory that the work of a historian should be a stepping stone on which future generations could expand.

Thomas B. Brewer[1]

Dr. Amelia W. Williams's doctoral dissertation "A Critical Study of the Siege of The Alamo and of the Personnel of Its Defenders" is probably the most cited secondary source found in articles and books on the Texian Alamo. Since the study's publication in the *Southwestern Historical Quarterly* in the early 1930s, historians have considered it to be the definitive investigative work on the exalted event. Even before its appearance in the scholarly journal, Dr. Eugene C. Barker, Williams's committee chairman, declared: "Miss Williams is also an experienced and industrious investigator.... In my judgment she has definitively settled many puzzling questions about the number and the identity of the defenders of the Alamo. This is a real contribution to the history of Texas."[2] Indeed, Williams's study did appear to be a true contribution at that time because it was the first time a systematic approach had been used in attempting to identify all of the men who had died at the Alamo.

Williams's research first impacted the world of Texas history during the 1936 centennial celebration of the Texas Revolution. The study determined the names of the Alamo heroes that were carved in stone and cast in bronze in San Antonio and Gonzales in honor of Texas's 100th birthday as an independent nation and state. L. W. Kemp, chairman of the

The Alamo, early twentieth century
Photo courtesy Library of the Daughters of the Republic of Texas at the Alamo

Advisory Board of Texas Historians, wrote Williams: "The names of the men who fell at the Alamo, as best as can be determined, will be carved on a $50,000 monolith to be erected in San Antonio. The selection of these names has been left up to me but of course I shall be guided solely by your recommendations in the matter."[3]

Williams was willing to have her Alamo list carved in stone for the centennial. Publication in a local newspaper, however, was another story. In March 1936 Williams became upset when she learned that J. C. Oslin, a writer for the *San Antonio Express,* had used, without her permission, her defender roster in an article. Williams penned Oslin's boss an indignant letter that declared: "He took my *entire list* of Alamo men. The very heart of my book that is on the press. This is what I call a sneak thief trick in the history [of the] writing world.... Your Mr. Oslin rearranged the list. I had it alphabetized. He arranged [it] as to the States from which the men came, but he used all my material – every bit. He even says it is my list."[4]

Williams's complaint seems to be without foundation, given that her list had been published in the *Southwestern Historical Quarterly* in 1934. The list was pretty much public record as long as any user cited

Williams's study as the source, which Oslin did. Clearly, Williams was protective of her list and had publication plans for it beyond the *Quarterly*. Moreover, she was well on the way to becoming the official gatekeeper for the Daughters of the Republic of Texas's honor roll of Alamo defenders.

Also that year the *Dallas Morning News* identified the reason Williams had completed the defender roster: "One of Dr. Williams's first contributions to Texas history was a reconstruction of the list [Williams's master thesis] of the men who left Gonzales in a company to fight in the Alamo.... This work received the praise of Dr. Eugene C. Barker, university authority on Texas history, and other historians of the State who believed Dr. Williams should go further into this same field of research. With this encouragement, she was prompted to make as complete as possible a study of the personnel of the Texas army at the Alamo when it fell."[5]

Three years later the *San Antonio Express Evening News* reported that Williams had received many letters claiming that this or that man died at the Alamo but was not on her list. Williams answered the complaint with words that in time would come back to haunt her: "However, for those names on the list, *I have not one but several official sources that indicate that each man died at the Alamo* [italics added].... I have never found a new name to be added to the roll, although I have found considerable material about some of the men. I have never had to discard but one man, that of John G. King of Gonzales."[6]

Today the Williams study is firmly entrenched as the "Bible" on the Texian Alamo. In 1992 a Texas State Historical Association sales pitch for old issues of the *Quarterly* described the work as: "Amelia Williams's classic five-part series on the Alamo." Alamo historian Bill Groneman used the Williams roll and its biographical data as his main source for *Alamo Defenders A Genealogy: The People and Their Words.* Also, Groneman was the author of all but a few of the Alamo defender entries for the *New Handbook of Texas,* a six-volume encyclopedia of Texas history published by the Texas State Historical Association. Thus Williams's list is reflected in that publication through Groneman's work. Susan Prendergast Schoelwer used the Williams data in "The Artist's Alamo: A Reappraisal of Pictorial Evidence, 1836-1850," the lead article for an Alamo thematic issue of the *Southwestern Historical Quarterly.* The most recent work in which Williams's study is reflected is *Alamo*

Sourcebook 1836 by Tim J. and Terry S. Todish. More importantly, the official Alamo defender roll for the state of Texas is based on Williams's Alamo list.[7]

Nevertheless, despite the study's acceptance, cracks have appeared in the work's facade of authority over the years since its publication. In 1956 Frank H. Wardlaw, director of the University of Texas Press, considered publishing the study but never did so. Perhaps letters like the one he received from Mrs. A. Waldo Jones of Atlanta, Georgia, influenced him. She wrote: "Mrs. R. G. Halter at the Alamo has told me that you are going to publish Dr. Amelia Williams' thesis, 'A Critical Study of the Siege of the Alamo,' and has suggested that I write you with respect to some errors therein regarding William Irvine Lewis, one of the heroes, so that they may be corrected before it goes to press."[8]

Then, Wardlaw may have had other reasons for rejecting Williams's study. According to Miss Jane Smoot, Williams's niece: "After her [Williams's] death I myself (one of her closest relatives) took her contract with him [Wardlaw] to [a] personal appointment in his office to ask him to carry on with their signed agreement. Mr. Wardlaw said that the public pulse had changed and that the University of Texas could no longer make as much money by printing scholarly works as it could profit from entertaining material, so he did not wish to honor his own contract." One would think that if Wardlaw did not want to publish Williams's work because of serious scholarship problems, it is doubtful he would have expressed that opinion to Smoot, a grieving relative. Also, it was and is the goal of a university press to publish scholarly works; even some that fail to make a profit, provided the work is important and the research is sound.[9]

A few years later writer Walter Lord encountered the Williams study while researching the Alamo for *A Time To Stand.* From that experience he wrote:

> The most widely known academic work is Amelia Williams' Ph.D. thesis. ... it has been the leading authority for dozens of subsequent articles and books. Miss Williams did indeed amass a mountain of material, but in a way her thesis has been the worst thing that ever happened to the history of the Alamo. Not because she did so little work, but because she did so much. The sheer bulk of her research has discouraged later students from checking up

on her and has led them all too often to take her statements at face value.

This is dangerous. As evidence supporting a Bonham-Travis friendship, for instance, she quotes from an alleged letter written by Travis urging Bonham to come to Texas. Actually her quotation is a paraphrase of a reminiscence by Bonham's nephew, recounting the family tradition.

Sometimes Miss Williams relies on pure trash. For example, she uses Frank Templeton's trivial novel *Margaret Ballentine or The Fall of the Alamo* as her source for making defender Hiram J. Williamson a West Point man, when any check of the Point's *Register of Graduates and Former Cadets* would show he never attended.

Most curious is her personal aversion to Travis, which has much to do with the rather priggish picture of him that exists today and which was especially evident in Laurence Harvey's portrayal in the recent John Wayne film. Miss Williams could get quite upset about Travis, as evinced by a letter she wrote her professor Samuel Asbury in 1933. From Travis's failure to mention Bowie in his desperate appeals for help, she declared she detected what she considered a mean streak, "a cruel, vindictive nature."[10]

Thomas Lloyd Miller was the next researcher to discover problems with Williams's scholarship. Miller observed: "Her list contains the names of eight Mexican-Texians; but more recent scholarship reveals that two of the eight names of Spanish-Texans, as well as the names of three Anglo-Texans should be stricken from the Alamo roll."[11]

Richard G. Santos is another historian who had a problem with Williams's defender list. In a footnote in *Santa Anna's Campaign Against Texas 1835-1836,* he observed: "This author has chosen to review and analyze only those figures given by people in San Antonio during or immediately after the siege and fall of the Alamo. For other figures not necessarily based on reliable sources but seemingly accepted in some circles, see Amelia Williams' 'Critical Study of the Siege of the Alamo....'"[12]

Miller's discovery and Santos's opinion would not have surprised historian Harbart Davenport, who appraised the dissertation for Williams before its submission to Dr. Barker's committee. His first criticism was:

"In preparing her corrected roster of those who fell at the Alamo, Miss Williams incorrectly estimated the weight of the evidence contained in the bounty, donation and headright [Texas land grant documents] files in the [Texas General] Land office, as compared with the copies of the muster rolls preserved in the same archive." As will be explained later, this error had a telling effect on the accurateness of Williams's Alamo list.[13]

Dr. Paul Hutton, an acclaimed historian at the University of New Mexico, was the first academic scholar to publicly condemn Williams's scholarship. He wrote:

> The line between the Alamo of fact and the Alamo of popular fancy is often blurred. While there has been an amazingly large body of historical and popular literature generated on the battle, there has never been an adequate serious study of it by a professional academic historian. Thus competent popular historians such as Walter Lord, who has written the best book on the battle, have not had the usual body of solid secondary materials to draw upon when writing. The academic work usually cited as the best study of the battle and its heroes, Amelia Williams's doctoral dissertation, is of stunningly poor quality. Academic historians have thus deserted the field, leaving the battle to the popularizers and propagandists.
>
> Those who have written on the battle, for the most part, have simply repeated false stories told before in books, articles, and newspaper accounts. The written historical record is a sad one.[14]

Hutton's critical bullet is on target, but he failed to cut the bull's eye. The "stunningly poor quality" of Williams's study involves much more than sloppy research. Time and space does not allow for a litany of every error, probable fabrication, and unfounded conclusion thus far discovered by this writer. The following examples, however, should adequately illustrate the unreliability of the Williams study and the reasons for it.

William B. Travis's Death

Travis's death has not generated controversy and debate equal to that of David Crockett's last minutes. There are, however, several versions of the Alamo commander's death. In 1928, previous to the completion of her dissertation, Williams accepted the version that is in vogue today. She wrote: "Concerning the death of the celebrated Travis, Crockett, Bowie, [and] Bonham, my conclusions backed by documentary evidence are: Travis fell while manning a cannon at [the] north west wall of [the] large area."[15]

In the following years, Williams, apparently without benefit of new evidence, changed her mind and validated the suicide version of Travis's death. She claimed: "Both Anselmo Borgarra (also found Bogarra), the messenger from the Mexicans at San Antonio to [Juan N.] Seguin at Gonzales, and Antonio Perez, their messenger to [Jose Antonio] Navarro and [Jose Francisco] Ruiz at San Felipe, reported that Travis shot himself when he saw the Mexicans pouring over the walls of the Alamo and realized all hope of saving his men was gone." Thus Williams concluded: "The fact that Travis's only wound was a pistol shot through the forehead, together with all attending circumstances, makes the reports carried by Borgarra and Perez seem very plausible."[16]

A review of the sources shows that Perez made no Alamo report at Gonzales, at least none that has survived. He was on a mission to inform Tejanos about Santa Anna's offer of pardons to all who would pledge allegiance to the centralist government. Perez found Bergara (the correct spelling) at the Jose Flores ranch. Bergara was there to escort Andres Barcena to safety at Beeson's on the Colorado River. Barcena was the man who entered Gonzales with Bergara. Perez arrived at Gonzales later and reported the pardon offer to Sam Houston. In regard to Travis's death, Bergara, who had obtained most of his information from Perez, only said: "Travis killed himself." The source reports no claim of Travis having shot himself in the forehead because enemy soldiers were "pouring over the walls of the Alamo and...all hope of saving his men was gone." That allegation appears to have come from Williams, not the source material.[17]

Nevertheless, Williams did have one source that claimed Travis had shot himself. Speaking to the unsupported story she attributed to Bergara and Perez, Williams wrote: "These reports have been ignored or discredited by all writers of Texas history, but there is evidence that some of Travis's closest friends believed them in 1836. On March 28, 1836, Andrew Briscoe gave an account of the fall of the Alamo to the editor of the *New Orleans Post and Union* in which he said: 'The brave and gallant Travis, to prevent his falling into the hands of the enemy, shot himself.' This account was copied by the *Arkansas Gazette*, April 12, 1836."[18]

Firstly, Briscoe's letter was written on March 16 and first appeared in the *Red River Herald*. The unsubstantiated story did not appear in the April 12, 1836 issue of the *Arkansas Gazette* as claimed by Williams. Secondly, Briscoe and Travis were well acquainted, but the one letter does not support Williams's conclusion that "some of Travis's closest friends" believed he committed suicide. For that claim she would have needed at least one more letter from a Travis friend that reported the same data as the Briscoe missive. As it is, the Briscoe document only shows that Briscoe may have believed a suicide rumor that was circulating about Travis. Briscoe's alleged reason (to not be captured) for the supposed suicide is different from the one (all hope of saving his men was gone) Williams attributed to Bergara and Perez. Also, Houston wrote a friend that it was rumored that Travis had stabbed himself to prevent capture, which contradicts Briscoe's claim of Travis shooting himself. The Houston version also suggests that someone may have seen a bayonet, knife, or sword wound on Travis's body.[19]

Another description of Travis's death is found in a report attributed to Joe, Travis's slave, who was sleeping near his master when the alarm was first sounded in the Alamo on the morning of March 6.

> ...Travis sprang up, seized his rifle and sword, and called to Joe to follow him. Joe took his gun and followed. Travis ran across the Alamo and mounted the wall, and called out to his men, "Come on, boys, the Mexicans are upon us, and we'll give them *Hell*." He discharged his gun; so did Joe. In an instant Travis was shot down. He fell within the wall, on the sloping ground, and sat up. The enemy twice applied their scaling ladders to the walls, and were twice beaten back. But this Joe did not well understand, for when his master fell he ran and ensconced himself in a house, from which he says he fired on them several times, after they got in. On the third attempt they succeeded in mounting the walls, and then poured over like sheep.... As Travis sat wounded on the ground General Mora, who was passing him made a blow at him with his sword, which Travis struck up, and ran his assailant through the body, and both died on the same spot.[20]

The Joe story is similar to a Susanna Dickinson report of Travis's death that was given at Gonzales and a few days later relayed to a Texas newspaper by John W. Smith, the Alamo storekeeper, and Andrew Ponton, the judge at Gonzales. Their description reads: "Col. Travis stood on the walls cheering his men, exclaiming, 'Hurra, my boys!' till he received a *second shot* [italics added], and fell; it is stated that a Mexican general, (Mora) then rushed upon him and lifted his sword to destroy his victim, who, collecting all his last expiring energies, directed a thrust at the former, which changed their relative positions; for the victim became the victor, and the remains of both descended to external sleep; but not alike to everlasting fame." It is highly unlikely that Dickinson witnessed Travis's death. Therefore, if her version is true or even partly true, she must have obtained the data from a Mexican officer. Also, it is important to understand that Joe did not witness Travis's death. Joe left him sitting upright on the sloping ground.[21]

Williams's claim of a "pistol shot through the forehead" comes from her transformation of a statement made by Francisco Ruiz. In 1860 Ruiz declared: "On the north battery of the fortress lay the lifeless body of Col. Travis on the gun carriage, shot only in the forehead." The claim of a "pistol shot through the forehead," which suggests entry and exit wounds is not supported by the Ruiz evidence. Thus, it appears that because Travis had already discharged his rifle, Williams assumed that the only way he could have shot himself in the head was with a pistol. Which makes sense, except that neither a pistol wound nor a caliber size of the ball is mentioned in the Ruiz account. Also, Joe reported that Travis was only armed with a rifle and sword. Moreover, there is valid evidence that indicates Ruiz was not in Bexar on March 6, 1836. Therefore, he did not identify Travis's body. If Travis had a wound someplace on his head, Ruiz obtained that information from somebody else who saw the body.[22]

Santa Anna's soldiers appear to have been firing "buck and ball" loads in their muskets. Thus, given Joe's statement, Travis's head wound, if he had one, may have been caused by a single buckshot pellet that did not cause immediate death. The Ruiz statement does not eliminate the possibility of a blade wound on Travis's body, which might not have been as obvious as the head wound.[23]

Furthermore, while there was no General Mora at the north wall, a "Colonel Esteban Mora" was one of the officers who "succeeded in gaining a foothold on the north side where the strife was bitterest, which encouraged the soldiers in their advance and resulted in their capture of the enemy's artillery on that side." Travis and Mora may have engaged in some kind of struggle. We just don't know. Mora, however, was not killed in the March 6 attack of the Alamo. He died at San Jacinto.[24]

Another Mexican report that throws new light on the older evidence is a letter that an unknown soldier wrote on March 7, 1836. The informant was a member of General Martin Perfecto de Cos's column that attacked the north wall. He claimed that what he had seen was "at close range." He wrote about Travis: "Their leader, named Travis, died like a brave man with his rifle in his hand at the back of a cannon." The soldier may have witnessed Travis's death, but that is not certain. He may have only seen Travis's body and assumed he "died like a brave man" because the body was located where the fighting was the most intense. Still, if the Mexican soldier saw Travis's body "with rifle in his hand," that would seem to eliminate the suicide stories and the death struggle with Mora. If Travis had killed himself with a pistol or knife, he would have had one of those weapons in hand. If he had died in a death struggle with Mora, he would have had a sword in his hand.[25]

In total, the evidence about Travis's death only supports a couple of conclusions. First, Travis did not shoot himself in the head or stab himself in the heart. Second, Travis was killed on one of the Alamo walls, next to a cannon. Remember, the *T & T Register* story claimed that Travis had been hit twice. The nature of the first wound is unknown, except that it did not appear to have killed Travis. The second wound knocked him down to a seated position on the sloping wall inside the fort but failed to kill him. Perhaps both wounds came from buckshot pellets. Had Travis been hit in the head with a musket or rifle ball, it is doubtful he would have remained seated on the slope. At that point Joe departed the scene. Travis must have moved from the sloping wall to a nearby cannon platform and received a third, fatal shot to his body. Or the killing wound may have come from a blade weapon of some kind.

What of the death struggle story—where did it come from? It may have been a piece of contrived fiction to refute the stories that Travis had killed himself and to turn his death into a moral victory. Look at the report's core element once again: "...it is stated that a Mexican general, (Mora) then rushed upon him, and lifted his sword to destroy his victim, who, collecting all his last expiring energies, directed a thrust at the former, which changed their relative positions; for the victim became the victor...." The tale seems to be one of those archetypal Alamo stories that, using Travis and Mora as symbols, proclaim that even though the event was a Mexican victory, the Mexican loss was so great that in the end it was as much a defeat as victory.

A second example of Williams changing the evidence to fit her interpretation of the events is found in her section on David Crockett's alleged "Tennessee Mounted Volunteers." She claimed: "Among the Comptroller Military Service Records, there are seven documents, all requisitions on the Provisional Government of Texas, signed by David Crockett and others of his band for board for a company of "Tennessee Mounted Volunteers" while they were resting at Washington and while they were on the way from that town to Bexar. These documents show that there were eighteen or more men in the company, including Colonel Crockett and Captain William B. Harrison, and that they went by the way of Gonzales to San Antonio."[26]

Williams used five documents to unite the Crockett and Harrison units into a single company at Washington-on-the-Brazos. One of the documents is a claim written by Dr. William P. Smith on April 24, 1836. Williams's published version of the Smith document reads:

> This is to certify that A. L. Harrison was a member of William B. Harrison's company of Mounted Volunteers when that company left Washington for San Antonio about January 20, last. He fell sick and was likewise under my medical care as a surgeon in the army of Texas.[27]

The actual Smith claim differs in two ways from what Williams reported. Smith wrote:

> This is to certify that A. L. Harrison was a member of Capt. William B. Harrison's company of Mounted Volunteers when the company left Washington for San Antonio about the 15th of last January – Said A. L. Harrison was likewise under my medical care as surgeon in the Army of Texas.[28]

Because Williams's papers contain a correct transcription of the Smith affidavit in what appears to be Williams's handwriting, it seems that she must have intentionally changed the wording of the document. First, she changed the date from "about the 15th of last January" to "about January 20, last." She probably changed the date because Crockett was in Nacogdoches on January 15, 1836. Thus Harrison and Crockett could not have ridden together to San Antonio if Harrison had left Washington-on-the-Brazos while Crockett was still in Nacogdoches.[29]

Williams's second alteration expanded Smith's statement of "Said A. L. Harrison was..." to "He fell sick and was..." Thus suggesting that Harrison became ill at Washington on or about January 20, 1836. This change appears to have been made to effect the understanding of a second A. L. Harrison document. According to Williams, Comptroller Military Service record 644 was a Colonel Sidney Sherman affidavit that reported that Harrison had lost a horse and gun in the service of Texas. Sherman wrote that the property had been appraised by "Captain W. B. Harrison, Col. Crockett, and Lieutenant Robert Campbell." Sherman, however, did not state when and where the evaluation had taken place. Williams, by changing the Smith affidavit to show that A. L. Harrison was sick and did not go to the Alamo, eliminated the possibility that the horse and gun were appraised at San Antonio. Thus, with Williams's versions of the documents, a reasonable interpretation would be that the evaluation most likely occurred sometime before Harrison's unit arrived at Washington-on-the-Brazos and supported Williams's claim that Captain W. B. Harrison and his men were members of Crockett's command.[30]

A military claim that Williams failed to find indicates that Harrison's "Nashville Volunteers," not the "Tennessee Mounted Volunteers," appear to have arrived at Washington-on-the-Brazos on January 23, 1836, and were still at that location on January 26. Whereas, Crockett and all but one of his men departed Washington on the morning of January 23, 1836. It would appear that the two companies probably missed each other by only hours.[31]

Moreover, Williams claimed that the Harrison and Crockett groups traveled to San Antonio by way of Gonzales. She, however, failed to cite any evidence for that belief. On the other hand, two military claims show that the Harrison company stopped in San Felipe. Harrison obtained forage and provisions from William Kerr and John Echols at San Felipe on January 28, 1836. Two additional claims for provisions reveal that Harrison's company trekked to Bexar by way of Mina (Bastrop). Harrison purchased provisions from James Gotier on January 30, 1836. The next day Harrison obtained supplies from John Eblin. Gotier lived southeast of Mina near the Gotier Trace that ran between Mina and San Felipe. John Eblin lived two miles below Mina and just across and upriver from present-day Smithville.[32]

Crockett commanded a small "Mounted Spy Company" that was organized on or about January 8, 1836, in Nacogdoches. Two claims show that on January 23 and 24, 1836, at Washington-on-the-Brazos, Crockett's unit comprised himself and five other men. At that time, Crockett and his scouts appear to have been riding for Goliad, rather than San Antonio. On January 9, 1836, while in San Augustine, about forty miles east of Nacogdoches, Crockett wrote his daughter. Of his travel plans, he wrote: "I have taken the oath of government and have enrolled my name as a volunteer and will set out for the Rio Grand[e] in a few days with volunteers from the United States." Houston was, at that time, sending all incoming troops from the United States to Goliad, which was serving as the staging area for his planned March invasion of Matamoros on the Rio Grande.[33]

The last documented location of Crockett before his arrival at Bexar sometime between February 5 and 11, 1836, was Gay Hill, the home of James Gibson Swisher, on the Goliad road, west of Washington-on-the-Brazos. The time frame for this location was most likely sometime between January 23 and 25. The other four men in Crockett's unit seem to have been riding ahead of Crockett at that point. Benjamin Archibald Martin Thomas appears to have joined Crockett on January 24. Crockett and Thomas's departure date from the Swisher home is unknown.[34]

One other piece of evidence suggests that the Crockett company rode to Goliad. Peter Harper, who had joined the unit on January 8 at Nacogdoches, transferred to Captain John Chenoweth's company of United States Invincibles on January 27. On that date, Chenoweth's unit, except for a number of men who had gone to the Alamo with James Bowie on January 17, was spread out between Goliad and Copano. Given the time frame, Harper most likely joined the unit at Goliad. Therefore, it appears that Harper and the other three men from Crockett's spy company were riding a day or so ahead of Crockett and Thomas.[35]

James Bowie's Offspring

A third document that Williams misrepresented concerns the death of James Bowie's wife. Williams quoted a Jose Antonio Navarro letter to

Samuel May Williams as saying: "Veramendi, my sister Josepha, his wife, and Ursula Bowie and her children, died unexpectedly in Monclova." Navarro actually wrote: "Verimendi, my sister Josefa, his wife and Ursula Bowie died unexpectedly at Monclova." It appears Williams added the element of "her children" in using the document.[36] The significance of this misrepresentation should be obvious. Any person who claimed, based on Williams's study, that Bowie had one or more children who died in 1833 in Mexico would be wrong on all counts.

Captain De Sauque and John

One of Williams's more complex misrepresentations involved John, the defender with no last name. African-Americans take great pride in believing John was a black man. Williams declared: "Francis De Sauque was a merchant of San Antonio and a true Texas patriot. It is now a well-known fact that Travis sent him from the Alamo on the evening of February 21 or 22 to get supplies for the soldiers at the fortress and plead for reinforcements. He left John M. Thurston, his clerk, and John, his Negro slave, at the Alamo. Both perished there; but De Sauque, cut off from his home by the arrival of the Mexicans, joined Fannin's troops at Goliad and was massacred with them. The Muster Rolls and all the land certificates, issued to De Sauque's heirs for land due him for his service, show these facts."[37]

The only information that is correct in Williams's claim is that De Sauque was a "true Texas patriot." He was not a resident and merchant of San Antonio. The land grants and muster rolls mentioned (but not cited by Williams) contain no evidence to support her statements about De Sauque, John M. Thurston, and John, the man without a last name.[38]

John M. Thurston was not De Sauque's clerk. Just why Williams believed Thurston was the clerk is not clear. The primary source for De Sauque, John, and Thurston dying at the Alamo is a list of Alamo defenders found in the March 24, 1836 issue of the *Telegraph and Texas Register.* The entries for those three men reads:

> F. Desanque [*sic*], of Philadelphia,
> John (cl'k in Desanque's store,)
> Thurstor [*sic*],[39]

Apparently, Williams believed that the entries read as follows: "John (cl'k in Desanque's store,) Thurstor," which she assumed was an identification of John Thurston as De Sauque's clerk. She was wrong. Still, several conclusions about the source are obvious: (1) John was De Sauque's clerk, (2) John's last name was unknown to the informant, (3) the first name of "Thurstor" was unknown to the informant.

John Thurston was not John, the clerk. Thurston arrived in Texas in early December 1835 as the first lieutenant of R. A. Wigginton's company of Louisville Volunteers. On December 21, 1835, Thurston received a commission as a second lieutenant in William B. Travis's Legion of horse. Thurston most likely entered the Alamo in Captain John H. Forsyth's company with Travis on February 5, 1836.[40]

De Sauque, a resident of Matagorda, was a former sea captain from Philadelphia. He was a friend to James W. Fannin Jr. and served as his commissary officer at Goliad. De Sauque was in Bexar in mid-February 1836 to set up a dry-goods shop in the city. Despite Williams's allegation that it was a "well-known fact," there is no evidence that De Sauque left the Alamo to obtain supplies and men for Travis.[41]

As to John's identity, Frank Templeton's novel *Margaret Ballentine or The Fall of the Alamo,* published in 1907, is the only source that identifies John as a black man. Templeton claimed: "John, the negro servant of Capt. De Sauque, was left by him with the officers at the post when he went off to recruit his company and was killed while fighting." Templeton most likely concluded that defender "John" was black because in the late nineteenth century the use of the single name of John was a disparaging tag applied to black men, much in the same way that "boy" was used in the twentieth century. In 1836, however, the single name of "John" was most often applied to an Indian man who lived on the edge of the white culture.[42]

Also, Templeton's unsupported claim about John appears to be the source of Williams's allegation that it was a "well-known fact" that Travis sent De Sauque out to locate men and supplies. While it is manifest that the novel was Williams's source for claiming John was a black slave, she did not cite the book. Ultimately, there simply is no primary evidence to substantiate the claim that John was a black man. Moreover, why did Williams, after having decided that "John" was John Thurston, swing about and also claim that "John" was a black slave? Who knows?[43]

Alamo Defender Identifications

Perhaps the most problematic section of Williams's study is her list of Alamo defenders—the roster that Dr. Barker lauded as "a real contribution to the history of Texas." Williams claimed: "I compiled a work list which contained every name mentioned on any previously made roll, or from any other source. Such a compilation yielded nearly 400 names, although contemporary authority is practically agreed that the number of Alamo victims was less than 200, most writers giving from 182 to 188. I set myself the task, however, to verify every name on this work, or to determine definitely that it should be discarded."[44]

In creating her list, Williams's first error was to ignore at least one valid Mexican source that identified the number of Alamo defenders. Colonel Juan N. Almonte put the number at two hundred fifty Texian dead. Williams should not have ignored Almonte's higher number unless she could have proved the number wrong. That she did not do.[45]

Williams' second mistake was her use of Texas General Land Office documents. She decided that any name listed on an Alamo muster roll was invalid unless the man's estate had been issued land grants for an Alamo death. She said that the "issued" land grant certificates or patents verified the muster roll entry for Alamo defenders. She failed to see and understand that the actual process worked in reverse of what she claimed. Land grant certificates for Alamo service were only issued after the service had been verified by a muster roll entry, sworn statements from two witnesses, or other creditable evidence. In sum, a muster roll identification alone was sufficient proof to the General Land Office that a man had died at the Alamo. In total, Williams's methods discarded many names for which there is acceptable evidence to show that the men died at the Alamo. In some cases, however, she did not have the evidence that now identifies some of the men in question. Then she rejected the valid names for no obvious reason.

New Alamo Defenders

There is I. L. K. Harrison, whose Alamo death is supported by the following James C. Neill affidavit, a document that Williams did have for her study. The statement is also further evidence that Captain William B. Harrison's men were not members of Crockett's mounted spy unit. If they had been in Crockett's unit, it seems that Neill would have identified I. L. K. Harrison as a member of Crockett's unit, instead of Captain Harrison's company. [46]

Neill wrote: "Col. Neill being called upon states that he knows of I. L. K. Harrison – states that he distinctly knows he was on the Roll of Capt. Harrison's company – when he [Neill] relinquished the Command to Col. Travis on the 14 Feby 1836 and that Capt. Harrison's company was enlisted for six months. Col. Neill has every reason to believe that I. L. K. Harrison was destroyed at the Alamo."[47]

There is Jacob Roth, a Nacogdoches area resident, who commanded a small East Texas company of fifteen to twenty men at the storming of Bexar in December 1835. Roth and company, after obtaining one hundred dollars from the Committee of Vigilance and Safety, departed Nacogdoches on November 17. The Roth unit traveled to Bexar with Captain Thomas H. Breece's company of New Orleans Greys and Captain John W. Peacock's United States Invincibles—a company later commanded by John Chenoweth. The three companies reached San Antonio on November 26, 1835.[48]

Little is known about Roth and his unit. He may have been Jewish. Roth, however, must have enjoyed some respect in the area because George A. Nixon, chairman of the Nacogdoches Committee of Vigilance and Safety, referred to Roth as "Major" Roth. David Cook and Leonard L. Williams are the only members of Roth's company thus far identified. Roth discharged both men on December 15, 1835, and they returned to Nacogdoches. Roth, however, appears to have joined the Bexar garrison under Lt. Colonel James C. Neill. Roth's name appears on the February 1, 1836 Alamo voters list for delegates to the March 1 convention held at Washington-on-the-Brazos.[49]

One of the many names that Williams could not obtain data about was "Rough, _____ ." Jacob Roth seems to have been the man whose name could only be remembered as "Rough."[50]

Roth's Alamo death is strongly endorsed by a petition that John Dorset submitted to the Nacogdoches probate court on January 31, 1838. According to Dorset:

> Jacob Roth, late a resident of said County, died while absent in the service of his country on or about the sixth of March Eighteen hundred and thirty six, leaving no will.
>
> Said deceased was possessed of little or no personal property, but was as your petitioner believes justly entitled

to a third of a League of land as a citizen of this Republic, and also some compensation from the Government for his services in the Army.

The said deceased was at the time of his death and had for a long time been a citizen of this county, and was also indebted to your petitioner, as well as to some other individuals, which requires that some one should be appointed to administer on the Estate of said deceased and that no one has been appointed so to do. [51]

New Orleans Greys

George Andrews, James Dickson, Thomas P. Hutchinson, James Holloway, John Morman, and John Spratt were members of the New Orleans Greys who died at the Alamo but are not on the current Daughters of the Republic of Texas honor roll of Alamo defenders. Williams eliminated five of the names because she could not verify their duty or deaths at the Alamo with other documents. These names come from a muster roll that is titled: "Muster Roll, Captain Thomas H. Breece's Co. Texas Volunteers, in the Army before Bexar 1835." The post-revolution status of each soldier is written to the left of each name. The men are identified as: (1) killed at the Alamo, (2) killed with Fannin, (3) living, (4) expelled, and (5) deserted. The roll appears to have been compiled by Breece in the fall of 1836.[52]

In regard to Breece's roll, Williams wrote: "Since it is a proved fact that the majority of Breece's men were Alamo victims, I verified this entire roll to test its accuracy, and found it to be unusually correct for a muster roll document. I found land certificates or other documents concerning all the names on the roll, except for John Spratt, George Andrews, and _____ Kedison." Williams stuck with her flawed methodology in explaining those three names.[53]

Williams eliminated John Spratt with nothing more than her opinion: "On some lists this name is given as William Spratt. Gray gives simply _____ Spratt, Muster Rolls, p. 25, ... gives *John Spratt* as an Alamo victim. No further information has been found. It is possible, though I believe hardly probable, that one Spratt fell at the Alamo."[54]

Williams used the same method to explain George Andrews. She wrote: "This leads me to suspect that the George Andrews of the roll should be George Anderson. In view of the fact that so many of the early lists included the name of Anderson as the quartermaster.... I have been forced to the tentative opinion that one George Washington Anderson did die at the Alamo, but I have no conclusive proof of the fact...."[55]

Williams, at least in this case of Andrews, was close to being right. She had no evidence to support her belief about Anderson; it was totally based on deductive reasoning and she was wrong. "Anderson" was A. Anderson, who had been involved in the revolution since late September 1835. Thus Anderson could not have been "George Andrews" who joined the fight with New Orleans Greys on November 26, 1835. Nor could Anderson have been George Washington Anderson, who was wounded at the Battle of San Jacinto. A. Anderson, a resident of Bexar, served as an express rider in September and October 1835, for Edward Gritten, an Englishman, who lived in San Antonio and who kept the Gonzales colonists informed of military events in Bexar. During the storming of Bexar in December 1835, Anderson was a member of Captain Peter L. Duncan's company that served as the Texian army's color guard unit.[56]

For the name "_____ Kedison" Williams wrote: "This name listed on Muster Rolls, pp. 2, 4, 25, and on all former rolls, made of Alamo victims. No further information has been found." Only one mistake here. Despite Williams's claim, the name "Kedison" is not on Breece's muster roll. Williams's failure to prove Kedison did not die at the Alamo means he is a probable Alamo defender.[57]

To eliminate the name of "John Moran" Williams claimed: "Morton, E. This name is a variant for either Edward Norton or John Morman. Both those men fought at the storming of Bexar, but both were honorably discharged on December 27, 1835. John Morman was killed at San Jacinto; Edward Norton was living in 1838 (see Lost Book of Harris County, p. 119)."[58]

For this investigator, it is hard to see any similarity between E. Morton and John Moran. Also, the Lost Book of Harris County contains no entry for John Morman. Neither does the book have entries for E. Morton or Edward Norton. And John Morman was not killed at the Battle of Sam Jacinto.[59]

Another example of Williams's failed methodology is analysis of the name "T. P. Hutchinson." A review of her sources clearly demonstrates the unreliability of her work and the reliability of the Breece muster roll. Williams dismissed T. P. Hutchinson with this explanation:

> *Hutcherson,* _____. This name is variously spelled
> Hutchinson, Hutcherson, Hutchison, and is found on Mus-
> ter Rolls, p. 25, and on every Alamo list that I have found.
> On Breece's company roll and on Frank Templeton's list
> the name is "T. P. Hutchinson"; everywhere else only the
> last name is given. Every land certificate, issued in the
> name of Hutcherson, or any of its possible variants, has
> been carefully examined, and all other available documents
> have been searched, but none of them show that any
> Hutcherson died at the Alamo. There were, however, two
> Hutchinsons at the storming of Bexar in December, 1835.
> There were Robert L. Hutchinson and Thomas J. Hutchin-
> son. Bounty certificate, Matagorda, 190, shows that Robert
> L. Hutchinson was honorably discharged, January 16, 1836.
> Thomas J. Hutchinson participated in the battle of San
> Jacinto and evidence is found (in related papers in I Milam,
> 1384, he signed his name) that he was living in 1841. My
> guess is that the service and record of Thomas J. Hutchin-
> son is what confused the list makers of the Alamo men and
> has caused them to include his name among the victims of
> the massacre of March 6, 1836.[60]

There are several problems with Williams's Hutcherson and Hutchinson analysis. She claimed that bounty land grant certificate, Matagorda,
190, identified a "Robert L. Hutchinson." There is no such bounty certificate. There are *no* land grants in the name of Robert L. Hutchinson or
any variant of the name. Next, Williams claimed that "papers in I Milam,
1384," contained the signature of a "Thomas J. Hutchinson." First class
headright Milam 1384 was issued to William Trampton in Austin County
on March 29, 1838, and does not include any document with the said
Hutchinson's signature or any information about a Thomas J. Hutchinson.[61]

Williams, despite the name "T. P. Hutchinson" or a variant of it being
on every Alamo list, eliminated Hutchinson from her Alamo roll because:
"Every land certificate, issued in the name of Hutcherson, or any of its
possible variants, has been carefully examined, and all other available
documents relating to soldiers of the Texas revolution have been
searched, but none of them show that any Hutcherson died at the
Alamo." She reinforced that by concluding that the name "Thomas J.

Hutchinson" is what has confused the list makers of the Alamo men and has caused them to include his name among the victims of the massacre of March 6, 1836." The problem with Williams's alleged research and analysis is that the list makers never included the name of "Thomas J. Hutchinson" on their lists. Thus, Williams's allegation of confusion make no sense.[62]

The name on "Captain Thomas H. Breece's Co. Texas Volunteers," the First Company of New Orleans Greys, was "T. P. Hutchinson." The next quoted document shows the Breece listing of Hutchinson was correct.

> Bexar Dec 27th 1835
> We the undersigned being appointed by the lst Company of Texas Volunteers from New Orleans to value the property of Francis William Jackson one of the members of the afore-said Company. We appraised his horse at $90 Saddle $35 & Rifle $30.
>
> > Robt. Musselman
> > Thos P. Hutchinson
> > John J. Baugh
> > N. O. Greys[63]

The document does not claim that Hutchinson died at the Alamo, but it does prove his existence as a member of the First Company of New Orleans Greys. Musselman and Baugh died at the Alamo. And as previously stated, a muster roll identification of an Alamo defender was sufficient evidence to General Land Office officials. In the case of Hutchinson there are no land grants in his name because no heirs ever surfaced to claim them. Undoubtedly, Hutchinson died at the Alamo, and his case clearly demonstrates the unreliability of Williams's methodology.[64]

Mr. Washington and a Little Irishman

Then there is James Morgan, who served under the alias of James Washington. The name "J. Washington" was on one of the General Land Office's muster rolls. Still, Williams ignored the name and did not explain why she rejected the name. After the revolution Thomas G. Masterson of Palacious, Matagorda County, requested that the Harris County probate court appoint him as administrator of his cousin James Morgan's estate. Masterson claimed that Morgan was killed at the Alamo under the name of "James Washington." One of the first reconstructed Alamo muster rolls includes the name "J. Washington." James, however, should not be confused with defender Joseph George Washington.[65]

The "Little Irishman" was identified by Major George Bernard Erath in his memoirs. Erath wrote:

> I set out from Bastrop with the surveyor, Thomas A. Graves, about the last of September [1835]. There were seventeen of us in the party, including four land speculators. We reached our destination in three days and commenced work, each compass running out a league of land a day. We intended to go farther east after surveying ten leagues, but, on the last day of our stay the Indians attacked one of the parties and killed Lang, an Irishman, who ran the compass. Such occurrences were not uncommon, especially near the Colorado, and even occurred in the midst of a settlement. A party of Indians always lurked around, waiting to find a solitary man to scalp, and would then put off immediately. As they generally did put off immediately after the killing, it seemed to me there was little danger in our whole party remaining a few days longer. One man of the party attacked had escaped and brought us the news; three men to be accounted for were missing, two besides Lang. We thought the dead ought to be found and buried, and after deliberation in camp found that all the hands and one land locator, Fiske, were in favor of this course, or, at least, to remain long enough to ascertain the fate of the missing men. So after a little opposition from Graves and the other land locators, we started the next morning, not to the settlements, but to the place of attack, guided by the man who had escaped. We paused there and, after another deliberation, Graves cut the matter short by declaring he had fitted out the expedition, would have to pay the hands, and did not propose to be at unnecessary expense in public service. So we turned back. Had we gone but a few hundred yards farther we would have found Lang's body. We kept a lookout for the other missing men, and one of them we found. He was quite wild from fright, mistook us for Indians, and ran from us for some time. He had grown up in some large city, a tailor by trade, and was

altogether unused to the frontier. The other man, McLellen, a little Irishman, carried a pistol and a Jacob's staff with him in flight, and escaped to the Colorado; he lived to be killed in the Alamo the following March.[66]

The "Little Irishman" appears to have been Ross McClelland. According to a Washington County first class headright document from July 1838: "Robert Merrett [and] Thomas S. Saul Proved that the deceased Ross McClelland was a resident citizen of Texas at the date of the Declaration of Independence, and that he was killed in the Alamo, a Single man."[67]

In the case of McClelland, Williams was guilty of nothing more than sloppy research. George Bernard Erath's memoirs were first published in the *Southwestern Historical Quarterly* (volumes 26 and 27) in 1923. Williams's failure to read the Erath narrative is an example of her failure to conduct a proper survey of all the biographical materials that contained information about the Texas Revolution that were available to her. Nor did Williams look to the many probate records that were available at the county level. A review of Williams's footnotes shows that she did little research outside of Austin. She depended on source materials she could find in state archives and at the University of Texas. Otherwise, she used sources that were sent to her by other scholars and historians.

Incorrect Alamo Defenders

In addition to the Alamo defenders that Williams eliminated for no good reason, she put men on her Alamo roll that did not die at the Alamo, or at least her sources fail to prove their deaths. This analysis does not reflect a complete review of Williams's list, but the number of names examined is sufficient to prove that Williams's roll is unreliable.

There is Johnny Kellogg, who, according to Williams, was: "Age, 19; rank, private; resident of Gonzales. Sources: I Bastrop, 240; I Bexar, 553; Miles S. Bennett, *The Quarterly of the Texas State Historical Association,* II: 240; Rather, Ibid., VIII, 159. This man was the son of John Kellogg, Sr., of Gonzales, and he was one of the thirty-two who went to the Alamo on March 1."[68]

Remember, Williams said: "I set myself the task, however, to verify every name on this work [her work list of four hundred names], or to determine definitely that it should be discarded." Also, in 1939, when

Williams was questioned about the accuracy of her list, she claimed that she had "several official sources" for each man on her roll.[69]

The name Johnny Kellogg appears on none of the Alamo rolls. The only source that identifies Kellogg as an Alamo defender is a secondary one, an article by Miles S. Bennett, who came to Texas after the revolution and joined his father in the Gonzales area. Williams misrepresented her sources by claiming that Ethel Zivley Rather's "De Witt's Colony" article identified Kellogg as an Alamo defender. The Rather work is not a legitimate source because Rather's source for Kellogg's death at the Alamo was the Bennett article, which Williams had already cited as a source.[70]

The only evidence in the land grant documents cited by Williams that speaks to Kellogg's death comes from Harrisburg residents William P. Harris and John W. Moore: "Harris said he first knew him [Benjamin Kellogg, not Johnny] in Oct. 1835 on his return from the Army of Texas, has also known him to have been in the army since that time, as also that he was a married man. Moore stated that he [his] first acquaintance was at Gonzales previous to the Declaration of Independence, also knew him in the service, knows he is dead and also that he was a man of family." Harris also knew Kellogg in Harrisburg when Kellogg worked on the steamboat *Cayuga* for eleven days between August 15 and September 8, 1836. Harris was the boat's captain.[71]

According to the court case of A. S. Miller versus Mary S. Rogers: "Kellogg died at Harrisburg in 1836, and Mrs. Kellogg, in 1837 or 1838, moved with her child upon the Thomas R. Miller homestead place, and lived there until her death, in 1839, leaving one son [Johnny Kellogg], then two or three years old, by Kellogg."[72]

Lastly, none of the evidence cited by Williams identifies a "John Kellogg, Sr., of Gonzales" as being Johnny Kellogg's father. Actually, there is no evidence of a John Kellogg Sr. or a Johnny Kellogg at Gonzales during the time of the Alamo. The "Kellogg" in question was Benjamin Kellogg, who had a son named Johnny, who was born after the fall of the Alamo. Benjamin was a private in Captain Albert Martin's Gonzales volunteer company during the siege of Bexar in October and November 1835. The company appears to have disbanded after Stephen F. Austin turned the Texian army over to Edward Burleson on November 24, 1836. Thus, it appears that Miles Bennett was not only wrong about Kellogg dying at the Alamo, he also got the man's first name wrong, confusing

Benjamin, the father, with Johnny, the son, who was born in 1836 and probably named for his uncle, John Gaston, who did die at the Alamo.[73]

To prove that Jose Maria Guerrero died at the Alamo, Williams cited: "I San Patricio, 320; I Bexar, 143, 237." Nevertheless, Texas land historian Thomas Lloyd Miller examined the cited land grant documents and concluded: "Miss Williams erred in this case. She cited three General Land Office Headright files to prove his [Guerrero] death in the Alamo. The writer carefully examined each file. Perhaps due to a printing error, the files do not concern Guerrero at all; I San Patricio 320 is for Josefa Guerra; I Bexar 143 is for Juan de Dios Neito; I Bexar 237 is for Manuel Martinez y Marquis."[74]

There was no printing error. In the 1870s Guerrero received a Texas pension for having taken part in the siege and storming of Bexar as a member of Philip Dimmitt's company. Clearly, Guerrero did not die at the Alamo.[75]

Williams claimed that "Jerry" or Jeremiah Day, James Hannum, and Isaac Robinson died at the Alamo. Other documents identify the three men as members of Philip Dimmitt's Goliad company. In reality, Robinson was killed by Indians near Bastrop in 1838. Williams used her father and son theory again for Day, stating that her sources indicated that Jeremiah Day was the father of Jerry Day. Williams's sources, however, do not identify Jeremiah as the father of Jerry. Jeremiah and Jerry were the same man. Day died sometime after the revolution, but he was alive on October 26, 1836, when William Delany and he "valued a gray horse of Charles Thomas Jackson into the public service at fifty dollars for which the government is responsible."[76]

In the case of James Hannum, the name "Hannum" or a variant is not found on any of the Alamo lists that Williams investigated. Just how Williams came up with this name remains a mystery. Nevertheless, she claimed that private James Hannum, aged twenty-one died at the Alamo. Her sources were "Milam, 1212; Refugio, 154; I Milam, 53, 202."[77]

First class headright grant Milam 202 was issued to Lucian Hannum, a single man, rather than James Hannum. Lucian was identified as deceased, but the file does not identify him as an Alamo defender. Bounty grants Milam 1212 and Refugio 154 were indeed issued to the heirs of James Hannum. Milam 1212 reported that Hannum died while in the service of Texas and identified him as a private in Captain Philip Dimmitt's company, a unit that was stationed in Goliad. Refugio bounty grant 154 and Milam headright 53 contain no data that identifies Hannum as an Alamo victim. Also, James Hannum's age is not found in any of the grant documents. Lastly, Dimmitt's morning report for December 14, 1835, reports: "REMARK - DIED - This Morning James Hannum, Private."[78]

Likewise, Jesse B. Bowman, Jesse G. Thompson, George Brown, James Brown, and Charles H. Clark are alleged Alamo victims whose Alamo deaths are not supported by the sources cited by Williams.

An examination of Williams's Jesse B. Bowman information further reveals her methodology. She wrote: "BOWMAN, JESSE B.: Rank, private. Sources: I Lamar, 109; I Bowie, 119; I Red River 670; Court of Claims Vouchers, No. 17, File (A-B)."[79]

Again there are a number of problems with Williams's alleged Bowman sources. The three first class headright files involve one grant that was obtained under Red River County certificate number 538. The patent files identify the assignee as "Jesse B. Boman." The Red River County clerk returns, however, show the name as Jesse T. Bowman, who arrived in Texas in March 1835. Nevertheless, the three files contain no mention of Boman or Bowman dying at the Alamo and contain no data that could be interpreted to mean he died at the Alamo.[80]

There is no Court of Claims file for Jesse B. Bowman or a variant of the name. Also, the name Jesse B. Bowman or a variant is not found on the government's muster rolls. The only evidence Williams found of a Bowman dying at the Alamo is the name "J. B. Bowman," which appears on a list that reports the names that were on the first Alamo monument, which was destroyed in 1881. She, however, cited no evidence that proved J. B. Bowman was Jesse B. Bowman, or other evidence to show that Jesse B. died at the Alamo. Yet, Williams said she had verified every name on her final list with other official evidence.[81]

Analysis of Williams's source material for Jesse G. Thompson is similar to the Jesse B. Bowman situation. Williams claimed that her primary sources for Thompson's death at the Alamo were: "Bexar, 519; Fort Bend, 51, 53; Colorado, 97; C. M. S. R. No. 7093; *Court of Claims Vouchers,* No. 954, File (S-Z); Muster Rolls, pp. 2, 28 (_____ Thompson is given)."[82]

Bounty land grants Bexar 519, Fort Bend 51, and Fort Bend 53 were issued to "Jesse Thompson," a different man, not Jesse G. Thompson, and contain no data that reports an Alamo death for Thompson. Bexar 519, however, does report that Thompson served in the Texian army from March 7, 1836, to June 7, 1836. Colorado 97 was issued to Jesse G. Thompson and contains no claim of his death at the Alamo. Bounty grant Milam 1512, however, was issued to Jesse G. Thompson for fighting in the Battle of San Jacinto on April 21, 1836. The C. M. S. R. No. 7093 claim shows that Jesse G. Thompson received his last pay for military service on May 30, 1836. In sum, not one of the documents cited by Williams identifies Jesse G. or Jesse Thompson as an Alamo soldier. To the contrary, the records show that "Jesse" and "Jesse G." were separate men, both of whom were living after the fall of the Alamo. The muster rolls identify a man named Thompson as having died at the Alamo, but his first name remains to be discovered.[83]

In regard to George Brown, Williams claimed he was a thirty-six-year-old private, born in England, who resided in Gonzales. Her sources for those claims were: "I Liberty, 317; Muster Rolls, pp. 2, 256. The muster rolls are not definite for this name. They give merely '_____ Brown.' The records show four George Browns in the Texan army in 1836, but the headright files and C. M. S. R. No. 728, show that but one of them died at the Alamo." An examination of the muster rolls shows that the name "Brown" does not appear on page two. The name "Browne," however, is found on page three. There is no page 256. The last page of the Muster Rolls book is 255.[84]

The first class headright grant for Liberty 317 was issued to Mrs. George Brown and contains no data that reports the death of a "George Brown" at the Alamo. Also, the file does not give Mr. Brown's age, rank, birthplace, or Texas residence. There are two C. M. S. R. claims identified as 728. The first originated on July 4, 1836, and was authorized by George W. Poe for D. B. Posey for military service and supplies. The second originated on July 30, 1836, and was authorized by Captain A. G. W. Pierson for Albert G. Perry for military services. This investigator was unable to locate a military claim in the name of George Brown for service or death at the Alamo.[85]

The situation with James Brown is similar to that of George Brown. Williams claimed that James was a thirty-six-year-old private from Pennsylvania. Her sources were: "Bexar, 962; I Nacogdoches, 399, 681; I Washington, 193; Muster Rolls, pp. 2, 20, 256 (the muster rolls give only the last name); James E. Winston, 'Pennsylvania and the Independence of Texas,' *Southwestern Historical Quarterly,* XVIII, 266; *Telegraph and Texas Register,* March 24, 1836; the *Register of Spanish Archives*, General

Land Office, shows that this man registered in De Leon's Colony, April 17, 1835."[86]

Bounty grant Bexar 962 was issued to James Bowie, not James Brown. First class headright Nacogdoches 399 was issued to Henry B. Rodney. First class Nacogdoches 681 was issued to Philip Mason. There is no first class headright Washington 193. The last first class grant for the Washington land district is 92. The James E. Winston article does not identify Brown as being from Pennsylvania. Winston only stated that reports of the fall of the Alamo appeared in the Philadelphia newspapers in April 1836. According to Winston one of those articles claimed that a man named "Browne" had died at the Alamo. The *Telegraph and Texas Register* of March 24, 1836, only listed a "Browne." A man named James Brown did obtain a land grant in De Leon's Colony in 1835, but none of Williams's other sources identify this man as having died at the Alamo. Nor do any of the sources give the man's age and rank. Also, despite the fact that Williams's muster roll page numbers for the name Brown are not valid, it appears she used the same single listing of the name of Brown to refer to both James Brown and George Brown. If James was "Browne," then George could not have been "Browne," and vice versa.[87]

Nevertheless, a man named Brown appears to have died at the Alamo. He was Robert Brown, whom Travis mentioned in a letter to Sam Houston. Travis wrote: "Lieutenant Simmons of cavalry acting as infantry, Captains Carey, Dickinson and Blair of the artillery, rendered essential service, and Charles Despallier and Robert Brown gallantly sallied out and set fire to houses which afforded the enemy shelter, in the face of the enemy fire."[88]

Williams acknowledged that Robert had been in the Alamo. She, however, believed, without any solid evidence, that he had departed the compound as a courier. She wrote: "The registers at the Land Office list but one Robert Brown in the Texan army in 1836. ... he was a single man who came to Texas in October, 1835, and that he rendered service during the San Jacinto campaign by guarding baggage at Harrisburg." This man's army discharge, however, shows that he is not the Alamo Robert Brown. The document shows that the "San Jacinto" Robert B. joined the Texian army on March 5, 1836, and was discharged on June 5, 1836. Thus, it appears that the name "Browne" in the Muster Rolls book refers to Robert Brown.[89]

Just as Williams had ignored conclusive evidence about Robert Brown's death at the Alamo, she turned away from the evidence that gave the location of Charles Clark's demise. She reported that Clark was Charles H. Clark, a "private; native of Missouri, came to Texas about November, 1835, probably with the New Orleans Grays. He was a single man, and his heir, a nephew, John C. (Charles) Clark, applied for lands due to him in December, 1837." She claimed her sources were: "Milam, 1425; Travis, 648; I Robertson, 1435; *Court of Claims Vouchers*, 891."[90]

An examination of Williams's Clark sources reveals a different picture than the one she presented. Court of Claims file 1549 (*Court of Claims Vouchers*, 891) reports that Clark had been a member of Captain Thomas H. Breece's company of New Orleans Greys and was killed at Goliad with Fannin. The two bounty grants, Milam 1425 and Travis 648, were issued for Clark's death at Goliad, not the Alamo. Robertson first class grant 1435 does not exist.[91]

James Robertson is another example of Williams's egregious misrepresentation of sources. Williams claimed:

> ROBERTSON, JAMES: Age, 32; rank, private; native of Tennessee, came to Texas from Louisiana. Sources: Goliad, 227; Bexar, 1917; Fannin, 1304; Lost Book of Harris, 96, 250. This last reference states that at the Storming of Bexar, December, 1835, James Robertson was a member of B. P. Despallier's company. The Muster Rolls do not show that B. P. Despallier was in command of a company at Bexar, but several other similar statements have been found in which Despallier is called captain. See Muster Rolls, p. 24.[92]

Land grants Goliad 227 and Bexar 1917 were issued to J. B. Robertson, who was still living after the revolution. Fannin 1304 was issued to J. W. Robertson for military service from February 1, 1836, to May 1, 1836. Page 96 of the Lost Book of Harris County does not contain an entry that reports that a James Robertson died in the second battle for San Antonio. Also, this man was not a member of a unit commanded by Blas P. Despallier. Robertson served in Captain Peyton Splann's company during the siege and storming of Bexar in 1835. In regard to "Captain" Blas P. Despallier, there is no page 250 in the Lost Book of Harris County. That book's last page is 141. Page 24 of the Muster Rolls book, which Williams cited, shows Despallier was a private in Captain William G. Cooke's company of New Orleans Greys.[93]

Biographical Data

Then, the biographical data for many of Williams's correct names are wrong. Probably the best example of her flawed methodology is her evidence concerning Jonathan Lindley. Williams claimed Lindley was "Jonathan L. Lindley," a thirty-one-year-old Englishman, a Gonzales resident, and member of the Gonzales Thirty-two. The age of thirty-one and birthplace of England appears to have been taken from a muster roll entry for Charles Linley, who died with Fannin at Goliad. Williams said that land grants identified Lindley as a Gonzales resident and a member of the Gonzales reinforcement group. Yet, none of the grants she cited for Lindley contains that data. Nor do any of Williams's sources contain proof that Lindley's middle initial was an "L."[94]

As to Jonathan Lindley's true identity, his Quaker family moved from England to Ireland in the late 1600s. The family came to America in 1713 as part of the Irish Quaker immigration of that period. Jonathan was a stock raiser who came to Texas in 1833 from either Illinois or Tennessee. He selected a Mexican land grant in the Vehlein colony in East Texas. He participated in the siege and storming of Bexar as a private in Captain John Crane's company. Afterward, Lindley joined the Bexar garrison as an artilleryman on December 14, 1835.[95]

Lindley is not the only man for whom Williams's biographical claims fail to hold up under a close inspection. However, the purpose of this chapter is not a total review and correction of every error, fabrication, and fallacious conclusion found in Williams's dissertation. The goal has been the presentation of sufficient evidence to show that Williams's methods were flawed and that her study is unreliable.

Still, one important question remains. Just how did Williams's Alamo study become so flawed? Her methods and her post-publication attitude suggest that she did not pursue her graduate work with a single goal of searching for the truth and new knowledge. After obtaining her doctoral degree at a public institution and having her study published in the *Southwestern Historical Quarterly*, she saw her Alamo defender list as her personal property, instead of a scholarly contribution to Texas and United States history. Also, with the Daughters of the Republic of Texas's acceptance of the roster, Williams's actions indicate that she seems to have appointed herself as the gatekeeper of the Alamo honor roll.[96]

In 1939 George P. Carrel asked the DRT's Alamo Committee to add the name of Nathaniel Massie Kerr to the Alamo list. Nathaniel was the brother of defender Joseph Kerr. Nathaniel died of some unknown illness on or about February 19, 1836, four days before Santa Anna's centralist army stormed into San Antonio. Joseph Kerr died in the final assault on March 6. Initially, the Alamo Committee was going to add Nathaniel Kerr to their defender list.[97]

Williams quickly killed the idea. She wrote: "...I think Nathaniel Kerr was as true a hero as his brother; he paid the same supreme price – His life. But according to my historical training, I am compelled to exclude his name from my roll.... Moreover, if we here in Texas begin to distort our historical judgment to appease our sentiment, we should have to enroll hundreds of names on battle muster rolls without having any actual data for so doing."[98]

Williams's words of rejection for Nathaniel Kerr are highly hypocritical, given that when she submitted her dissertation to the University of Texas, she knew that she had identified at least ten men as having died at the Alamo without any valid "data" and had excluded a number of individuals from the roll when the evidence for their inclusion was sufficient. A 1941 Williams letter suggests that she knew exactly what she was doing; that her Alamo list was a ticking time bomb she had to retain control over.

In 1941 Stuart McGregor, editor of the *Texas Almanac*, wrote Williams requesting permission to publish her list in the next edition of the almanac.[99] Williams's answer to McGregor is enlightening. She observed:

...Then, what is my point of view? Your letter indicates that you do not understand it. It is simply this. For a hundred years, first one and then anther [person] has mulled around trying to reconstruct a correct list of the men who died at the Alamo, March 6, 1836. After more than three years of hard work, eight months of which time I was constantly at work on the list, I was able to make a list of some 187-189 names. Houston and other contemporaries claim that was the number of men who were killed at the Alamo. My own opinion is that there possibly were others, but I failed to find sufficient proof of the fact. After the publication of this reconstructed list that I had made, I have had many, many letters disputing this or that name. Most of these contentions I have been able to prove erroneous; others I have either not had time to work on sufficiently to prove or disprove. There are some five or six names that should be added to the main list or probably to the list of couriers. In fact, it is my opinion that the entire list should be carefully and painstakingly worked through. Such a job will require a very great deal of work, a thorough knowledge of the problem, a complete verification of all former lists, or disproving certain names as belonging on the list. This I have done, and I have all the evidence of this. Who ever "brings my list down to date," will have to do the same thing, not only for all other former lists, but for mine also – that is if his list is historically correct. Because *I cannot vouch for all the names on my list being accurate* [italics added], until I have had the time to do the work that I have indicated as necessary, I have thought, *and I still think* it a pity for it to be published in the Texas Almanac.[100]

Some historians might defend Williams by arguing that the graduate work standards of the 1930s were different from today, that her study is no better or worse than others of the period. Perhaps misrepresentation, alteration, and fabrication of data were routine and acceptable behaviors at the University of Texas in the 1930s. That possibility, however, is extremely doubtful. Williams's own words and actions work against her. In the end, she claimed that her list was "an annotated and documented roll of the Alamo victims" when she clearly knew that with many of her defender names that was not the case.[101]

On the other hand, as Walter Lord wrote: "Miss Williams did amass a mountain of material." And to Williams's credit, her study does contain correct information about the Texian Alamo and its defenders. For that she deserves recognition. The Alamo historian must start with her study. Therefore, historians and writers should understand that if they are going to rely on Williams's work, they best verify her sources and conclusions before going to press. Otherwise, depending on what is used from the work, the users will fall into the group described by historian Paul Hutton: "Those who have written on the battle, for the most part, have simply repeated false stories told before in books, articles, and newspaper accounts."[102]

More importantly, because of Williams's methods, the official Alamo honor roll of defenders is flawed. In 1905 the Texas government placed "custody and care" of the Alamo in the hands of the Daughters of the Republic of Texas to "be maintained...as a sacred memorial to the heroes who immolated themselves upon that hollowed ground."[103] Are the Daughters of the Republic of Texas really operating the Alamo as a "sacred memorial" when their official roll honors men who did not die at the Alamo and does not honor men who did die "upon that hallowed ground"?

Chapter Two Notes

1   Thomas B. Brewer, "The 'Old Department' of History at the University of Texas, 1910-1951," *Southwestern Historical Quarterly*, LXX: 240-241. This article reveals that the teaching of history during Williams's time at UT was a man's game. Despite Williams's Alamo study and her work with Dr. Eugene C. Barker on *The Writings of Sam Houston*, there is no mention of her in the article. A true mistake on the part of Brewer.

2   Dr. Eugene C. Barker statement, September 20, 1931, Amelia Worthington Williams Papers, CAH; hereafter cited as the Williams Papers.

3   L. W. Kemp to Amelia W. Williams, December 4, 1937, Houston, Williams Papers.

4   "Amelia Williams Note," on back and front of A. W. Grant to Amelia Williams, San Antonio, March 12, 1936, Williams Papers.

5   *The Dallas Morning News,* January 12, 1936.

6   *San Antonio Express Evening News*, June 16, 1939.

7   *Southwestern Historical Quarterly*, XCVI: 419, Bill Groneman, *Alamo Defenders: A Genealogy, The People and Their Words* (Austin: Eakin Press, 1990), 4-125; Ron Tyler, Douglas E. Barnett, Roy R. Barkley, Penelope C. Anderson, Mark F. Odintz, eds., *The New Handbook of Texas* (6 vols.; Austin: Texas State Historical Association, 1996); Susan Prendergast Schoelwer, "The Artist's Alamo: A Reappraisal of Pictorial Evidence, 1836-1850," *Southwestern Historical Quarterly*, LCI: 403-456; Tim J. and Terry S. Todish, *Alamo Sourcebook 1836: A Comprehensive Guide to the Alamo and the Texas Revolution* (Austin: Eakin Press, 1998), 76-91.

8   A. Waldo Jones to Frank H. Wardlaw, August 13, 1956, Atlanta, William I. Lewis file, Daughters of the Republic of Texas Library, San Antonio; hereafter cited as DRTL.

9   Miss Jan Smoot to Kent Biffle, of *The Dallas Morning News*, July 18, 1995, Austin, author's copy.

10   Walter Lord, "Myths and Realities of the Alamo," in Stephen B. Oates, ed., *The Republic of Texas, by the editors of the American West and the Texas State Historical Association* (Palo Alto, California: American West Publishing Company, 1968), 19.

11   Thomas Lloyd Miller, "Mexican-Texans at the Alamo," *The Journal of Mexican American History,* II: 33. Miller also had praise for Williams: "In spite of the few corrections which have been made to the Williams roll, she made a tremendous historical contribution and all scholars studying the subject must begin with her work."

12   Richard G. Santos, *Santa Anna's Campaign Against Texas, 1835-1836* (Waco: Texian Press, 1968), 84, n. 88.

13 Harbart Davenport, "Notes on 'Siege and Fall of the Alamo' by Amelia Williams," Williams Papers.

14 Paul Hutton, "Introduction" in Susan Prendergast Schoelwer, with Tom W. Glaser, *Alamo Images* (Dallas: DeGolyer Library and Southern Methodist University Press, 1985), 4.

15 Amelia W. Williams to Morris Sheppard, March 6, 1928, Austin, Williams Papers.

16 Amelia W. Williams, "A Critical Study of the Siege of the Alamo and of the Personnel of Its Defenders," *Southwestern Historical Quarterly*, XXXVII: 41-42.

17 Examination of Andrew Barsena and Anselmo Bergara, March 11, 1836, Gonzales, Jenkins, ed., *Papers*, V: 45-46; E. N. Gray letter, March 11, 1836, Gonzales, Jenkins, ed., *Papers,* V: 48-49; C. B. Stewart to Ira R. Lewis, March 16, 1836, Washington-on-the-Brazos, Jenkins, ed., *Papers*, V: 93; Delores Beeson affidavit, November 3, 1853, Colorado County, Anselmo Bergara file, M & P-TSL; Alexander Horton, "The Life of A. Horton and Early Settlement of San Augustine County," *The Quarterly of the Texas State Historical Association,* XIV: 311.

    At the time, Houston reported that Ben, Colonel Juan N. Almonte's black cook, brought the pardon proclamation to Gonzales. In his 1858 memoir, Juan N. Seguin said that Bergara and Barcena were members of his company that he had "left for purposes of observation in the vicinity of San Antonio." In this case Seguin's veracity is doubtful as it is not supported by the other evidence. In regard to his role in the defense of the Alamo, Seguin's self-serving book is often contradicted by his later statements about the Alamo. See Chapters Three and Four for this writer's interpretation of Seguin's role in the defense of the Alamo.

18 Williams, "A Critical Study," 41-42.

19 A. Briscoe to editor, March 16, 1836, *Red River Herald,* date unknown; B. B. Goodrich to Edmund Goodrich, March 15, 1836, Washington-on-the-Brazos, Jenkins, ed., *Papers,* V: 81; Houston to Raguet, March 13, 1836. Goodrich, a member of the convention and brother of Alamo defender John C. Goodrich, reported: "Col. Travis, the commander of the fortress, sooner than fall into the hands of the enemy, stabbed himself to the heart and instantly died."

20 Alamo account, *Telegraph and Texas Register*, San Felipe, March 24, 1836; Gray, *From Virginia,* 137. The informant who described the death struggle to Joe is unknown. Susanna Dickinson may have told Joe of the incident. The death struggle report first appeared in the *T&T Register*, and she was the paper's source for the description. Dickinson was in the Alamo chapel and did not view much of the battle. Thus she would have had to obtain the information from a Mexican soldier, most likely Colonel Juan N. Almonte. On the other hand, Joe may have told the story to Dickinson. Joe's

informant may have been Captain Manuel Barragan, of the Rio Grande Presidial company of cavalry, who captured and saved Joe from being killed.

21 *Telegraph and Texas Register*, March 24, 1836.

22 Francisco Ruiz, "Fall of the Alamo and Massacre of Travis and His Brave Associates," *The Texas Almanac* (Galveston: The Galveston News, 1860), 80-81. See Chapter Eight for additional analysis of the Ruiz account. The evidence indicates that Ruiz was not in San Antonio on March 6. Therefore, the report is not an eyewitness account and cannot be trusted.

23 Doctor Greg Dimmick interview, October 19, 1998, Nixon, Texas. Dimmick is a member of the Houston Archaeological Society. This group has been excavating the route of the Mexican army's April and May 1836 withdrawal in Wharton County for the last four years. Dimmick reported that they have found numerous English Brown Bess musket cartridges comprised of a single musket ball and a number of buckshot pellets, which proves the Mexican soldiers were shooting "buck and ball" loads in their muskets.

24 Ramon Martinez Caro, "Verdadera Idea De La Primera Campana De Texas Y Sucesos Ocurridos Despues De La Accion De San Jacinto" in Carlos E. Castaneda, trans. and ed., *The Mexican Side of the Texan Revolution* (1928; reprint: Austin and Dallas: Graphic Ideas Incorporated, 1970), 105; *Republica de Tejas Commandencia militar de Galveston Lista de los oficioles mejicanos muertos en la accion de San Jacinto, el 21 ded abril de 1836*, Jenkins, ed., *Papers*, VI: 84.

25 *El Mosquito Mexicano*, Mexico City, April 5, 1836. The missive from the unknown soldier was dated "Bexar, March 7, 1836."

26 Williams, "A Critical Study," 165-166.

27 Ibid., 251-252. A copy of Williams's original study was reviewed to make sure the version in the SWHQ was not a printing error. There was no error.

28 A. L. Harrison file, AMC-TSL.

29 Nacogdoches Enlistments, January 14, 1836, Jenkins, ed., *Papers*, IV: 13-14; Evaluation of David Crockett's horse and equipment, January 15, 1836, Nacogdoches, David Crockett file, AMC-TSL.

30 S. Sherman affidavit, transcription copy, April 24, 1836, Headquarters in Camp on Brazos, Williams Papers, CAH. The original Sherman claim could not be located in the archives division of the Texas State Library. Also, there is a problem with the transcription. The HQ of the Texian army on April 24, 1836, was not on the Brazos River. The HQ was near the San Jacinto battleground. Nevertheless, Military Warrant Ledger, call number 304-2511, Archives Division, TSL, contains an entry on pages 37 and 38 for a military supplies and service claim, voucher 203, for A. L. Harrison that was authorized by Sidney Sherman on April 24, 1836.

31 Martin & Clem & Co., July 23, 1836, Summary of Claims dated from October 26, 1835, to March 19, 1836, Martin and Clem & Company file, AMC-TSL; William B. Harris to Martin and Clem, January 23, 1836,

Washington, Quarter Master Records, 401-1227-13, TSL; David Crockett to John Lott, January 23, 1836, Washington-on-the-Brazos, David Crockett file, AMC-TSL; B. A. M. Thomas to John Lott, January 24, 1836, John Lott file, AMC-TSL.

32 William B. Harrison to William Kerr, January 28, 1836, San Felipe, William Kerr file, AMC-TSL; William B. Harrison to John Echols, January 28, 1836, Quarter Master Records, 401-1218-25, TSL; William B. Harrison to James Gotier, January 30, 1836, James Gotier file, AMC-TSL; William B. Harrison to John Eblin, John Eblin file, AMC-TSL; Kenneth Kesselus, *Bastrop County Before Statehood* (Austin: Jenkins Publishing Company, 1986), 183.

33 Sam Houston to Peter Harper, February 9, 1837, Columbia, Peter Harper file, AMC-TSL; David Crockett to Son[-in-law] and Daughter, January 9, 1836, San Augustine, Jenkins, ed., *Papers,* III: 453-454; Sam Houston to All Volunteers and Troops for the Aid of Texas in her Conflict, December 27, 1835, Washington-on-the-Brazos, Jenkins, ed., *Papers,* III: 335; Sam Houston to James Power, December 28, 1835, Washington-on-the-Brazos, Jenkins, ed., *Papers,* III: 350; Sam Houston Army Order, December 30, 1835, Headquarters, Jenkins, ed., *Papers*, III: 373.

Peter Harper was most likely a couple of days ahead of Crockett. Crockett and B. A. M. Thomas would have arrived at Goliad in late January when there were about thirty-five Texian soldiers under the command of Francis W. Thornton. Those troops would have believed that San Antonio was under the threat of an immediate attack by a large Mexican force and that Lt. Colonel James C. Neill was in need of mounted scouts. That information may in turn have influenced Crockett and his men to join the Texian force at Bexar.

Or Crockett may have encountered Houston on the road to Goliad as Houston was returning to Washington-on-the-Brazos, and Houston may have ordered Crockett to the Alamo because Neill needed mounted scouts. Houston, however, left no record of such an event.

There are two sources that report that Crockett traveled through Bastrop on his way to San Antonio. First, there is the John Berry story in Andrew Jackson Sowell, *Early Settlers and Indian Fighters of Southwest Texas* (Austin: Ben C. Jones and Company, 1900), 46. Berry's wife claimed that her husband, John Berry, had repaired a broken rifle stock for Crockett while in Bastrop (Mina) on the way to San Antonio. Mrs. Berry's veracity is compromised by two elements in the account. First, she claimed that John B. repaired the rifle's stock with a "large silver band." Silver is a soft metal that would not have been used to repair a broken stock. Second, she claimed that Crockett did not wear an animal skin cap. Crockett did wear such a cap. It appears that Berry told the Crockett tale to enhance her and her husband's small place in Texas history, not an uncommon human behavior.

The second source is Noah Smithwick's *The Evolution of a State*, which claims: "I [Smithwick] was taken down with fever while in Bastrop, but was convalescent when Crockett came on, and wanted to return with him to San Antonio, but, seeing that I was not in condition to do so, he persuaded me to wait for another party to arrive a few days later."

Contrary to the great trust that has been placed in the Smithwick book, military service records, Noah Smithwick file, AMC-TSL, show that he was a member of Captain I. W. Burton's Texas Ranger company from January 29, 1836, to April 29, 1836. The unit was stationed in East Texas, near the United States border. If Crockett had traveled through Bastrop, it would have been around January 26 or 27. It would have been impossible for Smithwick to have been sick in Bastrop on those dates and have enlisted in Burton's company on the Sabine River on January 29, 1836.

William C. Davis, Crockett's most recent biographer, in *Three Roads to the Alamo: The Lives and Fortunes of David Crockett, James Bowie, and William Barret Travis*, 718, reports: "[Thomas Ricks] Lindley's itinerary maintains that Crockett was in the Goliad-Copano area, more than one hundred miles off the most direct route to Bexar. Lindley's evidence is a claim filed for an expense incurred by Peter Harper, who had been part of Crockett's contingent, the inference being that if Harper was near Goliad or Copano, then so was Crockett. This may be true, and it may not. Since the most direct road from Gay Hill to Bexar was the old Gotier Trace to its junction with the *Medio* road [La Bahia road], then south across the San Antonio road and thence via Gonzales, this has been chosen as his most likely route."

Mr. Davis's triple biography is mammoth and excellent. Also, Mr. Davis has been very supportive and appreciative of this investigator's work, for which I am extremely thankful. In this case, however, Mr. Davis's direct route to San Antonio claim is off base. Had Crockett taken the Gotier Trace, it would have taken him to Mina (Bastrop), not Gonzales. The San Antonio road that Davis wrote of did not go through Gonzales. The most direct and safest route to Bexar from Gay Hill would have been for Crockett to have traveled southwest on the Medio road to its junction with the San Antonio to Columbus road. At that intersection Crockett could have turned west and the road would have taken him through Gonzales, straight to Bexar. Also, on that road the chance of being attacked by Indians was much less than on the road from Mina to Bexar. There is, however, no evidence that indicates Crockett passed through Gonzales.

34 John M. Swisher, *The Swisher Memoirs* (San Antonio: The Sigmond Press, 1932), 18; James C. Neill to Convention, February 5, 1836, Bexar, Jenkins, ed., *Papers*, IV: 265; G. B. Jameson to Henry Smith, February 11, 1836, Bexar, Jenkins, ed., *Papers*, IV: 303; Crockett to Lott, January 23, 1836; Thomas to Lott, January 24, 1836; "Muster Roll of Capt. Chenoweth's Co," Muster Rolls book, Archives Division, Texas General Land Office, Austin; said archive is hereafter cited as the GLO. Historians have long wondered just how the Muster Rolls book was created. The GLO book was copied from the original Adjutant General muster rolls sometime before those rolls were destroyed in the burning of the Adjutant General building during the mid-1850s. A notice that appeared in the November 26, 1836 issue of the *Telegraph and Texas Register* indicates that the original Adjutant General's

rolls were most likely created in 1837. The notice reads: "The undersigned being appointed a committee by the House of Representatives of the Republic of Texas to obtain the names of as many of the officers and soldiers who were in service under the commands of Austin, Burleson, Dimmit, Travis, and Fannin – do hereby request that all persons who are in possession of information relative to said service will furnish the undersigned, the Secretary of War, or the editor of the *Telegraph*, with a certificate list of the names of such as can be procured. [John] Chenoweth, [Elkanah] Brush, [John Wheeler] Bunton." The three men were veterans of the revolution.

The Crockett claim reads: "This is to certify that John Lott furnished myself and four other volunteers on our way to the army with accommodations for ourselves & horses." At that point the army was forming at Copano and Goliad. Thus, it appears that the group spent the night of January 22 at Lott's place and departed the following morning. As Gay Hill was only a short ride from Washington-on-the-Brazos, Crockett probably arrived there on the twenty-third.

B. A. M. Thomas's claim shows that he did not depart Lott's establishment until the morning of January 24. He would have most likely joined Crockett at Gay Hill on that date.

The February 5 Neill letter contains the signatures of all the company commanders at San Antonio on that date. Because Crockett's name is not on the document, it appears he had not arrived at Bexar as of February 5. The Jameson missive placed Crockett in Bexar on February 11. He most likely arrived before the eleventh, but the evidence for an earlier date is weak. Antonio Menchaca, one of James Bowie's men, who left the Alamo during the siege, reported in his *Memoirs* that Crockett was in Bexar on February 10, 1836. That date is most likely correct, but Menchaca also claimed that Crockett entered the city on January 13, 1836, which is wrong.

35 Ibid.

36 Williams, "A Critical Study," 97; Jose Antonio Navarro to Samuel M. Williams, September 26, 1833, Bexar, Samuel May Williams Papers, Rosenberg Library, Galveston, Texas. Translation of the Navarro letter was done by Mr. Ismael Magna, Mexican Consul of Galveston, date unknown. A special thanks to Casey Edward Greene, Head of Special Collections at the Rosenberg Library, for furnishing this writer with copies of the original Navarro letter and the translation.

37 Williams, "A Critical Study," 298; Note titled "John" and page from Williams's early draft of her defender roll listing defenders 181 to 183, Box 2N494, Williams Papers. Williams's research notes reveal that, about John, she first wrote: "John – Negro slave boy of Desauque I find no warrant, headright or other information." The first draft of her summary on John reads: "183 _____ John, the negro slave boy who belonged to Francis De Sauque was left at the Alamo by his master. He died there. Why he was not spared as were the other negroes is not known. All lists include the name. No certificate for land to his heirs, if he had any, can be found."

38 Milam I-883, Jasper B-23, Bexar B-413, Land Grant records, GLO.

39 *Telegraph and Texas Register*, March 24, 1836, San Felipe.

40 John Thurston to Noah J. Byars, December 20, 1835, Noah J. Byars file, AMC-TSL; J. M. Thurston to Sam Houston, December 18, 1835, Andrew Jackson Houston Papers, TSL; Bernard Bee affidavit, October 28, 1837, Houston, John M. Thurston file, AMC-TSL; John H. Forsyth to William Newland, February 4, 1836, Gonzales, William Newland file, AMC-TSL; John H. Forsyth to William A. Matthews, February 4, 1836, Gonzales, William A. Matthews file, AMC-TSL; William B. Travis to Henry Smith, January 29, 1836, Burnam's Crossing on the Colorado River, AP-TSL; James C. Neill et al. to Convention, February 5, 1836, Bexar, Jenkins, ed., *Papers*, IV: 263-265.

41 George M. Collinsworth to Governor Henry Smith, January 10, 1836, Matagorda, Henry Smith Papers, CAH; George Wheelright affidavit, November 20, 1837, Houston, R. R. Royall file, AMC-TSL.

42 Frank Templeton, *Margaret Ballentine or The Fall of the Alamo* (Houston: State Printing Company, 1907), 235; James O. Breeden, ed., *A Long Ride in Texas: The Explorations of John Leonard Riddell* (College Station: Texas A&M University Press, 1994), 51; David R. Goldfield, *Promised Land: The South Since 1945* (Arlington Heights, Ill.: Harlan Davidson, 1987), 107. Riddell, on meeting an Indian named John, wrote: "The soldiers and Texans universally gave Indians the name John." Templeton's appendix has some valuable data not found elsewhere, but it must be used with caution.

43 Ibid.

44 Williams, "A Critical Study," 238.

45 Samuel E. Alsbury, "The Private Journal of Juan Nepomuceno Almonte February 1 - April 16, 1836," *Southwestern Historical Quarterly*, XLVIII, 23.

46 Copy of the Neill statement in Dr. William's handwriting, Williams Papers, Box 2N494, CAH.

47 James C. Neill affidavit, February 2, 1838, Houston, I. L. K. Harrison file, M & P-TSL.

48 George A. Nixon to R. R. Royall, November 14, 1835, Nacogdoches, Box 2/19, Council Papers, TSL; J. Roth receipt, November 17, 1835, Nacogdoches, Henry Raguet Papers, CAH; John Chenoweth affidavit, n.d., Houston, Edward Nelson file, AMC-TSL.

49 Nixon to Royall, November 14, 1835; J. Roth affidavit, December 15, 1835, Bexar, Leonard L. Williams file, AMC-TSL; J. Roth affidavit, December 15, 1835, Bexar, David Cook file, AMC-TSL; Alamo voting list, Bexar, Election Returns Collection, TSL.

50 Williams, "A Critical Study," 301.

51 Petition of John Dorset for Administration of Jacob Roth, January 31, 1838, Final Record Book A: 128, Nacogdoches County, Texas.

52 "Muster Roll, Captain Thomas H. Breece's Co., Texas Volunteers, in the Army before Bexar, 1835," Muster Rolls book, 25, GLO. Williams identified James Dickon as James Dimkins (Dimplins). Ernest Beerstecher Jr., "Historical Probate Extracts," *Texana*, VII: 271 shows that the name was James Dickon. Williams did not address the name of James Holloway in her study.

53 Williams, "A Critical Study," 287.

54 Ibid., 291.

55 Ibid., 287.

56 Edward Gritten to *Alcalde, Ayuntamiento* and People of Gonzales, October 4, 1835, Bexar, Jenkins, ed., *Papers*, II: 38; Edward Gritten claim for expenses for A. Anderson express to Gonzales, Edward Gritten file, AMC-TSL; Alamo voting list, February 1, 1836; "List of men who have this day volunteered to remain before Bexar, November 24, 1835," Austin Papers, CAH; "Return of Killed and Wounded in the Actions of 20th and 21st of April 1836," Jenkins, ed., *Papers*, VI: 14-14; Peter L. Duncan muster roll, n.d., siege of Bexar, 1835, Austin Papers, CAH; Peter L. Duncan to Luke Moore, December 13, 1835, Bexar, Luke Moore file, AMC-TSL.

57 Williams, "A Critical Study," 288; "Breece Muster Roll."

58 Williams, "A Critical Study," 301; Lost Book of Harris County, 119 and name index, Box G-629, GLO; Gifford White, Lost Book of Harris County, typescript copy, 119 and name index, Manuscript Collection, TSL; San Jacinto List, Jenkins, ed., *Papers*, VI: 14-15.

59 Ibid.

60 Williams, "A Critical Study," 300.

61 *Texas General Land Office Land Grant Index*, Volume H, 1673-1674, GLO.

62 Williams, "A Critical Study," 300; "Breece Muster Roll."

63 Robert Musselman, Thomas P. Hutchinson, and John J. Baugh affidavit, Francis William Jackson file, AMC-TSL; Groneman, *Alamo Defenders*, 11 and 82. A total review of Williams's citations for Baugh and Musselman was not conducted. Her sources appear to prove the two men died at the Alamo.

64 Ibid.

65 "List of the names of those who fell in the Alamo at San Antonio de Bexar March 6, 1836," Muster Rolls book, 2, GLO, this roll lists a "J. Washington"; Ernest Beerstecher Jr., "Historical Probate Extracts," *Texana*, VIII: 86; reports an entry for "James Washington"; Alamo voting list, February 1, 1836. The last document lists the name George Washington. Also, the Nacogdoches Enlistments, January 14, 1836, list Joseph G. Washington. It is believed that Joseph G. Washington arrived at San Antonio with David Crockett. Both men enlisted at the same place on the same date. Washington, however, voted at Bexar on February 1. Crockett did not, which suggests they were not together. It is possible that Washington was riding ahead of Crockett and reached San Antonio before Crockett.

66 Lucy A. Erath, "Memoirs of Major George Bernard Erath," *Southwestern Historical Quarterly*, XXVI: 230-231. The long quote from Erath was included because it is the only known information about the life of Ross McClelland, other than his death at the Alamo.

67 Robert Merrett and Thomas S. Saul statement, July 1838, Washington County Board of Land Commissioners records, p. 81, Washington County Courthouse, Brenham, Texas.

68 Williams, "A Critical Study," 267.

69 Ibid., 238; *San Antonio Evening News*, June 16, 1939.

70 Miles S. Bennett, "The Battle of Gonzales, the 'Lexington' of the Texas Revolution," *The Quarterly of the Texas State Historical Association*, II: 314; Ethel Zively Rather, "De Witt's Colony," *The Quarterly of the Texas State Historical Association*, VIII: 158-159.

71 William P. Harris and John W. Moore affidavit, September 26, 1857, copy of entry from the Lost Book Harris County, Benjamin Kellogg Court of Claims file, C-4531, GLO; William P. Harris affidavit, September 8, 1836, Harrisburg, Benjamin Kellogg file, AMC-TSL.

72 A. S. Miller et al. v. Mary S. Rogers, *Texas Reports*, XLIX: 402.

73 Williams, "A Critical Study," 267.

74 Ibid., 263; Miller, "Mexican-Texans," 34.

75 Jose Maria Guerrero file, PC-TSL.

76 Williams, "A Critical Study," 254; Ibid., 263; Ibid., 276; "Morning Report of the Troops Stationed at the Fort of Goliad, Commanded by Capt. P. Dimitt," December 14 and 21, 1835, Philip Dimmitt Morning Report Papers, CAH; Goliad Declaration of Independence, December 20, 1835, Jenkins, ed., *Papers*, III: 269; Beerstecher Jr., "Historical Probate," 72; Isaac Robinson affidavit, May 21, 1838, Harris County, Isaac Robinson file, AMC-TSL; William and Jeremiah Day affidavit, Charles Sheam file, AMC-TSL. The "Day" who died at the Alamo was Freeman H. K. Day, who entered the Alamo with one of the Gonzales reinforcements. According to the March 24, 1836, *Telegraph and Texas Register,* one _____ Robinson from Scotland died at the Alamo. A correct identification of Robinson needs to be attempted.

77 Williams, "A Critical Study," 237-242; Ibid., 263.

78 Milam I-202, Milam B-1212, and Refugio B-1544, GLO; "Morning Report of the Troops Stationed at the Fort of Goliad, Commanded by Capt. P. Dimmitt, December 14, 1835."

79 Williams, "A Critical Study," 249.

80 Jesse T. Bowman entry, Certificate Number 538, Red River County Clerk Returns, GLO; Lamar I-109, GLO; Red River I-670, GLO; Bowie I-119, GLO.
    The Texas General Land Office Muster Rolls book show that one J. T. Bowman served in Captain "Jno. M. Bradley's" company of San Augustine Volunteers that was mustered on April 30, 1836. A second Bradley muster

roll, same book, dated December 12, 1835, however, does not list any person named Bowman. A third Bradley roll, dated November 21, 1835, found in the Austin Papers at the CAH, also fails to list a Bowman.

The only early Alamo victim list that includes the name Bowman is the roll found in Gray's *From Virginia*, 138. Gray listed a "Col. Bowman," which appears to be an error. Given that the name is listed between the name of William B. Travis and James Bowie, it appears Gray wrote Bowman instead of Bonham.

81   Clinton De Witt Baker, ed., *A Texas Scrap-Book* (New York and New Orleans: A. S. Barnes & Company, 1875), 112-113. The name "J. B. Bowman" does appear on three secondary Alamo lists, which were complied after the publication of Baker's book. In the mid-1870s the Texas government attempted to compile a correct roll of Alamo soldiers. Two of the lists can be found in the "Alamo Strays" box in the Archives Division of the Texas State Library. One list is a holographic document that the old veteran Francis W. Johnson signed off on. The second list is found in a newspaper article from an unknown Austin newspaper published in the summer of 1874. Both of these lists appear to have obtained the Bowman name from the early Alamo monument listing. The third list is found in John J. Linn's *Reminiscences of Fifty Years in Texas* that was first published in 1883. The book was actually ghost written (Jenkins, ed., *Texas Books*, 346) by Victor M. Rose. Linn was never in a position during the revolution to have obtained firsthand knowledge of the Alamo and its fall. Thus the Bowman name on his list was most likely taken from Baker's book.

According to the "Records of the Permanent Council," January 15-16, TSL and James W. Robinson to the Council, January 16, 1836, San Felipe, Jenkins, ed., *Papers*, IV: 42, there was one James H. Bowman in San Antonio in mid-January 1836. Thus the name on the first Alamo monument may have been "J. H. Bowman" and is represented as "J. B." in *A Texas Scrap-Book* because of a copy error or a typesetting mistake.

Furthermore, while it is negative evidence, the Jesse B. Bowman name or a variant of it is not found on any (all being primary documents) of the siege of Bexar muster rolls, the storming of Bexar rolls, the Alamo rosters, or the February 1, 1836 Alamo voting list. Neither did the Republic of Texas or the state of Texas issue any bounty or donation land grants in the name for service and death in the revolution.

A list found in Frederick C. Chabot's *The Alamo: Mission, Fortress and Shrine* (San Antonio: Frederick C. Chabot, 1941), 68-69, attributed to Mrs. Letta A. Small, custodian of the Alamo, is the earliest list this writer has found that includes Jesse B. Bowman, who is listed in a category titled: "Native States Unknown." This list appears to be the Daughters of the Republic of Texas's official list prior to their acceptance of Dr. Williams's roster.

J. B. Ferrell and Bob N. Bowman, in "Jesse B. Bowman, 1785-1836: Defender of the Alamo," Jesse B. Bowman file, DRT Library, report: "On file at the county courthouse at Cooper, Texas, is a contract between Jesse

Bowman and Ambrose Douthit, which said that Jesse Bowman agreed to give Douthit 1/2 of his citia and labor of land. In return Douthit agreed to draw up all paper work and pay for having his land surveyed and any other expenses involved. This land was to be located in the neighborhood of the Red River. This contract was dated Feb 13, 1836." The Bowman family believes the contract is a forgery because they think Bowman was part of the Bexar garrison at that time and died at the fall of the Alamo. However, given that there is no valid evidence proving that Bowman was part of the San Antonio garrison, it would appear the contract is authentic.

For the Bowman family's point of view about their ancestor Jesse B. Bowman, one should read Bob and Doris Bowman, *The Search for an Alamo Soldier* (Lufkin: Best of East Texas Publishers, 1997), 11-67.

82   Williams, "A Critical Study," 281.

83   Bexar B-519, Fort Bend B-51, Fort Bend B-53, Colorado B-97, Milam B-1512, GLO; Jesse G. Thompson file, AMC-TSL; "List of the names of those who fell in the Alamo at San Antonio de Bexar March 6, 1836," Muster Rolls book, 2, GLO. The name "_____ Thompson" appears after Dr. Pollard.

84   Williams, "A Critical Study," 249; "List of the names of those who fell in the Alamo at San Antonio de Bexar March 6, 1836," Muster Rolls book, 2, 3, 255, GLO.

85   Liberty I-317; Military Warrant Ledger, 304-2511, TSL.

86   Williams, "A Critical Study," 249.

87   Bexar B-962; Nacogdoches I-399; Nacogdoches I-681; Washington I-92, GLO; James E. Winston, "Pennsylvania and the Independence of Texas," *Southwestern Historical Quarterly,* XVIII: 266; *Telegraph and Texas Register,* March 24, 1836; James Brown, Spanish Land Grant Index, GLO.

88   Travis to Houston, February 25, 1836.

89   Williams, "A Critical Study," 309-310; Robert Brown army discharge, June 5, 1836, Headquarters, La Bahia [Goliad], Robert Brown file, AMC-TSL.

90   Williams, "A Critical Study," 251.

91   Charles Clark C-1549, Court of Claims collection, GLO; Milam B-1425 and Travis B-648, GLO.

92   Williams, "A Critical Study," 276.

93   Goliad B-227, Bexar B-1917, Fannin B-1304, GLO; Lost Book of Harris County, 96 and 141; "New Orleans Greys, Capt. Wm. G. Cooke, in the Army before Bexar 1835," Muster Rolls book.

94   Williams, "A Critical Study," 161-163 and 269; Nacogdoches enlistments, January 14, 1836, Muster Rolls book, 115, GLO. Charles Linley, age thirty-one, a Nacogdoches resident, was England born and joined the Texas army on January 14, 1836. One of Williams's sources for Jonathan Lindley is C. M. S. R. No. 9189, which shows that Lindley joined the Bexar garrison on December 14, 1835. Williams's belief that Charles Linley and Jonathan Lindley were the same man is impossible to understand.

95 Albert Cook Myers, *Immigration of the Irish Quakers into Pennsylvania 1682-1750* (1902; reprint; Baltimore: Genealogical Publishing Company, 1985), 179; Jonathan Lindley, entry 369, folder F, Montgomery County Clerk Returns, GLO; Jonathan Lindley probate inventory, Vol. A, 135-136, Montgomery County, Texas; *Telegraph and Texas Register,* March 24, 1836; Gray, *From Virginia*, 140-141; "List of Men who have this day volunteered to remain before Bexar," Jonathan Lindley pay certificate, Jonathan Lindley file, AMC-TSL; Jonathan Lindley file, *New Handbook of Texas* records, Texas State Historical Association, University of Texas, Austin, Texas.

96 "Williams note," Grant to Williams, March 12, 1936. Williams believed only she had a right to publish and use material from her study. Never mind that it had already been published in a journal, which made it available to the public for fair use.

97 Leita Small to George P. Carrel, January 6, 1939; George P. Carrel to the Alamo Committee, January 11, 1939, San Antonio; Amelia Williams to George P. Carrel, January 19, 1939, Austin; Leita Small to Amelia Williams, January 21, 1939; all letters are in the Williams Papers, CAH.

98 Amelia W. Williams to Stuart McGregor, February 10, 1941, Austin, Williams Papers, CAH.

99 Williams to Carrel, January 19, 1939.

100 Ibid.

101 Williams, "A Critical Study," 237.

102 Oates, ed., *The Republic of Texas*, 19; Schoewer and Glaser, *Alamo Images,* 4.

103 Alamo — Providing for the Purchase, Care and Preservation of. S. H. B. No. 1, Section 2, January 26, 1905, *General Laws of Texas*, chapter 7. 28th, 29th, 30th Legislatures: 1903, 1905, 1907.

Travis's Bones:
Reinforcement of the Alamo

Do hasten on aid to me as rapidly as possible, as from the superior number of the enemy it will be impossible for us to keep them out much longer. If they overpower us, we fall a sacrifice at the shrine of our country, and we hope posterity and our country will do our memory justice. Give me help, oh my Country! Victory or death!

William B. Travis[1]

Alamo history, as it currently stands, reports only one reinforcement of the Alamo garrison during the thirteen-day siege. That relief came from thirty-two mounted men from Gonzales who entered the Alamo at 3:00 a.m. on March 1, 1836. Twentieth-century citizens of Gonzales crowned the group as the "Immortal Thirty-two." That nomination includes the myth that the men knew their action was suicidal but willingly entered the Alamo to die for Travis and Texas independence. Also, the rest of Texas stood accused of having deserted Travis and his band of men at the Alamo. New evidence shows that the reinforcement of the Alamo was not that simple or that simple minded. Nor did all of Travis's countrymen desert him.[2]

Travis, in the March 3, 1836 missive that reported the arrival of the Gonzales relief, also wrote: "I hope your honorable body [Convention assembled at Washington-on-the-Brazos] will hasten on reinforcements, ammunitions and provisions to our aid as soon as possible.... If these things are promptly sent and large reinforcements are hastened to this frontier, this neighborhood will be the great and decisive ground." Travis, even more emphatic, wrote his good friend Jesse Grimes: "I shall have to fight the enemy on his own terms, yet I am ready to do it, and if my countrymen do not rally to my relief, I am determined to perish in the defense of this place, and my bones shall reproach my country for her neglect."[3]

The Alamo neighborhood did not become the "decisive ground" in the way Travis had hoped, but new evidence shows that far more men than thirty-two answered Travis's plea for assistance. The following analysis is not a complete accounting of the siege and storming of the Alamo. Rather, the work is an attempt to identify who went into the Alamo the first day, who entered during the siege, who attempted to enter, and who left during the siege. The story of those men, women, and children commenced on February 23, 1836, the day that Santa Anna's centralist army stormed into Bexar to avenge the 1835 Texian victory over the forces of General Martin Perfecto de Cos and to make an example of the Alamo defenders.[4]

William Barret Travis
Photo courtesy Texas State Library & Archives Commission

First Day — Tuesday, February 23, 1836

Sunrise of the first day likely found many of the Alamo soldiers just going to bed. Others may have been at breakfast, eating flour tortillas with their eggs instead of the usual American biscuits. A small number of men were on duty at the Alamo. The garrison had celebrated George Washington's birthday the previous night, and the wild fandango, as was the Texian way, had continued through the night. Drinking, gambling, dancing, and romantic adventures with the young women of Bexar were the only rewards of service at the frontier post.[5]

Already the vanguard of General Santa Anna's Army of Operations Against Texas was within striking distance of the Texian rebels. The night before, General Joaquin Ramirez y Sesma, with one hundred sixty mounted infantrymen, had departed from the Medina River, about

Mexican dragoon
Photo courtesy Joseph Musso collection

eighteen miles west of San Antonio. Their mission was to prevent any escape of the Texians. Sometime during the advance, Trinidad Coy, a Texian spy, was captured by the Mexican advance. Coy, probably hoping to give Travis and Bowie some time, told the Mexican general that an ambush awaited his troops. Santa Anna had ordered his generals to be cautious in approaching the enemy in order to prevent an early defeat that might demoralize his untested soldiers. Therefore, Ramirez y Sesma halted at 7:00 a.m. on Alazan Creek, a mile or so west of the city, to await his commander and the larger force. The Mexican presence in Texas, however, had not gone unnoticed.[6]

Years later Francisco Ruiz reported: "...the forces under the command of Travis, Bowie, and Crockett having on the same day, at 8 o'clock in the morning, learned that the Mexican army was on the banks of the Medina river, they concentrated in the fortress of the Alamo." Travis and Bowie, at that point, appear to have believed that the enemy force was under the command of Ramirez y Sesma, rather than Santa Anna.[7]

Despite their shocked surprise, fatigue, and hangover headaches, the rebels managed to pull things together. One or more soldiers were left in the San Fernando church bell tower to watch for the enemy. Otherwise, the defenders, their family members, and a number of Mexican-Texians (Tejanos and Tejanas) hurried behind the Alamo walls. The relocation was far from smooth.[8]

In 1878 Ruben M. Potter, the second historian to pen an account of the fall of the Alamo, reported:

> The first sight of the enemy created as much confusion with as little panic at the Alamo as might be expected among men who had known as little of discipline as they did of fear. Mr. [Nat] Lewis, of San Antonio, informed me that he took refuge for a few hours in the fort when the invaders appeared, and the disorder of the post beggared description.... Some of the volunteers, who had sold their rifles to obtain the means of dissipation, were clamoring for guns of any kind; and the rest, though in arms, appeared to be mostly without orders or a capacity for obedience. No "army in Flanders" ever swore harder. He saw but one officer who seemed to be at his proper post and perfectly collected. This was an Irish Captain, named [William B.] Ward, who though generally an inveterate drunkard, was

now sober, and stood quietly by the guns of the south battery ready to use them. Yet amid the disorder of that hour no one seemed to think of flight.[9]

Dr. Horatio "Horace" A. Alsbury, the garrison's Spanish translator, was one of the Texians who moved his family into the Alamo. In addition to Alsbury, there was his wife, Juana Navarro Alsbury, her infant son, Alijo Perez Jr., and Mrs. Alsbury's sister, Gertrudis Navarro. Juana and Gertrudis were the nieces of Juan Martin Veramendi, James Bowie's father-in-law. Their father was Jose Angel Navarro, one of the city's leading centralists. Both women, however, had been reared in the federalist home of Veramendi and were viewed as sisters to Bowie's dead wife, Ursula Veramendi.[10]

Dr. Alsbury, after getting his family settled in the Alamo, departed for Gonzales with the news that the Mexican army was in the vicinity of San Antonio. Merchant Nat Lewis, however, did not join the garrison. Lewis, known as *Don Pelon* because of his bald head, left on foot that morning for Gonzales. At that juncture, the Alamo force numbered one hundred fifty-six effectives. There were fourteen or more men in the Alamo hospital, and Bowie was beginning to feel the effects of the typhoid pneumonia that would soon put him on his deathbed.[11]

Still, Bowie and Travis, despite a mid-February argument over who was to command the garrison in the absence of Lt. Colonel James C. Neill, worked to unite people, materials, and provisions to meet the enemy. Ignacio Perez, a local government contractor, sold Travis thirty head of cattle that were quickly herded into the courtyard on the east side of the Alamo to join an unknown number of horses. Eighty or ninety bushels of corn were found in houses abandoned by the citizens of Bexar. Most of the corn came from Gabriel Martinez's small hut located on the east side of the Alamo.[12]

Also, the defenders dismantled Antonio Saez's blacksmith shop that was located near the Alamo and carried the materials into the compound to help fortify the sprawling structure. In the days before Santa Anna's arrival, Saez had aided the Texians by repairing their arms and cutting up pieces of iron to be used in the place of canister shot for the Alamo cannon.[13]

The Alamo defenders were well armed. The compound's artillery commanders had twenty-one cannon of various calibers. Eighteen guns were combat-ready on the walls. The Alamo armory was stocked with 816 rifles and muskets and over 14,600 cartridges. Except for cannon-balls of certain calibers, the artillerymen had plenty of ball, grape, and "cut-iron" shot. Each defender had a bayonet for his musket. Others had swords or large butcher knives for the close fighting. Cannon and rifle powder, however, were in short supply.[14]

Provisions and weapons were in order, but Travis and Bowie still had little intelligence that identified the exact whereabouts of the enemy. The two commanders, however, knew that the opposing army would be moving in their direction Thus, Travis, probably around high noon, sent Captain Philip Dimmitt and Lieutenant Benjamin Noble, who had arrived in mid-February with supplies, out to locate the Mexican force.[15]

About the same time, Santa Anna's army joined its detachment of mounted infantry in the Alazan hills. After the revolution, Santa Anna, forgetting his order about caution, claimed the storming of the Alamo could have been avoided had Ramirez y Sesma obeyed his orders to dragoon the Texians without delay. Yet, at the time, the Mexican com-mander-in-chief was content to linger on the Alazan.[16]

As the Mexican army took a lunch break, additional men, women, and children scurried into the Alamo for safety. Other citizens hurriedly packed and left the city for their lower San Antonio River ranch houses or headed east to the Anglo-Celtic colonies.[17]

Captain Almaron Dickinson, however, settled his artillery company in the fortress and then left to get his family. Riding up to his temporary home, he found Susanna, his young wife, and Angelina, their baby girl, ready to move. Susanna handed Angelina up to Almaron, then she jumped up behind him for a fast ride to the Alamo.[18]

The invading army, after a stop of an hour and a half, resumed its advance. Between 2:30 and 3:00 p.m. the Texian bell tower sentry saw dust clouds rising from the road that ran west to Leon Creek. Travis was quickly notified of the sighting. Needing more information because Dimmitt and Noble had not returned, Travis sent John W. Smith, the Alamo's storekeeper, out to scout the Leon Creek road. Smith was a San Antonio merchant and carpenter who knew the area well. Soon after Smith's departure, the enemy marched into view near the city's grave-yard, west of the city.[19]

Travis and Bowie could see they were going to need armed assistance to win the coming fight. They then sent John Johnson to Colonel James

W. Fannin Jr., commander of the Texian force at Goliad, on the San Antonio River, about ninety miles southeast of Bexar. Johnson carried a note that read:[20]

> We have removed all our men into the Alamo, where we will make such resistance as is due to our honor, and that of the country, until we can get assistance from you, which we expect you to forward immediately. In this extremity, we hope you will send us all the men you can spare promptly. We have one hundred and forty-six men [correct number was 156], who are determined never to retreat. We have but little provisions, but enough to serve us till you and your men arrive. We deem it unnecessary to repeat to a brave officer, who knows his duty, that we call on him for assistance.[21]

Colonel Juan N. Almonte, Santa Anna's senior aide-de-camp, reported the Texian actions as seen from the Mexican advance: "The enemy, as soon as the march of the division was seen, hoisted the tri-colored flag with two stars, designed to represent Coahuila and Texas. The President with all his staff advanced to Camp Santo (burying ground). The enemy lowered the flag and fled, and possession was taken of Bexar without firing a shot. At 3 P.M. the enemy filed off to the fort of the Alamo."[22]

In 1890 Juan N. Seguin also described the defenders' move to the Alamo. He wrote: "As we marched [down] 'Potrero Street' (now called 'Commerce') the ladies exclaimed 'poor fellows, you will all be killed, what shall we do?' "[23]

A number of Texian sharpshooters lagged behind to cover the defenders' stroll to the Alamo. David Crockett may have commanded the Texian shooters. At least one of the men, James M. Rose, was in Crockett's spy company. Colonel Jose Vicente Minon commanded an advance element of Santa Anna's force as they dodged the Texian rifle balls in front of the church of San Antonio. Santa Anna later reported: "...the national troops took possession of this city with the utmost order, which the traitors shall never again occupy; on our part we lost a corporal and a scout, dead, eight wounded."[24]

Meanwhile, outside the city a local Mexican encountered Dimmitt and Noble. He told the two Texians that Bexar was invested by the Mexican army. Later, a Tejano sent by Dimmitt's Mexican wife told the men they would be killed if they attempted to return because "two large bodies of Mexican troops were already around the town." Dimmitt and Noble's location at that time is unknown. They were, however, most likely on the Laredo road that ran south of Bexar—the wrong road on which to have spotted the enemy. Santa Anna entered San Antonio by the Leon Creek road, west of the city. The two Alamo soldiers then rode to the "Rovia," a nearby location, to wait and see what developed.[25]

Two other Alamo men were prevented from returning to the fortress that first day. A. J. Sowell, a Gonzales blacksmith, and Byrd Lockhart, a Gonzales surveyor, had departed the Alamo that morning in a search for cattle and other provisions. The enemy arrived while they were out on the supply-gathering expedition. Thus, Sowell and Lockhart rode to Gonzales, a loss of two more men for Travis.[26]

Another man who was caught outside of the Alamo that day was Luciano Pacheco. He went into the Alamo with Juan N. Seguin. Seguin then realized he had left an important trunk at his city home. He sent Pacheco out to get the trunk. By the time Pacheco had retrieved the luggage, the Mexican troops had taken possession of the city streets. Thus, Pacheco could not get back into the Alamo. Pacheco, however, was most likely not a loss for Travis. He had probably never been included in Travis's count.[27]

Travis, probably after he had entered the Alamo, wrote a short note to Judge Andrew Ponton at Gonzales: "The enemy in large force is in sight. We want men and provisions. Send them to us. We have 150 men and are determined to defend the Alamo to the last. Give us assistance.... Send an express to San Felipe with news night and day." An experienced man with a good horse was needed for the eighty-mile shot to Gonzales. It would, however, take almost an hour before a rider hit the road with Travis's plea for reinforcements.[28]

Santa Anna's centralist force probably entered the city's main plaza around 3:30 p.m. From the Alamo, Travis welcomed the enemy soldiers with an iron ball blast from the Alamo's eighteen-pounder. One diarist in the Mexican force reported that the Texians had two cannon aimed toward the city, an eighteen pounder and an eight pounder. Unfazed, Santa Anna had his troops spread out until occupation of the city, except for the Alamo, was complete. Cavalry commander Ventura Mora took half of the cavalry to mission Concepcion to secure that location. By 4:00 p.m. a blood-red flag had been hoisted from the church's bell tower; the

Old Mexican Cathedral on Plaza.

San Antonio de Bexar, Main Plaza
Photo courtesy Library of the Daughters of the Republic of Texas at the Alamo

banner's meaning was clear—no quarter, no mercy, and a Texian surrender would have to be unconditional. Travis responded with untroubled defiance by firing a round shot at the red flag with the eighteen-pounder. At that time, Colonel Juan N. Almonte was on his way to the Alamo with a flag of truce to initiate negotiations with the Texians. Almonte, however, understood the finality of the cannon blast and retreated. Minutes later a five-inch howitzer set up below Bexar began lobbing bronze bombs into the air over the Alamo compound.[29]

Travis, either before firing on the flag or right afterward, sent out his letter to Gonzales. The courier was Dr. Launcelot Smither, an old settler who spoke Spanish and knew the lay of the land. At that point Bowie and Travis appear to have believed that they faced two thousand Mexican soldiers, commanded by General Ramirez y Sesma.[30]

Bowie, however, was not ready to fight and wanted to know what the enemy had to offer the Texians. On February 2, 1836, Bowie had boldly declared to Governor Henry Smith that he would "rather die in these ditches than give it [the Alamo] up to the enemy." Also, in the same missive and seldom mentioned by Alamo historians, Bowie observed: "Our force is very small, the returns this day to the Comdt. is only one hundred and twenty officers & men. It would be a waste of men to put our brave little band against thousands." Thus, Bowie, with that thought in mind and apparently too sick to write, dictated a short note in Spanish to Juan Seguin. Bowie wanted to know if it was true that the enemy had requested a parley before Travis had fired on the flag. Bowie then signed the message with an unsteady hand and had Green B. Jameson, the garrison's sharpshooting engineer, meet with Almonte under a white flag.[31]

Of the meeting on the bridge over the San Antonio River, Almonte reported: "I conversed with the bearer...he informed me of the bad state [150 effectives versus 1,541 troops] they were in at the Alamo, and manifested a wish that some honorable conditions should be proposed for a surrender." Almonte sent Bowie's note to Santa Anna, who instructed

Mexican lancer
Photo courtesy Joseph Musso collection

another aide, Jose Batres, to answer Bowie and Jameson. Batres wrote: "...the Mexican army cannot come to terms under any conditions with rebellious foreigners to whom there is no other recourse left, if they wish to save their lives, than to place themselves immediately at the disposal of the Supreme Government from who alone they may expect clemency after some considerations are taken up." The "considerations" would have been the immediate execution of Travis, Bowie, most of their officers, and the United States volunteers.[32]

As the day edged toward the night, Travis maintained his boldness and sent Captain Albert Martin out with another offer for the Mexican officer. According to Almonte: "He [Martin] stated to me what Mr. Travis said, 'that if I wished to speak with him, he would receive me with much pleasure.' I answered that it did not become the Mexican government to make any propositions through me, and that I had only permission to hear such as might be made on the part of the rebels. After these contestations night came on, and there was no more firing."[33]

Sometime during the negotiations with Almonte, Travis's scout John W. Smith returned to the Alamo. Seguin, in his old age, said that Smith returned at "about five o'clock saying 'there comes the Mexican army composed of cavalry, infantry, and artillery!'" Travis, however, already had a pretty good idea of what he and his men faced across the San Antonio River.[34]

Soon afterward Travis is said to have called his soldiers together for a short address. Little is known about the talk. Historian Reuben M. Potter claimed: "When informed of this [the Mexican demand for an unconditional surrender], Travis harangued his men and administered to them an oath that they would resist to the last."[35]

That night Santa Anna's soldiers set up a second artillery battery for two long nine-pounders on the river. The site was on the west side, near the Veramendi house, Bowie's Bexar home.[36]

In the Alamo, Travis undoubtedly worried about the people in his charge. He only had 150 men to fight over 1,500 of the enemy. Six men had departed since Travis and Bowie had written Fannin that morning. At the minimum fourteen men were in the fort's hospital. Escape was impossible and the defenders knew it. They could not abandon the women and children. Their only chance was the possibility that sufficient reinforcements might arrive in time to ensure a Texian victory. Even at that, many of the defenders would surely die.[37]

Besides the Alamo soldiers, a large number of civilians were in the Alamo. Some were family members. Anthony Wolf's two boys, aged eleven and twelve, were there. Men on the Texas frontier considered such boys as being close to full grown. Texian mothers, however, might have viewed sons in that dangerous situation as their "darling baby boys."[38]

Other citizens were a number of Tejanos who, as volunteers, had fought against the Mexican army in the siege and storming of the town in 1835. They, however, were not members of Bexar garrison or soldiers in the Texian army on entering the Alamo. The group appears to have included Juan N. Seguin, Antonio Menchaca, Ambrosio Rodriguez, Eduardo Ramirez, Pedro Herrera, Salvador Flores, Manuel Flores, Simon Arreola, Cesario Carmona, Vicente Zepeda, Jose Maria Arocha, _____ Silvero, Matias Curvier, Antonio Fuentes, and Antonio Badillo. Addition of the men's family members probably made their total twenty or more.[39]

The last civilians to enter the Alamo that day appear to have been members of the Gregorio Esparza family who entered an hour before sunset. The accounts vary, but it appears that John W. Smith, sometime that morning, had advised the family to enter the Alamo. Gregorio, who was twenty-seven, was probably a member of Bowie's makeshift crew. Besides Gregorio, there was his wife, Ana Salazar Esparza, and their four children: Maria de Jesus, ten years old; Enrique, eight years old; Manuel, five years old; and Francisco, an infant.[40]

Enrique Esparza, in his old age, would remember others who had been in the Alamo. He listed: Juana Losoya Melton, wife of defender Eliel Melton; Concepcion Losoya, Juana's mother, and her sons, Juan and Toribio; Vitorina de Salina and three little girls; Madame Candeleria; a woman named Trinidad Saucedo; and an old woman called Petra Gonzales. There may have been other women and children in the Alamo, but their names have not survived in the known records and accounts of the fall of the Alamo.[41]

In addition to the soldiers, dependents, and civilians in the fortress that first day, the compound housed individuals who were not there by choice but because of forced circumstance—the slaves. Joe, in his early twenties, was Travis's manservant. Sam and Betty, who belonged to Bowie, were most likely house servants from the Veramendi house, Bowie's home in San Antonio. Joe later identified another slave, a black female, whose name and owner are unknown.[42]

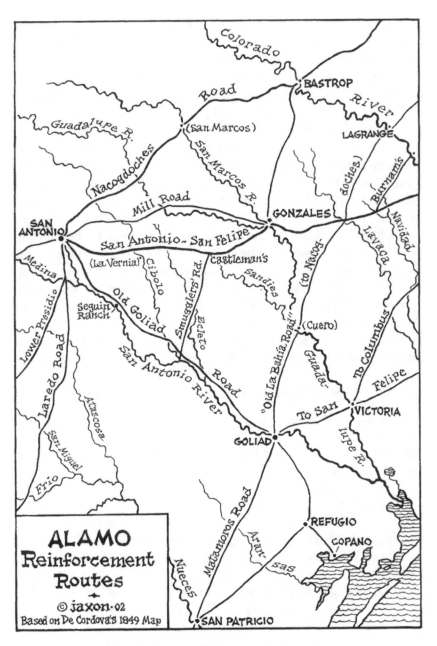

Alamo reinforcement routes
Map courtesy of Jack Jackson

As the Alamo inhabitants consumed their first supper in the old mission that night, Dr. Alsbury, A. J. Sowell, and Byrd Lockhart arrived at Gonzales, on the Guadalupe River, eighty miles due east of San Antonio. The Gonzales ranger company was quickly notified. The provisional government had only created the unit on February 4. Three commissioners, Matthew Caldwell, Byrd Lockhart, and William A. Matthews, had been instructed to raise and organize two platoons of twenty-eight men each, for a total company strength of fifty-six rangers. The company was to be commanded by a captain. Each platoon was under the direct command of a first lieutenant. The captain was paid $60 per month, the lieutenants $55. The noncommissioned officers were the first sergeant or orderly sergeant, second sergeant, and a corporal for each platoon. Each platoon would have had a first lieutenant and a second lieutenant. The platoons would have been divided into two squads of fourteen troopers each, with a lieutenant as the squad leader. The officers would have been chosen by company election. The term of enlistment was three months. Privates received $1.25 per day for themselves, horse, arms, and ammunition and $5.00 per month for provisions. The force was part of the ranger battalion commanded by Major R. M. "Three-Legged Willie" Williamson, Travis's former law partner and probably his best friend in Texas.[43]

Second Day — Wednesday, February 24

Travis probably knew it on the first day, but clearly the weight of the garrison's critical situation wore heavy on him the second day. For on that day he wrote the most famous letter sent from the Alamo during those fateful thirteen days. The document reads:

> Commandancy of the Alamo,
> Bexar, Feby. 24th, 1836
>
> To the People of Texas & all Americans in the world – Fellow Citizens & Compatriots – I am besieged by a thousand or more Mexicans under Santa Anna. I have sustained a continual bombardment & cannonade for 24 hours & have not lost a man. The enemy has demanded a surrender at discretion, otherwise, the garrison are to be put to the sword, if the fort is taken. I have answered the demand with a cannon shot, & our flag still waves proudly from the walls. I shall never surrender or retreat. Then, I call on you in the name of Liberty, of patriotism & every thing dear to

the American character, to come to our aid with all dispatch. The enemy is receiving reinforcements daily & will no doubt increase to three or four thousand in four or five days. If this call is neglected, I am determined to sustain myself as long as long as possible & die like a soldier who never forgets what is due his own honor & that of his country. VICTORY or DEATH.
  William Barret Travis
  Lt. Col. Comdt.
P.S.
The Lord is on our side. When the enemy appeared in sight we had not three bushels of corn. We have since found in deserted houses 80 to 90 bushels and got into the walls 20 or 30 head of Beeves.[44]

Today the dramatic missive is admired as the paramount expression of American sacrifice in a combat situation. Writer Jeff Long, however, saw the letter in a different light. He wrote: "Certainly it was Travis's masterpiece, romantic, pointed, and abundant with ego. Travis repeated its suicidal melody in the next (and last) four dispatches he sent from the Alamo, but never quite captured the high tragedy of this February 24 message."[45]

The key word in Long's statement is "pointed," for it is doubtful that Travis or contemporary readers thought of the letter as romantic. Travis had a concise and singular point to get across: If a sufficient number of armed men did not arrive in time, he and his men would have to fight to the death. In a time when there were only two methods of communication, speech and the written word, Travis used language to *emotionally move* the people. The missive, more than reflecting Travis's ego, showed his urgent need to influence citizens of a like mind to speed to the garrison's rescue. At least one contemporary writer left his impression of Travis's missive. William F. Gray wrote: "Another express is received from Travis, dated the 24th, stating that Santa Anna, with his army, were in Bexar, and had bombarded the Alamo for twenty-four hours. An unconditional surrender had been demanded, which he had answered by a cannon shot. He was determined to defend the place to the last, and called *earnestly* [italics added] for assistance."[46]

Long's use of the phrase "suicidal melody" is certainly without foundation. Travis was the stereotypical man caught in the wrong place at the wrong time. He had not wanted to go to Bexar and had done everything, short of disobeying orders, to return to his home in San Felipe. If events had gone Travis's way, he might have died trying to reinforce the Alamo, but he would not have died as its commander.[47]

During that second day the Gonzales rangers continued their recruitment. Unfortunately, little information has survived concerning the Gonzales company. Initial organization of the unit appears to have occurred around February 8, 1836. Though Albert Martin was in the Alamo at the start of the siege, he seems to have been the unit's captain. Thomas Jackson was first lieutenant of the company. George C. Kimbell was the second lieutenant.[48]

A muster roll was supposed to have been submitted to the government, but only a partial list exists today. The roster was completed after the fact on June 20, 1838. The document does not appear to be complete and may not be totally correct. The roll identifies twenty-two men as being mustered on February 23 by Byrd Lockhart. Despite the date, most of the men probably joined the unit between February 8 and 23, 1836.[49] The men were:

George C. Kimbell	John Ballard
William A. Irwin	James Nash
Jesse McCoy	William Morrison
William Fishbaugh	Galba Fuqua
John C. King	Andrew Duvalt
Daniel McCoy Jr.	John Harris
Jacob C. Darst	Andrew Kent
Frederick E. Elm	Isaac Millsaps
Prospect McCoy	William E. Summers
Marcus Sewell	David Kent
Robert White	John Davis[50]

Joseph Kent and James Gibson, while not listed, also appear to have been members of the unit. Clearly, there were other men in the company, but at this time evidence has not been found that identifies those soldiers.[51]

Although the unit was organized at Gonzales, all of the members were not from that settlement or the Green De Witt colony. Sewell and Harris were from Nacogdoches. Millsaps and Summers were from the upper Lavaca River on the western edge of Stephen F. Austin's colony.

White and Duvalt had been members of James W. Fannin's Brazos Guards during the siege of Bexar; thus they were also most likely from Austin's colony. After the Texian victory at San Antonio in December 1835, a number of the Brazos Guards remained in the city and reorganized as the Bexar Guards. The unit disbanded on February 14, 1836, with White, Irwin, and Ballard traveling to Gonzales. Irwin, first sergeant of one of the Gonzales ranger units, had been a member of Captain George English's company at the siege and storming of Bexar. That company was from San Augustine in East Texas. Ballard had been a member of James Cheshire's company in the same actions in 1835. Cheshire's unit came from Bevil's Settlement in far East Texas, between the Neches and Sabine Rivers.[52]

Dr. Smither arrived at Gonzales sometime that day. After meeting with Judge Ponton, Smither quickly penned a note that described the conditions at San Antonio and in the Alamo when he had departed at 4:00 p.m. on February 23. He wrote: "In a few words there is 2000 Mexican soldiers in Bexar, and 150 Americans in the Alamo. [Ramirez y] Sesma is at the head of them, and from best accounts that can be obtained, they intend to show no quarter. If every man cannot turn out to a man every man in the Alamo will be murdered." This document and Travis's note of the twenty-third to Ponton were then sent to San Felipe as Travis had requested—riding "night and day."[53]

Third Day — Thursday, February 25

Albert Martin appears to have been the courier who carried Travis's February 24 missive to Gonzales. John W. Smith most likely accompanied Martin. They probably left the Alamo sometime during the early morning hours of February 25 under the cover of darkness. The east side road to Gonzales was still open at that time. Nevertheless, there would have been enemy cavalry patrols. The Mexican horsemen, however, might have been napping as they were probably not that used to night duty.[54]

At Gonzales a courier was sent to Mina (Bastrop) with the news that Smither had detailed in his short note. The rider probably arrived that evening and reported to Major Robert M. Williamson, the ranger commander. Williamson was known as "Three-Legged Willie" because of a peg leg. Soon afterward, he issued orders to Captain J. J. Tumlinson, the commanding officer of the first detachment of rangers at Mina. In part the orders read: "...they [Alamo defenders] implore aid from their fellow citizens and solicit it speedily – Provisions and men is the cry, are the frontiers of Colorado safe? Are there no hostile Indians bearing materially upon the frontier of Texas? If there be none you will forthwith fall down to Bastrop and wait further orders from me. It would be well for the inhabitants of Bastrop to keep out spies in the direction of San Antonio lest a foraging party of Mexicans surprise them, every inch of ground must be disputed by us until we can communicate and march against and crush them . . . . "[55]

John Johnson, the Alamo's first rider to Fannin, arrived at Goliad, probably in the afternoon. John Sowers Brooks, an aide-de-camp to Fannin, wrote: "An express from San Antonio de Bexar received here a few moments since, with intelligence that the Mexican army under Santa Anna, were in sight of that place and preparing to attack it. He heard the firing of cannon after he had gained some distance towards us." Brooks then wrote that they would march to Bexar in the morning with "320 men, and 4 pieces of artillery, – 2 sixes and 2 fours."[56]

Fannin was busy with administrative duties when Johnson rode into the old Spanish fort in Goliad. The Colonel's first mention of the Alamo situation is found in the closing note of a letter dealing with military expenditures written that day to the acting governor and the council. Fannin wrote: "I am well aware that my present movement toward Bexar is anything but a military one. The appeal of Cols. Travis & Bowie cannot however pass unnoticed – particularly by troops now on the field – Sanguine, chivalrous Volunteers – Much must be risked to relieve the besieged."[57]

Government officials at San Felipe learned of the Alamo situation that evening. Travis's note of the twenty-third to Ponton and Smither's note arrived at San Felipe at 9:00 p.m. that evening.[58]

Albert Martin and John W. Smith most likely arrived at Gonzales in late afternoon or early evening. Martin quickly added a note to Travis's letter of February 24 that reads: "send this to San Felipe by Express night & day – Since the above was written I heard a very heavy cannonade during the whole day. Think there must have been an attack made upon the Alamo. We were short of Ammunition when I left. Hurry on all the men you can in haste." Smither added a message to the missive that reads: "When I left there was but 150 determined to do or die tomorrow I leave for Bejar with what men I can raise [& we] will be [on our way] at all events –

"Col Almonte is there the troops are under the command of Gen Seisma [*sic*]

"N b I hope every one will Randeves [*sic*] at gonzales as soon as poseble [*sic*] as the Brave soldiers are suffering do not neglect the powder is very scarce and should not be delad [*sic*] one moment."[59]

That night, at 10:00 p.m., someplace near San Antonio, Philip Dimmitt and Benjamin Noble departed the area for Dimitt's Point, east of Lavaca Bay. Dimmitt later wrote: "I left the Rovia at 10 p.m., on the 25th and heard no more firing from which I concluded the Alamo had been taken by storm."[60]

Dimmitt was close to being right. February 25 was a busy day for the Alamo. That morning two or three hundred of the enemy crossed the river below the Alamo and attacked it from the south, using houses in that area for cover. The Mexican troops were able to advance to within one hundred yards of the Alamo's southern artillery batteries. The action lasted two hours, with the defenders ousting the centralist troops from the wooden structures with point-blank canister and grapeshot fire.[61]

Later that night Travis and his officers conducted a council of war to discuss their situation and options.[62] Afterward Travis wrote to Sam Houston, the "Commander-in-Chief of the Army of Texas." Travis detailed the day's action and closed with: "... The Hon. David Crockett was seen at all points, animating the men to do their duty. Our numbers are few and the enemy still continues to approximate his works to ours. I have every reason to apprehend an attack from his whole force very soon; but I shall hold out to the last extremity, hoping to secure reinforcements in a day or two. Do hasten on aid to me as rapidly as possible, as from the superior number of the enemy, it will be impossible for us to keep them out much longer. If they overpower us, we fall a sacrifice at the shrine of our country, and we hope posterity and our country will do our memory justice. Give me help, oh my Country! Victory or Death!"[63]

Juan N. Seguin and Matias Curvier were selected to carry the letter to Gonzales. They probably left the Alamo on foot that night as the defenders engaged the enemy outside the walls. Almonte reported the following: "The enemy, in the night, burnt the straw and wooden houses in their [Mexican cavalry] vicinity [Gonzales road east of the Alamo], but did not attempt to set fire with their guns to those in our rear." This action may have been a diversion to cover the departure of the Tejano couriers to Gonzales. Once outside, Seguin and Curvier appear to have obtained horses from Antonio Cruz, who lived near the Alamo. Cruz joined them on their mission to Gonzales.[64]

Santa Anna must have been reading Travis's mind that night. He closed down the southeast and eastern avenues to the Alamo. Almonte wrote: "In the night two batteries were erected by us on the other side of the river in the Alameda of the Alamo – the battalion of Matamoros was also posted there, and the cavalry was posted on the hills to the east of the enemy, and in the road from Gonzales at the Casa Mata Antigua."[65]

Colonel Juan N. Seguin — Post Revolution
Photo courtesy Texas State Library & Archives Commission

Fourth Day — Friday, February 26

Almonte's journal entry for the day starts off with: "The northern wind continued very strong; the thermometer fell to 39, and during the rest of the day remained at 60. At daylight there was a slight skirmish between the enemy and a small party of the division of the east, under command of General Sesma." A cavalry patrol seems to have encountered Seguin, Curvier, and Cruz as they broke through the Mexican line on their way to Gonzales.[66]

At Mina Major R. M. Williamson departed for Gonzales. He most likely rode out at daylight, leaving Edward Burleson in charge of military affairs for the settlement.[67]

About the same time, at Washington-on-the-Brazos, acting governor James W. Robinson dispatched a rider to find Sam Houston, who was on the road between Nacogdoches and Washington-on-the-Brazos. The note was addressed to "Gen. Sam Houston Wherever he may be. Send this by express day & night." Robinson detailed the Alamo's critical situation and asked: "Come quickly and organize our countrymen for Battle. Call the militia out en mass, send your orders East by this Express for that purpose."[68]

Officials at San Felipe, however, were not going to wait on the slow-moving Houston. A courier was sent off to Mina with orders for Captain J. J. Tumlinson's ranger company to reinforce the Alamo immediately. Clearly, Robinson and other officers of the government understood that the Alamo command did not have much time. If the courier to Mina departed San Felipe early that morning, he probably arrived at Mina that night or the next morning.[69]

At Goliad, Fannin was not able to pull men and equipment together until that afternoon. First, he issued a call for a volunteer company of horsemen. The unit, commanded by Captain Francis De Sauque and Captain John Chenoweth, was to ride immediately to the Seguin ranch, thirty-three miles southeast of Bexar on the San Antonio River to await Fannin's main force of infantry and artillery. The special mounted unit was made up of Chenoweth's company of United States Invincibles and mounted men from the other Goliad units commanded by Fannin. John Smith, orderly sergeant of Captain William Wadsworth's company, a unit from the Georgia battalion, later wrote that Wadsworth had "received an order from Col. Fannin to raise a company to get to the Alamo. In company with Mr. David Murphy [*sic*] Capt Chenoweth & others the company was raised." The company included, but was not limited to men from Chenoweth's own company, the United States Invincibles.[70]

The muster roll of the United States Invincibles included the following men who appear to have been available for Fannin's special mounted relief force for the Alamo:

John Chenoweth	C. Mallon	William Badgett
M. G. Frazier	J. D. Elliott	S. M. Edwards
A. A. Petrasseweiz	F. Petrasseweiz	J. B. Calicothe
N. Debichi	W. A. Moore	T. B. Cox
E. F. Mitchson	L. R. Oneal	Thomas H. Roberts
S. S. Curtis	W. T. Green	S. W. McNeilly
Hugh Frazier	William Hunter	G. J. W. Thayer
B. H. Smith	W. H. Sanders	Peter Harper
B. M. Clark	C. Mallon[71]	

David Murpree's name is not on the Chenoweth roll, but he was a member of the company. After the storming of Bexar, he remained in San Antonio to care for John W. Peacock, the unit's original captain, who had been severely wounded in the attack on Bexar. After Peacock's death in early February 1836, Murpree rejoined the company at Goliad.[72]

This muster roll reports every man as having been killed, except John Chenoweth, Peter Harper, B. H. Smith, and C. Mallon. The list, however, does not identify when and where the men were killed. Also, Hugh Frazier, T. B. Cox, and S. S. Curtis, though identified as being killed, were not killed during the revolution. Harper had originally been a member of Crockett's small company of mounted spies. Harper, William Hunter, B. H. Smith, B. M. Clark, and C. Mallon joined the Invincibles on January 27.[73]

Before Fannin's quickly formed mounted relief departed for Bexar, it appears that Fannin sent Edwin T. "Tom" Mitchell to the Gonzales committee of safety, informing them of his plans for reinforcing the Alamo. He requested that the Gonzales soldiers "...effect a junction with him below Bexar, at some convenient point." The "convenient point" appears to have been the Cibolo Creek crossing on the San Antonio/Goliad road, about halfway between San Antonio and Goliad. Then, sometime after the Chenoweth and De Sauque force rode out for the Alamo, Fannin's main force crossed the San Antonio River on their march to Bexar.[74]

John Sowers Brooks, Fannin's adjutant, described the event with these words: "We marched at the time appointed, with 420 men, nearly the whole force at Goliad, leaving only one company of Regulars to guard the Fort. Our baggage wagons and artillery were all drawn by oxen (no broken horses could be obtained) and there were but a few yokes of them. In attempting to cross the San Antonio River, three of our wagons broke down and it was with the utmost labor and personal hazard, that our four pieces of cannon were conveyed safely across. We remained there during the day, with our ammunition wagon on the opposite side of the River."[75] Unable to repair their equipment before dark, Fannin's men spent the night on the east side of the river. Reinforcement activities, however, continued at Gonzales.

Major R. M. Williamson, who had left Mina that morning, probably arrived at Gonzales that evening. As the senior military officer he assumed command of the relief activities at that settlement. Later Seguin and his two men would have arrived with Travis's letter of February 25 to Houston.[76]

Houston, however, was still someplace on the road between Nacogdoches and Washington-on-the-Brazos. Yet, after four days, the reinforcement of the Alamo was in motion at the settlements that could send men the quickest. Time was the key element and it was precious. The second factor was the number of Texians that could be brought to the Alamo with sufficient arms and provisions. Bowie, in attempting an honorable surrender on February 23, understood that the Alamo's only hope was the immediate arrival of a force large enough to bottle up Santa Anna in the city on the west side of the San Antonio River.[77]

Travis also knew their backs were against the wall. Giving up was not an option. He did the only thing he could. He assumed the aggressive posture of a trapped animal, hoping to make the enemy realize that the cost would be high if they stormed the Alamo. The question was: Would the stratagem work long enough for a sufficient number of Texian soldiers to reach the Alamo in time?[78]

Chapter Three Notes

1   Travis to Houston, February 25, 1836.

2   Walter Lord, *A Time To Stand* (1961; reprint, New York: Bonanza Books, 1987), 126-127; Long, *Duel,* 224-226; Stephen L. Hardin, *Texian Iliad: A Military History of the Texas Revolution, 1835-1836* (Austin: University of Texas Press, 1994), 133; Michael Lind, *The Alamo* (New York and Boston: Houghton Mifflin Company, 1997), 176; Rita Kerr, *The Immortal 32* (Austin: Eakin Press, 1986), 1-51.

3   Travis to Convention, March 3, 1836.

4   The fall of the Alamo was extremely "decisive" in that the defeat and the subsequent murder of the Goliad soldiers enraged the Texians, which resulted in the San Jacinto victory.

5   R. M. Potter, "The Fall of The Alamo," *Magazine of American History,* January 1878, 7-8. This article is an expanded version of an article that was first published in the *San Antonio Herald* in 1860. While many believe that Potter's study of the Alamo defeat was the first written. That is not the case. John Henry Brown, an old Texas Ranger and newspaperman, wrote a pamphlet titled *The Fall of the Alamo* in September 1843. In December 1853, Brown wrote a second pamphlet titled *Facts of the Alamo, Last Days of Crockett and Other Sketches of Texas.* Copies of the works cannot be located today. Potter found a place in Texas history by writing about the Texas revolution. However, when given the opportunity to participate in that fight he refused. On March 6, 1836, Potter was at Velasco on the Texas coast. He was the chairman of a public meeting of the citizens of Velasco and Quintana that concerned an expected navel blockade of the Texas coast. By summer 1836 he had returned to Matamoros.

      There is no primary source that shows that the Alamo defenders actually celebrated Washington's birthday, but given that most of them were from the United States, the party probably took place.

6   Almonte, "Private Journal," 16-17; Jose Enrique de la Pena, Campaign Diary, 13, Jose Enrique de la Pena collection, CAH; "Trinidad Coy: As Recalled by His Son Andres Coy," *San Antonio Light,* November 26, 1911; Antonio Lopez de Santa Anna to General Joaquin Ramirez y Sesma, December 27, 1835, San Luis Potosi, English translation, Box 2/23/1063, MS-TSL.

      Order number four of the Santa Anna document reads: "On starting your march from Laredo to Bejar you will walk with the most possible precautions not to be surprised by a nocturnal ambush in your camp, taking care that this march be executed in accordance with the military strict laws."

      Order number five starts with: "If the enemy should come out to meet you and present battle, you will examine above everything else the position they have taken, and if it should be so advantageous that you would see it impossible to defeat them, you will avoid the attack, directing your maneuver towards Bejar through one of its flanks if the territory permits it, or to initiate a false retreat of about 2 or 3 leagues."

7   Ruiz, "Fall of the Alamo," 80; John Sutherland, *The Fall of the Alamo* Annie B. Sutherland, ed. (San Antonio: The Naylor Company, 1936), 15-16; L. Smither to All the Inhabitants of Texas, February 24, 1836, Gonzales in Michael R. Green, "To The People of Texas & All Americans in The World," *Southwestern Historical Quarterly,* XCI: 503-504.

Sutherland, though he was not in San Antonio on February 23, also reported that Travis learned the Mexican army was near the city on the morning of the twenty-third.

Also, the Ruiz account is compromised by the fact that he was not in San Antonio on March 6, 1836. See Chapter Eight of this book for the evidence that shows why Ruiz was out of town on the day the Alamo fell. Still, his claim in regard to when Travis and his men learned of the Mexican army being in the area appears to be correct.

8   Juan N. Seguin to William Winston Fontaine, June 7, 1890, Nuevo Laredo, W. W. Fontaine Papers, CAH; Potter, "The Fall," 6; Sutherland, *The Fall of the Alamo,* 6, Amelia W. Williams Papers, CAH.

In this original Sutherland manuscript (1860), he wrote that one had to climb to the top of the church's bell tower by a scaffold that had been erected by the Mexicans after the siege and storming of Bexar in 1835. Given that during the storming of Bexar, Texian artilleryman William Langenheim hit the bell tower's cupola with two twelve-pound cannonball shots, the scaffold was probably in place to assist workmen in repairing the tower.

9   Potter, "The Fall," 7-8. If the Alamo defenders were selling weapons, they were most likely Brown Bess muskets that were captured from the Mexican army in December, not their personal weapons.

10   Joint Resolution for the relief of H. A. Alsbury, December 29, 1838, in H. P. N. Gammel, *The Laws of Texas 1822-1897* (10 vols., Austin: The Gammel Book Company, 1898), II: 30; "Testimony of Mrs. [Susanna Dickinson] Hannig Touching the Alamo Massacre, September 23, 1876, MS-TSL; Webb, Carroll, and Branda, eds., *Handbook,* I: 36.

11   Herbert S. Kimble affidavit, August 22, 1837, Springfield, Tennessee, P. J. Bailey file, M & P-TSL; Charles Merritt Barnes, "The Alamo's Only Survivor," *San Antonio Express,* May 12 and 19, 1907; Susanna [Dickinson] Hannig interview, *San Antonio Express,* April 27, 1881; Potter, "The Fall," 6-7; Antonio Menchaca, *Memoirs,* Yanaguana Society Publications, 23; Frederick C. Chabot, *With The Makers of San Antonio* (San Antonio: Artes Graficas, 1937), 328; William B. Travis and James Bowie to James W. Fannin Jr., February 23, 1836, Jenkins, ed., *Papers,* IV: 419; James S. Brooks to A. H. Brooks, February 25, 1836, Goliad, Jenkins, ed., *Papers,* IV: 426; Jesse B. Badgett interview, *The Advocate* (Little Rock), April 15, 1836; Juana Alsbury account in Bill Groneman, *Eyewitness to the Alamo* (revised edition, Plano, Texas: Republic of Texas Press, 2001), 70.

The Travis and Bowie letter to Fannin reported they had 146 men. Brooks, Fannin's adjutant, reported that the Alamo was manned with 156 effectives. A few hours later Travis's letter to Gonzales reported 150 men ready for combat. Hannig reported that there were about "160 sound persons in the Alamo." The number of "146" is probably a printing error.

12 William Barret Travis to the Public, February 24, 1836, Bexar, Jenkins, ed., *Papers,* IV: 423; William Barret Travis to Ignacio Perez, February 23, 1836, Bexar, Ignacio Perez file, AMC-TSL; Gabriel Martinez claim, June 1, 1850, Department of State Papers, No. 39, File 60, TSL, copy in Amelia Williams Papers, Box 2N494, CAH.

13 Antonio Saez file, PC-TSL.

14 Thomas Ricks Lindley, "Alamo Artillery: Number, Type, Caliber, and Concussion," *Alamo Journal,* 82 (July 1992); "Statement and manifest of the Artillery, arms, munitions and other effects taken from the Enemy," March 6, 1836, Bexar, Expediente XI/481.3/1655, *Archivo Historico Mexicano Militar,* Mexico City. Thanks to historian William C. "Jack" Davis for a copy of this Mexican document.

15 "Testimony of Mrs. Hannig," September 23, 1876. She claimed that the Alamo, "had provisions enough to last the besieged 30 days." Antonio Lopez de Santa Anna to General Vicente Filisola, February 27, 1836, Bexar, English translation, Box 2/23/1063, MS-TSL. Santa Anna wrote: "...they [Alamo defenders] only had time to hastily seek refuge at the Alamo fortification which had been beforehand, well fortified and with plenty of supplies." James Bowie to Henry Smith, February 2, 1836, Bexar, Jenkins, ed., *Papers,* IV: 237. Bowie wrote: "We are still labouring night and day, laying up provisions for a siege, encouraging our men, and calling on the Government for relief." Philip Dimmitt to James Kerr, February 28, 1836, Dimitt's Point, Jenkins, ed., *Papers,* IV: 453; R. R. Royall to Governor and Council, February 2, 1836, Matagorda, Jenkins, ed., *Papers,* IV: 243. Royall reported that supplies had just landed at his port and that he had instructed Dimmitt to furnish the troops at Bexar and Goliad the much-needed supplies.

Dimmitt and Noble's departure time from the Alamo is an estimate based on the fact that they were sent out before the sighting of the Mexican force in mid-afternoon.

16 Almonte, "Private Journal," 16-17; Antonio Lopez de Santa Anna, "Manifesto Relative to His Operations in Texas Campaign and His Capture" in Carlos E. Castaneda, trans. and ed., *The Mexican Side of the Texas Revolution* (1928; reprint: Austin and Dallas: Graphic Ideas Incorporated, 1970), 13.

17 Antonio Balle affidavit, November 12, 1874, San Antonio, Antonio Balle file, PC-TSL; Juan Rodriquiz affidavit, October 24, 1874, San Antonio, Juan Rodriquiz file, PC-TSL.

18 J. M. Morphis, *History of Texas, From its Discovery and Settlement* (New York: United States Publishing Company, 1874), 174.

19 Almonte, "Private Journal," 16-17; Seguin to Fontaine, June 7, 1890.

20 Alamo voting list, February 1, 1836; Sutherland, *The Fall of the Alamo,* 22; John Sutherland statement, November 28, 1836, William Brookfield file, AMC-TSL; Lt. Colonel J. C. Neill to John Johnson, March 6, 1836, [Gonzales] and J. Snively, acting secretary of war, to John Johnson, June 22, 1837, Houston, RV 1101, GLO. According to Sutherland, the courier to Goliad was named Johnson. Given that a total analysis of the Sutherland account and other reliable evidence shows that Sutherland was not in San Antonio on February 23, Johnson may or may not have been the courier. Sutherland, however, did furnish a supporting statement for one John Johnson in regard to "one elegant Bay horse pressed by Jn. Johnson to carry the express from Bexar to Washington [on-the-Brazos] respecting the fall of the Alamo." Sutherland rode with Johnson to the convention sometime after General Houston's arrival at Gonzales and claimed he had seen Johnson take the $200 horse. If Johnson was Travis's courier to Goliad, then after arriving at that location, he must have continued on to Gonzales. The February 1 Alamo voting roll shows a soldier named John Johnson who did not die at the Alamo. The copy of Johnson's March 6 Alamo discharge signed by Lt. Colonel J. C. Neill at Gonzales indicates that Johnson traveled to Gonzales after riding to Goliad. On March 7, 1836, Johnson joined a Captain Splane's company and continued to serve as an express rider. Therefore, Travis's first courier to Goliad was probably Johnson.

21 William B. Travis and James Bowie to James W. Fannin Jr., February 23, 1836, Bexar, Jenkins, ed., *Papers,* IV: 419.

22 Almonte, "Private Journal," 17. Almonte was the bastard son of priest Jose Maria Morelos and an Indian woman named Brigida Almonte. He was born on May 15, 1803. Almonte, because of the nature of his birth, was often called Morelos's nephew. In 1834 Almonte conducted an inspection of Texas for Santa Anna. He wrote two reports for the government concerning the Texas tour, one public and one secret. Many Texians considered the inspection tour a deception to spy on Texas for a future military invasion. Seems they were correct.

23 Seguin to Fontaine, June 7, 1890.

24 Santa Anna to Vicente Filisola, February 27, 1836, Bexar, Jenkins, ed., *Papers,* IV: 448; Susanna (Dickinson) Bellis affidavit, July 16, 1857, Caldwell County, James M. Rose file, C-7115, Court of Claims Collection, GLO; Jose Vicente Minon military service records, XI/111/1-135, *Archivo Historico of Secretaria de la Defensa National,* Mexico City, this data found in Jack Jackson research notes made on a visit in July 2000. Mr. Jackson furnished this writer a copy of his notes.

Susanna Dickinson identified James M. Rose as one of David Crockett's men. She also reported that during the first Mexican attack Rose barely escaped a Mexican officer. The fighting in the plaza on February 23 seems to be the only incident in which the Mexican soldiers and the Alamo defenders were in such close contact.

25 Dimmitt to Kerr, February 28, 1836. This investigator was unable to identify the site known as the "Rovia" or learn the meaning of the name. Dr. Jesus F. de la Teja, professor of history at Southwest Texas State University, San Marcos, Texas, believes (phone conversation June 17, 1999) that the site was most likely a regular camping place on or near the Laredo road.

Alan C. Huffines in *Blood of Noble Men: The Alamo Siege & Battle* (Austin: Eakin Press, 1999), 24, claims that the "Rovia" site was probably Rosilla Creek on the Goliad road. Huffines cites no source for his opinion. It appears he simply selected a geographical feature in the area that had a name that started with an "r."

26 Andrew Jackson Sowell, *Rangers and Pioneers of Texas* (1884; reprint; New York: Argosy-Antiquarian, Ltd., 1964), 136; "A list of the Gonzales Ranging Company of Mounted Volunteers mustered into service on the 23rd of February 1836, by Byrd Lockhart acting Commissioner for that purpose and Aid[e] de Camp to the acting Governor of Texas, attached to Travis' command," Muster Roll book, 1, GLO; Laura J. Irvine, "Sketch of Guadalupe County," *American Sketch Book* (Austin: Sketch Book Publishing House, 1882), 8; J. E. Grinstead, "An Orphan of the Alamo," *San Antonio Express*, November 5, 1916.

27 Luciano Pacheco file, PC-TSL.

28 W. B. Travis to Andrew Ponton, February 23, 1836, Bexar, Jenkins, ed., *Papers,* IV: 420.

29 Pena, Campaign Diary, 13; James Bowie to Santa Anna, February 23, 1836, Bexar, Jenkins, ed., *Papers,* IV: 414; Almonte, "Private Journal," 16-17; Travis to Houston, February 25, 1836. This investigator's belief that the howitzer was operating from a site below the city is based on the fact that Bowie addressed his missive to the "Commander of the invading forces below Bejar."

Jose Enrique de la Pena was not in San Antonio on February 23. He wrote that the data concerning events in San Antonio between February 23 and March 2 he had added to his campaign diary came from a diary that had been sent to him. The writer of that diary is unknown. The Alamo's 18-pounder was on the northwest corner. The 8-pounder was probably mounted at the southwest corner.

In Alan C. Huffines' *Blood of Noble Men: The Alamo Siege & Battle*, 26-27, illustrator Gary S. Zaboly depicts the no-quarter flag with a skull and crossbones as if it were a pirate banner. Zaboly's source for his flag was a sketch attributed to Captain Jose Juan Sanchez Navarro in *La Guerra de Tejas: Memorias de un Soldado,* an alleged account of the Texas revolution by a participant.

Zaboly notes that the only other source that includes his Mexican pirate standard is an oil painting. Zaboly wrote: "One additional clue to the use of a blood-red banner with skull and crossbones appears in Henry McArdle's frequently reproduced 1905 oil, *Dawn at the Alamo.* At center top a Mexican soldier, shot, is falling backwards and letting go of a red flag with skull and crossbones decorating it. McArdle had been gathering, for several decades, much of his research data from a number of sources, including veterans of the Texian Revolution. Perhaps one of the latter remembered this flag, which nearly parallels what Navarro had drawn."

Mr. Zaboly's opinion notwithstanding, an examination of McArdle's research materials for the painting (McArdle's *Alamo Scrapbook*, TSL) reveals another answer for the skull and crossbones in his painting. The flag of no quarter is only identified as a blood-red banner. There is no mention of the flag having a skull and crossbones in the center. A photograph of McArdle's original crayon sketch of the red flag and the falling Mexican soldier shows only a red flag, no skull and crossbones. Thus, it appears that McArdle added the skull and crossbones to the final painting as symbols of death to explain the meaning of the banner. Otherwise, a red flag would have only had meaning to those viewers who knew exactly what the standard represented. To others, the banner would just have been a red flag, without meaning.

In sum, there is no valid source for the red flag with the skull and crossbones. If the Sanchez Navarro drawing is authentic, which this investigator believes is not the case, the skull and crossbones are probably a symbol for death, not an element that actually appeared on the Mexican banner. More likely, the creator of the Sanchez Navarro drawing based the flag on the McArdle flag.

30 L. Smither to All the Inhabitants of Texas, February 24, 1836, Gonzales in Green, "To the People of Texas & All Americans in the World," 503-504; Nathaniel Townsend to Jn. Adriance, February 26, 1836, San Felipe, John Adriance Papers, CAH.

The Smither missive reports that he left San Antonio at 4:00 p.m. on February 23. The Townsend letter reports that: "An express came in at 9 o'clock last night [February 25] from Bexar in 53 hours, from Col. W. B. Travis...." Townsend then quoted part of Travis's letter to Andrew Ponton at Gonzales. The fifty-three-hour travel time shows that the express had departed Bexar at 4:00 p.m. on February 23. Most historians believe that Dr. John Sutherland was Travis's first courier to Gonzales. See endnote number 34, Chapter One and Chapter Eight for an explanation as to why Sutherland was not an Alamo express rider.

31 Bowie to Smith, February 2, 1836; Almonte, "Private Journal," 17; J. C. Neill affidavit, December 13, 1835, Bexar, Green B. Jameson file, AMC-TSL.

The belief that Bowie dictated the short note to Juan Seguin is based on a comparison of the note's handwriting to a sample of Bowie's handwriting. The Bowie signature on the note, which is uneven, matches known examples of Bowie's signature. The text of the document does not match Bowie's handwriting. The text handwriting, however, does match an example of Seguin's handwriting.

The J. C. Neill statement is in Jameson's siege and storming of Bexar army discharge. In it Neill mentions Jameson's skill with his rifle.

32   Almonte, "Private Journal," 17; Vicente Filisola, Wallace Woolsey, editor and translator, *Memoirs for the History of the War in Texas* (2 vols., Austin: Eakin Press, 1986, 1987), II: 149-150; Santa Anna to Joaquin Ramirez y Sesma, December 7, 1836, San Luis Potosi, Jenkins, ed., *Papers,* III: 114. Travis believed that he faced 2,000 enemy soldiers, but at that point in time this was not the case.

33   Ibid. Some individuals think that after Martin returned to the Alamo and informed Travis of the conversation with Almonte, Travis responded by firing another cannon shot at the Mexican force. That does not appear to have been the case because Almonte reported: "After these contestations night came on, and there was no more firing."

34   Seguin to Fontaine, June 7, 1890.

35   Potter, "The Fall," 6.

36   Almonte, "Private Journal," 17; Travis to Convention, March 3, 1836.

37   Jesse Badgett interview, April 15, 1836. Badgett reported that the garrison had fourteen men on the sick list when he departed for the convention, which was about February 19. The six men who left on February 23 were (1) John Johnson, Goliad courier, (2) Nat Lewis, merchant, (3 & 4) A. J. Sowell and Byrd Lockhart, who were out searching for cattle, (5 & 6) Philip Dimmitt and Benjamin Noble, scouts.

　　In 1876 Susanna Dickinson reported there were fifty to sixty wounded men from the siege and storming of Bexar in the Alamo. That appears to have been a mistake on her part or the person who interviewed her misunderstood what she said. She may have said fifteen or sixteen.

38   [Susanna Dickinson] "Survived the Alamo Massacre," *San Antonio Express,* February 24, 1929.

39   Barnes, "The Alamo's Only Survivor"; Pedro Herrera army discharge claim (ADC), August 1, 1836, AMC-TSL; Simon Arreola ADC, July 31, 1836, AMC-TSL; Cesario Carmona ADC, February 14, 1837; Vicente Zepeda ADC, January 15, 1837, AMC-TSL; Jose Maria Arocha ADC, January 17, 1839, AMC-TSL; Matias Curvier file, PC-TSL; James L. Fushears to William Steele, February 6, 1875, San Antonio, AJC-TSL; Manuel Flores bounty grant, Travis 46, GLO; Filisola, *Memoirs,* II: 178.

　　The discharge claims and the one land grant identify the individuals as members of Seguin's company. The start and end dates for the military service indicate that the men were in service at the start of the Alamo siege on February 23.

　　Historian R. M. Potter claimed: "J. N. Seguin, a native of San Antonio, who had been commissioned as the senior Captain of Travis' corps, joined him at the Alamo, and brought into the garrison the skeleton of his company, consisting of nine Mexican recruits, natives, some of the town aforesaid and others of the interior of Mexico." Bluntly said, Potter did not know what he was talking about, and it suggests that he never talked with Seguin about the Alamo.

Seguin had been offered a cavalry commission, but he rejected it. Instead, he was elected the first judge of San Antonio. Nevertheless, Seguin claimed in his 1858 *Personal Memoirs* that he accepted the commission. To the extent that Seguin had a company in the Alamo, the men were volunteers. The true organization of Seguin's unit took place after he had departed the Alamo as courier.

Filisola reported that the Alamo garrison contained: "... some twenty people and tradesmen of the city of Bexar itself." Filisola was not aware that most of those individuals left the fortress during the siege.

40 "Children of the Alamo," *Houston Chronicle,* November 9, 1901; *San Antonio Express*, November 22, 1902; Groneman, *Alamo Defenders*, 43-47.

In the 1902 article, Enrique Esparza, Gregorio's son, reported that his father belonged to "[Placido] Benavides' company in the American army." Enrique placed his father's unit in Goliad before his father returned to San Antonio. If that remembrance is accurate, then Gregorio Esparza most likely served under James Bowie because Benavides and his men were aligned with Bowie when he was at Goliad.

41 Ibid.; Barnes, "The Alamo's Only Survivor"; John S. Ford, "Memoirs of John S. Ford - 1815-1836," John S. Ford Papers, CAH. In addition to the names given by Esparza, Ford reported: Dolores Cervantes and Desidora Munoz. Ford's sources for the two women is unknown.

42 John S. Ford, "The Fall of the Alamo," *Texas Mute Ranger,* April 1882; [Joe's account] in "Letter from Texas," *Frankfort* [Kentucky] *Commonwealth,* May 25, 1836.

43 Barrett et al. to Governor, February 4, 1836, San Felipe, Jenkins, ed., *Papers*, IV: 249; "A list of the Gonzales Ranging Company," February 23, 1836; George C. Kimbell pay certificate, November 29, 1839, AMC-TSL; James George pay certificate, January 15, 1839, AMC-TSL; William Dearduff pay certificate, January 15, 1839, AMC-TSL; John G. King pay certificate, January 15, 1839. The four certificates identify the men as rangers in "Major Williamson's command."

This Gonzales ranger company should not be confused with the twenty-member ranger unit G. W. Davis was authorized to organize at Gonzales in November 1835. Davis's company was to operate from "the big spring, on the head of St. Marks [San Marcos] river." This investigator has not been able to find any evidence that verifies Davis actually organized the company. As the siege of Bexar was taking place at that time there would have been few men available for a ranger company in Gonzales.

44 William Barret Travis to the People of Texas & all Americans in the World, February 24, 1836, Alamo, Jenkins, ed., *Papers*, IV: 423. Travis's battle cry, "Victory or Death," had been the watchword for General George Washington's assault on the British garrison at Trenton, New Jersey, in the American Revolution. Also, this is the only Travis missive from the Alamo that he signed with his full name. The other letters are signed W. Barret Travis.

45 Long, *Duel*, 190.

46 Gray, *From Virginia*, 120.

47 Ibid.

48 "A list of the Gonzales Ranging Company," February 23, 1836; George C. Kimbell pay certificate, November 29, 1839, AMC-TSL; Thomas Jackson pay certificate, March 4, 1840, AMC-TSL; "Muster Roll of the Gonzales Volunteer Militia Company," [October or November 1835], Austin Papers, CAH. Albert Martin was the commanding officer of the volunteer militia unit. Jackson should not be confused with Thomas R. Jackson, the quartermaster officer for Travis's Legion of Cavalry.

49 "A list of the Gonzales Ranging Company," February 23, 1836; Matthew Caldwell to Joseph Kent for military supplies and services, February 8, 1836, number 387, Audited Military Claims ledger, 304-2511, TSL; Matthew Caldwell to G. W. Cottle for military supplies and services, February 9, 1836, number 302, AMC-ledger; Matthew Caldwell to John Davis for military services, February 12, 1836, number 378, AMC-ledger; John Fisher to Sarah DeWitt for military supplies, February 21, 1836, number 107, AMC-ledger; Matthew Caldwell to Dolphin Floyd for military supplies, February 24, 1836, number 368, AMC-ledger. The actual Kent, Cottle, Davis, DeWitt, and Floyd claims have been lost or destroyed. The ledger, however, has entries that show, except for the DeWitt claim, the claims were authorized by Matthew Caldwell, one of the officials who organized the Gonzales ranger companies.

50 "A list of the Gonzales Ranging Company," February 23, 1836; Thomas B. Zumwalt affidavit, July 24, 1880, Kerr County and David B. Kent affidavit, July 22, 1880, Kerr County, RV 1419, GLO. David Kent did not make the ride to San Antonio with the Gonzales rangers. Instead, on or about March 1, 1836, he carried an express from Gonzales to Texanna near the coast on the Lavaca River and returned with Captain George Sutherland's company. At the time Kent was eighteen years old.

51 Caldwell to Kent, February 8, 1836; Matthew Caldwell to James Gibson for military services and supplies, February 23, 1836, number 371, AMC-ledger; Nathaniel Addson file, RV 683, GLO. Bevil's Settlement came to be named Jasper after the revolution.

52 [Marcus Sewell] Entry 579, "Proceedings of the Land Commissioners," RHRD Number 114, Nacogdoches County Records, East Texas Research Center, Stephen F. Austin University, Nacogdoches, Texas; Certificate 650, "Heirs of John Harris," in Carolyn Reeves Ericson, *Nacogdoches Headrights* (New Orleans: Polyanthos, 1977), 20; "List of votes taken at the Precinct of Upper La Vaca for the purpose of electing two Delegates to the Convention to convene lst March at the town of Washington," February 1, 1836, Upper Lavaca River, Election Returns, TSL; "Roll of Brazos Guards," November 21, 1835, Bexar, Austin Papers, CAH; J. C. Neill to Robert While, February 14, 1836, Bexar, Robert White file, AMC-TSL; J. C. Neill to John T. Ballard, February 14, 1836, Bexar, John T. Ballard file, AMC-TSL; J. C. Neill to

William A. Irwin, February 14, 1836, Bexar, William A. Irwin file, AMC-TSL; "List of men who have this day volunteered to remain before Bexar," November 24, 1835, Austin Papers, CAH; George English entry in Tyler, Barnett, Barkley, Anderson, Odintz, eds. *The New Handbook of Texas*, II: 870.

53 "L. Smither to All the Inhabitants in Texas," February 24, 1836; Townsend to Adriance, February 26, 1836.

54 Albert Martin to the People of Texas and all Americans [February 25, 1836, Gonzales], Green, "To the People of Texas & All Americans," 493; Almonte, "Private Journal," 17-18.

It is speculation on this investigator's part that Smith departed the Alamo on the night of February 24, rather than on the afternoon of February 23. First, the available evidence indicates that John Sutherland's report that Smith and he had departed the Alamo on the twenty-third is fiction. Second, Seguin said only Smith was sent out to scout the Leon Creek road on the afternoon of February 23 and that Smith returned to the fortress about five o'clock. Third, given that Launcelot Smither, Travis's rider to Gonzales, left at 4:00 p.m., there would have been no reason for Travis to have also sent Smith to Gonzales that day. Fourth, since Smith returned to the Alamo with Albert Martin, it makes sense that he probably left the Alamo with Martin.

55 R. M. Williamson to Governor and Council, February 25, 1836, Mina, Jenkins, ed., *Papers*, IV: 434-435.

56 John S. Brooks to A. H. Brooks, February 25, 1836, Goliad, Jenkins, ed., *Papers,* IV: 426.

57 James W. Fannin Jr. to Acting Governor James W. Robinson, February 25, 1836, Goliad, Jenkins, ed., *Papers*, IV: 429-230.

58 Townsend to Adriance, February 26, 1836.

59 "Martin to the People of Texas and all Americans" [February 25, 1836].

60 Dimmitt to Kerr, February 28, 1836. Just what route Dimmitt and Noble took to return to their home is unknown. Because they are not mentioned in any of Goliad documents from that time frame, they most likely went by way of Gonzales.

61 Travis to Houston, February 25, 1836; Almonte, "Private Journal," 17-18.

62 Ibid.; Jesus F. de la Teja, *A Revolution Remembered: The Memoirs and Selected Correspondence of Juan N. Seguin* (Austin: State House Press, 1991), 79. Seguin claimed the date as February 28, but that appears to have been a mistake on his part.

63 Travis to Houston, February 25, 1836.

64 De la Teja, *A Revolution Remembered*, 79; Seguin to Fontaine, June 7, 1890; Almonte, "Private Journal," 18; Matias Curvier file, PC-TSL; Antonio Cruz Arrocha account, Box SM-2, Gentilz Collection, Daughters of the Republic of Texas Library, Alamo, San Antonio, Texas.

Curvier stated that he left the Alamo with a letter from Travis to Houston.

Seguin, in his memoirs, claimed he had been sent to Fannin at Goliad, instead of Houston at Gonzales. At that time, the brief biography was written for political reasons, to defend past Seguin actions. Also at that time, Houston was being attacked by old veterans for his lack of leadership during the revolution. Seguin and Houston were old friends and political allies in the new Democratic party. Seguin may have claimed that Travis sent him to Fannin, instead of Gonzales, in order to protect Houston's reputation. Also, for Seguin, there was no need of claiming he had attempted to reinforce the Alamo and had failed. Most likely, his enemies would have claimed it was another example of his flawed character.

65 Almonte, "Private Journal," 18.

66 Ibid.

67 Edward Burleson affidavit [February 29, 1836], Thomas G. McGehee file, AMC-TSL. Burleson stated that the provisional government had ordered him to organize the militia and raise volunteers for the draft. This investigator's belief that Williamson left Bastrop that morning is speculation based on the fact that Williamson had learned of the Alamo situation the day before and would have hurried to Gonzales once Burleson had been notified of the events.

68 James W. Robinson to Sam Houston, February 26, 1836, Washington-on-the-Brazos, Jenkins, ed., *Papers*, IV: 445; W. B. Travis to Andrew Ponton, February 23, 1836, Bexar, Acting Governor James W. Robinson copy, February 26, 1836, Washington-on-the-Brazos, Don Carlos Barrett Papers, CAH. Robinson copied Travis's short note to Ponton and added two notes to the bottom of the copy, which was sent to D. C. Barrett. It reads:
Washington Feb. 26th 1836
Send copies in every direction and let the militia turn out in mass.
    James W. Robinson
    Acting Governor
N. B.
The militia will rendezvous at Gonzales.

69 Alexander Thomson and G. A. Pattillo to James W. Robinson [February 26, 1836], Washington-on-the-Brazos, Jenkins, ed., *Papers*, IV: 472. Jenkins missed it, but the original document is dated February 26.

70 James W. Fannin Jr. to James W. Robinson, February 27, 1836, Goliad, Jenkins, ed., *Papers*, IV: 455-456; Fannin to Francis to De Sauque and John Chenoweth, March 1, 1836, Goliad, Jenkins, ed., *Papers*, IV: 477-478; John S. Brooks to Mother, March 2, 1836, Goliad, Jenkins, ed., *Papers*, IV: 485-488; De la Teja, *A Revolution Remembered*, 79-80; "Muster Roll Capt. Chenoweth's Co., Mustered into service February, 1836," Muster Roll book, 68; "John Smith petition for a first class headright land grant," n.d., M&P-TSL.

71 "Muster Roll Capt. Chenoweth's Co.," February 1836.

72 "John Smith petition," n.d.; J. W. Peacock affidavit, January 27, 1836, Bexar, J. W. Peacock file, AMC-TSL; J. C. Neill affidavit, February 3, 1836, Peacock file.

73 "Muster Roll Capt. Chenoweth's Co.," February 1836; Houston to Smith, January 17, 1836; Neill et al. to Convention, February 5, 1836, Bexar, Jenkins, ed., *Papers*, IV: 263-265; Houston affidavit, February 9, 1837. G. J. Thayer, H. O. Marshall, and W. G. Frazier died with Fannin at Goliad according to land grant records.

74 James W. Fannin Jr. to "troops at Gonzales," February 25, 1836, Goliad, in Foote, *Texas and The Texians*, II: 224-225; "Ben Highsmith account," Sowell, *Early Settlers*, 9-10; Fannin to De Sauque and Chenoweth, March 1, 1836, Jenkins, ed., *Papers*, IV: 477-478; Juan N. Seguin, *Personal Memoirs of John N. Seguin, From The Year 1834 to the Retreat of General Woll From the City of San Antonio, 1842* (San Antonio: Ledger Book and Job Office, 1858), 9; Alamo voting list, February 1, 1836; "Information Derived From J. W. Andrews," *Lamar Papers*, IV, Part II: 237.

 Highsmith claimed that Tom Mitchell entered the Alamo with David Crockett and a number of men from Gonzales. Tom Mitchell appears to have been Edwin T. Mitchell. Mitchell's brother Doctor Warren J. Mitchell was the commanding officer of the Georgia Battalion with Fannin at Goliad. Edwin T. Mitchell's name does not appear on the February 1, 1836, Alamo voting list. Thus, given that Mitchell was most likely a member of the Georgia Battalion at Goliad, it seems the only way he could have joined the Gonzales force is that he was sent to Gonzales as a courier. Warren J. Mitchell died at Goliad. J. W. Andrews listed a third brother, Goodwin Mitchell, as dying with Fannin. Currently, Goodwin Mitchell is not included on the Goliad list of victims.

75 Brooks to Mother, March 2, 1836.

76 R. M. Williamson to William B. Travis, March 1, 1836, Gonzales, found in Spanish translation in *El Nacional* (Mexico City), *Suplemento al Numero 79*, March 21, 1836, see Thomas W. Streeter, *A Bibliography of Texas*, number 1647. In this missive Williamson stated that the last courier from the Alamo had arrived at Gonzales four days earlier, which would have been February 26.

77 Houston et al. Treaty, February 23, 1836; Gray, *From Virginia*, 121.

78 Barrett, Clements, Thomson, and Pattillo to Robinson, January 31, 1836. The military committee of the Texian government had ordered: "...that the Commandant [of Bexar, J. C. Neill] be required to put the place [Alamo] in the best possible state for defense, with assurances that every possible effort is making to strengthen, supply and provision the Garrison, and in no case to abandon or surrender the place unless in the last extremity."

Chapter Four

Three-Legged Willie's Entreaty:
"Hold On Firmly"

Dear Colonel Travis – You cannot conceive my anxiety:
today it has been four whole days that we have not the slightest
news relative to your dangerous situation and we are therefore
given over to a thousand conjectures regarding you.

Major R. M. Williamson[1]

Getting sufficient armed men to San Antonio to prevent the destruction of Travis and his men would not be an easy task for their like-minded countrymen. After the start of the Texian insurrection in October 1835, the advance on Bexar by General Stephen F. Austin's volunteer army from Gonzales took eleven days. The gathering of men, arms, equipment, animals, and provisions was not done with ease or speed. Also, given human nature, the organization of companies and the election of officers was not done quickly or without friction.

The move to San Antonio would have taken longer, except for several factors. Austin, expecting armed conflict, had issued a declaration of war on September 18. Thus militia companies and volunteer units were already organizing when a detachment of centralist soldiers rode into Gonzales and demanded the return of a bronze cannon (a six-pounder) that the Green De Witt colonists had been loaned for protection against Indian attack. That attempt at "gun control" kicked off the hostilities on October 2, 1835. When Austin arrived at Gonzales on October 10 to take command, many of the militia companies and volunteer units were already on site or on the road to that settlement. More importantly, the colonists were unified behind a single general, Austin; a single political purpose, support of the federal constitution of 1824; and a single military mission, expulsion of the centralist Mexican army from Texas.[2]

Robert "Three-Legged Willie" Williamson
Photo courtesy The Center for American History,
The University of Texas at Austin

The 1836 siege of the Alamo, however, was a far different situation. Organization and delivery of an adequate reinforcement to the Alamo would be even harder than the formation of Austin's 1835 federalist army of volunteers. Two enormous obstacles stood in the way of getting relief to Bexar. After the December 1835 victory in San Antonio, the colonists began fighting over the political objective of the war. The provisional government split into two persuasions and the military forces into three factions. Lieutenant Governor James W. Robinson and the council, using Colonel James W. Fannin Jr. and his volunteers, were operating in the name of Mexican federalism. Governor Henry Smith, Sam Houston, and James Bowie, with only the Alamo soldiers on their side, supported independence and separation from Mexico, so that the country could be annexed to the United States. James Grant and F. W. Johnson, using the American volunteers from the storming of Bexar, hoped to unite with northeastern Mexican federalists and create a new republic made up of several Mexican states and Texas that would not be joined to the U.S. The result was that in January 1836, when Houston should have been organizing a defensive line along the San Antonio River, Texas was plagued by three military commanders: Houston, Johnson, and Fannin, who were, albeit for different political goals, attempting to turn a defensive war into an offensive campaign by attacking the port city of Matamoros. If any of the commanders had ever studied Napoleon's rules of war, they appear to have forgotten what the great general said about offensive war and leadership. Firstly: "The passage from the defensive to the offensive is one of the most delicate operations of war." Secondly, he observed: "Nothing is more important in war than unity in command. When, therefore, you are carrying on hostilities against a single power only, you should have but one army acting on one line and led by one commander."[3]

Travis had summed up the Texas situation pretty well on his way to San Antonio in January 1836, when he wrote Henry Smith: "The people are cold & indifferent. They are worn down & exhausted with the war, & in consequence of dissensions between contending rival chieftains, they have lost all confidence in their own govt. & officers. You have no idea of [the] exhausted state of the country – volunteers can no longer be had or relied upon. A speedy organization, classification & draft of the Militia is all that can save us now."[4]

Governor Smith seems to have either ignored Travis's advice or was too busy with his own political schemes to understand what was happening in the country. On February 5, at a time when San Antonio was garrisoned by perhaps one hundred fifty men, Smith wrote: "This country can never prosper until a few of that baneful faction [F. W. Johnson, James Grant, James W. Robinson, and the Council] are immolated on the altar of their own perfidy. The convention will, I hope, afford the grand corrective. Owing to their base management, much confusion prevails among our volunteer troops on the frontier, but, by using much vigilance, I have now got Bexar secure."[5]

Lieutenant Governor Robinson and the Council were equally blind to their own behavior and the manpower needs of the Alamo. On January 31 Robinson and the Council's military committee, on hearing of Houston's recommendation that the Alamo be destroyed and the troops moved to Gonzales, demanded that Houston be required "to put the place in the best possible state for defense, with assurances that every possible effort is making to strengthen, supply and provision the Garrison, and in no case to abandon or surrender the place unless in the last extremity."[6]

Then, in direct opposition to what they had recommended for the Alamo, they wrote: "The advisory Committee are of opinion that no further necessity exists of increasing the number of troops now at Bejar, beyond those that are already there, or on their way to the place."[7]

Thus, the evidence shows that Smith, Robinson, and the Council believed that two hundred men were sufficient to defend the Alamo. That belief was shared by many of the Texians. Many years later Lancelot Abbotts, an old Texian who had been at the convention, observed: "A public meeting was called for the purpose of enlisting volunteers for the relief of the Alamo. At this time there was living in Washington a doctor by the name of Biggs, or Briggs [Benjamin Briggs Goodrich, brother of Alamo defender John C. Goodrich], who was a big, burly, brave Manifest Destiny man. He made a speech, in which he declared his unbelief in the dispatch [Travis's March 3 letter] and the utter impossibility of any number of Mexicans to take the Alamo, when defended by near 200 men."[8]

Austrian George Bernard Erath, a veteran of San Jacinto, later reported:

> After the fall of Bexar, in the month of December, 1835, the people became overconfident in their own ability and Mexican insignificance. A land speculating element of immigration, who did not remain, induced them to lean too much to private interest, and when the Alamo was besieged, no entreaties could bring men in the field, believing the handful of men under Travis sufficient to repulse 7,000 Mexicans who advanced from the Rio Grande. When Travis and his men fell and were put to the sword by Santa Anna's proclamation for the extermination of the American

people from the soil of Texas, terror took the place of self-confidence and boasting.[9]

Moseley Baker described General Houston's failure in preparing the country for Santa Anna's advance into Texas. He wrote:

> While the coming of Santa Anna was daily expected in the month of January, 1836, you [Houston] deliberately took your departure for Nacogdoches, on a plea of going to pacify the Indians, without having previously organized a single company for the defense of the country. You remained absent, and was still so, when the Mexicans actually invaded the country and besieged the immortal Travis in the Alamo, and he in calling for assistance writes to the Convention, on account, as he [Travis] himself says, "of the absence of the commander-in-chief." But sir he called in vain – you had left no one whom to look for orders in your absence, and before the people could recover from their consternation – the Alamo had fallen.... [10]

A speedy reinforcement of the Alamo would be hampered by the lack of a general officer to coordinate relief activities and by the Texians' delusional belief that two hundred men could hold out against Santa Anna's two thousand soldiers. Regardless, a small number of patriots attempted to save Travis and his troops.

Fifth Day — Saturday, February 27

In the morning, at San Antonio, a party of Mexican solders, commanded by Lieutenant Manuel Manchaca, a member of the permanent second company of Tamanlipas cavalry and a San Antonio native, left the city for the Seguin and Flores ranches, southeast of the city on the San Antonio River, to collect corn, cattle, and hogs for Santa Anna's mess tables. The ranches appear to have been selected because those families had sided with the rebels.[11]

Sometime during the day, however, Fannin's advance relief force, commanded by Captains John Chenoweth and Francis De Sauque, beat Manchaca to the punch and arrived at the Seguin ranch. The Texian troops quickly collected corn, cattle, horses, and mules for the trip to San Antonio. When the collection was finished, they rode back toward Goliad to wait for Fannin's infantry and artillery at the Cibolo Creek crossing of the Bexar/Goliad road.[12]

At Gonzales, Major Williamson continued to recruit men for the Gonzales ranger company. At that time the unit was probably nowhere near its authorized complement of fifty-six troopers. Still, other men appear to have joined the company by that date. They were John Cain, Isaac Baker, Freeman H. K. Day, William Dearduff, James George, William George, William Garnett, George W. Cottle, Thomas Jackson, William P. King, Claiborne Wright, Benjamin Kellogg, George Taylor, Edward Taylor, James Taylor, William Taylor, Andrew J. Sowell, Ben McCulloch, Benjamin Kellogg, and _____ Rigault, a Spanish Creole. Ben Highsmith may have been a member of the unit.[13]

Weapons, ammunition, and provisions were collected. One government claim shows that Second Lieutenant Kimbell purchased fifty-two pounds of coffee at Stephen Smith's store "for the use of the men that has volunteered to go to Bexar to the Relief of our Boys [at the Alamo]." At that point the coffee likely broke down to more than a pound per man for the ride to San Antonio.[14]

Also, Fannin's courier, Edwin T. Mitchell, probably arrived sometime that evening with Fannin's request that the Gonzales men "effect a junction with him below Bexar, at a convenient point." The Cibolo Creek crossing of the Goliad/San Antonio road, halfway between the two settlements, appears to have been the rendezvous location.[15]

Fannin's force, however, had other problems to attend to that day. Shortly after daylight, the command discovered their oxen had wandered off during the night and could not be located. Then a soldier arrived from Refugio with the news that Colonel F. W. Johnson's small cavalry unit had been annihilated in an ambush. Only Johnson and two other men had escaped to report the centralist advance from Matamoros. After hearing the depressing report, one of Fannin's volunteer captains requested, in the name of his company, that a council of war be called to reconsider the idea of reinforcing the Alamo. Fannin convened a meeting of the company officers. After a decision had been made, he wrote acting governor Robinson: "...The Council of war...unanimously determined, that, in as much as a proper supply of provisions and means of transportation could not be had; and, as it was impossible, with our present means, to carry the artillery with us, and as by leaving Fort Defiance without a proper garrison, it might fall into the hands of the enemy, with provisions, etc., now at Matagorda, Dimmitt's Landing and Cox's Point and on the way to meet us; and, as by report of our spies.... We may expect an attack upon this place, it was deemed expedient to return to this post and complete the fortifications, etc., etc."[16] The war council's decision was a good one because a local Tejano, a Santa Anna loyalist, was at that time riding to Bexar to inform the general that Fannin and his men were on the road to San Antonio.[17]

That afternoon Fannin, after having learned more of the enemy advance, again wrote Robinson and bemoaned: "...we hope that before this time the people have risen and are marching to the relief of Bexar & this post – but should the worst happen – on whose head should the burden of censure fall – not on the heads of those brave men who have left their homes in the United States to aid us...but on those whose all is Texas & who notwithstanding the repeated calls have remained at home without raising a finger to keep the Enemy from their thresholds – What must be the feelings of the Volunteers now shut [up] in Bexar?"[18]

As Fannin wrote of his reinforcement concerns, Henry Smith, at San Felipe, issued an "Appeal to the People of Texas" that pleaded:

> I call upon you as an officer, I implore you as a man, to fly to the aid of your besieged Countrymen and not permit them to be massacred by a mercenary foe. I slight none! The call is upon ALL who are able to bear arms, to rally without one moment's delay, or in fifteen days the heart of Texas will be the seat of War.... Do you possess honor? Suffer it not to be insulted or tarnished! Do you possess patriotism? Evince it by your bold, prompt and manly action! If you possess even humanity, you will rally without a moment's delay to the aid of your besieged countrymen![19]

That morning a courier from San Felipe most likely rode into Mina (Bastrop) with the Council's orders for Captain John James Tumlinson's rangers to reinforce the Alamo. The messenger reported to Edward Burleson, the former commanding general of the volunteer forces at the storming of Bexar. The orders also contained instructions for Burleson "to organize the militia and to raise volunteers for the draft."[20]

Later that afternoon or evening, Tumlinson's ranger company probably departed Mina for Gonzales to join the Gonzales ranger unit. The Mina rangers had been organized in mid-January 1836, the men enlisting for twelve months. A muster roll for the company does not exist, but other sources identify the following members: Captain John James Tumlinson, Lieutenant Joseph Rogers, Timothy McKean, William Johnson, Felix W. Goff, Robert Owen, James E. Edmiston, Joseph Cottle, Joseph Weakes, Hugh M. Childers, James Curtis Sr., James Curtis Jr., Gany Crosby, Joshua Gray, Thomas Gray, Novet Haggard, James Haggard, William Leech, J. G. Dunn, Andrew Dunn, and James P. Gorman. Other probable members were Robert E. Cochran, Lemuel Crawford, James Kenny, James Northcross, Charles S. Smith, James E. Stewart, and Ross McClelland.[21]

That night at Bexar a "courier extraordinary" left to locate General Vicente Filisola, second in command of the Texas campaign, who was on the road to San Antonio. The rider carried a Santa Anna letter that reported events at San Antonio up to that date. Among other things, the Mexican general wrote: "From the moment of my arrival I have been busy hostilizing the enemy in its position, so much that they are not even allowed to raise their heads over the walls, preparing everything for the assault which will take place when at least the first brigade arrives, which is even now sixty leagues away. Up to now they still are stubborn, counting on the strong position which they hold, and hoping for much aid from the colonies and from the United States of the North, but they shall soon find out their mistake." One has to wonder if Santa Anna had received a copy of Travis's missive of February 24 that was addressed to "To the People of Texas & all Americans in the world."[22]

Sixth Day — Sunday, February 28

The morning was cold at San Antonio, registering forty degrees shortly after daylight. The Tejano spy from Goliad arrived during the day and informed Santa Anna that a Texian force had departed Goliad for Bexar.[23]

Later in the day Captain J. J. Tumlinson and his Mina rangers rode into Gonzales. Soon afterward, Major Williamson, Captains Martin, Smith, Seguin, Tumlinson, and Lieutenants Jackson and Kimbell probably conducted a council of war to determine the manner in which they would reinforce the Alamo. The officers appear to have decided that Martin, Smith, and Tumlinson would take the relief force to the Cibolo Creek crossing on the Bexar/Gonzales road, twenty miles east of the city. At that location they would wait for Fannin's force. Seguin and his two men

The Gonzales/San Antonio road running west from Sandies Creek

would ride to the Cibolo Creek crossing on the Bexar/San Antonio road to rendezvous with Fannin's men and guide them to the Cibolo ford on the San Antonio/Gonzales road. The two ranger companies combined, including the returning Alamo couriers, appear to have totaled sixty men.[24]

Sometime later, probably late afternoon or evening, Captain Albert Martin, Captain John James Tumlinson, John W. Smith, and Juan Seguin departed Gonzales with fifty-six mounted men. One or two point men probably rode some distance in front of the force to detect any enemy horsemen that might be riding toward them on the same road. Three or four hours later the relief force reached John Castleman's home at the intersection of the San Antonio road and Sandies Creek, about twenty miles west of Gonzales. Seguin, Antonio Cruz, and Matias Curvier split from the group and rode almost due south to the Cibolo crossing on the Goliad/Bexar road to intercept Fannin's advance force. The Tejanos traveled on an old smuggler's road that ran from the well-known water hole at Castleman's to the mouth of Cibolo Creek. Captain Martin, Captain Tumlinson, Smith, and the other rangers continued west toward Bexar. They most likely reached "Forty-mile hole" on Ecleto Creek, about forty miles east of San Antonio, in late afternoon or early evening. They probably camped there for the night.[25]

About the same time, Seguin and his men arrived at the Cibolo Creek crossing on the Bexar/Goliad road. Seguin wrote: "...I met, at the Ranch of San Bartolo, on the Cibolo, Captain Desac [*sic*], who, by orders of Fannin, had foraged on my ranch, carrying off a great number of beeves, corn, & c. Desac informed me that Fannin could not delay more than two days his arrival at the Cibolo, on his way to render assistance to the defenders of the Alamo. I therefore determined to wait on him. I sent Fannin, by express, the communication from Travis, informing him at the same time of the critical position of the defenders of the Alamo. Fannin answered me, through Lieutenant Finley, that he had advanced as far as 'Rancho Nuevo,' but, being informed Of the movements of General Urrea, he had countermarched to Goliad to defend that place...."[26]

Lieutenant Finley and an unknown number of men returned to Goliad with the provisions taken from the Seguin ranch. After the revolution, Erasmo Seguin, Juan's father, filed a claim for "one hundred and twenty-five beeves, twenty-five fanegas of corn, two yoke of oxen, one cart, seven horses, and five mules" taken for Fannin's command at Goliad.[27]

At Goliad, Fannin and his remaining men were safely back in the old presidio that they had named "Fort Defiance." John S. Brooks later wrote his mother: "Our situation became delicate and embarrassing in the extreme. ... it was concluded to return to Goliad, and place the Fort in a defensible condition. We are hard at work, day and night, picketing, ditching, and mounting cannon, & c. We are hourly in expectation of an attack."[28]

Northeast of Goliad, Captain Philip Dimmitt arrived at his store and warehouse on Lavaca Bay at 8:00 p.m. that evening. He quickly sent a rider with a message to James Kerr who lived inland on the Lavaca River. Dimmitt reported the conditions surrounding his departure from the Alamo and closed with: "...On the 24th there was heavy cannonading, particularly at the close of the evening. I left the Rovia at 10:00 p.m., on the 25th, and heard no more firing, from which I concluded the Alamo had been taken by storm. On the night of the 24th, I was informed that there were from four to six thousand Mexicans in and around Bexar. [General Jose C.] Urrea was at Carisota, on the Matamoros road, marching for Goliad. If immediate steps are not taken to defend Guadalupe Victoria

[Victoria, Texas—100 miles east of Bexar], the Mexicans will soon be upon our families."[29]

Time was running out, not only for the Alamo, but for the rest of Anglo-Celtic Texas. At San Felipe, John A. Wharton, Houston's adjutant general, sent a rider to Brazoria, on the lower Brazos River, with a plea for Alamo relief. He wrote: "I advise all that live in the upper part of the Jurisdiction who can procure horses, to leave immediately for Gonzales.... I consider it unnecessary to make appeal to your patriotism, as the information from Bexar, speaks louder than words." Still, Moseley Baker took his own good time in organizing a company to march to the Alamo. Lt. Colonel James C. Neill, however, moved quickly. He obtained six hundred dollars from Henry Smith and left for Gonzales.[30]

Up the road at Washington-on-the-Brazos, where the March convention was to take place, William Fairfax Gray, a recent arrival from the United States, took notice of events. He observed that the weather was "cold and drizzling." In regard to the Alamo, Gray wrote: "Another express is received from Travis, dated the 24th... An unconditional surrender had been demanded, which he had answered by a cannon shot. He was determined to defend the place to the last, and called earnestly for assistance. Some are going, but the *vile rabble* here cannot be moved."[31]

Seventh Day — Monday, February 29

Sam Houston, commander-in-chief of the Texian military forces, arrived at Washington-on-the-Brazos to take a seat at the convention as a delegate from Refugio. Mr. Gray, who appears to have known nothing of Houston's experiences in Texas, noted: "Gen'l Houston's arrival has created more sensation than that of any other man. He is evidently the people's man, and seems to take pains to ingratiate himself with everybody. He is much broken in appearance, but has still a fine person and courtly manners; will be forty-three years on 3rd of March – looks older." Houston, instead of concerning himself with the organization of a relief force for the Alamo, met with John Forbes and prepared a report on the unnecessary treaty they had negotiated with the peaceful Indians of East Texas.[32]

While Houston ignored the Alamo's critical situation, Albert Martin, J. J. Tumlinson, and John W. Smith and their rangers, after riding from Ecleto Creek, probably camped on the Cibolo Creek ford, twenty miles east of Bexar—a five- or six-hour ride to the Alamo. That evening they readied their weapons, horses, and other equipment for the ride to the Alamo. Lastly, they probably had a cold supper to avoid detection by any enemy spies in the area. Sometime after sundown Martin and Smith departed the Cibolo with at least thirty-four men. It appears that Tumlinson and the Mina rangers decided to wait on Fannin before riding to the Alamo. A number of the Gonzales rangers also appear to have decided to wait on Fannin. Those individuals were First Lieutenant Thomas Jackson, Second Lieutenant George Kimbell, Andrew Kent, Abe Darst, Wash Cottle, Albert Fuqua, John Gaston, and Fannin courier Edwin T. Mitchell.[33]

At Mina, Edward Burleson detached Thomas McGehee, Martin Walker, Andy Mays, David Heldeman, and Michel Sishum from Jesse Billingsly's volunteer company to operate as spies to scout the San Antonio road between Mina and Bexar to give the Mina citizens quick notice of any enemy advance. McGehee commanded the scout detachment. They remained out in that service until March 20, when they joined Houston's army at Beeson's Crossing (Columbus) on the Colorado River.[34]

In the Alamo that night, Travis, concerned that seven couriers had been sent out for assistance and not a single man had returned, put another man on the road to Gonzales. The rider was Samuel G. Bastian, a former resident of Alexandria, Louisiana, who probably departed shortly after dark for Gonzales "to hurry up reinforcements."[35]

On the Mexican side that night, Santa Anna posted the Jimenez battalion to the east side of the Alamo. Near midnight Santa Anna sent General Ramirez y Sesma with the Dolores cavalry and the Jimenez infantry to locate and attack Fannin's force, which was supposed to be on the march to San Antonio. The general's last words to Ramirez y Sesma were: "Try to fall on them at dawn in order that you may take them by surprise. In this war you know there are no prisoners."[36]

Eighth Day — Tuesday, March 1

The first hours of the day found John W. Smith, Albert Martin, and thirty-four mounted men, after having crossed the San Antonio River someplace north of the town, positioned north of San Antonio on the west side of the river and about a thousand yards northwest of the Alamo. That approach to the Alamo appears to have been the only avenue to the fortress that was not obviously blocked by Mexican soldiers.

The Texians were someplace above two sugarcane mills that were due west of the Molino Blanco, a gristmill on the river about eight hundred yards north of the Alamo. There was an enemy encampment at the Molino Blanco. A second Mexican detachment was located next to the Alamo *acequia* (irrigation ditch) eight hundred yards northeast of the old mission. Sam Bastian, who had left the Alamo the previous evening, had encountered the Gonzales men and joined them to enter the Alamo. Smith and Martin, however, were well acquainted with the area as they had entered the city from the Texian camp at the Molino Blanco during the storming of Bexar in December 1835.[37]

Sometime before 3:00 a.m., with a cold norther blowing at their backs, the Texians edged their horses toward the Alamo across the San Antonio River. The rebels, however, before crossing the river, were detected by the Mexicans. The rangers probably rode into, if not over, an enemy encampment or a roving patrol. At that point, they probably made a run for the Alamo.[38]

Sam Bastain, _____ Rigault, the Spanish Creole, and two other men were separated from the unit by enemy soldiers. Bastian described the event with these words: "...When near the fort we were discovered and fired on by the Mexican troops. Most of the party got through; but I and three others had to take to the chaparral to save our lives." A fifth ranger, John Ballard, was also separated from the company. He, however, appears to have made his way back to the Cibolo ford. Otherwise, Martin, Smith, and thirty men rode into the Alamo at 3:00 a.m. that morning.[39]

The norther, which probably included a dark sky and perhaps rain, served the mounted rangers well that morning. Gray, at Washington-on-the-Brazos, described the weather with these words: "In the night the wind sprung up from the north and blew a gale, accompanied by lightning, thunder, rain and hail, and became very cold. In the morning the thermometer was down to 33 degrees...." At daylight in Bexar, Almonte reported that the temperature was thirty-six degrees.[40]

The available evidence indicates the enemy did not know exactly what had occurred on their northern line. Almonte, if he was aware of it, made no mention of the rebels' mad ride through the Mexican line. In 1837 Ramon Martinez Caro, Santa Anna's civilian secretary, reported: "...two small reinforcements from Gonzalez that succeeded in breaking through our lines and entering the fort. The first consisted of four men who gained the fort one night, and the second was a party of twenty-five who introduced themselves in the daytime." Thirteen years later General Vicente Filisola, second in command of the Texas campaign, wrote about "...32 people of the Town of Gonzalez who under the cover of darkness joined the group two days before the attack on the fort."[41]

Alamo artillery
Top: gunade twelve-pounder, bottom: Spanish twelve-pounder

Either Martin or Smith probably carried a letter from Major R. M. Williamson to Travis. Most certainly they told Travis that couriers had been sent east, north, and south from Gonzales to spread the news of the Alamo's investment. Also, Travis would have learned that men were assembling at Gonzales to join Fannin's force at the Cibolo ford on the Gonzales road and that those men would soon ride into the Alamo.[42]

Sometime before daylight, Ben Highsmith, who probably entered the Alamo with Martin and Smith, rode from the Alamo and headed for Goliad. Travis was worried that Fannin might not come to the Alamo's relief. In 1897 Highsmith said that Travis had ordered Fannin "to blow up the fort at Goliad and come to him with his men."[43]

Later that day John Ballard, who had been separated from the Martin and Smith detachment of Gonzales rangers during the night, joined Tumlinson's command at the Cibolo ford. The other four men, Bastian, Rigault, and the two unnamed men, remained in the thick brush north of the Alamo on the west side of the river. Bastian claimed: "He [Rigault] went into the town and brought us intelligence. We were about three hundred yards from the fort concealed by brush, which extended north for twenty miles. I could see the enemy's operations perfectly."[44]

General Ramirez y Sesma's expedition to cut off Fannin's main force returned to Bexar during the day. The general had sent riders as far as the tinaja, or water hole, which may have been near the ford on Salado Creek. That was the site where Fannin's advance would probably have been if they had continued their march to Bexar. The Mexican horsemen returned to their camp outside the city, and the infantry to a position in the city. Then Ramirez y Sesma informed Santa Anna that he had not found any evidence of an enemy advance from Goliad.[45]

South of Bexar, among the Tejano ranches on the San Antonio River, Seguin appears to have raised a volunteer company of Mexican-Texians.[46] The Tejano volunteers were probably the following men:

Manuel Flores	Antonio Manchaca
Nepomuceno Flores	Ambrosio Rodriquez
Jose Maria Arocha	Eduardo Ramirez
Lucio Enriques	Matias Curvier
Antonio Curvier	Simon Arreola
Pedro Avoca	Pedro Herrera
Manuel Tarin	Tomas Maldonado
Cesario Carmona	Jacinto Pena

Nepomuceno Navarro	Andres Barcenas
Juan Abamillo	Damacio Jimenes
Guadalupe Rodriquez	Andres Nava
Salvador Flores	Antonio Cruz
Ignacio Guerra	Jose Alemeda
Antonio Balle	Juan Rodriquez
Vicente Zepeda	Juan Ximenes
Phillip Coe	Manuel Maria Flores
Juan A. Badillo	Macedonio Arocha[47]

Antonio Manchaca, Jose Maria Arrocha, Ambrosio Rodriquez, Eduardo Ramirez, Matias Curvier, Pedro Herrera, Lucio Enriques, Simon Arrerlo, Cesario Carmona, Ignacio Gurrea, Vicente Zepeda, and one or all of the Flores men appear to have been in the Alamo with Seguin at the start of the siege. These men and perhaps other Tejanos seem to have exited the Alamo sometime after Seguin's departure for Gonzales.[48]

In 1902 Enrique Esparza, the son of Alamo defender Gregorio Esparza, claimed that Santa Anna had called an armistice of three days and that a number of the Mexican-Texians left the Alamo. That year Esparza said only one woman, Trinidad Saucedo, had exited the fort. In 1907 Esparza identified _____ Menchaca, _____ Flores, _____ Rodriquez, _____ Ramirez, _____ Arocha, and _____ Silvero as having left the Alamo during the alleged armistice. Also, Madame Candelaria most likely left with the Tejanos. They probably departed at night and melted back into the Bexar population—except for the men who appear to have moved downriver to the Tejano ranches.[49]

The total force that awaited Fannin and his artillery at the Cibolo Creek ford on the Bexar/Goliad road is unknown, but it was probably around fifty to eighty mounted men. Colonel Fannin, however, had turned back, but that fact was not known outside of Goliad. Fannin, at 5:00 p.m., penned a missive to Chenoweth and De Sauque. He informed them of what had happened at Goliad since their departure and of the council of war's decision to remain at Goliad. Lastly he did not rule out an attempt to reach the Alamo. He wrote: "If you can...communicate with Gonzales and know how many volunteers will form a junction & if informed speedily I will push out 200 [men] and cooperate."[50]

At that time twenty Tennessee men were speeding toward Bexar to join the Alamo defenders. The men were part of a unit that had originally been a company of thirty-five men commanded by a Captain William Gilmore. The men enlisted for six months in the Volunteer Auxiliary Corps on January 14, 1836. On February 9, 1836, Gilmore's company purchased clothing from the Jones and Townsand store in San Felipe. Later that day the command split into two groups. One of the company's members, W. P. Grady, wrote: "...at San Felipe his captain became dissatisfied and returned to Tennessee leaving him with twenty other men in the country."[51] The rupture appears to have been over which Texas political faction the men would support. A written agreement shows that ten or more of the men sided with acting governor James W. Robinson and the council:

> We the undersigned do agree to proceed on to the Army of
> Texas under the directions of the governor & council –
>
> 1. Samuel Sprague   6. R. R. Pritty
> 2. Daniel Murphy   7. J. F. Pittman
> 3. John W. Thomson   8. C. S. Hardwick
> 4. Nathaniel Hazen   9. David G. Jones
> 5. Charles Linley   10. Clark M. Harmon
>
> Samuel Sprague has been selected to head the company
> whose many [names] are attached to this paper.[52]

Nevertheless, government officials at San Felipe continued to think of the unit as "Gilmore's" company. On February 9 the acting governor ordered the group to report to the commanding officer at Copano, who was Captain Chenoweth. On February 14 Robinson wrote Sam Houston that "most of Gilmore's men" had left for Goliad.[53]

The "Gilmore" company, however, did not depart for Goliad. In late May 1836 James Gillespie, one of Gilmore's men who commanded a company at San Jacinto, wrote of their pre-San Jacinto activities:

> ...We left home about the 25 of November 1835 [and] was in Texas on Christmas and received the right of citizenship and enrolled our names as volunteers about the 15 January. We were then ready to do any service the country demanded. We remained you know in Nacogdoches sometime and were furnished with means to move on towards the frontier of the country, by the _____ of a few individuals, among whom we rank you among the most _____ the small fund we received was exhausted before we got to Washington [-on-the-Brazos]. We were then again on our

own hook. We consulted Genl.Houston whom we found at _____, as to what course was most advisable to pursue. He gave us no satisfaction as we thought. We then went to San Felipe the seat of government, hoping that the government would make some disposition of us but unfortunately we found the Governor & Council at war with each other, neither capacitated to act without the consent of the other. The governor I first understood him wanted us to go to San Antonio. The Council thought we ought to go to Labahea [Goliad] and join Fannin, but neither gave us the means to go to either place & the fact is neither wanted us & both seemed to be jealous of us. We found out in a few days that we were trifled with and Gilmore who was then our captain disbanded the company and he himself went home together with a few others while those of us who were determined to try Texas a little longer rambled about the country waiting to see if our service would be needed. As soon as we heard of the approach of the Mexican army towards Bexar we hastened towards that place. This was about the first of March....[54]

As Gilmore's men rode toward San Antonio, the people of Gonzales were busy with their own relief activities. James B. Bonham, Travis's first lieutenant, left Gonzales for the Alamo, probably in the late afternoon. He carried two letters. One missive appears to have been from Governor Henry Smith. The second was a letter of encouragement and hope from Williamson to Travis. Bonham, who had probably been at the convention when he learned of the Alamo situation, also had a verbal message from Sam Houston for the garrison.[55]

Ninth Day — Wednesday, March 2

At Washington-on-the-Brazos, William F. Gray noted in his diary that the morning was clear and cold. That evening a rider arrived with Travis's letter of the twenty-fifth to Houston. Gray observed: "Col. Fannin was on the march from Goliad with 350 men for the aid of Travis. This, with the other forces known to be on the way, will by this time make the number in the fort some six or seven hundred. It is believed the Alamo is safe."[56]

At San Antonio, the weather was also cold. According to Almonte: "Commenced clear and pleasant – thermometer 34 – no wind." Lieutenant Manuel Menchaca and a party of soldiers were dispatched to the Seguin ranch to obtain a supply of corn that was reported to be there.[57]

At Goliad, Ben Highsmith arrived in the evening with Travis's most recent message to Fannin. In response, Fannin appears to have called a council of war to reconsider the idea of reinforcing the Alamo.[58] Sometime that day John S. Brooks, Fannin's adjutant, wrote his mother. In regard to the Alamo, he wrote: "If the division of the Mexican army advancing against this place has met any obstructions.... 200 men will be detached for the relief of Bexar. I will go with them. Our object will be to cut our way through the Mexican army into the Alamo, and carry with us such provisions as it will be sufficient to hold out until we are relieved by a large force from the Colonies.

"We have just received additional intelligence from Bexar. The Mexicans have made two successive attacks on the Alamo in both of which the gallant little garrison repulsed them with some loss. Probably Davy Crockett 'grinned' them off."[59]

Sometime after Brooks had completed the letter, a group of Fannin's men, mostly former members of Captain Thomas H. Breece's company of New Orleans Greys, perhaps as many as fifty men, left for the Alamo. The Greys had disbanded after the fall of Bexar in December, some remaining under command of Lieutenant Colonel James C. Neill. Most of the Greys, however, joined the Johnson and Grant Matamoros expedition that moved down the road to Goliad. Now the men who had remained in Bexar were part of the Alamo garrison. Fannin's Greys were not just going to the Alamo to help fellow soldiers, they were going to save their friends and former mess mates. Brooks, however, despite his words to his mother, did not ride to the Alamo that day.[60]

Tenth Day — Thursday, March 3

At 11:00 a.m. Bonham entered the Alamo. He rode in without being attacked, having passed between the Powder House, three hundred yards east of the Alamo on a high hill near the Gonzales road, and the enemy emplacement, eight hundred yards northeast of the Alamo, on the Alamo ditch.[61]

Within minutes, Travis was reading a letter from his good friend Williamson, which reads:

Gonzales, March 1, 1836
Dear Colonel Travis,

You cannot conceive my anxiety: today it has been four whole days that we have not the least news relating to your dangerous situation and for that time we found ourselves given up to a thousand conjectures about it. From this municipality 60 men have now set out, who in all human probability are found, at this date, with you. Colonel Fannin with 300 men and 4 artillery pieces has been en route to Bejar for three days now. Tonight we are waiting for some reinforcements from Washington, Bastrop, Brazoria and San Felipe, numbering 300, and not a moment will be lost in providing you assistance. Regarding *the other letter of the same date, let it pass*[;] you must know what is means; if the populace gets hold of it, let them guess [at] it – It is from your true friend *R. M. Williamson* –

P.S. For God's sake sustain yourselves until we can assist you. – I remit to you with major Bhanham [Bonham] a communication from the interim governor. A thousand regards to all your people, and tell them for "Willie" to maintain themselves firm until I go there – Williamson. Write us soon, soon.[62]

Thus, Travis was confronted with good news and bad news. Fannin had left Goliad to reinforce the Alamo, but he had yet to arrive there. Where was he? Then, there was the bad news. Bonham told Travis that Houston would not be coming to their aid anytime soon. Houston had instructed Bonham to "urge Colonel Travis ... to fall back and unite his forces with the main army to more successfully defend the country against the invaders."[63]

Nevertheless, Fannin's former New Orleans Greys had probably joined the Chenoweth and De Sauque company and Seguin's Tejano unit the previous evening or that morning at the Cibolo ford on the Bexar/Goliad road. That afternoon the combined force rode northwest to join J. J. Tumlinson's rangers at the Cibolo ford on the Gonzales road. Seguin probably guided the combined force cross country, traveling on the east side of Cibolo Creek. The terrain was open prairie and the distance was about thirty-five miles.[64]

Also, this date, the Tennessee men known as Gilmore's company probably joined the relief group that was massing at the Cibolo ford. Just how many of the men joined the mounted reinforcement is unknown, but at least two of the men died at the Alamo.[65]

At Goliad, Ben Highsmith, after a good night's rest and a couple of meals, departed for the Alamo. He knew it was important to let Travis know of Fannin's plans.[66]

In the afternoon, between 4 p.m. and 5 p.m., reinforcements arrived at San Antonio. The troops, however, were the Mexican battalions of "Zapadores, Aldama, and Toluca." The men were exhausted from their forced march from the Medina River. Santa Anna now had the troops he had been waiting on for the final attack on the Alamo.[67]

Travis, soon after the arrival of the Mexican units, wrote the Convention at Washington-on-the-Brazos, saying: "In the present confusion of the political authorities of the country, and in the absence of the commander-in-chief, I beg leave to communicate to you the situation of this garrison." He detailed what had occurred since the start of the siege and requested reinforcements and provisions. He acknowledged that Fannin was supposed to be on the way with aid, but he feared that was not the case. Of his men, Travis wrote: "The spirits of my men are still high although they have had much to depress them.... Their [the enemy] threats have no influence on me or my men, but to make all fight with desperation and that high-souled courage that characterizes the patriot, who is willing to die in defense of his country's liberty and his own honor."[68]

The Alamo force appears to have increased to two hundred men by that time. Travis had started with 150 effectives on the evening of February 23. Five couriers had departed. Fourteen or more Tejanos had left. Three couriers and thirty men from Gonzales had joined the garrison. The total as of March 3 should have been around one hundred and sixty-four men. Where did the other thirty-six men come from? Given that Santa Anna's soldiers were not going to take any prisoners, the Alamo sick and wounded may have been included in the count of two hundred. Regardless of their condition, the sick and wounded would have to fight to live. Also, a group of ten to thirty men had left the city on February 14, 1836, to locate headright sites on Cibolo Creek. David P. Cummings, a young surveyor from Pennsylvania, was one of those men. Susanna Dickinson reported that Travis had sent a rider to find the men who were out on the Cibolo. The group appears to have returned to the Alamo, probably during the early days of the investment, most likely on February 24. Travis would not have identified the men as a relief force because they were already members of the garrison.[69]

Still, the Alamo was far short of the number of soldiers needed to repulse Santa Anna's centralist force. Travis, knowing that Houston was involved in political activities and would not be coming to their aid, needed to know the whereabouts of Fannin's three hundred men and four cannon. The Goliad troops were the only men close enough to the Alamo to do Travis's people any good. Thus he sent three of his mounted spies (scouts) out to find Fannin.[70]

There is limited but tantalizing evidence that David Crockett commanded the scouting mission to locate Fannin. In 1876 Susanna Dickinson reported that Crockett was one of three spies who had been sent out and had returned to the Alamo three nights before the final attack on the Alamo. Crockett probably volunteered for the mission as he was an experienced scout who did not like being shut up in the Alamo.[71]

Moreover, Crockett had been concerned for some time about the government's failure to send troops to the Bexar garrison. Sometime in February, probably around the middle of the month, James Bowie and Crockett sent a courier to the east to raise volunteers for Bexar. They selected a skinny young man named David Harmon to ride to Jefferson with their plea for men to be sent to San Antonio.[72]

Almost fifty years later, Harmon wrote of his mission. He reported: "A day or two after our arrival at San Antonio, one morning, in company with Payton Bland, David Crockett & George Evans (afterward Maj. Evans, [who was] killed in the Alamo; Maj. Evans was a member of David Garner's company when we left Jefferson).[73] – When we went out to look after our horses, that were staked out on the high ground, or second bank [probably the east side of the San Antonio River near the Alamo], we met up with two soldiers (I can't remember their names) – who asked Col. Crockett if he thought there was any chance for a fight, [for] if not they were going home.

"Col. Crockett said there had been plenty of men there to take the town, but that the men were going away as fast as they came, and remarked that if he (Crockett) was in command he would have given them 'Sheet'[74] long ago, meaning that he would whip them [reinforcements] out [of the colonies] – & [he] said that they needed some

David Crockett
Photo courtesy of Texas State Library and Archives Commission

one to carry orders back to hurry up the drafted men & all soldiers at home."[75]

Thus, when the time came during the siege for someone to go out and "whip" reinforcements into the Alamo, it appears that Crockett volunteered for the job. Also, it was a chance for him to do what he did best: scout and talk. A better man could not have been found to locate and motivate Fannin's American volunteers to ride to the aid of the Alamo than the old "half horse, half alligator" himself, who had a reputation for "whipping his weight in wildcats." Sure the Crockett tales were fiction. Nevertheless, the Goliad men were already boasting about how David Crockett had "grinned down" the Mexicans. Crockett had a reputation that would have appealed to the men from the United States; he was one of them, having come to Texas for the same reasons. If he could not talk them into the Alamo, nobody could. Sometime after dark, Crockett and two other men left the Alamo. One man's task was to carry a packet of letters to Gonzales. Crockett and the third man's mission was to locate Fannin's force and guide it back to the Alamo.[76]

That night Santa Anna wrote General Jose C. Urrea to congratulate him on his rout of "the colonists at San Patricio." In closing the missive, the "Napoleon of the West" mentioned that he was busy planning his final assault on the Alamo.[77]

Sometime before midnight, Crockett and his scouts probably located the combined force (Tumlinson's rangers, Seguin's Tejanos, Chenoweth and De Sauque's men, Gilmore's men, and about fifty other Fannin men) that were camped at the Cibolo ford on the Gonzales road, twenty miles east of the Alamo. Travis's letter to the convention, with at least three other missives, was sent on to Gonzales. Also, Crockett would have informed the combined force that Houston was not coming to the Alamo's aid. Nevertheless, he would have told them that additional men were forming at Gonzales and that Major Williamson was probably en route with more men as they talked. Chenoweth and De Sauque would have told Crockett that Fannin would join Williamson's force, provided Fannin received timely notice. That is, if he was not engaged with another Mexican force at Goliad.[78]

Eleventh Day — Friday, March 4

Sometime before daylight, part of the combined force broke through the enemy perimeter and entered the Alamo. The Texians appear to have approached, like the March 1 group, from upriver of the Alamo, near the sugarcane mills. As with the first unit, the force did not go undetected. In 1838 Bennett McNelly, former second sergeant of Breece's Greys company, put it this way: "...on the 4th [March] was driven across the prairie by enemy...." The exact number of men who made it into the Alamo is unknown. The *Arkansas Gazette* of April 12, 1836, however, reported: "Col. Crockett, with about 50 resolute volunteers, had cut their way into the garrison, through the Mexican troops only a few days before the fall of San Antonio." Word of the reinforcement reached Goliad by March 10. Joseph B. Tatom wrote his sister about the Alamo, reporting: "...I believe they have been reinforced by about fifty militia...."[79]

Again, the Mexicans did not know exactly what had occurred. Colonel Almonte's journal only contains a simple note: "The enemy attempted a sally in the night at the Sugar Mill, but were repulsed by our advance." It appears that Almonte believed that the "enemy" came from the Alamo. That makes no sense. There would have been no reason for men from the Alamo to have gone on a mission to the mills during the night. General Filisola, writing many years later, appears to have confused the second relief with the March 1 entry. He wrote: "...32 people of the Town of Gonzalez who under the cover of darkness joined the group two days before the attack on the fort...." His date for Crockett's group is exactly right, but the number is wrong.[80]

Historians, however, might argue that a reporter in Arkansas could not have known about a reinforcement of the Alamo. Regardless, the paper's source for Crockett leading the men into the Alamo appears to have been Jesse B. Badgett, one of the Alamo's convention delegates. But how would Badgett have learned of the relief? Badgett's source for the information would most likely have been his brother, William Badgett, a member of Chenoweth's company, who appears to have taken part in the March 4 reinforcement. At first it was believed that William had been killed at the Alamo. Jesse, however, informed the *Arkansas Advocate*, the *Gazette's* competitor, that William had not been killed and that as of March 20, he was with Houston's army on the Colorado River.[81]

Conclusive identification of all the men who entered the Alamo with Crockett that morning is probably impossible. Still, evidence exists for the following men.

Former New Orleans Greys from Breece's company:[82]

George Andrews	Henry Thomas
Robert B. Moore	William Howell
Thomas P. Hutchinson	John Spratt
James Holloway	Stephen Dennison
Conrad Eigenauer	Henry Courtman

Chenoweth's United States Invincibles:[83]

W. A. Moore	Dr. E. F. Mitchusson
Thomas H. Roberts	W. T. Green
W. H. Sanders	J. D. Elliott
A. A. Petrasweiz	William Hunter
N. Debichi	L. R. O'Neil
S. W. McNeilly	M. B. Clark

Samuel M. Edwards
Gonzales Mounted Rangers:[84]

George B. Kimbell	Thomas R. Jackson
James Taylor	Edward Taylor
William Taylor	Andrew J. Kent
Jacob Darst	George W. Cottle
Galba Fuqua	John Gaston
William George	James George
Freeman H. K. Day	

Mina (Bastrop) Mounted Rangers:[85]

Robert E. Cochran	Lemuel Crawford
James Kenny	James Northcross
Charles S. Smith	James E. Stewart
Ross McClelland	

Juan N. Seguin's men:[86]

Juan Abamillo	Juan A. Badillo
Damacio Ximenes	Andres Nava
Guadalupe Rodriquez	

William Gilmore's Tennessee Volunteer unit:[87]

John M. Thomson	George Olamio

Miscellaneous Fannin men:[88]

Edward Mcafferty	Francis H. Gray
Edwin T. Mitchell	

The total is fifty-three men. The roster may contain a few errors and may not include all of the men who entered the Alamo with Crockett on the morning of March 4, 1836. Still, there is at least one piece of primary evidence that puts each man in the Alamo or strongly suggests each man was an Alamo defender.

The reinforcement was only partially successful in that perhaps only about one-third of the combined force made it into the Alamo. That result appears to have convinced the remaining men that the enemy line around the Alamo was too strong for their small force to break through. Also, they probably had a few wounded men. The force, however, seems to have remained in the area. They most likely returned to the Cibolo ford on the Gonzales road to await the arrival of additional men from Gonzales and Goliad.[89]

In probably late afternoon, Santa Anna met with his generals, battalion colonels, and one major. The group discussed the commander-in-chief's plan for the final assault of the Alamo.[90] Almonte later wrote: "A meeting of Generals and Colonels was held...After a long conference [Martin Perfecto] Cos, [Manuel F.] Castrillon, Orisnuela [Gregorio Urunuela], and [Jose Maria] Romero were of the opinion that the Alamo should be assaulted – first opening a breach with the two cannon of _____ and the two mortars, and that they should wait the arrival of the two 12 pounders expected on Monday the seventh. The President, Gen. Ramirez [y Sesma], and I were of the opinion that the 12 pounders should not be waited for, but the assault made. Colonels [Francisco] Duque and [Agustin] Amat, and the Major of the San Luis battalion did not give any definite opinion about either of the two modes of assault proposed. In this state things remained – the General not making any definite resolution."[91]

Travis may have also met with his officers that afternoon. As least they would have had much to consider. The large compound was encircled by almost 2,400 enemy soldiers, comprised of about 2,000 footsoldiers and artillerymen and about 380 horsemen. Major Williamson and Fannin should have arrived with a large force by that time, but they were nowhere to be seen.[92]

During the night, Santa Anna had the third and last Mexican artillery battery installed north of the Alamo. Lieutenant Ignacio Berrospe, an engineer officer, supervised the construction. The fortification was put in place to hammer the Alamo's north wall for the final assault.[93]

Sometime that evening, John W. Smith left the Alamo for the last time. He rode east, probably to locate what remained of the combined force. If he found them, their officers probably told him they would not attempt to enter the Alamo without additional men. Getting killed while trying to enter the fortress would not have helped Travis and his men. Regardless of what may or may not have happened at the Cibolo ford, Smith continued on to Gonzales to search for help.[94]

There were men at Gonzales but not many. Captain Jesse Billingsly arrived sometime during the day with his company of Mina Volunteers. Lt. Colonel James C. Neill had arrived sometime after March 1 and had assumed command of all the troops at that settlement. The town had two bronze cannon, a four-pounder and a six-pounder, guns that had been captured at the storming of Bexar in December 1835. Neill had the guns mounted on carriages made from the front and back wheels of a cotton wagon. Also, he collected provisions, equipment, clothing, and medicine for the ride to the Alamo.[95]

Also, at Gonzales that day, Travis's letters of March 3 and a missive from Crockett calling for assistance were most likely given to a courier to take to San Felipe and Washington-on-the-Brazos. The rider was William Bull, who was paid five dollars by Joseph D. Clements, a Gonzales resident, to deliver the express mail.[96]

Twelfth Day — Saturday, March 5

At San Antonio Colonel Almonte reported that the day was clear and moderate with a thermometer reading of fifty degrees. Ideal weather for the heavy labor of working hot cannon. He continued in his diary: "A brisk fire was commenced from our north battery against the enemy, which was not answered, except now and then." At high noon the temperature was almost seventy degrees.[97]

Sometime that day, perhaps in the morning, Ben Highsmith arrived from Goliad. He later reported that as he approached the Alamo he saw that it was circled by cavalrymen "...on the look out for messengers whom they knew the Texan commander was sending from the doomed fort." Highsmith, seeing that he had no chance to join Travis, departed for Gonzales. The enemy, however, saw the young Texian and pursued him. The chase continued for six miles—two miles beyond Salado Creek. Young Ben, who must have been riding an extremely strong and fast horse, escaped his pursuers.[98]

In the afternoon Santa Anna called his senior officers together. The Mexican general had made a decision about the Alamo. At 2:00 p.m. he issued "secret" attack orders to the "Generals, Chiefs of Sections, and Commanding Officers." The assault was to be conducted by four separate columns from the north, south, east, and west. The attack was to take place the following morning just before daylight in order to catch the Alamo defenders by surprise, when their sleep was the most sound.[99]

Santa Anna's secret plan was soon compromised to some extent. That evening Angel Navarro crossed the river and approached the Alamo. He requested that Juana Alsbury and Gertrudis Navarro, his daughters, be allowed to leave the compound. Undoubtedly, Navarro's appeal made Travis realize that a major assault on the fort would soon take place. Thus, he took advantage of the opportunity to send a message out with Mrs. Alsbury, who went out to talk with her father. Little valid evidence of this incident has survived.[100] General Filisola, however, left this description: "On that same evening about nightfall it was reported that Travis Barnet [*sic*], commander of the enemy garrison, through the intermediary of a woman, proposed to the general in chief that they would surrender arms and fort with everybody in it with the only condition of saving his life and that of all his comrades in arms. However, the answer had come back that they should surrender unconditionally, without guarantees, not even of life itself, since there should be no guarantees for traitors. With this reply it is clear that all were determined to lose their existence, selling it as dearly as possible. Consequently they were to exercise extreme vigilance in order not to be surprised at any time of the day or night." Mrs. Alsbury, after hearing from Santa Anna or his representative, returned to the Alamo.[101]

Later that night the last courier from the Alamo left for Goliad. The rider was a young man named James L. Allen. Allegedly, he was selected because he had a "fleet mare." Yet, he had no saddle. He rode bareback "with his arms about the animal's neck and bending low the better to conceal himself...." Apparently, he passed through the enemy lines unnoticed because of their preparation for the final attack on the Alamo. Allen would later tell Fannin that the Mexicans had erected an artillery battery four hundred yards from the Alamo and that "every shot goes through the walls."[102]

The Mexican artillery remained quiet that night. Thus, the people in the Alamo obtained some much-needed sleep. The defenders, sleeping or not, probably knew that an attack, a fatal one, could occur at any time. Travis's men would have been doing everything possible to repair the damage to the north wall, which was most likely nothing more than shoring up the interior side with a dirt embankment. Also, given the cannonball pounding the north wall had been taking, Travis would have realized that the main thrust of the attack would be at that point. Thus, he most likely shifted weapons, ammunition, and men to positions that would allow them to react quickly to wherever they were needed.[103]

That afternoon or evening John W. Smith would have arrived at Gonzales. The force there had not grown much larger. Besides Billingsly's company, Sidney Sherman had arrived with a company of American volunteers from Kentucky. Moseley Baker's San Felipe company of foot soon joined the Gonzales force.[104]

The Last Day — Sunday, March 6

At about a half-hour before daylight, Santa Anna's soldiers, with rockets bursting in the dark sky to signal the assault, stormed the Alamo fortress from the south, the north, the west, and the east with a force of about 1,500 men. Ramirez y Sesma, with part of the Dolores cavalry, was stationed in the *alameda* (cottonwood grove) about a hundred yards southeast of the Alamo. Colonel Ventura Mora, with the rest of the cavalry, was stationed north of the Alamo, probably near the Mexican artillery battery.[105]

In a brief description, Colonel Almonte reported: "At 5 A.M. the columns were posted at their respective stations, and at half past 5 the attack or assault was made, and continued until 6 A.M. When the enemy attempted in vain to fly, they were over taken and put to the sword, and only five women, one Mexican soldier (prisoner,) and a black slave escaped from instant death. On the part of the enemy the result was, 250 killed, 17 pieces of artillery – a flag; muskets and fire arms taken. Our loss was 60 soldiers and 5 officers killed, and 198 soldiers and 25 officers wounded – 2 of the latter General officers. The battalion of Toluca lost 98 between the wounded and killed."[106]

Sam Bastian and his comrades appear to have watched the final assault from their hiding place northwest of the Alamo. Bastian reported: "Disguising myself, and in company with Rigault, the creole, we stole into the town. Everything was in confusion. In front of the fort the Mexican dead covered the ground, but the scene inside was awful." After they had completed their dangerous visit, Bastian claimed: "We now thought it time to look after ourselves, and made for the chaparral, where our companions were [waiting]. We had nearly reached the wood when a mounted lancer overtook us. Rigault awaited and shot him dead, and so we made our escape." Ultimately, these men appear to have fallen back to Gonzales.[107]

The remaining members of the combined force that camped at or near the Cibolo Creek ford on the Gonzales road also realized the Alamo had fallen. Some of these men retreated to Gonzales, arriving on March 8. Others appear to have joined Fannin at Goliad. Juan Seguin may have sent a part of his Tejano company to his ranch and the Flores ranch on the San Antonio River to evacuate their families to Nacogdoches. Seguin and his remaining men then rode to Gonzales with John Chenoweth and Francis De Sauque.[108]

Cibolo Creek ford on the Gonzales/San Antonio road
and author's good friend Donald Hoffman

Aftermath

On March 7, probably in the morning, John W. Smith, unaware that the Alamo had fallen, departed Gonzales with fifty volunteers to return to the Alamo. The force seems to have ridden to Bexar on the upper road, which was also known as the "Mill" road. That route ran northwest from Gonzales, then southwest to San Antonio, through the area that became the town of Seguin, Texas.[109]

The Gonzales-bound element of the combined force, under command of Chenoweth, De Sauque, and Seguin, arrived at that settlement on March 8.[110]

Two men from the combined relief group appear to have ridden northeast from San Antonio to Nacogdoches. The March 29, 1836 issue of the *Arkansas Gazette* carried this report:

> San Antonio retaken, and the Garrison massacred. – Just as our paper was ready for press, a gentleman who arrived this morning, from Red River, informs us, that, on Thursday night last [March 24], he spent the night, on the Little Missouri, with a man and his family, who had fled from the vicinity of San Antonio after that post was besieged by the Mexicans. This man, he says, informed him, that on his arrival at Nacogdoches, he was overtaken by two men (one of them badly wounded), who informed him that San Antonio was retaken by the Mexicans, and the garrison put to the sword – that if any others escaped the general massacre, besides themselves, they were not aware of it.[111]

While it may appear that these two men survived the fall of the Alamo as members of the garrison, one must remember that those men who attempted to enter the Alamo and failed were also participants in the fight for the Alamo. Perhaps the men were in the Alamo. Still, given that one man was seriously wounded, a March 6 escape from the Alamo, which was surrounded by Mexican horsemen, seems unlikely. The two survivors had most likely participated in the March 4 reinforcement of the Alamo. As for their identities, time has yet to reveal that secret. There are, however, two possibilities, Louis and Stephen Rose, which will be discussed in a following chapter.

History reports that the citizens of Gonzales did not learn of the Alamo's fall until Anselmo Bergara and Andres Barcena arrived at Gonzales at 4:00 p.m. on March 11. In reality, Bergara and Barcena probably only confirmed what surviving members of the failed relief had already told Lt. Colonel Neill and the people of Gonzales. Undoubtedly, citizens started departing the area on March 9. John G. King, a member of the combined relief force whose son William P. King had entered the Alamo with one of the reinforcements, immediately packed up his family and headed east. On March 10 he was near Peach Creek, about ten miles east of Gonzales.[112]

On the night of March 8 or in the early morning hours of March 9, John W. Smith and his volunteers approached Bexar from its west side. One of Smith's men was Connel O'Donnel Kelly, who had escaped General Jose C. Urrea's soldiers at San Patricio.[113] He described the last relief attempt of the Alamo: "I joined Moseley Baker's company [at San Felipe]; went to Gonzales, where volunteers were called to go to the assistance of Travis, and volunteered as one to go; went to the Leon [Creek], where we saw about one thousand Mexican camp fires, when they, the Mexicans, opened fire on us, and our party being too small, retreated to the Cibolo, under Capt. [John] W. Smith, where we remained but a short time, and returned to Gonzales, [March 11] where Gen. Sam Houston had just arrived from Washington...our captain [Smith] informed him that the Alamo had fallen."[114]

Thus ended the reinforcement of the Alamo. In the end eighty-two or more men had entered the mission fortress as reinforcements during the thirteen-day siege. Those brave men were neither suicidal nor stupid. The first thirty, members of the Gonzales ranger company, entered the Alamo thinking that many more men would soon join them under the leadership of General Sam Houston. The fifty-two that David Crockett apparently guided through Mexican lines probably believed that a large force under the command of Major Williamson and Colonel Fannin would soon join them in the Alamo.

Few of the reinforcement survivors ever wrote of the relief action. Undoubtedly, some felt great guilt because their friends had died and they had lived. Thus, the painful event was best repressed. Others were probably ashamed of their failure to save Travis and his men. For many the Alamo was a tragic failure best forgotten after the San Jacinto victory. Then others may have been afraid they would be branded as cowards for not having made it into the Alamo to die. Such a view may be hard for many to understand from the comfort of the twenty-first century, but after the fall of the Alamo, Charles and Tom Turner learned the hard way. In September 1836 Tom wrote their mother of their Alamo experience:

> You have no doubt heard of the troubles of late in Texas. Believe me when I say that Charles and I was not involved in any of it. By not fighting, we have opened the door to the people's verbal attacks. We find it difficult to get even a Small amount of kindness from them people. It is hard to fight for Something that you do not believe in. When those men fought at the Alamo (Bejar), Charles and I was to leave and help them but did not. By the time we started to leave, it was all over for them. I think that God must have saved our lives that Day. Are we to blame? Who would think that Texas could win? If Texas can keep what she had won, in later years, people will remember me as a coward, and call useless dying an Act of glory. We will be home year next...."[115]

Turner's missive clearly defined his situation. As he said, the difference between the Alamo defenders and the Turner brothers was a belief—the idea that there could be an independent Texas for which the defenders were willing to die. Still, the collective death of the Alamo defenders was not some kind of suicide compact as portrayed in the "Moses Rose" tale of Travis drawing a line in the dirt and asking his men to cross and die a glorious death with him. The Alamo garrison had been ordered by their government on January 31, 1836, "...in no case to abandon or surrender the place unless in the last extremity." As with all good soldiers, Travis, Bowie, Crockett, and all their men obeyed that order until the evening of March 5 when it became clear that the "last extremity" was fast approaching.[116]

Abandoning the fort, however, was impossible and time had run out. The defenders could only look to the east and wait. Susanna Dickinson summed up their situation with these words: "The enemy gradually approached by means of earth works.... Besieged were looking for reinforcements which never arrived." In the end, the men of the Alamo, with the combat assistance of one black woman and a number of teenage boys, marched into the "last extremity" with the courage of their fathers and grandfathers who had fought and died to create the United States of

America. Nevertheless, they probably would have preferred to be home in their warm beds, but that was not their fate that morning.[117]

Susanna Dickinson, ca. 1850s
Photo courtesy of Archives Division — Texas State Library

Chapter Four Notes

1 Williamson to Travis, March 1, 1836.

2 Stephen F. Austin circular, September 18, 1835, San Felipe, Jenkins, ed., *Papers*, I: 455-456; Stephen F. Austin to Consultation, October 10, 1835, Gonzales, Jenkins, ed., *Papers*, II: 81-82; William T. Austin, "Account of the Campaign of 1835 by William T. Austin, Aide to Gen. Stephen F. Austin & Gen. Ed. Burleson," *Texana*, IV: 300-302.

3 D. C. Barrett et al. to James W. Robinson, February 15, 1836, San Felipe, Jenkins, ed., *Papers*, IV: 340-341; D. C. Barrett and J. D. Clements to James W. Robinson, February 15, 1836, San Felipe, Jenkins, ed., *Papers*, IV: 341-342; Stephen F. Austin to Provisional Government, December 22, 1835, Velasco, Jenkins, ed., *Papers*, III: 284-286; Stephen F. Austin to R. R. Royal, December 25, 1835, Quintana, Jenkins, ed., *Papers*, III: 315-317; Houston to Smith, January 17, 1836; Henry Smith to Sam Houston, December 17, 1835, San Felipe, Jenkins, ed., *Papers*, III: 239-240; Sam Houston to James Bowie, December 17, 1835, San Felipe, Jenkins, ed., *Papers*, III: 222-223; Citizens' and Soldiers' Meeting [at San Antonio], January 2, 1836, Bexar, Jenkins, ed., *Papers*, IV: 153-155; Sam Houston to John Forbes, January 7, 1836, Washington-on-the-Brazos, Jenkins, ed., *Papers*, III: 436-437; Sam Houston to James Bowie, January 10, 1836, north of Goliad, in Yoakum, *History*, II: 57-58; Henry Smith to William Bryan, February 5, 1836, San Felipe, Jenkins, ed., *Papers*, IV: 268-269; Napoleon, "Military Maxims of Napoleon," in General T. R. Phillips, ed., *Roots of Strategy* (Harrisburg, Penn.: Stackpole Books, 1985), 413 and 227.

4 Travis to Smith, January 28, 1836.

5 Smith to Bryan, February 5, 1836.

6 D. C. Barrett et al. to James W. Robinson, January 31, 1836, San Felipe, Jenkins, ed., *Papers*, IV: 204-205.

7 Ibid.

8 Abbotts to Steele, January 2, 1876; Abbotts to Johnson, April 3, 1880.

9 Lucy A. Erath, ed., *The Battle of San Jacinto* (Houston: The Union National Bank, 1936), 7.

10 Baker to Houston, October 1842, Evergreen.

11 Almonte, "Private Journal," 19; Muster roll for the Second Company Permanent of Tamanlipas, October 1, 1835, Box 2S319, Bexar Archives, CAH. In this account the Menchaca name is misspelled as Menchacho.

12 Fannin to De Sauque and Chenoweth, March 1, 1836; F. Hord to J. P. Borden, May 17, 1839, Box 2-10/2, General Land Office Correspondence, TSL; De la Teja, *A Revolution Remembered,* 79. The arrival time at the Seguin ranch is an estimate based on when Chenoweth and De Sauque departed Goliad. Given that collection of the livestock and provisions at the

Seguin ranch most likely took most the day, Chenoweth and De Sauque probably had scouts north of the ranch watching the Bexar road for any approach of the enemy. Thus, the Texians probably detected the approach of Lieutenant Manchaca and the Mexican troops. Manchaca, after his arrival at the ranch, may have learned of the Texians' mission. Whatever the situation was at the ranch, there is no evidence that Texians encountered Menchaca's detachment.

13   "A List of Votes taken at an Election held on the lst day of February 1835 [1836] for the purpose of Electing two Delegates...," February 1, 1836, Gonzales, Election Returns, TSL; Alamo List (Gonzales men) in *Telegraph and Texas Register,* (San Felipe) March 24, 1836; Bennet, "The Battle of Gonzales, the 'Lexington' of the Texas Revolution," II: 314; James Taylor and Edward Taylor affidavit (copy), March 3, 1836, Cibolo Creek and J. C. Taylor affidavit (copy), September 6, 1890, Deed Records, Vol. 10: 203, Montgomery County Records, Conroe, Texas; George Taylor affidavit, February 2, 1836, and J. C. Taylor affidavit, August 7, 1890, Deed Record E, Somervell County Records, Granbury, Texas; James Taylor, Edward Taylor and William Taylor affidavit (copy), March 3, 1836, Cibolo Creek, and J. C. Taylor affidavit (copy) August 7, 1890, Deed Records, Vol. 19: 596, Liberty County Records, Liberty, Texas; Petition pertaining to the deaths of brothers James and William George at the Alamo, n.d., Bexar, and Interrogation of Benjamin McCulloch, n.d., Bexar, Court of Claims file, C-3103, GLO; Samuel Bastian account, n.d. but circa 1887-92, in John Henry Brown, *Indian Wars and Pioneers of Texas* (Austin: L. E. Daniel, 1896), 138.

The Taylor documents place the Taylors and David Crockett on the Cibolo Ceek on March 3, 1836, in a ranger company described as being with Fannin's command.

William George is not listed on the official Alamo list of defenders. The evidence for his Alamo death, however, is as good as the evidence the Daughters of the Republic of Texas officials accepted for Damacio Jimenes, the last addition to the list.

Ben McCulloch's answers to the interrogation about James and William George cannot be located. Still, the fact that the children of James George asked McCulloch to verify that their father and uncle had died at the Alamo suggests that McCulloch was part of the company. Otherwise, how would he have been in a position to have known that James and William George died at the Alamo.

Clearly, there were other men who joined the Gonzales company, but their names are currently lost to history. For example, Benjamin Kellogg was probably part of the reinforcement but did not enter the Alamo or die in the attempt.

14   G. C. Kimbell to Stephen Smith, February 27, 1836, Stephen Smith file, AMC-TSL.

15   Foote, *Texas and The Texians,* II: 225; Seguin, *Personal Memoirs,* 9.

16   James W. Fannin Jr. to James W. Robinson, January 28 [27], 1836, Goliad, Jenkins, ed., *Papers*, IV: 455-456. This document appears to be a second version of Fannin's letter to Robinson. The first version is found in *Papers*, IV: 443-444. Based on content analysis of both documents, it appears that they are incorrectly dated February 28, 1836.

17   Almonte, "Private Journal," 19.

18   Fannin to Robinson, February 27, 1836, second version of this letter.

19   Henry Smith to Public, February 27, 1836, San Felipe, Jenkins, ed., *Papers*, IV: 450.

20   Thomson and Pattillo to Robinson, February 26, 1836; Burleson affidavit, February 29, 1836. That the San Felipe rider arrived at Mina on February 27 is based on the fact that the order for sending Tumlinson's company to the Alamo was written on February 26, and the ride from San Felipe to Mina could have been made in twenty-four hours or less.

21   William F. Fisher statement in regard to J. J. Tumlinson's ranger service, February 27, 1837, Columbia, J. J. Tumlinson file, AMC-TSL; James P. Gorman file, PC-TSL; J. P. Gorman to Mrs. J. B. Robertson, May 11, 1873, Bastrop, Texas Veterans Association Papers, Box 2H119, CAH; J. J. Tumlinson affidavit, Hugh M. Childress file, AMC-TSL; J. J. Tumlinson affidavit, July 12, 1836, location not given, James Curtis Sr., file, AMC-TSL; J. J. Tumlinson affidavit, July 25, 1836, James Curtis Jr., file, AMC-TSL; J. J. Tumlinson affidavit, April 17, 1836, Gany Crosby file, AMC-TSL; J. J. Tumlinson affidavit, April 27, 1836, Joshua Gray file, AMC-TSL; J. J. Tumlinson affidavit, April 16, 1836, Thomas Gray file, AMC-TSL; J. J. Tumlinson affidavit, May 17, 1836, Novet Haggard file, AMC-TSL; J. J. Tumlinson affidavit, April 27, 1836, James Haggard file, AMC-TSL; J. J. Tumlinson affidavit, June 6, 1836, William Leech file, AMC-TSL; R. M. Coleman affidavit, Andrew Dunn file, AMC-TSL; L. W. Alexander to Edward Clark, La Grange, June 2, 1858, L. W. Alexander file, Unpaid Claims Collection, TSL; J. J. Tumlinson affidavit, April 25, 1836, Joseph Cottle file, AMC-TSL; J. J. Tumlinson affidavit, n.d., Joseph Weakes file, AMC-TSL; J. J. Tumlinson affidavit, April 17, 1838, Houston, Robert Owen file, AMC-TSL; William Johnson file, PC-TSL; Felix W. Goff file, PC-TSL; Erath, "Memoirs of Major George Bernard Erath," 231; Merrett and Saul statement, July 1838; J. J. Tumlinson listings on the Republic of Texas Claims Name Index, TSL; Alamo voting list, February 1, 1836.

The Republic of Texas Claims Name Index lists A. R. Bowen, George M. Kerby, Flood McGrew, James Edmunson, and Henry P. Redfield as members of Tumlinson's ranger company. This investigator, however, was not able to determine when these men served in the company because the records are not available to the public at this time. Thus, it is possible that some of the men participated in the Alamo reinforcement.

The names of Bastrop Alamo defenders Robert E. Crochran, Lemuel Crawford, James Kenny, James Northcross, Charles S. Smith, Ross McClelland, and James E. Stewart do not appear on the February 1, 1836, voting list, making it appear that they entered the fort after that date. Thus, they appear to have been members of the Tumlinson ranger unit.

The departure date and time for the Mina rangers is speculation based on the fact that the company was already organized and would have wasted no time in riding to Gonzales.

22 Almonte, "Private Journal," 19; Santa Anna to Vicente Filisola, February 27, 1836, Bexar, Jenkins, ed., *Papers,* IV: 447-449.

23 Almonte, "Private Journal," 19.

24 "Ben Highsmith account" in Sowell, *Early Settlers,* 9-10; Captain A. J. Sowell, "Frontier Days of Texas: Pathetic Incidents of the Battle of the Alamo – The Losing of the Little Cannon that Brought on the Texas Revolution," *The San Antonio Light,* August 18, 1912; Seguin to Fontaine, June 7, 1890; [Letter from Gonzales about reinforcement of the Alamo], *Telegraph and Texas Register,* San Felipe, March 5, 1836; Sutherland, "The Fall of the Alamo," Williams Papers, CAH; Seguin, *Personal Memoirs,* 9; Williamson to Travis, March 1, 1836; "A list of the Gonzales Ranging Company," February 23, 1836; Colonel Edwin Morehouse affidavit concerning John Ballard's service in the Gonzales ranger company, May 24, 1836, John Ballard file, AMC-TSL.

This investigator's belief that the Tumlinson unit joined the Gonzales rangers at Gonzales and rode to Bexar with them is based on three pieces of evidence. First, Major R. M. Williamson claimed that as of March 1, 1836, sixty men had left Gonzales for the Alamo. Second, the Gonzales rangers muster roll indicates they did not have sixty men. Third, the Morehouse affidavit shows the Tumlinson company was outside of San Antonio on March first.

Highsmith reported that: "David Crockett went into the Alamo with George Kimble, A. J. Kent, Abe Darst, Tom Jackson, Tom Mitchell, Wash Cottle, and two 16-year-old boys named Albert Fuqua and John Gaston." Mitchell was Edwin T. Mitchell, a member of Fannin's command at Goliad, who had been sent to Gonzales as a courier. Crockett was in the Alamo on the morning of March 1 when the first relief group from Gonzales entered the Alamo. He, however, was out of the Alamo on March 3 on the Cibolo Creek, twenty miles east of the Alamo. Thus, it appears that Kimbell and the other men did not enter the Alamo on March 1, but rather on a later date. That a council of war was conducted at Gonzales is speculation. However, given the situation, it would have been a reasonable action on the part of Williamson and the other officers.

25 McComb to _____, October 5, 1835, Gonzales, Jenkins, ed., *Papers,* II: 48; R. F. Hord to J. P. Borden, May 17, 1839, Box 2-10/2, General Land Office Correspondence, TSL.

26 Seguin, *Personal Memoirs,* 9; Seguin to Fontaine, June 7, 1890. Seguin also said that Fannin ordered him to fall back to Gonzales where General Sam Houston was located. At that time Houston was on the road to Washington-on-the-Brazos from Nacogdoches. Also, in his *Memoirs,* Seguin claimed

that he had been sent to Goliad, not Gonzales. In that case, Seguin does not appear to be telling the truth. Seguin, however, made it clear in his letter to Fontaine that he had been sent to Gonzales and that he played a part in getting reinforcements to the Alamo. The complete identity of Finley is unknown at this time.

27 Erasmo Seguin affidavit, November 9, 1839.

28 John S. Brooks to Mother, March 2, 1836, Goliad, Jenkins, ed., *Papers,* IV: 485-486.

29 Dimmtt to Kerr, February 28, 1836.

30 John A. Wharton to Citizens of Brazoria, February 28, 1836, San Felipe, Jenkins, ed., *Papers,* IV: 458; Moseley Baker to Gail Bordon, February 29, 1836, San Felipe, Jenkins, ed., *Papers,* IV: 460; J. C. Neill to Henry Smith, February 28, 1836, James C. Neill Papers, Daughters of the Republic of Texas Library; Moseley Baker to John R. Jones et al., March 8, 1836, Gonzales, Jenkins, ed., *Papers,* V: 22-23.

31 Gray, *From Virginia,* 120.

32 Ibid., 121; "'Old Setter' Two Chapters on Political Quackery with Especial Reference to Sam Houston," 1844, *The Papers of Mirabeau Buonaparte Lamar,* IV: 64. The anonymous writer of the Lamar document reported that Houston's main concern during the convention was obtaining land titles for the Texas Cherokee and obtaining military assistance from the Cherokee. Houston was not that popular with the colonists. He obtained his military positions through the political process—first, the Consultation; second, the Convention. Whereas, Stephen F. Austin and most of the other military leaders of the revolution obtained their command positions by being elected by the men they commanded.

After Texas independence was declared on March 2, Houston reported that March 2 was his birthday. There is, however, no other source that verifies March 2 was actually Houston's date of birth.

On the other hand, there is one piece of evidence that indicates that Houston's birthday was not March 2, 1793. In Haley, *Sam Houston,* 90, we learn that in September 1832, before going to Texas, Houston picked up a United States passport that described him as "General Samuel Houston, a Citizen of the United States, Thirty-eight years of age, Six feet, two inches in stature, brown hair and light complexion." If Houston's birthday had been March 2, 1793, he would have been thirty-nine in September 1832, not thirty-eight as listed on the passport.

33 Travis to Convention, March 3, 1836; Joaquin Ramirez y Sesma to Santa Anna, March 15, 1836, Cibolo Creek, Jenkins, ed., *Papers,* V: 85; "Connel O'Donnel Kelly" account in James M. Day, compiler, *The Texas Almanac 1857-1873: A Compendium of Texas History* (Waco: Texian Press, 1967), 600; Morehouse affidavit, May 24, 1836; Sowell, *Early Settlers,* 9-10.

That Smith and Martin used the Gonzales road route to the Alamo is speculation based on these sources. After the fall of the Alamo, when

Ramirez y Sesma arrived at the Cibolo ford on his way to Gonzales, he made note of the evidence he saw that indicated a large number of men had been at the Cibolo ford in recent days.

Ballard attempted to enter the Alamo with Martin and Smith but failed to do so. On March 1, 1836, he joined Tumlinson's unit. Travis, in his March 3 letter, mentioned that only men from Gonzales got into the Alamo. Thus, it appears the Tumlinson rangers remained at the Cibolo to wait on Fannin's force. Ben Highsmith identified Kimbell, Jackson, Kent, Darst, Mitchell, Cottle, Fuqua, and Gaston as having entered the Alamo with David Crockett. Other evidence shows that Crockett left the Alamo as a scout and returned on the night of March 3. Thus, the men listed by Highsmith do not appear to have entered the Alamo with the March 1 group.

34 Burleson affidavit, February 29, 1836; Michael Sessum file, PC-TSL; David Haldeman affidavit, March 1, 1882, David Haldeman file, RV 1091, GLO; Kesselus, *Bastrop County Before Statehood*, 170-171.

35 Samuel Bastian interview, Brown, *Indian Wars*, 138.

36 Almonte, "Private Journal," 19; Filisola, *Memoirs*, II: 172-173; Santa Anna to Joaquin Ramirez y Sesma, February 29, 1836, Bexar, Jenkins, ed., *Papers*, IV: 469. For some unknown reason, Almonte identified the Jimenez battalion as the Allende battalion, a unit for which there is no other evidence to show it was in San Antonio at that time.

37 Travis to Convention, March 3, 1836; Sowell, *Early Settlers*, 9-10; Almonte, "Private Journal," 19-20.

Santa Anna, clearly aware of and concerned about the reinforcement's entry route, inspected the sugar mill site at high noon on March 1.

General Filisola, in *Memoirs*, II: 81, described the area: "To the North, between the San Antonio River and Alamo creek, the settled part of the city of Bexar extends as far as eight hundred varas [a vara is thirty-three and one third inches] along a collection of streets made up of mud huts, the framework of which is of wood, and it ends in some sugarcane fields where there are two small sugar mills called Zambrano and Garza."

38 Ibid.; Morehouse affidavit, May 24, 1836; Bastian interview, Brown, *Indian Wars*, 137-138. A "norther" is a Canadian cold front that blows into Texas from the north.

39 Bastian interview, Brown, *Indian Wars*, 138; Morehouse affidavit, May 24, 1836; Travis to the Convention, March 3, 1836.

40 Gray, *From Virginia*, 121; Almonte, "Private Journal," 19.

41 Almonte, "Private Journal," 17 and 19; Caro, "A True Account of the First Texas Campaign" in Castaneda, trans. and ed., *The Mexican Side*, 104; Susanna (Dickinson) Belles affidavit, December 9, 1850, Houston, David P. Cummings file, C-1936, Court of Claims collection, GLO; Filisola, *Memoirs*, II: 178.

Caro's group of four that entered the Alamo at night were probably from the Martin and Smith reinforcement of March 1. The Mexicans most likely only saw four men because of the darkness. The daytime group of twenty-five men were probably Alamo soldiers who had been scouting for headright sites on the Cibolo. According to Susanna Dickinson, Travis sent a courier out to locate and bring those men back to the Alamo. Almonte reported that during the night of February 24 thirty men from Gonzales entered the Alamo. Given that the Alamo soldiers who had been on the Cibolo would have approached the city from the east, the Mexicans probably assumed they had come from Gonzales, when in fact they had been on the Cibolo.

42 Williamson to Travis, March 1, 1836; Fannin to De Sauque and Chenoweth, March 1, 1836.

43 Sowell, *Early Settlers*, 9-10; "List of Men who have this day volunteered to remain before Bexar," November 24, 1835, Bexar, Austin Papers, CAH; "Colonel J. C. Neill's Alamo Return," Ca. December 31, 1835, Bexar, Muster Rolls book, 20; Alamo voting list, February 1, 1836. That Highsmith left at the time given in the narrative is speculation based on the data for the time frame that he detailed to Sowell. Highsmith is alleged to have taken part in the siege and storming of Bexar, and afterward joined the Alamo garrison. The name "_____ Highsmith" is listed as a member of R. M. Coleman's company on the list of men who volunteered to remain at Bexar on November 24, 1835. The name Highsmith does not appear on Neill's Alamo return of about December 31, 1835, or the February 1, 1836 Alamo voting list, which suggests that, like many soldiers, he returned to his home after the fall of Bexar on December 11, 1835.

44 Morehouse affidavit, May 24, 1836; Bastian interview, Brown, *Indian Wars*, 138. The location of the Texians on the west side of the San Antonio River is speculation based on the sources and period maps.

45 Almonte, "Private Journal," 19. A *tinaja* is a water hole in impervious rock.

46 De la Teja, *A Revolution Remembered*, 80 and 136, Appendix document 20; Hipolito Montoyo file, Jose Alemeda file, Juan Rodriquiz file, Philip Coe file, and Antonio Balle file, PC-TSL; Lucio Enriques file, Andres Barcenas file, Ignacio Guerra file, and Nepomuceno Flores file, AMC-TSL; Macedonio Arocha file, RV 951, GLO; Bexar bounty grant, 1238 and Bexar donation grant, 1161 and 1204 for Manuel Maria Flores, Archives, Texas General Land Office, Austin. Seguin never claimed that he organized his company from the San Antonio River ranches. However, when he reported to Sam Houston at Gonzales after the fall of the Alamo, Seguin had a twenty-five-member company of Tejanos. It is only logical that the unit was organized while Seguin was at the family ranch.

47 Ibid.

48 Barnes, "The Alamo's Only Survivor."

49 Ibid.; Petition to State of Texas for Pension for Andrea Castanon de Villanueva (Madame Candelaria), March 1889, and John S. Ford to Governor L. S. Ross, March 25, 1889, San Antonio, M & P-TSL; Candelario

Villanueva deposition, August 26, 1859, San Antonio, Timothy M. Matovina, *The Alamo Remembered: Tejano Accounts and Perspectives* (Austin: University of Texas Press, 1995), 35-36; Walter B. Stevens, *Through Texas – A Series of Interesting Letters* (St. Louis: St. Louis Globe-Democrat, 1892), 77. The Arocha that left the Alamo appears to have been Jose Maria Arocha. Macedonio Arocha joined Seguin's unit on March 1, 1836.

Most likely a definitive answer in regard to Madame Candelaria's presence in the Alamo during the siege will never be determined. Candelario Villanueva, her future husband, claimed in his Republic of Texas pension application that he had been a member of Seguin's company but was prevented from being in the Alamo because Seguin had sent him to "lock up" Seguin's house, and "whilst performing that duty Santa Anna's soldiers got between" him and the Alamo. If that statement is true, Madame Candlaria may have entered the Alamo while her "to-be" husband hurried to the Seguin home. Another possibility is that both entered the Alamo and departed with the other Bexar citizens during the siege. After all, it would have done little good for Seguin to have locked his home. Once Santa Anna learned that Seguin was in the Alamo, he would have had the house broken into by his troops.

The 1889 petition shows the signatures of a number of influential San Antonio citizens, including Mary Maverick, wife of Alamo delegate to the March 1 convention Samuel Maverick, John S. Ford, and Alamo custodian Tom Rife, who believed that the old woman had been in the Alamo. Rife, however, in 1892 denounced Candelaria as a liar, claiming that she had not been in the Alamo. Rife failed to explain what had caused him to change his mind about the woman.

Given the praise from San Antonio citizens found in an 1871 petition (same file as the 1889 petition) to the legislature, Candelaria appears to have been the Mother Theresa of San Antonio.

50 De la Teja, *A Revolution Remembered*, 79-80; Fannin to De Sauque and Chenoweth, March 1, 1836.

51 Nacogdoches Enlistments, Muster Roll book, 114-115; Forbes to Robinson, January 12, 1836, Nacogdoches, Jenkins, ed., *Papers,* III: 498; Townsend Receipt, February 9, 1836, San Felipe, Jenkins, ed., *Papers*, IV: 297; James W. Robinson to Sam Houston, February 14, 1836, San Felipe, Jenkins, ed., *Papers*, IV: 337; W. P. Grady petition, n.d., M & P-TSL; "Gilmore unit members agreement with Acting Governor Robinson and Council," [February 16, 1836?], Records of the Permanent Council, TSL.

52 "Gilmore unit members agreement," February 16, 1836.

53 Robinson to Houston, February 14, 1836.

54 James Gillespie to Thomas J. Rusk, May 29, 1836, Victoria, Jenkins, ed., *Papers*, VI: 407-408. Given that acting governor James W. Robinson had ordered all reinforcements to rendezvous at Gonzales, the Gilmore unit most likely traveled to San Antonio through Gonzales.

55 Lieutenant James B. Bonham Republic of Texas pay record, May 15, 1838, James B. Bonham file, AMC-TSL; Williamson to Travis, March 1, 1836; Thomas Ricks Lindley, "James Butler Bonham: October 17, 1835 - March 6, 1836," *The Alamo Journal*, August 1988.

    The Bonham pay document identifies Bonham as a "lieutenant of cavalry." Contrary to what many historians and writers believe, Travis did not send Bonham out as a courier during the February and March 1836 siege of the Alamo. Travis, on March 3, 1836, wrote: "Colonel Bonham, my special messenger, arrived at La Bahia fourteen days ago, with a request for aid, and on the arrival of the enemy in Bexar, ten days ago, I sent an express to Colonel F...." The rider sent to Goliad on February 23 appears to have been John Johnson.

56 Gray, *From Virginia*, 123-124.

57 Almonte, "Private Journal," 19-20.

58 Sowell, *Early Settlers*, 9-10; Brooks to Mother, March 2, 1836.

59 Brooks to Mother, March 2, 1836.

60 "Muster Roll, Captain Thomas H. Breece's Co."; Webb, Carroll, and Branda, eds., *Handbook*, II: 273; Brooks to Mother, March 2, 1836; Bennett McNelly petition, April 23, 1838, Houston, M & P-TSL.

61 Travis to Convention, March 3, 1836.

62 Williams to Travis, March 1, 1836.

63 Bonham Jr., "James Butler Bonham: A Consistent Rebel," 129.

64 The belief that the reinforcement force used this route is speculation. However, given the circumstances, it would have been the safest route to Cibolo ford on the San Antonio/Gonzales road. Second, it was the most direct route to join the ranger company from Bastrop. Lastly, with Santa Anna sending local militia units to obtain provisions from the Seguin and Flores ranches, riding on the Goliad/Bexar road would have been too dangerous.

65 The men were John W. Thomson and George Olamio. Thomson is on the current Alamo list. Olamio is not listed. See note 87 for more information on Olamio.

66 Sowell, *Early Settlers*, 9.

67 Almonte, "Private Journal," 20.

68 Travis to Convention, March 3, 1836.

69 Travis to Ponton, February 23, 1836; Thomas B. Rees to Gerard Burch, Goliad, March 8, 1836, Jenkins, ed., *Papers*, V: 28-29; B. H. Duval to William P. Duval, March 9, 1836, Goliad, Jenkins, ed., *Papers*, V: 33-34; Joseph B. Tatom to Sister, March 10, 1836, Goliad, Jenkins, ed., *Papers*, V: 44; John Cross to Brother and Sister, March 9, 1836, Goliad, John Cross papers, DRT Library; David P. Cummings to Father, February 14, 1836, San Antonio, Jenkins, ed., *Papers*, IV: 334; Susanna (Dickinson) Belles affidavit, December 9, 1850, Houston, David P. Cummings file, Court of Claims

records, C-001936, GLO.

Historians, in spite of Dickinson's claim that Travis had sent an express rider to get Cummings, continue to claim that Cummings returned to the Alamo with the first Gonzales reinforcement that entered the Alamo on March 1.

Colonel Juan N. Almonte, "Private Journal," 17, reported that thirty men from Gonzales entered the Alamo on the night of February 24. Given that the returning Cummings group would have entered the Alamo from the east, having traveled on the Gonzales road, it is easy to understand why Almonte might have believed they were reinforcement from Gonzales.

70　Williamson to Travis, March 1, 1836; "Testimony of Mrs. Hannig," September 23, 1876; Travis to Convention, March 3, 1836. In regard to Fannin, Travis wrote: "Col. Fannin is said to be on the march [R. M. Williamson letter of March 1] to this place with reinforcements, but I fear it is not true, as I have *repeatedly* sent to him for aid without receiving any."

71　"Testimony of Mrs. Hannig," September 23, 1876, Morphis, *History of Texas, from its Discovery and Settlement*, 174-177. According to Morphis, Susanna Dickinson reported: "I heard him [Crockett] say several times during the eleven days of the siege: 'I think we had better march out and die in the open air. I don't like to be hemmed up.'"

72　David Harmon affidavit and J. B. Pevito affidavit, RV 1205, VD-GLO. Pevito described Harmon's enlistment with these words: "I saw David Harmon the applicant go off from his home, on Cow Bayou as a soldier to join the army. His father went with him to see him mustered in. Dave was quite young & a mere stripling of a boy, & I asked his father at the time where he was going with David, & he said that David was young but he had to learn, & he was going to see him mustered in the army."

73　J. C. Neill's Alamo roster, Muster Rolls book, 20; "List of the names of those who fell in the Alamo at San Antonio de Bexar," Muster Rolls book, 2; Alamo voting list, February 1, 1836; *The Telegraph and Texas Register*, March 24, 1836. Neill's return and the February 1, 1836 Alamo voting list, show Major Evans's first name to be George. The *T&TR* list and the page two list in the Muster Rolls book show Evans's first name as Robert. The page two list appears to have been taken from the *T&TR* list. Neill's Alamo roster and the voting list are the more reliable lists. Thus, it appears that Evans's first name was George, as so identified by David Harmon's affidavit.

74　"Sheet" appears to be a euphemism for feces or Harmon's pronunciation of Crockett's pronunciation of shit.

75　Ibid.; Robert Whittock affidavit, RV 1153, VD-GLO. It appears that the additional men Harmon was able to enlist were in Captain William W. Logan's company. They joined Sam Houston's army at Beeson's Ferry on the Colorado River after the Alamo had fallen.

76　Ibid.; Sowell, *Early Settlers*, 9; James Taylor and Edward Taylor affidavit, March 3, 1836; J. C. Taylor affidavit, September 6, 1890, George Taylor affidavit, February 2, 1836 and J. C. Taylor affidavit, August 7, 1890; James Taylor, Edward Taylor, and William Taylor affidavit, March 3, 1836; "War News: Texas and Florida," *Arkansas Gazette* (Little Rock), April 12, 1836; Adina de Zavala, *The Alamo: Where the Last Man Died* (San Antonio: The Naylor Company, 1905), 35; Mark Derr, *The Frontiersman: The Real Life and the Many Legends of Davy Crockett* (New York: William Morrow and Company, Inc., 1993), back flap of the dust jacket; W. D. Grady petition to the Legislature of the State of Texas, n.d., M & P-TSL.

The Zavala book quotes part of a late nineteenth-century poem by James Jeffrey Roche that reports Crockett entered the Alamo with the Gonzales reinforcement. W. D. Grady stated that he had been employed as a printer with the *Texas Telegraph and Register* at San Felipe when expresses from Travis and Crockett arrived from the Alamo. William Patton, Crockett's nephew, is a good guess as the person who carried the package of letters to Gonzales. Patton appears to have been with Crockett at the Alamo, but he did not die there. At least the family never made any claims that Patton died with Crockett.

77 Jose Urrea, *Diario De Las Operaciones Militares De La Division Que Al Mando Del General Jose Urrea Hizo La Campana De Tejas* (Victoria de Durango: Imprenta Del Gobierno & Cargo de Manual Gonzalez, 1838), 54-55.

78 Sowell, *Early Settlers*, 9; James Taylor and Edward Taylor affidavit, March 3, 1836; J. C. Taylor affidavit, September 6, 1890, George Taylor affidavit, February 2, 1836, and J. C. Taylor affidavit, August 7, 1890; William B. Travis to Jesse Grimes, March 3, 1836, Alamo, Jenkins, ed., *Papers*, IV: 504-505; William B. Travis to David Ayres, March 3, 1836, Alamo, Jenkins, ed., *Papers*, IV: 501; William B. Travis to Rebecca Cummings, March 3, 1836, Alamo, reference to the letter in Holley, *Interviews*, 20; Williamson to Travis, March 1, 1836; Fannin to De Sauque and Chenoweth, March 1, 1836.

The Taylor documents place Crockett on the Cibolo Creek on the night of March 3, 1836. The affidavits claim that Crockett was so sick at the time he could not execute his signature on the document. Thus he signed with an "X." Crockett did suffer from malaria. A sudden attack of the illness can be brought on by extreme stress, which Crockett would have been under while he was on the Cibolo. If that was the case, he could have experienced shaking chills that would have prevented him from writing his name.

79 Almonte, "Private Journal," 20; Bennett McNelly affidavit, April 23, 1838, Houston, M & P-TSL; "War News: Texas and Florida," *Arkansas Gazette*, Little Rock, April 12, 1836; Joseph B. Tatom to Sister, March 10, 1836, Goliad, Jenkins, ed., *Papers*, V: 44-45; C. O. Edwards to John Dollar, July 12, 1881, Oakville, Texas Veterans Association Papers, Box 2N251, CAH.

Tatom probably obtained his information from a member of the combined March 4 reinforcement, who had returned to Goliad. Tatom, however, incorrectly believed that the addition of fifty soldiers to the Alamo increased the total number of Alamo defenders to 200 men. Tatom's number seems to be based on the belief that Travis only had 150 men. That number was close to correct on February 23. The 150 figure, however, does not take into account the fourteen men in the hospital, the thirty men who entered with Martin and Smith on March 1, and the thirty men who probably returned to the Alamo from Cibolo Creek on February 24. Thus, the actual Alamo number appears to have been: 150 effectives, plus 14 in the hospital, plus 30 that returned from the Cibolo, and 81 reinforcements, minus 14 Tejanos who departed the Alamo and 7 couriers, which equals 254 total men on March 6.

The C. O. Edwards letter appears to speak to the March 4 relief effort. In describing the military actions he had been involved in, Edwards wrote: "I was in no noted Battle. I was always out on post or in advance or in [the] rear of the main army and was subject to order at all times. I was in several pretty warm skirmishes. One on the Salado and at the Alamo hill before the capture of the Alamo. And as the Army moved on eastward I was stationed on the Brazos at Fort Bend...." Alamo hill would appear to have been Powder House hill about a half mile due east of the Alamo on the Gonzales road. If that is the case, it would appear that the March 4 reinforcement encountered Mexican patrols on Salado Creek about five miles from the Alamo and at Powder House hill before they were able to swing around to the north to approach the Alamo from the west. A careful search of Texas State Library and General Land Office documents has failed to locate any more data on Edwards.

80 Almonte, "Private Journal," 20; Filisola, *Memoirs,* II: 178. Filisola reported that a group of 32 men from Gonzales entered the Alamo two days before the final assault. The morning of March 4 would have been exactly two days before the March 6 attack. By the time Filisola wrote his book, the "Gonzales Thirty-two" were established as the only reinforcement to enter the Alamo. It appears that Filisola had an informant that reported the March 4 entry, and Filisola wrongly assumed it had to be the group of thirty-two.

81 "Muster Roll, Capt. Chenoweth's Co."; Jesse Badgett interview, April 15, 1836.

82 "Muster Roll, Captain Thomas H. Breece's Co"; "A list of votes Received at Refugio Mission by the Volunteers at that point...," February 1, 1836, and San Patricio voting list, February 1, 1836, Election Returns, TSL; Alamo voting list, February 1, 1836; Conrad Eigenauer pay document for death at Alamo on March 6, 1836, May 29, 1838, Houston, AMC-TSL; Conrad Eigenauer Court of Claims file, C-002495, GLO; Robert Musselman, Thomas P. Hutchinson, and John J. Baugh affidavit, December 29, 1835, in Francis William Jackson file, AMC-TSL; Joseph H. Barnard, "A List of the Men under the Command of Col. J. W. Fannin at Goliad in March 1836, corrected from the list published in the *Telegraph* of Nov. 9, 1836," Joseph H. Barnard Papers, CAH.

The names of these ten men from the original Greys company do not appear on the February 1 Alamo voting list, which shows they were not members of the Bexar garrison as of that date. Eigenauer voted at Refugio. Stephen Dennison voted at San Patricio.

There is one source that reports Eigenauer was wounded on March 19, 1836, at the battle of Coleto and died that night. That claim comes from Hermann Ehrenberg's *Texas Und Seine Revolution*, a memoir of the Texas war, published in Germany in 1843. Ehrenberg had been a member of the Greys. After the unit broke up, he joined the Mobile Greys. Ehrenberg's report of Eigeneauer's death is suspect because it claims that Ehrenberg did not know Eigenauer until he discovered him dying during the night of March 19, 1836, on the Coleto battleground. The truth is they traveled together from New Orleans to the siege and storming of Bexar in 1835, and both voted in the February 1 election at Refugio. Also, Barnard, one of Fannin's doctors, did not identify Eigenauer as one of the men wounded on March 19.

Ehrenberg's chapter on Fannin's activities during the Alamo siege in late February and early March is lacking in data that Ehrenberg should have known. His Alamo chapter is best described as lurid fiction.

Ehrenberg may have been one of the men who joined the mounted force under the command of Chenoweth and De Sauque that Fannin sent to the Alamo. Ehrenberg's obituary, apparently written by his close friend and business partner Samuel Peter Heintzelman (James E. Crisp, "In Pursuit of Herman Ehrenberg: A Research Adventure," *Southwestern Historical Quarterly*, CII: 435), which appeared in the *New York Times*, January 10, 1867, reported that Ehrenberg had been "the only survivor of the Fannin Massacre at the Alamo." If Ehrenberg was part of Fannin's reinforcement of the Alamo, he was not the only survivor of that action, but he may have been at the time of his death.

83 Muster Roll, Capt. Chenoweth's Co.; Alamo voting list, February 1, 1836; John Chenoweth affidavit, May 3, 1837, Brazoria, Samuel M. Edwards Probate, Brazoria County Probate Records, Brazoria, Texas; Refugio voting list, February 1, 1836; San Patricio voting list, February 1, 1836; Kevin R. Young, *Texas Forgotten Heroes* (Goliad: Goliad County Historical Commission, 1986).

The Chenoweth muster roll identifies these men as having been killed. An inspection of the Goliad list shows they were not killed while with Fannin's command at Goliad. And given that the company rode to the Alamo and later fell back to Gonzales, the only action in which they could have been killed was in their reinforcement of the Alamo or the fall of the Alamo on March 6. William Badgett, who is listed as not being killed, Adolf A. Petrasweiz, W. H. Sanders, and William Hunter, who are listed as killed, all voted at Refugio on February 1. Thus, the dead men were not part of the Alamo on February 1, 1836.

Also, Samuel M. Edwards is identified as having died with Fannin at Goliad. Nevertheless, Chenoweth first identified Edwards as having died with Fannin, then he crossed that out and wrote that Edwards had died at the "Alimo."

84 "A List of the Gonzales Ranging Company...," February 23, 1836; Sowell, *Early Settlers*, 9-10; George B. Kimbell pay certificate, November 29, 1839;

James George pay certificate, January 15, 1839; Thomas R. Jackson pay certificate, March 4, 1840; Horce Eggleson affidavit, January 3, 1841, probate number 21, Gonzales County probate records, Archives, Gonzales County Courthouse, Gonzales, Texas; James Taylor and Edward Taylor affidavit, March 3, 1836; J. C. Taylor affidavit, September 6, 1890, George Taylor affidavit, February 2, 1836 and J. C. Taylor, August 7, 1890; James Taylor, Edward Taylor, and William Taylor affidavit, March 3, 1836; Petition in regard to the deaths of brothers James and William George at the Alamo, n.d., Bexar, and Interrogation of Benjamin McCulloch, n.d., Bexar, Court of Claims file, C-3103, GLO. In total, this list is a best guess compilation based on the sources. Some of the men may have entered the Alamo on March 1 with John W. Smith and Albert Martin.

85 Alamo voting list, February 1, 1836; Erath, "Memoirs of Major George Bernard Erath," 231; Merret and Saul statement, July 1838; Thomson and Pattillo to Robinson, February 26, 1836. The names on this list do not appear on the February 1 Alamo voting list. Thus, it appears they entered the Alamo after that date. While it is not certain they rode to the Alamo with Captain J. J. Tumlinson's ranger company, it is the most likely method of entry for them.

86 Travis to Convention, March 3, 1836; Candelario Villanueva Deposition, August 26, 1859, Matovina, *The Alamo Remembered*, 35; James L. Thuchearz to William Steele, February 6, 1875, San Antonio, Adjutant General Correspondence, TSL.

On March 3 Travis wrote that only three San Antonio Mexican-Texians were in the Alamo. Speculation suggests the three were probably Antonio Fuentes, Gregorio Esparza, and Toribio Losoya. Esparza and Losoya would have remained with their families. Fuentes appears to have been aligned with Bowie, not Seguin. Enrique Esparza, Gregorio's son, later reported that he had seen Fuentes in the fort. Therefore, it is most credible that if more than three Tejanos died in the Alamo, they entered with the March 4 relief. Also, some of these men may have been in the Alamo and left during the siege, only to return with Seguin and Crockett.

87 Nacogdoches Enlistments, Muster Roll book, 114-115; Forbes to Robinson, January 12, 1836; Townsend Receipt, February 9, 1836; Robinson to Houston, February 14, 1836; "Gilmore unit members agreement with Acting-Governor Robinson and Council," [February 16, 1836?]; William Gilmore affidavit, April 12, 1859, Giles County, Tennessee, John W. Thomson (Thompson) file, Court of Claims file, GLO; Williams "A Critical Study of the Siege of the Alamo," 291. Williams concluded that: "It is possible that George Olamio was an Alamo victim." In this case Williams was probably right. At that time she was not aware of the total evidence indicating that a portion of the Gilmore company took part in a reinforcement of the Alamo.

88 "A List of the names of Volunteers who were admitted as Colonists in San Patricio – February 1836 under the Command of Col. Johnson, Grant,

Cooke, and Burk," San Patricio Colonists file, M & P-TSL; Alamo voting list, February 1, 1836; Francis H. Gray certificate number 837, June 6, 1851, in "Exhibit of all the Bounty, Donation, and Headright Certificates issued to administrators since the establishment of Adjutant General by an act of the Legislature of 1846"; Francis H. Gray, Robertson Bounty and Donation file, Number 573, GLO.

89 "Connel O'Donnel Kelly" account, Day, compiler, *The Texas Almanac 1857-1873*, 600; Ramirez y Sesma to Santa Anna, March 15, 1836. Ramirez y Sesma on arriving at the Cibolo crossing found evidence that a large force had been assembled at the ford. He even found horse equipment that had the name of Alamo defender Richard Storr on the items.

90 Almonte, "Private Journal," 20.

91 Ibid.

92 John S. Brooks to James Hagarty, March 9, 1836, Goliad, Jenkins, ed., *Papers*, V: 31; Travis to Convention, March 3, 1836; Almonte, "Private Journal," 22; Filisola, *Memoirs*, II: 149-152.

93 Almonte, "Private Journal," 21; Ignacio Berrospe military service records, XI/111/4-782, p. 100, *Cancelados, Archivo Historico of Secretaria de la Defensa Nacional*, Mexico City, from Jack Jackson's research notes, July 2000. Mr. Jackson was kind enough to share his research with this investigator.

94 John W. Smith and Nathaniel Lewis testimony for James L. Ewing heirs, first class headright land grant certificate 475, March 30, 1838, Finley Ewing Jr. Papers, DRT Library, Alamo. The belief that Smith encountered the remaining members of the relief force is speculation based on the belief they returned to the Cibolo Creek ford on the Gonzales road.

95 Jesse Billingsley to L. C. Cunningham, March 4, 1836, Gonzales, L. C. Cunningham file, AMC-TSL; J. C. Neill affidavit, March 4, 1836, Gonzales, Joseph S. Martin file, AMC-TSL; J. C. Neill affidavit, March 3, 1836, Gonzales, A. Matthews file, AMC-TSL; J. C. Neill affidavit, December 7, 1839, Austin, Samuel Williams file, AMC-TSL; J. C. Neill affidavit, November 21, 1837, Houston, Joseph D. Clements file, AMC-TSL.

96 Joseph D. Clements affidavit, November 22, 1837, Joseph D. Clements file, AMC-TSL; W. D. Grady petition, M & P-TSL.

97 Almonte, "Private Journal," 22.

98 Sowell, *Early Settlers*, 9. That Highsmith returned to the Alamo on March 5 is speculation based on the evidence. It is possible he returned on March 6.

99 Almonte, "Private Journal," 22-23; Santa Anna Order, March 5, 1836, Bexar, Jenkins, ed., *Papers*, IV: 518-519.

100 Gray to _____, March 11, 1836, Gonzales, Jenkins, ed., *Papers*, V: 48-49; Filisola, *Memoirs*, II: 176-177; Nacogdoches Meeting, March 26, 1836, Jenkins, ed., *Papers*, IX: 159-161; "Testimony of Mrs. Hannig," September 23, 1876; Mrs. James McKeever to W. P. Hardeman, July 25, 1893,

Houston, Alamo Papers, Box 2-23/591, TSL; extract from Miss Louise Alsbury's DRT membership application, Alamo Papers.

The Nacogdoches document reports: "... during a temporary suspension of the bombardment they [Alamo defenders] sought repose the enemy became apprized of their situation by the supposed treachery of a Mexican in the Fort...." Hannig claimed that Mrs. Alsbury departed the Alamo "about two days before the assault," and betrayed the garrison. McKeever claimed that Alsbury had been "taken from the Alamo under a flag of truce the day before the Fort was besieged by the Mexicans." Louise Alsbury reported that Alsbury "was in the Alamo until the day before the fort was stormed by the Mexicans, when she was taken out by Santa Anna under a flag of truce at the request of her father. Most likely, Hannig (Dickinson) was not aware that Alsbury had returned to the Alamo. Also, it is unbelievable that Alsbury would have left her infant son and her sister in the Alamo. The alleged betrayal seems unlikely as Mrs. Alsbury returned to the Alamo and witnessed the March 6 assault.

101 Filisola, *Memoirs*, II: 176-177.

102 Robert H. Davis, "Bob Davis Uncovers an Untold Story About the Alamo," [newspaper unknown], February 28, 1932, James L. Allen file, DRT Library; Mrs. B. N. Pittman to E. C. Baker, April 4, 1932, Hochheim, Amelia W. Williams Papers, Box 2N493, CAH; Brooks to Hagarty, March 9, 1836.

The claim that Allen rode bareback is suspicious because there were probably close to one hundred horses and sets of horse gear in the Alamo when he left. Also, Allen was not a teenage boy as many accounts claim. He was a twenty-one-year-old adult.

103 Filisola, *Memoirs*, II: 176-177; Travis to Convention, March 3, 1836; Jesse Badgett interview, April 15, 1836; Nacogdoches Meeting, March 26, 1836, 159-161. The Nacogdoches report claims that each Alamo defender had from five to ten loaded weapons on the morning of March 6.

104 *Telegraph and Texas Register*, San Felipe, March 12, 1836; J. H. Kuykendall, "J. H. Kuykendall's Recollections of the [San Jacinto] Campaign," in Dr. Eugene C. Barker, *The Quarterly of the Texas State Historical Association*, IV: 292.

105 Filisola, *Memoirs*, II: 149-152; "Testimony of Mrs. Hannig," September 23, 1876; Santa Anna Order, March 5, 1836; Almonte, "Private Journal," 22-23; Thomas Ricks Lindley, "Storming the Alamo Walls," *The Alamo Journal*, June 2000; Thomas Ricks Lindley, "At the Alamo Walls Again," *The Alamo Journal*, December 2000. This investigator's two *Journal* articles offer an analysis of the evidence that speaks to the March attack.

106 Almonte, "Private Journal," 23; General Juan de Andrade report in Filisola, *Memoirs*, II: 178; Colonel Pedro Ampudia's "Inventory of Artillery, munitions, and other weapons captured at the fall of the Alamo," March 6, 1836, number 39, XI/481.3/1655, *Secretria de la Defensa Nacional*, Mexico City. See Chapter Eight of this book for the most accurate analysis of the number of Mexican dead and wounded at the Alamo.

107 Bastian interview, Brown, *Indian Wars*, 138. Bastian confused Gonzales with Goliad, but given the time that had passed since the fall of the Alamo and his interview, that is not an unreasonable mistake.

108 De la Teja, *A Revolution Remembered*, 79-80; Bennett McNelly affidavit, April 23, 1838; John Chenoweth affidavit, January 2, 1841, M & P-TSL; Juan Rodriquiz affidavit, October 24, 1874, San Antonio, and Juan N. Seguin affidavit, October 28, 1874, San Antonio, Juan N. Rodriquiz file, PC-TSL.

Seguin, in his 1858 memoir, claimed that, after his arrival at Gonzales after the fall of the Alamo, General Sam Houston sent Captain Salvador Flores and twenty-five men to the San Antonio River ranches to protect the inhabitants from Indian attack. Whereas, Rodriquiz, Seguin's orderly, claimed that Seguin sent him, Juan Jose Flores, and anther man named Guillermo back to the Seguin ranch to protect the Seguin family and ranch. Rodriquiz further claimed he remained at the Seguin ranch on that duty until October 1836. Seguin's affidavit supports Rodriquiz's claims. There is no evidence from Sam Houston that verifies Seguin's claim that Houston had sent twenty-six men to protect the ranches.

Jose Alemeda, however, claimed in his Republic of Texas pension application that he was one of twenty men, under Salvador Flores, that Seguin sent from Gonzales to evacuate the Tejano ranches. Francisco Miranda and Mateo Cassillas also claimed in their pension applications that they were members of the unit sent to escort the Tejano families to the east.

The Tejano families would have probably used the Contraband road that ran from the mouth of Cibolo Creek to the road's junction with the Gonzales/Bexar road at Castleman's home on Sandies Creek.

109 Moseley Baker to John R. Jones, Thomas Gray, William Pettus, March 8, 1836, Gonzales, Jenkins, ed., *Papers*, V: 22-23; "Connel O'Donnel Kelly" account, Day, compiler, *The Texas Almanac 1857-1873*, 600.

110 De la Teja, *A Revolution Remembered*, 79-80; Bennett McNelly affidavit, April 23, 1838; John Chenoweth affidavit, January 2, 1841, M & P-TSL.

111 "Later – San Antonio Retaken and the Garrison Massacred," *The Arkansas Gazette,* Little Rock, March 29, 1836.

112 Barsena et al. deposition, March 11, 1836, Gonzales, Jenkins, ed., *Papers*, V: 45-46; Captain John Bird affidavit, November 29, 1837, San Felipe, and John G. King pay certificate, January 15, 1839, John G. King file, AMC-TSL. King was paid for military service from February 24, 1836, to March 6, 1836, as a member of Major R. M. Williamson's command.

113 "Connel O'Donnel Kelly" account, Day, compiler, *The Texas Almanac 1857-1873*, 600.

114 Ibid. The belief that John W. Smith returned to San Antonio by the upper road from Gonzales is based on the fact that if he had used the lower road, his group would have encountered Seguin, Chenoweth, and De Sauque,

who were riding to Gonzales. At that point, Smith would have learned the Alamo had fallen.

115 Tom Turner to Dearest Mother, September 8, 1836, Liberty, Jenkins, ed., *Papers*, VIII: 415-416.

116 D. C. Barrett et al. to James W. Robinson, January 31, 1836. The wording of "last extremity" as a term for death was also used by soldiers in General George Washington's army during the American Revolution.

117 "Testimony of Mrs. Hannig," September 23, 1876.

Chapter Five

Moses, the Climbing Rose:
Thorny Problems

> *I wish to say something in self-defense and for the truth of*
> *history, concerning my published account of the escape of a man*
> *whose name was Rose from the Alamo, March 3, 1836.... I*
> *have not seen any published contradiction of it by any reliable*
> *authority; neither do I know of any reliable person who has*
> *publicly contradicted it.*
>
> William P. Zuber[1]

In the summer of 1990, a new history of the Battle of the Alamo surfaced in bookstores. The narrative was Jeff Long's *Duel of Eagles: The Mexican and U.S. Fight for the Alamo.* The book, with the Battle of the Alamo and the alleged "warts" of Alamo commanders William B. Travis, James Bowie, and David Crockett forming the narrative's core, was promoted by the publisher as "a rich, powerful, and comprehensive history that removes the myths from the battle for Texas; we have the true story, as dramatic as any legend, of what led to the Alamo and what followed from it."[2]

Ironically, for a narrative that is supposed to be a myth-buster, Long accepted the biggest Alamo myth of all of them, the story of Travis's line in the dirt, as the truth.[3] The tale alleges that on the afternoon of March 3, Alamo commander William B. Travis, realizing that there was no hope of a Texian victory, called his troops together and informed them of their impending fate. He is supposed to have scratched a line in the dirt with his saber and asked those who would join him in a gallant death to cross over the line. All of the men, except Moses Rose, an old Frenchman from James Bowie's volunteers, are alleged to have hurried across the line. A short time later Rose escaped over an Alamo wall and humped it to

Grimes County. There Rose told his story to Abraham and Mary Ann Zuber, old friends, whose son William P. Zuber published an account of the tale in the 1873 *Texas Almanac*.[4]

Brass rod in the flagstone at the Alamo, symbolic of Travis's line

At that time acceptance of the Rose report varied from Texan to Texan. Rufus Grimes, brother of Alamo defender Albert C. Grimes, expressed his strong support with these words: "The account is entitled full credit.... Wm. P. Zuber is a man of undoubted veracity and when Rose escaped from the Alamo he made his way to the house of Abram Zuber an old friend and acquaintance then living in Rvans Prairie in this county (Grimes) where he staid [*sic*] until his feet got well enough to travel again (his feet & legs were full of cactus thorns) traveling in the night."[5]

The artist (painter) H. A. McArdle, however, felt the Rose narrative was pure fiction. McArdle, after presenting a critical analysis of the story to brand it as a fabrication, reflected: "Mr. Zuber feels he has worked in 'a just and truthful case.' What? The defense of a craven and dastard – and to cast a reflection on the courage and patriotism of the martyrs of the

Alamo, who, according to Rose, required a speech, etc – and after eight days' siege – to keep them from running away."[6]

Despite Zuber's promotion and defense of the tale until his death in 1913, the argument remained unsettled.[7] The early 1930s brought two academic historians to the subject. Ruby Mixon, in researching a master's thesis on William B. Travis, did her best to verify the Rose story. She felt the accounts of Travis's last three days were "a veritable Gordian knot" of legend, fact, and fiction. She concluded that it was probably impossible to determine the truth about Travis's alleged sword line in the dirt.[8]

Dr. Amelia W. Williams, in her doctoral dissertation, expressed her opinion with a singular footnote: "Historians have been divided in their opinion concerning the story, the most careful students having discredited it. At best they consider it a legend, plausible perhaps, but almost certainly the creation of a vivid imagination."[9]

Thus the certitude of the Rose story remained in doubt until as Walter Lord, author of *A Time To Stand* (considered by many to be the best book on the Alamo), observed: "Then in 1939 came a thunderbolt." The "electric" evidence out of the blue was land grant testimony found by R. B. Blake, a Nacogdoches researcher. Blake claimed the documents revealed that in 1838 one Louis Rose of Nacogdoches identified six Alamo defenders in probate court proceedings. Rose allegedly placed himself in the Alamo on March 3 and claimed he had departed the fortress on that date. Blake assumed that Louis Rose had to have been Moses Rose.[10]

At that point, J. Frank Dobie, famed folklorist, eminent Texas pundit and raconteur, who was always quick to recognize a Texas tale that had legs, entered the fray with an article titled "The Line That Travis Drew." He referred to the Louis Rose testimony and a secondhand account of the line story attributed to Susanna Dickinson by Rufus Burleson. Thus Dobie, as only he could, concluded: "The old story, the cherished story, the heroic story of the line that Travis drew seems to me vindicated sufficiently for credence. The mere absence of documentary proof never repudiated it anyhow."[11]

More objective individuals were far from convinced by the 1838 Louis Rose statements. An editorial writer for the *Wichita Times* wrote: "This new evidence does not give the story absolute confirmation, but it should be comforting to those who want so much to believe. Probably there never will be definitive proof of either the truth or falsity of the story; but those who want to believe have a good basis for believing, and they will greatly outnumber the scholarly doubters."[12]

Claude Elliott, Southwest Texas State Teachers College professor, was one of the scholarly skeptics. He reviewed *In the Shadow of History*, published by the Texas Folklore Society, which contained the Dobie article and R. B. Blake's "A Vindication of Rose and His Story," that showcased the 1838 land grant testimony.[13]

Elliott declared with authority:

> Mr. Dobie first gives a history of the Travis story and tacitly admits that it is untrue when he says: "Reading the documented historians you'd think nothing could be so unless it happened," and then states that he believes the story. In regard to "A Vindication of Rose and His Story" it should be said that it falls short of a real vindication. An analysis of this ingenious and admirable bit of detective work shows that there is very good reason to believe that Rose lived and, aside from going under the names of Louis, Lewis, Moses, and Stephen, was fairly reliable. In spite of all this the fertile imagination of W. P. Zuber, to whom we are solely indebted for the Rose story, must be dealt with.[14]

Simply put, the Louis Rose data is not an independent verification of the Rose story because Blake never proved Louis Rose and Moses Rose were the same person. Still, Lord was convinced Louis and Moses were one and the same and the tale was true. He concluded: "So Rose was there. But did he leave under the dramatic circumstances described by Zuber? Freshly uncovered information suggests that the did." The new evidence Lord discovered was an alleged statement by Susanna (Dickinson) Hannig, allegedly given in 1876 to an agent of the Texas Adjutant General's office. Lord felt the Hannig document was reliable and independent evidence that verified Travis's talk to his soldiers and Rose's escape.[15]

Today the "line story" is a historical fact that stands on three legs of evidence. Those limbs being: the original Moses Rose tale as told by William P. Zuber, the 1838 Louis Rose land grant testimony as interpreted by R. B. Blake, and the alleged Susanna Hannig affidavit as interpreted by Walter Lord. A quick read of the evidence, as presented by Blake and Lord, strongly suggests that the "line" yarn stands on a solid foundation. An expanded and critical examination of the data, however, will show that the house of Moses/Louis Rose is constructed on unstable sand.

First, let us "deal" with the "fertile imagination of W. P. Zuber." His account first appeared in 1873. Twenty-two years later he furnished an expanded version for Mrs. Anna M. J. Pennybacker's *A New History of Texas for Schools, 1895. Alamo Traces* presents a combination of the 1873 report and the 1895 version because few Alamo researchers have seen the entire account. The parts in brackets are the elements that were not included in the 1873 version.[16]

An Escape From The Alamo

Prairie Plains, Grimes County, Texas May 7th, 1873
Editor, *Texas Almanac:*
I regard the following account worthy of preservation, as it enhances a report of the last scene in the Alamo that has ever been made known to the survivors of those who fell in that fortress.

Moses Rose, a native of France, was an early immigrant to Texas, and resided in Nacogdoches, where my father, Mr. Abraham Zuber, made his acquaintance in 1827. I believe that he never married. My father regarded and treated him as a friend, and I have often heard him say that he believed Rose to be a man of strict veracity. In 1830, I saw him several times at my father's residence, in what is now San Augustine County. He was then about forty-five years old, and spoke very broken English. [He had been a soldier in Napoleon's army in the invasion of Russia and the retreat from Moscow. He was one of the early settlers at Nacogdoches, Texas, and that was his home, as long as he lived. Mr. Frost Thorn, of Nacogdoches, employed him as a messenger between that town and Natchitoches, Louisiana. Said Thorn generally kept four wagons running between the two towns, carrying cotton and other produce to Natchitoches and returning with goods from Nacogdoches. He arranged with settlers on the road to repair his wagons and supply his teamsters with provender and provisions, on short credit. Rose's duty was to bear the money and pay the debts thus contracted. At the same time, he carried the mail between the two towns on private contract, there being no government mail on this route. My father visited Texas in 1827, and became acquainted with Rose at Nacogdoches. He also knew him later, and believed him to be an honest, truthful man. I also knew him in what is now San Augustine County, in 1830. He was a close observer and had a retentive memory.][17]

Rose was a warm friend of Col. James Bowie, and accompanied or followed him to the Alamo in the fall of 1835, and continued with him till within three days of the fall of the fort.

During the last five days and nights of his stay, the enemy bombarded the fort almost incessantly, and several times advanced to the walls, and the men within were so constantly engaged that they ate and slept only at short intervals, while one body of the enemy was retiring to be relieved by another, yet they had not sustained a single loss.

The following is the substance of Rose's account of his escape and the circumstances connected therewith, as he related them to my parents and they related them to me:

About two hours before sunset, on the third day of March, 1836, the bombardment suddenly ceased, and the enemy withdrew an unusual distance. Taking advantage of that opportunity, Col. Travis paraded all of his effective men in a single file; and, taking his position in front of center, he stood for some moments apparently speechless from emotion. Then, nerving himself for the occasion, he addressed them substantially as follows:

MY BRAVE COMPANIONS – Stern necessity compels me to employ the few moments afforded by this probably brief cessation of conflict in making known to you the most interesting, yet the most solemn, melancholy, and unwelcome fact that perishing humanity can realize. But how shall I find language to prepare you for its reception? I cannot do so. All that I can say to this purpose is, be prepared for the worst. I must come to the point. Our fate is sealed. Within a very few days – perhaps a very few hours – we must all be in eternity. This is our destiny, and we cannot avoid it. This is our *certain* doom.

I have deceived you long by the promise of help. But crave your pardon, hoping that after hearing my explanation, you will not only regard my conduct as pardonable, but heartily sympathize with me in my extreme necessity. In deceiving you, I also deceived myself, having been first deceived by others.

I have continually received the strongest assurances of help from home. Every letter from the Council and every one that I have seen from individuals at home, has teemed with assurances that our people were ready, willing, and anxious to come to our relief; and that within a very short time we might confidently expect recruits enough to repel any force that would be brought against us. These assurances I received as facts. They inspired me with the greatest confidence that our little band would be made the nucleus of an army of sufficient magnitude to repel our foes, and to enforce peace on our terms. In the honest and simple confidence of my heart, I have transmitted to you these promises of help, and my confident hopes of success. – But the promised help has not come and our hopes are not to be realized.

I have evidently confided too much in the promises of our friends. But let us not be in haste to censure them. The enemy has invaded our territory much earlier than we anticipated; and their present approach is matter of surprise. Our friends were evidently not informed of our perilous condition in time to save us. Doubtless they would have been here by the time they expected any considerable force of the enemy. When they find a Mexican army in their midst, I hope they will show themselves true to their cause.

My calls to Col. Fannin remain unanswered, and my messengers have not returned. The probabilities are that his whole command has fallen into the hands of the enemy, or been cut to pieces, and that our couriers have been cut off.[18]

I trust that I have now explained my conduct to your satisfaction and that you do not censure me for my course.

I must again refer to the assurances of help from home. They are what deceived me, and they caused me to deceive you. Relying upon those assurances, I determined to remain within these walls until the promised help should arrive, stoutly resisting all assaults from without. Upon the same reliance, I retained you here, regarding the increasing force of our assailants with contempt, till they outnumbered us more than twenty to one, and escape became impossible. For the same reason, I scorned their demand of a surrender at discretion and defied their threat to put every one of us to the sword, if the fort should be taken by storm.

I must now speak of our present situation. Here we are, surrounded by an army that could almost eat us for breakfast, from whose arms our lives are, for the present, protected by these stone walls. We have no hope for help, for no force that we could ever reasonably have expected, could cut its way through the strong ranks of these Mexicans. We dare not surrender; for, should we do so, that black flag, now waving in our sight, as well as the merciless character of our enemies, admonishes us of what would be our doom. We cannot cut our way out through the enemy's ranks; for, in attempting that, we should all be slain in less than ten minutes. Nothing remains then, but to stay within this fort, and fight to the last moment. In this case, we must, sooner or later, all be slain; for I am sure that Santa Anna is determined to storm the fort and take it, even at the greatest cost of the lives of his own men.

Then we must die! Our speedy dissolution is a fixed and inevitable fact. – Our business is, not to make a fruitless effort to save our lives, but to choose the manner of our death. But three modes are presented to us. Let us choose that by which we may best serve our country. Shall we surrender, and be deliberately shot, without taking the life of a single enemy? Shall we try to cut our way out through the Mexican ranks, and be butchered before we can kill twenty of our adversaries? I am opposed to either method; for in either case, we could not but lose our lives, without benefiting our friends at home – our fathers and mothers, our brothers and sisters, our wives and little ones. The Mexican army is strong enough to march through the country, and exterminate its inhabitants, and our countrymen are not able to oppose them in open field. My choice, then, is to remain in this fort, to resist every assault, and to sell our lives as dearly as possible.

Then let us band together as brothers, and vow to die together. Let us resolve to withstand our adversaries to the last; and, at each advance, to kill as many of them as possible. And when, at last, they shall storm our fortress, let us kill them as they come! Kill them as they scale our walls! Kill them as they leap within! Kill them as they kill our companions! And continue to kill them as long as one of us shall remain alive!

By this policy, I trust that we shall so weaken our enemies that our countrymen at home can meet them on fair terms, cut them up, expel them from the country, and thus establish their own independence, and secure prosperity and happiness to our families and our country. And, *be assured*, our memory will be gratefully cherished by posterity, till all history shall be erased, and all noble deeds shall be forgotten.

But I leave every man to his own choice. Should any man prefer to surrender, and be tied and shot; or to attempt an escape through the Mexican ranks, and be killed before he can run a hundred yards, he is at liberty to do so.

My own choice is to stay in this fort, and die for my country, fighting as long as breath shall remain in my body. *This I will do, even if you leave me alone.* Do as you think best – but no man can die with me without affording me comfort in the moment of death.

Colonel Travis then drew his sword and with its point traced a line upon the ground extending from the right to the left of the file. Then, resuming his position in front of the center, he said, "I now want every man who is determined to stay here and die with me to come across this line. Who will be the first? March!"

The first respondent was Tapley Holland, who leaped the line at a bound, exclaiming, "I am ready to die for my country!" His example was instantly followed by every man in the file, with the exception of Rose. Manifest enthusiasm was universal and tremendous. Every sick man that could walk arose from his bunk and tottered across the line. Col. Bowie, who could not leave his bed, said, "Boys, I am not able to go to you, but I wish some of you would be so kind as to remove my cot over there." Four men instantly ran to the cot, and, each lifting a corner, carried it across the line. Then every sick man that could not walk made the same request, and had his bunk removed in like manner.

Rose, too, was deeply affected, but differently from his companions. He stood till every man but himself had crossed the line. A consciousness of the real situation overpowered him. He sank upon the ground, covered his face, and yielded to his own reflections. For a time he was unconscious of what was transpiring around him. A bright idea came to his relief; he spoke the Mexican dialect very fluently, and could he once get safely out of the fort he might easily pass for a Mexican and effect an escape. He looked over the area of the fort; every sick man's berth was at its wonted place; every effective soldier was at his post, as if waiting orders; he felt as if dreaming.

He directed a searching glance at the cot of Col. Bowie. There lay his gallant friend. Col. David Crockett was leaning over the cot, conversing with its occupant in an undertone. After a few seconds Bowie looked at Rose and said, "You seem not to be willing to die with us, Rose." "No," said Rose, "I am not prepared to die, and shall not do so if I can avoid it." Then Crockett also looked at him, and said, "You may as well conclude to die with us, old man, for escape is impossible."

Rose made no reply, but looked up at the top of the wall. "I have often done worse than to climb that wall," he thought. Suiting the action to the thought he sprang up, seized his wallet of unwashed clothes, and ascended the wall. Standing on its top, he looked down within to take a last view of his dying friends. They were all now in motion, but what they were doing he heeded not. Overpowered by his feelings he looked away and saw them no more.

Looking down without, he was amazed at the scene of death that met his gaze. From the wall to a considerable distance beyond the ground was literally covered with slaughtered Mexicans and pools of blood.

He viewed this horrid scene but a moment. He threw down his wallet and leaped after it; he alighted on his feet, but the momentum of the spring threw him sprawling upon his stomach in a puddle of blood. After several seconds he recovered his breath, he rose and took up his wallet; it had fallen open and several garments had rolled out upon the blood. He hurriedly thrust them back, without trying to cleanse them of the coagulated blood which adhered to them. Then, throwing the wallet across his shoulders he walked rapidly away.

He took the road which led down the river around a bend to the ford, and through the town by the church. He waded the river at the ford and passed through the town. He saw no person in town, but the doors were all closed, and San Antonio appeared as a deserted city.

After passing through town he turned down the river. A stillness as of death prevailed. When he had gone about a quarter of a mile below the town his ears where saluted by the thunder of the bombardment, which was then renewed. That thunder continued to remind him that his friends were true to their cause, by a continual roar, with but slight intervals, until a little before sunrise on the morning of the sixth, when it ceased and he heard it no more.

At twilight he recrossed the river on a footlog about three miles below town. He then directed his course eastwardly towards the Guadalupe river, carefully bearing to the right [south] to avoid the Gonzales road.

On the night of the third he traveled all night, but made but little progress as his way was interrupted by large tracts of Cactus or prickly pear which constantly gored him with thorns and forced him out of his course. On the morning of the fourth he was in a wretched plight for traveling, for his legs were full of thorns and very sore. The thorns were very painful, and continued to work deeper into the flesh till they produced chronic sores, which are supposed to have terminated his life.

Profiting by experience, he traveled no more at night, but on the two evenings following he made his bed on the soft mesquite grass. On the sixth of March he crossed the Guadalupe by rolling a seasoned log into the water and padding across with his hands. He afterwards crossed the Colorado in the same manner.

[On landing, after ascending a bluff, he found himself a deserted house, at which he found plenty of provisions and cooking vessels. There he took his first nourishment after leaving the Alamo. Travel had caused the thorns to work so deep in his flesh that he could not bear the pain of pulling them out, and he had become lame. There he rested two or three days, hoping that his lameness would subside, but it rather grew worse. Thenceforth he traveled on roads, subsisting, except in the instance to be noted, on provisions which he found in deserted houses. The families were retreating before the threatened advance of the enemy, and between the Guadalupe and Colorado every family on his route had left home. Between the Colorado and the Brazos he found only one family at home. With them he stayed during a considerable time; but probably from want of knowledge or skill, they did nothing to relieve his sore legs. While he was with them, two travelers of whom he had no previous knowledge, called and lodged during a night. The landlord entertained them with an account of Rose's escape. They seemed to be much interested in the account; but, on the next morning, just as they were leaving they obtained a private interview with the landlord, and told him that they lived in Nacogdoches and knew this Frenchman, Rose; that he was a man of very bad character, that he was an imposter, and had never seen the Alamo, and that he (the landlord), for the honor of his family, ought to ship him immediately. I judged that they, themselves, were bad men, and tendered this pretended friendly advice to their landlord, hoping thereby, to induce him not to charge them for their lodging. After their departure, the landlord told Rose what the men had said of him, and he determined never again to tell that he had been in the Alamo. This was during Houston's retreat from the Colorado, and several squads of deserters from the army overtook and passed Rose. The first of these told him that an impostor by the name of Rose had imposed himself upon an old gentleman as being escaped from the Alamo, but that two men from Rose's home had informed the old gentleman of the imposition, and he had promptly driven the impostor from his premises. Succeeding squads told the same story, and before reaching the Brazos, Rose heard this caricature of part of his own history four times, but he did not tell any of his informants that he was the man, nor that his name was Rose. Years later, I learned that the report of his reputed imposition preceded him to Nacogdoches, and that several malicious persons there circulated the slander. I further learned that, not being able to disprove it by eyewitnesses, he was averse to talking on the subject. This reticence, though natural to a slandered man who could not positively prove his innocence, was imprudent. The people of Nacogdoches knew that he had been in the Alamo, but his sullenness exacted a suspicion that he was not merely an impostor, but a deserter and traitor. As I shall yet show, he at one place exhibited conclusive evidence of his innocence, yet his stubborn reticence caused his adventures to be forgotten, and this, I judge, was what prevented his escape from being recorded in the early histories of Texas.

After crossing the Brazos Rose found several families at home, and from them obtained direction to my father's residence.]

He continued his journey toilsomely, tediously and painfully for several weeks, in which time he encountered many hardships and dangers which for want of space can not be inserted here. He finally arrived at the residence of my father on Lake Creek, in what is now Grimes County.

My parents had seen, in the Telegraph and Texas Register, a partial list of those who had fallen at the Alamo, and in it observed the name of Rose. Having not heard of his escape, they had no doubt that he had died with his companions. On his arrival, my father recognized him instantly, and exclaimed, "My God! Rose, is this you, or is it your ghost?" "This is Rose, and not a ghost," was the reply.

My mother caused her washing servant to open Rose's wallet, in her presence, and found some of the garments glued together with the blood in which they had fallen when thrown from the Alamo.

My parents also examined his legs, and by the use of forceps extracted an incredible number of cactus thorns, some of them an inch and a half in length, each of which drew out a lump of flesh and was followed by a stream of blood. Salve [which my mother made] was applied to his sores and they soon began to heal.

Rose remained at my father's between two and three weeks, during which time his sores improved rapidly, and he hoped to be well. He then left for home. We had reliable information of him but once after his departure. He had arrived at his home in Nacogdoches, but traveling on foot had caused his legs to inflame anew, and his sores had grown so much worse that his friends thought that he could not live many months. That was the last we heard of him.

During his stay at my father's Rose related to my parents an account of what transpired in the Alamo before he left it, of his escape, and of what befell him afterwards, and at their request he rehearsed it several times (till my mother could have repeated it as well as he). Most of the minutia here recorded were elicited by particular inquiries. In the following June I returned home from the Texas army, and my parents several times rehearsed the whole account to me.

[God had endowed my mother with close observation and extraordinary memory and I had inherited them. Hence what Rose had stated became stamped upon her memory and mine. I admired the sentiments of Travis' speech even as they had come to me third-handed and not in the speaker's own language. I regretted the apparent impossibility of the speech being preserved for posterity. In 1871 I determined to commit it to paper and try by rearrangement of its disconnected parts to restore its form as a speech. I had enjoyed a slight personal acquaintance with Colonel Travis, had heard repetitions of some of his remarks as a lawyer before courts, and had read printed copies of some of his dispatches from the Alamo. After refreshing my memory by repeated conversations with my mother, I wrote the sentiments of the speech in what I imagined to be Travis's style, but was careful not to change the sense. I devoted several weeks of time to successive rewritings and transpositions of the parts of that speech. This done, I was surprised at the geometrical neatness with which the parts fitted together.]

Of course it is not pretended that Col. Travis' speech is reported literally, but the ideas are precisely those he advanced, and most of the language is also nearly the same.

Hoping that this letter may meet your approval and be interesting to your readers. I am, gentlemen, most respectfully, your humble correspondent,

W. P. Zuber

Prairie Plains, Grimes County, Texas, May 9, 1871

I have carefully examined the foregoing letter of my son, William P. Zuber, and feel that I can endorse it with the greatest propriety. The arrival of Moses Rose at our residence, his condition when he came, what transpired during his stay, and the tidings that we afterwards heard of him, are correctly stated. The part which purports to be Rose's statement of what he saw and heard in the Alamo, of his escape, and of what befell him afterwards is precisely the substance of what Rose stated to my husband and myself.

Mary Ann Zuber[19]

If one does not have a detailed knowledge of how the Alamo was garrisoned, the events that surrounded its fall, and the Texas landscape in 1836, the Rose story may seem conceivable and truthful. On the other hand, a number of Alamo-knowledgeable individuals have accepted the story without serious examination. Lon Tinkle, author of *13 Days to Glory: The Siege of the Alamo,* wrote that the Zuber tale was "of all the incomplete and unproved stories about the Alamo, the most dramatic and most plausible." The story is certainly dramatic. Plausible is another story. But then one must forgive Tinkle; his goal appears to have been the creation of an exciting and heroic narrative, not an authoritative history. Had Tinkle been more careful he might have seen that the Zuber chronicle contains a number of elements that defy reason and historical fact.[20]

More recently Alan C. Huffines, a graduate student, observed: "At some time on the evening of March 5, Travis may have assembled the garrison and told them what he believed was about to happen. Then in true federalist fashion he offered the defenders a choice: to stand and fight or leave. The decision was up to them. The accounts dealing with this event are presented here, but their validity is still challenged. Historians generally do not want to believe that something this melodramatic happened. There are three choices here: (1) All are experiencing mass-hallucination, (2) They are lying, (3) They are telling the truth." Mr. Huffines gives the impression that he believes in number three.[21]

In line with Huffines's observation, author, teacher, and living-historian J. R. Edmondson wrote in his book, *The Alamo Story*, "The debate [about Moses Rose] goes on.... Ultimately Travis's line must remain a legend. It can neither be proven nor disproved.

"But some seem overly eager to deny it."[22]

In taking a close and cutting look at Zuber's story, let us start with certain claims. First, the allegation that Travis said the Mexican army was flying a black flag of no quarter. That is incorrect. On March 3, 1836, in a letter to a friend, Travis wrote: "If independence is not declared, I shall lay down my arms and so will the men under my command. But under the flag of independence, we are ready to peril our lives a hundred times a day, and to drive away the monster who is fighting us under a blood-red flag, threatening to murder all prisoners and make Texas a waste desert."[23]

Second, Zuber claimed that Moses Rose had never married. Jumping ahead a little, there is the question of Louis Rose. As will be fully explained in the next chapter, Louis is supposed to have been Moses. If that is the case, there is a conflict. Louis Rose's 1835 character certificate reports that he entered Texas with a family. Either Zuber was (1) wrong in his claim that Rose was not married, (2) Moses Rose was not Louis Rose, (3) Louis was the head of a family that did not include a wife.[24]

Next, there is Rose's alleged friendship with James Bowie and Rose's arrival at the Alamo. Zuber wrote: "Rose was a warm friend of Col. James Bowie, accompanied or followed him to the Alamo in the fall of 1835, and continued with him till within three days of the fall of the fort."[25]

James Bowie
Photo courtesy of Texas State Library and Archives Commission

Therefore, let us look at what Bowie did during the revolution previous to his arrival at the Alamo and see if Rose can be found in those activities. Bowie was in Nacogdoches in early October 1835. After having received only sixty-eight votes as a candidate for the Consultation, thus losing the election, he departed sometime between October 7 and 9 and returned to his home in San Antonio. William T. Austin, General Stephen F. Austin's aide-de-camp, reported: "The army then took up the line of march and reached the Salado at day light on the morning of the [October] 20th inst.... Col. James Bowie joined the army last night during the march to this position, he had very lately left San Antonio, where he married & had resided for several years previously, this gentleman fully

189

confirmed the information previously received in relation to the defensive preparations made by the enemy."[26]

Bowie entered the army as a single individual and appears to have used his reputation and "force of personality" to obtain positions of authority. Austin gave him command of the army's first division on October 22, 1835. Bowie resigned the command position on November 2 because of dissatisfaction with Austin's leadership.[27]

Austin then appointed Bowie as his adjutant general on November 4. Austin probably made the move so he could keep a close eye on Bowie's behavior. Two days later Austin reorganized the army, an act that included an election for a regimental commander to replace Colonel John W. Moore. Echoing his loss at Nacogdoches, Bowie received 5 votes out of the 527 that were cast. Bowie, obviously angry over the defeat and his inability to dominate Austin, resigned as Austin's adjutant and left town. He joined Sam Houston at San Felipe. There he encountered Anson Jones, a future president of the Republic of Texas.[28]

Jones described the meeting with these words: "I was introduced to Bowie – he was dead drunk; to Houston – his appearance was anything but decent or respectable, and very much like that of a broken-down sot and debauchee. The first night after my arrival, I was kept awake nearly all night by a drunken carouse in the room over that in which I 'camped.' Dr. [Branch T.] Archer and Gen. Houston appeared to be the principal persons engaged in the orgy, to judge from the noise. What made the whole thing more unpleasant to me, was, that the whole burden of the conversation, so far as it was, at times, intelligible, appeared to be abuse and denunciation of a man for whom I had the highest respect, Gen. Stephen F. Austin, then in command before San Antonio de Bexar, for not breaking up the siege of that place, and retreating to the east of the Colorado."[29]

In the end Bowie and Houston, being unable to take Austin's army away from him, had to settle for second best. They had Austin taken away from the army. The Consultation selected Austin to represent Texas in the United States. Bowie returned to Bexar with the courier that carried the results of the Consultation to General Austin. George M. Patrick, the express rider, wrote: "Genl. Sam Houston had told me that Col. James Bowie would accompany me to San Antonio, [that] I must not leave him. When my papers were handed [to] me, I announced the fact at once to Genl. H. [that] my horse and myself had been ready all night, only waiting the delivery of the papers. [Houston replied,] 'But now, oh *horrors,* you must not leave, Patrick, Col. B. will be ready in 15 minutes.' You [Moses Austin Bryan] have been tried in patience by drinking friends, but never more surely than I was tried on that occasion[.] Surely. After a painful lapse of about one hour the Col. with assistance was mounted. [Bowie said] 'Now Patrick you have been kind enough to wait for me, keep up with me, and I guarantee to make up the lost time, never mind your horse, I have plenty of horses at De Wees on the Colorado.' Good as his promise he made things quite lively enough for me."[30]

The volunteer army at Bexar replaced Austin with Edward Burleson on November 24. Courier Patrick also left a statement in regard to that change of command: "You [Bryan] know my Dear Sir why Col. Jas Bowie wanted to be in camps.... When Genl. Austin resigned the command of the army, but unfortunately for his prospects; he had access to strong drink from the city of San Antonio the night of our arrival. On the morning of the electing a successor of your uncle, Col. B. was drunk which secured the election of Genl. Burleson which doubtless was all for the best."[31]

Nevertheless, Bowie somehow secured a position on Burleson's command staff, replacing F. W. Johnson, Burleson's original appointment as the army's adjutant general. Bowie, however, did not remain with the army for long. After participating in the Grass Fight on November 26, he moved down the road to Goliad. He appears to have returned to San Antonio sometime in mid-December. On December 17 Houston issued orders for Bowie to organize a volunteer force to proceed to Matamoros and "if possible reduce the place and retain possession [of it] until further orders." Bowie received the orders on or about December 27, when he reached Houston's headquarters in Washington-on-the-Brazos.[32]

Bowie appeared before the General Council in San Felipe on December 28 and 29. He presented his views on the status of the volunteer forces at Bexar and recommended that those troops be used in an expedition against Matamoros. On January 6 he reviewed Houston's orders for the attack on Matamoros with the Council. Afterward, he departed for Goliad. He and a "Captain Blount" arrived at Goliad on January 11, 1836.[33]

In mid-January Houston joined Bowie in Goliad. On January 17 Houston received a missive from Lt. Colonel James C. Neill, the commander at San Antonio, that reported a major attack on that city was expected within days. Bowie immediately collected an unknown number of mounted volunteers and rode to San Antonio, arriving the next day, January 18. Bowie's men appear to have come from Captain John Chenoweth's company of United States Invincibles, a unit that Bowie probably recruited in the summer of 1835 in the Jackson, Mississippi area. If there was one unit in the revolution that could be called Bowie's company, it was the Invincibles. The muster roll of that unit, however, does not list a man named Rose.[34]

Also, the name of Moses Rose or a variant is not found on any of the known siege of Bexar muster rolls or the James C. Neill's muster roll of about December 31, 1835. More importantly, the February 1, 1836 Alamo voting list contains Bowie's name and a number of names of men from Chenoweth's company, but no "Rose." The only Alamo list that shows a man named Rose is the March 24, 1836 issue of the *Telegraph and Texas Register.* That roll does not include a first name for Rose. Therefore, the name may refer to James M. Rose, who entered the Alamo with David Crockett. In sum, if one Moses Rose went to the Alamo with James Bowie, his name should be on many of the known documents, but it is not found on a single one.[35]

Next, there is the entire Travis "line" speech, which is extremely compromised by the fact that Zuber admitted he had created the speech and that one paragraph was fiction.[36] In 1877 Zuber wrote Texas Adjutant General William Steele:

> One feature in my "Escape from the Alamo," (see Texas Almanac, 1873,) I must confess, gives it the appearance of fiction. That is, Travis's address to his companions in arms. This certainly needs an explanation; which I now give.
>
> Rose was, if I am not mistaken, but a poor scholar, if a scholar at all. Yet he distinctly remembered the substance of Colonel Travis's certificate. But, both the distinctions & the exception were omitted by the printer. That one paragraph contains every word of fiction in my article in the Almanac.
>
> In conclusion, please permit me to explain that the object of the foregoing lines is, First, to establish the following facts; to wit:
>
> 1. That, on the afternoon of the third day of March, 1836, Travis, in a formal address, explained to his

command, their real situation; & offered to every man who might be disposed to accept it, an opportunity to risk the chances of surrender or escape.

2. That every man, with but one exception, determined to remain & did in the fort, & sell his life as dearly as possible.

3. That Rose alone accepted the offer, & effected his escape.[37]

Given that Zuber failed to mention the "line in the sand" in his "by the number" explanation, it appears the one paragraph that he admitted was fiction was the one in which Travis's sword line in the dirt is described.

Furthermore, several other features in the story indicate that the entire document is fiction. Is there any truth to the Zuber/Rose allegation that Travis called the troops together and informed them there was no hope of relief and offered them the opportunity to escape? A new Alamo document coupled with Travis's March 3 letter to the Convention at Washington-on-the-Brazos and Susanna (Dickinson) Hannig's adjutant general testimony brands the Zuber tale as bad fiction.

According to the Zuber/Rose account, "two hours before sunset" on March 3, Travis told his men: "Our fate is sealed. Within a few days – perhaps a very few hours – we must all be in eternity." Travis is alleged to have told the defenders that Fannin had not answered his call for help, that his messengers had not returned, and that no aid was on the way to the Alamo. The truth, however, is the opposite. On March 3, Travis had every reason to think that help was coming, including assistance from Colonel James W. Fannin.[38]

On the morning of March 1, John W. Smith and Albert Martin, two of Travis's couriers had returned with thirty men from Gonzales. Then, in broad daylight on the morning of March 3, James B. Bonham, Travis's "Special messenger" to Fannin, galloped into the Alamo untouched by the enemy. Bonham carried a March 1 missive from Major R. M. Williamson, Travis's good friend, who was in command of the relief effort at Gonzales.[39] The important document, quoted earlier in Chapter Four, is repeated here:

> You cannot conceive my anxiety: today it has been four
> whole days that we have not the least news relating to your

dangerous situation and for that time we found ourselves given up to a thousand conjectures about it. From this municipality 60 men have now set out, who in all human probability are found, at this date, with you. Colonel Fannin with 300 men and 4 artillery pieces has been en route to Bejar for three days now. Tonight we are waiting for some reinforcements from Washington, Bastrop, Brazoria and San Felipe, numbering 300, and not a moment will be lost in providing you assistance. Regarding *the other letter of the same date, let it pass*[;] you must know what it means; if the populace gets hold of it, let them guess [at] it. – It is from your true friend *R. M. Williamson.* –

P.S. For god's sake sustain yourselves until we can assist you. – I remit to you with major Bhanham [Bonham] a communication from the interim governor. A thousand regards to all your people and tell them for "Willie" to maintain themselves firm until I go there — Williamson. Write us soon, soon.[40]

Also, Travis's last letters from the Alamo, dated March 3, are certainly upbeat. Travis, to his friend Jesse Grimes, wrote: "I am still here, in fine spirits and well to do, with 145 men, I have held this 10 days against a force variously estimated from 1,500 to 6,000, and shall continue to hold it till I get relief from my countrymen, or I will perish in its defense." Hardly the words of man who believed all hope of survival and victory was lost.[41]

Thus it is unbelievable that Travis, on the afternoon of March 3, would have declared to his troops that he had been betrayed by his friends and that there was no hope of relief and victory. That conclusion is confirmed by a statement from Susanna (Dickinson) Hannig's 1876 adjutant general's affidavit, which reads: "The Mexicans came unexpectedly into San Antonio & witness [Hannig] & her husband & child retreated into the Fort. Enemy began throwing bombs into Fort, but no one hurt till the last day, i.e. the assault, except one horse killed – Had provisions enough to last the besieged 30 days .... The enemy gradually approached by means of earth-works thrown up. *Besieged were looking for reinforcements which never arrived* [italics added]."[42]

Equally implausible and impossible is Rose's alleged departure from the Alamo and Bexar and his journey to the Zuber home in southeast

Texas. Zuber reported that an unarmed Rose jumped from an Alamo wall and strolled down to the San Antonio River, crossed the bridge at what is now Commerce Street, and continued on through downtown Bexar, passing the San Fernando cathedral on the main plaza. That route would have put Rose within pistol shot of Santa Anna's headquarters, regardless of the date he left the Alamo. This amazing walk was supposed to have been completed in the clear light of late afternoon, without Rose seeing a single Mexican soldier or citizen of Bexar. Such an act would have been impossible on any day of the siege, but it was especially inconceivable on the afternoon of March 3, 1836.[43]

Thursday, March 3 may not have been the most active day of the siege. Still, Colonel Juan N. Almonte's diary entry for the date reports a situation that conflicts with the one communicated by Zuber. Almonte

Mexican dragoon officer
Photo courtesy of Joseph Musso collection

195

wrote: "Commenced clear, at 40 [degrees], without wind. The enemy fired a few cannon and musket shots at the city.... The General-in-Chief went out to reconnoiter. A battery was erected on the north of the Alamo within musket shot. Official despatches were received from Gen. [Jose] Urrea, announcing that he had routed the colonists at San Patricio – killing 16 and taking 21 prisoners. The bells were rung. The battalions of Zapadores, Aldama, and Toluca arrived." Jose Enrique de la Pena's authentic and unpublished diary manuscript (Campaign Diary) reports that the Zapadores entered Bexar "between 4 and 5 in the afternoon."[44]

Furthermore, on Thursday, February 25 the *"batalion de Cazadores"* had been stationed in houses "half a rifle shot" south of the Alamo. Then, after dark, according to Almonte: "Two [artillery] batteries [probably only two guns] were erected by us on the other side of the river in the Alameda of the Alamo – the battalion of Matamoros was also posted there...." In total, the area that Rose was supposed to have strolled through unarmed, unseen, and untouched was swarming with Mexican soldiers who would have killed or captured him in the proverbial blink of an eye.[45]

In regard to Rose's departure from the city, Zuber claimed that Rose left the Bexar area "three miles below the town" at twilight on March 3. He remained south of the Gonzales road and walked all night. Rose, however, allegedly made little progress because of numerous cactus collisions that forced him off course. Thereafter, the account claims that Rose only traveled during the day. He reached the Guadalupe River below Gonzales sometime during the day on March 6 and floated across the river on a log. On the east side of the river he found a deserted house, where he remained two or three days. From that point on Rose only traveled on roads. On those arteries he found empty houses because the citizens had retreated in advance of the threat of the enemy. This scenario, however, conflicts with common sense and historical truth.[46]

The route described by the Zuber account is seventy-five or more miles. A modern infantryman can travel fifteen miles a day. When required, such troops can double time thirty miles a day. A couple of days of such intense marching, however, renders soldiers unsuitable for immediate and effective combat. Also, while the account does not state it, Rose would have had to have slept a large part of the day on March 4. Otherwise, we must accept that despite his "old age" and the thorns that "continued to work deeper into his flesh," he walked for twenty-four

Texas prickly pear cactus

hours before stopping to make "his bed on the soft mesquite grass." Quite a feat. In reality, given the conditions described by Zuber, the journey should have taken Rose five days or about sixty hours at twelve hours per day. Yet Zuber would have his readers believe that the trip was accomplished in forty-eight hours or less; a twenty-four-hour walk and, say, twelve hours per day on March 5 and 6. Then, one must consider that if Rose slept all day on March 4, the trip only required about thirty-six hours.[47]

Secondly, the Zuber story locates Rose on the Gonzales to Columbus road on March 8 or 9, when according to Zuber: "The families were retreating before the threatened advance of the enemy, and between the Guadalupe [River] and Colorado [River] every family on his route had left home." The claim is absurd. Sam Houston did not arrive at Gonzales to take command of the Texian forces until 4:00 p.m. on March 11. The retreat from Gonzales and the "Runaway Scrape" did not start until about 11:00 p.m. on March 13. If Rose had been where Zuber said he was on March 8 or 9, he would have probably encountered Houston and his staff or other Texians on the way to Gonzales.[48]

Thus the conflicts and inconsistencies show why knowledgeable officials and scholars in the late nineteenth century and the early twentieth century did not accept Zuber's tale of Moses Rose as the truth. Texas Adjutant General William Steele was the first to challenge Zuber on the story. In 1877 Steele wrote Zuber, requesting his help in compiling an official list of the Alamo defenders. At the same time, Steele wrote Zuber that the Moses Rose escape story did not match the data the adjutant general's office had obtained from Susanna (Dickinson) Hannig.[49] Unfortunately, Steele's copy of this letter is missing from his letter book in the Texas State Library. However, we do have Zuber's response, and it is extremely revealing. Zuber wrote:

I must confine this letter to Rose, who escaped from the Alamo. In 1871, I wrote a tolerably lengthy account of the escape of Rose, & his travels from the Alamo to the residence of my father, in what is now Grimes County. To this account, I supplied quite a number of notes of explanations; showing, as I believe that some parts of the narrative, which, at first view might appear incredible, were, in reality very reasonable statements. Said account was designed for publication in the Texas Almanac; but, judging it too lengthy for an insertion in that periodical, I withheld it, & yet have the manuscript in possession. I however proposed a condensed copy thereof, without notes; which, with my mother's certificate, was published in the Texas Almanac for 1873. That copy, I believe, contains all the important information which I am able to give on the subject; & therefore respectfully refer you to it.

But, to clear away some apparent doubts which seem to have arisen, I deem it proper to furnish you with some additional particulars.

But, in the first place, please permit me to digress a little. On the night of the 13th of March, 1836, Captain (afterwards lieutenant Colonel) Joseph L. Bennett, with his company, (afterwards Captain Gillaspie's Company,) encamped on the east bank of the Colorado river; very near the site of the present town of La Grange. I was a private in said company, kept a diary, & witnessed & noted what I am about to state.

On that night, about nine o clock, Colonel J. C. Neill rode into camp & in a conversation with Captain Bennett, confirmed the rumors which we had heard, that the Alamo had fallen. He had borne an express from Colonel Travis to San Felipe or Washington [-on-the-Brazos], & was returning; when, on the 7th of March, I believe, at the ford of the Cibolo, between Gonzales & San Antonio, he met Mrs. Dickinson & her infant, & Colonel Travis's servant, Joe. They, then & there informed him of the slaughter of his brave companions in arms. They stated to him, that they had, three days prior to the final assault been sent for safety, into the city & placed under the care of a priest, who prepared a place for Mrs. Dickinson & her babe, in the upper part of the church; probably the cupola or belfry; where he concealed them in safety, till the fort had fallen, & the fighting had ceased. Of course, Colonel Neill returned with Mrs. Dickinson, to the Colorado. He first went to Bastrop to inform the citizens of the great calamity, & was proceeding down the river, for the same purpose.[50]

Zuber's defensive tale of Mrs. Dickinson being secreted in the San Fernando church tower and Neill finding her on Cibolo Creek is false. More than that, it appears to be an outright lie to cover his trail of lies about Moses Rose. Thus, the evidence shows that Zuber, when questioned about the veracity of the Moses Rose escape story, responded with an explanation that contains only one truth: Dickinson and Neill were real persons associated with the Alamo. Is it not reasonable to assume, since Zuber defended his Rose narrative with a lie, that the Rose story is also a fabrication? Such is the nature of liars and lies. Once a lie is told and questioned, it requires many secondary lies to stay afloat.[51]

Total acceptance of the Rose tale continued to elude Zuber. On April 22, 1901, he read a paper defending the Rose narrative to the annual reunion of the Texas Veterans Association and the Daughters of the Republic of Texas. Zuber opened with: "I wish to say something in self-defense and for the truth of history, concerning my published account of the escape of a man whose name was Rose from the Alamo, March 3, 1836. The occasion of what I have to say is that I have been reliably informed that my account of that escape has been contradicted. I have not seen any published contradiction of it by any reliable authority, neither do I know of any reliable person who has publicly contradicted it; yet I am led to believe that such contradictions, though unreliable, have made an impression upon the minds of some well-meaning persons. Therefore I feel called upon to present the case more fully."[52]

Then, after reviewing the story's provenance, Zuber said: "The men in the fort (all but Rose), were killed, none surviving to tell the story. Mrs. Dickinson and Travis's negro were shut up in rooms, and could not see what was done outside the fort, nor much that was done in it. None of the Mexicans knew all that was done, and the official reports of the Mexican officers were not distinguished for veracity. Then, how can any person at this late period disprove Rose's statement of what occurred about the fort?"[53]

Given Zuber's allegations in the previous statement, one would think he had been in the Alamo during the last days. He could not have known what Dickinson or Joe did or did not do while in the Alamo. Also, the statement conflicts with Zuber's 1877 letter to Adjutant General William Steele. Remember, Zuber said that Dickinson had been taken out of the Alamo before March 3. But in 1901 Steele had been dead since mid-January 1885, so Zuber did not have to worry about what he had written Steele, or any contradiction from Dickinson, who had died in 1883. Thus Zuber was right about one thing. In 1901 there was probably no living person who could have contested his Moses Rose tall tale.[54]

Another challenge Zuber addressed in the talk was the time of John W. Smith's departure from the Alamo with Travis's March 3 letters. Zuber wrote: "Rose left the Alamo on the afternoon of March 3d, and historians say that the courier, Captain Smith, left on the *night* of the 3d. If it were certain that Smith left on the night *following* the 3d after Rose left, this would prove Rose's statement to be false; for Smith said nothing of Travis's speech. But Smith certainly left before that night. I have no doubt that he left on the 3d, and in the night; but his departure evidently was on the morning of the 3d, between midnight and daybreak – say soon after midnight."[55]

Old age surely had caught up with Zuber's ability to spin a tall tale. His story about Smith contains a major flaw that even Zuber should have seen. Travis wrote that "J. [James] B. [Butler] Bonham (a courier from Gonzales) got in this morning at eleven o'clock...." Travis also wrote: "A reinforcement of about one thousand men is now entering Bexar from the west and I think it more than probable that Santa Anna is now in town, from the rejoicing we hear." Travis appears to have been writing about the entry of the "battalions of Zapadores, Aldama, and Toluca" that marched into Bexar between 4:00 p.m. and 5:00 p.m. Thus, Travis was writing a long letter to the Washington-on-the-Brazos convention at the time Zuber claims Rose said Travis was drawing his line in the sand. Moreover, Smith could not have departed the Alamo on the morning of March 3 because Travis had yet to write the March 3 letters.[56]

Mrs. Adele B. Looscan, historian for the Daughters of the Republic of Texas, also noticed the Bonham data and challenged Zuber on his departure time for Smith. Then she concluded that Smith had departed "in the evening of 3d of March, in all likelihood after dark. Zuber responded the way many Alamo historians do when they are confronted with evidence opposing their opinions. He argued, without any evidence to support his view, that *Travis was wrong* about when Bonham entered the Alamo. Zuber wrote: "I believe that my note in the QUARTERLY of October, 1901, – *The Escape of Rose From the Alamo,* – proves that Travis being weary and pressed for time, made a blunder (surely not an extraordinary one), and that his meaning was 'yesterday morning,' 'last evening,' or 'tonight.' "[57]

Zuber then continued with a long-winded argument detailing why Smith could not have obtained "good roadsters" (strong American horses) to ride, so "he could not have performed the trip in less than four days; and therefore that, as he arrived at Washington on the sixth, he left the Alamo soon after midnight on the morning of March the third." Never mind that "four days" travel would have had Smith arriving in Washington-on-the-Brazos after midnight on March 7.[58]

Concluding his response to Looscan, Zuber said: "I deem the time of Smith's departure from the Alamo a subject of special importance, because it directly bears upon the proof of the reality of Travis's speech as orally reported by Rose and published by me." On that point Zuber was right. He was just wrong about when Smith left the Alamo.[59]

Almonte's diary was not readily available until 1945 when it appeared in the *Southwestern Historical Quarterly.* Thus Looscan and Zuber probably did not know it contained two March entries that verified Travis's report of a large enemy reinforcement entering San Antonio on the afternoon of March 3. The Jose Enrique de la Pena Campaign Diary, which shows that the Mexican troops entered Bexar between 4:00 p.m. and 5:00 p.m., was not even known when Looscan and Zuber were debating the Rose story. The manuscript has yet to be translated and published. The two Mexican sources, coupled with Travis's March 3 missive, leave no doubt about when Travis wrote the missive.

Moreover, in March 1838 John W. Smith, in the probate of Alamo defender James Lee Ewing's estate, testified that: "He [Smith] left him [Ewing] in the Alamo on the Friday night previous to its fall...." Friday night would have been the night of March 4, 1836. Clearly, Smith rode out of the Alamo after the alleged time of Travis's speech and Rose's escape.[60]

The evidence, however, suggests that Smith did not carry Travis's March 3 letters out of the Alamo. First, Travis's February 23 note to Andrew Ponton at Gonzales took fifty-three hours to reach San Felipe, and Washington-on-the-Brazos was about forty miles farther north. Thus if Smith had taken the missive out on the night of March 4, the letter would have had to have made the trip to the convention in forty hours or less. Second, given that Travis appears to have written his missive to the convention in late afternoon of March 3, it seems unlikely that he would have waited over twenty-four hours to send it out. However, if that were the case, one would think there would be a second letter or postscript that detailed the daytime events of March 4. There is no such document. Everything considered, the March 3 letters were most likely taken out of the Alamo by David Crockett on the night of March 3, when he and two other men rode to the Cibolo ford on the Gonzales road in search of Colonel James W. Fannin's relief group. At the ford the documents were probably transferred to another rider, perhaps Crockett's nephew William Patton, who carried them to Gonzales. William Bull appears to have been the final courier who carried the letters to Washington-on-the-Brazos. In the end, given Zuber's own requirement of proof (Smith's departure time), the Rose story is false.[61]

Given the totality of the evidence, the Moses Rose escape yarn appears to have been Zuber's creation, rather than the report of a true event. Or is that the whole story? One element in this long running argument that historians and Alamo aficionados have failed to notice is that the first report of Travis's alleged speech to his men on March 3 did not originate with Zuber. The story first appeared in the summer of 1836 with the publication of *Col. Crockett's Exploits and Adventures in Texas*, a spurious David Crockett diary. The alleged journal's entry for March 3 reads: "We have given over all hopes of receiving assistance from Goliad or Refugio. Colonel Travis harangued the garrison, and concluded by exhorting them, in case the enemy should carry the fort to fight to the last gasp, and render their victory even more serious to them than to us. This was followed by three cheers." While it is impossible to know for sure, the Crockett diary entry appears to be the springboard Zuber used to create the Moses Rose story.[62]

Zuber's inspiration for the "line" element of the Rose tale may have been an incident that occurred a few minutes previous to the Battle of San Jacinto. Zuber missed the fight because he was a member of the baggage guard. Still, there is every reason to believe he could have heard the episode reported around the victory campfires on the night of April 21 or sometime afterward. The incident was reported by L. L. Cunningham, a veteran of the fight, who wrote: "Before the battle, the officer of the day, when the men were drawn up, asked all those who were afraid to face a loaded cannon to step out of the ranks, and there were two as big and healthy looking men [as] I ever saw who stepped out of my regiment." Undoubtedly, the two men were given a hard time after the Texians' decisive victory.[63]

More likely, Zuber based his line story on an incident that took place on the Colorado River in the vicinity of Columbus on the morning of March 26, 1836. In 1844 Angelina Eberly told Mary Austin Holley that Captain Sidney Sherman had told her: "Our spies reported no danger of reinforcement [to Ramirez y Sesma's command]; Deaf Smith went as far as Gonzales. All [the Texians] were anxious to fight – the *Panic* was to advance, not retreat. Houston cursing them, and drawing a line [in the dirt], called out, 'All of you who are so full of fight step out to this line. *I will see whose faces will turn pale.*' With the exception of his staff, and those subservient to his will, all came up to the mark. All volunteered to whip the enemy. So report many officers. Seeing they were ready to meet the enemy. Houston ordered a retreat in fifteen minutes to San Felipe." Given the other verified reports of Houston's behavior on the Colorado River during the army's retreat, there is every reason to believe the Sherman report, a previously unknown and unused source on Houston.[64]

Walter Lord, author of *A Time To Stand*, was not aware of all of the evidence that has been presented in this chapter. He, however, knew about some of it, and despite the inconsistencies and impossible feats reported in the Zuber story of Rose's escape, Lord accepted the tall tale as the truth. Jeff Long simply followed in many of Lord's footsteps when he penned his anti-Alamo tome, *Duel of Eagles.* In total, the two writers' acceptance of the Rose story highlights a major problem in historical research methodology. Historians often operate on the fragile precept that any report by an old veteran, no matter how absurd or unbelievable, is the truth until it is proven otherwise.

Chapter Five Notes

1   W. P. Zuber, "The Escape of Rose From the Alamo," *The Quarterly of the Texas State Historical Association*, V: 1.

2   Long, *Duel*, data comes from the front flap of the book's dust jacket.

3   Long, *Duel*, 232-234, 337-338.

4   W. P. Zuber, "An Escape From the Alamo," *The Texas Almanac for 1873*, 80-85.

5   Rufus Grimes to E. M. Pease, Navasota, July 29, 1876, Alamo Strays Box, TSL.

6   "The Alamo Again: Facts in Regard to Its Defense and Fall Not Heretofore Published," *San Antonio Express*, December 17, 1905.

7   Zuber, "The Escape of Rose," W. P. Zuber, "Rose's Escape From the Alamo," in "Notes and Fragments," *The Quarterly of the Texas State Historical Association*, VI: 67-69.

8   Ruby Mixon, "William Barret Travis, His Life and Letters" (unpublished master's thesis, The University of Texas, 1930).

9   Williams, "A Critical Study," XXVII: 31.

10   Lord, *A Time*, 202.

11   J. Frank Dobie, "The Line That Travis Drew," *Dallas News*, March 31, 1940.

12   *Wichita Times*, Wichita Falls, April 7, 1940.

13   Claude Elliott, "Book Reviews," *Southwestern Historical Quarterly*, XLIII: 532-533.

14   Ibid.

15   Lord, *A Time*, 202.

16   W. P. Zuber, "An Account of the Adventures of Moses Rose, Who Escaped from the Alamo," in Anna M. J. Pennybacker, *A New History of Texas for Schools* (Palestine: Percy V. Pennybacker, 1895), 183-188; William Physick Zuber, Janis Boyle Mayfield, ed., *My Eighty Years in Texas* (Austin and London: University of Texas Press, 1971), 247-255.

17   Steven G. Kellman, "The Yellow Rose of Texas," *Journal of American Culture*, Vol. 2, Number 2, 46, and 48, endnote 7. Kellman believed that he found French military records (AF IV 858, plaquette 6900, cote 91-47, and page 192 of the third volume of the records of the 101st Regiment) that proved Louis Rose of Nacogdoches, Texas, had been a member of the French army. The documents identified a Louis Rose, who had been born on May 11, 1785, Laferee, Ardennes. This Rose had served in the 101st Regiment of the French army. The man started out as a private in 1806. By 1814 Rose had climbed the ranks to become a lieutenant. On March 12, 1814, Rose was named to the Legion of Honor for his part as the aide-de-camp to General Jacques de Monfort.

Remember that Louis Rose of Nacogdoches was illiterate. A soldier in Napoleon's army did not have to be able to read and write to be promoted to the rank of lieutenant. However, it is very unlikely that a lieutenant who was illiterate could serve as an aide-de-camp to a general. Also, the French military records show no service for Louis Rose in Russia. Therefore, it is unlikely that the French documents Kellman found pertain to Louis Rose of Nacogdoches.

Moreover, Zuber also claimed Rose had carried the mail between Nacogdoches and Natchitoches, Louisiana. Again, it is unlikely that Rose could have performed that job if he had been illiterate.

18 See Chapter Four for data on returning couriers. As of March 3, three couriers to Gonzales had returned. Also, James B. Bonham had entered the Alamo with news about reinforcement activities at Goliad and Gonzales.

19 Zuber, "An Account of the Adventures," Pennybacker, *A New History,* 183-188; Zuber, *My Eighty Years,* 247-255.

20 Lon Tinkle, *13 Days to Glory: The Siege of the Alamo* (New York, Toronto, London: McGraw-Hill Book Company, Inc., 1958), 179.

21 Huffines, *Blood of Noble Men,* 128, n. 8.

22 J. R. Edmondson, *The Alamo Story: From Early History to Current Conflicts* (Plano, Texas: Republic of Texas Press, 2000), 396.

23 William B. Travis to Jesse Grimes, March 3, 1836, Bexar, Jenkins, ed., *Papers,* IV: 504-505. Of course Zuber would have probably argued that Travis could not tell the difference between black and blood red.

24 Louis Rose character certificate, number 580, 1835 Entrance Certificates, Nacogdoches Archives, TSL.

25 Zuber, "An Escape," 80.

26 William T. Austin, "Account of the Campaign of 1835," 300-301.

27 Stephen F. Austin, "General Austin's Order Book for the Campaign of 1835," *The Quarterly of the Texas State Historical Association,* II: 2; James Bowie to Stephen F. Austin, Camp below Bexar, November 2, 1835, Jenkins, ed., *Papers,* II: 297; Samuel Maverick, *Samuel Maverick, Texan: 1803-1870,* Rena Maverick Green, ed. (San Antonio: Rena Maverick Green, 1952), 35-36. Bowie's inability to take orders from Austin was such that word of their quarreling reached Maverick, who was a prisoner within the city.

In the 1870s a number of Mexican-Texans filed pension applications (Republic of Texas Pension Collection, Texas State Library) in which they reported they had served under Bowie at the battle of Concepcion on October 28, 1835. The men were Mathias Maldonado, Ferman Martinez, Manuel Martinez, Joaquin Casas, Juan Reyes, Antonio Garza, Seferino Huizar, Luis Gomez, and Canuto Dias. A number of the men were from Goliad and initially had been members of a Tejano unit from Goliad that had been commanded by Placido Benavides, who was from Victoria. The unit probably included more men, but Bowie never completed a muster roll for his crew, or if he did complete a roster, it has not survived.

28 Austin, "Order Book," 34; Barr, *Texans in Revolt,* 30-31. Results of this election can be found in *Lamar Papers,* I: 259, the document is, however, incorrectly dated November 24, 1835.

29 Jones, *Memoranda and Official Correspondence,* 12-13. Jones wrote that he had made a public expression of his feelings about the "denunciation" of Stephen F. Austin by Houston, Bowie, and Archer. Then, Jones reported: "Col. John A. Wharton, came to me and assured me my life was in danger from some rude attack which was threatened, and advised me, that, however true and just my remarks might be, it was not the disposition of some parties to allow the utterance of them."

30 George M. Patrick to Moses Austin Bryan, August 8, 1878, Anderson, Box 2H120, Texas Veterans Association Papers, CAH; G. M. Patrick to Moses Austin Bryan, March 15, 1875, Anderson, Box 2N251, Texas Veterans Association Papers, CAH.

Bowie's horses would have been what a horse trainer of today would describe as "legged-up," that is: animals with strong legs and running endurance because they were ridden all the time.

In 1875 Patrick wrote this about James Bowie: "I traveled from Nacogdoches to San Felipe and thence, after the close of the Consultation to San Antonio, with dispatches to Genl. Austin, with Col. James Bowie, in which time I learned to esteem him as a social, cautious and in every respect an agreeable gentleman, instead of the overbearing, blood thirsty tyrant that he had been represented by others to be."

The James Bowie entry in William S. Speer and John Henry Brown, eds., *The Encyclopedia of the New West* (Marshall, Texas: The United States Biographical Publishing Company, 1881), 436-437, quotes Captain Archibald Hotchkiss as reporting: "Late in 1835 I traveled with him [Bowie] from San Antonio to San Felipe...." Hotchkiss said that previous to their departure, Bowie had traveled to the Rio Grande, burning the grass to prevent the advance of the Mexican cavalry. One individual, J. R. Edmondson, *The Alamo Story,* 230, believes that the Hotchkiss data proves the negative Patrick claims wrong. Hotchkiss, however, appears to have been wrong. A. Hotchkiss to the Council, November 5, 1835, Jenkins, ed., *Papers,* II: 333 shows that Hotchkiss was in San Augustine in far East Texas in early November 1835. If Hotchkiss rode to San Felipe with Bowie in 1835, it was probably in late December.

Also, Bowie most likely did not go on a grass-burning mission in November or any other time. Stephen F. Austin to James W. Fannin Jr., November 14, 1836, Mission Concepcion, Jenkins, ed., *Papers,* II: 407 shows that Austin ordered Salvador Flores and his company "to go on as far as beyond the Nueces to examine whether any troops are on the road, they will also burn the whole country as far as they go...."

31 Patrick to Austin, August 8, 1878.

32 Austin, "Order Book," 53-54; Edward Burleson to the Provisional Government, Bexar, November 27, 1835, Jenkins, ed., *Papers,* III: 5-6; Austin,

"Account of the Campaign of 1835," 318. William T. Austin claimed that Bowie was sent to Goliad to "Superintend the strengthening of the fortifications" of the old fort in anticipation of the Bexar troops retiring to Goliad.

33 *Journal of the General Council,* 145, 208, Box 2-9/18, TSL; Yoakum, *History of Texas,* II: 57-58. Captain Blount was most likely William S. Blount, a recent arrival to San Augustine.

34 Neill to Houston, January 14, 1836; Houston to Smith, January 17, 1836; Cooke account, *Lamar Papers,* IV: part I, 42-46; [John] Chenoweth's Co., Mustered into service February 1836, Muster Roll book, 68, GLO; J. H. Nash, January 18, 1836, Bexar, a claim for service as an express courier for James Bowie, Audited Military Claims Ledger, 19, TSL; Manuel Barragan to Martin Perfecto de Cos, June 29, 1835, Bexar, BA-CAH. The Barrgan missive reports that Bowie had left Texas for Mississippi "with the goal of recruiting adventurers."

The Invincibles originally came to Texas under the command of Captain John W. Peacock. From Nacogdoches, the company traveled to Bexar with two other units: Thomas H. Breece's company of New Orleans Greys and Jacob Roth's small unit from Nacogdoches. The three units reached San Antonio on November 26, 1836. Captain Peacock was seriously wounded in the storming of Bexar in December. Chenoweth was then selected to replace Peacock. The unit was reorganized starting on December 25, 1835. Houston assigned the unit to the Port of Copano to secure the area for the Matamoros expedition. In mid-January 1836 the company was spread out between Goliad and Refugio. A comparison of the February 1, 1836 Alamo voting list with Chenoweth's muster roll shows Captain William Charles M. Baker, Edward Nelson, Patrick Henry Herndon, and J. M. Hays rode with Bowie to San Antonio on January 17.

35 Muster Roll book, 1-4, 20-28, GLO; Alamo voting list, February 1, 1836; *Telegraph and Texas Register,* March 24, 1836; Muster Roll for M. B. Lewis's company, R. B. Blake Papers, Box 3G300, CAH; Thomas J. Rusk's company muster roll, R. B. Blake Papers, LXI: 303; Morning Report of the San Augustine Company, November 21, 1835, Captain Bradley's Company muster roll, November 21, 1835, "Report of the Strength & conditions of the Nacogdoches Independence Volunteer company," November 21, 1835, Austin Papers, CAH; Statement of Susanna (Dickinson) Bellows to Notary, J. Castanie, Harris County, Texas, November 21, 1853, James M. Rose Court of Claims file, number 7115, GLO. Bellows identified James M. Rose as being in David Crockett's unit.

36 W. P. Zuber to General William Steele, September 14, 1877, Iola, Grimes County, AJC-TSL.

37 Ibid.

38 Zuber, "An Escape," 81.

39 Travis to Convention, March 3, 1836; Williamson to Travis, March 1, 1836.

40 Williamson to Travis, March 1, 1836.

41 William B. Travis to Jesse Grimes, March 3, 1836, Bexar, Jenkins, ed., *Papers*, IV: 504-505.

42 "Testimony of Mrs. Hannig," September 23, 1876.

43 Zuber, "An Escape," 83.

44 Almonte, "Private Journal," 20; Jose Enrique de la Pena, Campaign Diary manuscript, 13, Jose Enrique de la Pena Collection, Box 2J146, CAH. This 109-page manuscript has never been translated or published. The handwriting appears to be identical to a sample of Pena's handwriting found in an authentic Pena document in the Mexican Military Archives. Historian Jack Jackson first discovered this new Pena document in July 2000 but was unable to obtain a copy. This investigator, with the important assistance of Lee Spencer-While of Freer, Texas, obtained a copy of the Pena document.

45 Almonte, "Private Journal," 20; Filisola, *History,* II: 170-171.

46 Zuber, "An Escape," 84; Zuber, *Eighty Years*, 253.

47 Douglas P. Hyatt interview, June 11, 1996. Mr. Hyatt, a retired U.S. Army lieutenant colonel, who served in World War II through the Vietnam War, informed this investigator that a day's march for a modern infantryman is fifteen miles.

48 Zuber, *Eighty Years,* 253; Houston to James W. Fannin Jr., March 11, 1836, Gonzales, Jenkins, ed., *Papers*, V: 52; J. H. Kuykendall, "Recollections of the Campaign," edited by Eugene C. Barker, *The Quarterly of the Texas State Historical Association*, IV: 292; Webb, Carroll, and Branda, eds., *Handbook,* II: 514-515.

49 Zuber to Steele, September 14, 1877. Because a copy of Steele's letter to Zuber cannot be found in the Texas State Library and Archives, just how Steele obtained his information from Susanna Hannig is uncertain. Steele may have interviewed her or obtained his data from records on hand at that time.

50 Zuber to Steele, September 14, 1877.

51 "Testimony of Mrs. Hannig," September 23, 1876. See Chapter Nine for a detailed explanation of Lt. Colonel James C. Neill's departure from the Alamo.

52 Zuber, "The Escape of Rose," 1.

53 Ibid., 3.

54 Webb, Carroll, and Branda, eds., *Handbook,* I: 501, II: 665.

55 Zuber, "The Escape of Rose," 4.

56 Travis to Convention, March 3, 1836; Almonte, "Private Journal," 19-20; Pena, Campaign Diary, 13.

57 William P. Zuber, "Last Messenger From the Alamo," *The Quarterly of the Texas State Historical Association*, V: 263.

58 Ibid., 264.

59   Ibid., 266.

60   John W. Smith and William Lindsey testimony for James L. Ewing heirs, first class headright certificate, number 475, Bexar Land District Clerk Returns, GLO.

61   Townsend to Adriance, February 26, 1836; "Testimony of Mrs. Hannig," September 23, 1876; Joseph D. Clements affidavit, Joseph D. Clements file, AMC-TSL; Davis, *Three Roads*, 416; P. Caldwell to William Patton, May 30, 1837, Camp Lavaca, William Patton file, AMC-TSL. William Patton appears to have entered the Alamo with Crockett, but he has never been identified as having died at the Alamo. The William Patton Texian army discharge shows that he served in the army from June 21, 1836, to May 30, 1837. This Patton should not be confused with Captain William H. Patton, who had an infantry company at the Alamo but did not die there.

62   Richard Penn Smith, *Col. Crockett's Exploits and Adventures in Texas* (1836; reprint: New York: Nafis & Cornish; Philadelphia: John B. Perry, 1845), 200.

63   L. L. Cunningham quote is found in George Alfred Hill, *The Centennial Celebration of the Battle of San Jacinto* (Washington, D.C.: U.S. Government Printing Office, 1936), 8.

64   Holley, *Interviews,* 20. The story of Houston's line in the sand at Columbus is somewhat verified by another Houston statement concerning his soldiers' readiness before the Battle of San Jacinto. The statement comes from Houston's February 28, 1859, U.S. Senate speech, as quoted in Sherman, *Defense of Gen. Sidney Sherman,* 8. Houston said: "After the men had taken refreshments, the rolls were called and it was found that a good many men had sore feet, and some were sick and had *pale faces* [italics added]; after deducting these we had only five hundred and forty (540) effective men."

Sidney Sherman answered Houston's statement with these words: "Fellow soldiers of San Jacinto, many years have elapsed since we met on the battlefield, and many of our companions have gone down to the grave. But those who survive! How do your brave hearts respond to this slander? which of you had *sore feet*? which of you all feigned to *be sick*? and who had *pale faces* on that glorious day? Will you not, one and all reply, if there was one who faltered on that day, or at any period before, it was the Commander-in-Chief?"

Chapter Six

Louis and Stephen Rose:
At the Walls of the Alamo

> *Louis Rose appeared before the Board of Land Commissioners as a witness for sixteen applicants for certificates, and in two instances the only corroborating witnesses were Mexican citizens. In other cases the corroborating witness was Adolphus Sterne, a member of the board. In no instance was the testimony of Rose rejected as lacking in credibility.*
>
> R. B. Blake[1]

For the first thirty-eight years of the twentieth century, William P. Zuber's story of Moses Rose's alleged escape from the Alamo was an unsubstantiated tale accepted by few historians. Now, in the early years of the twenty-first century, Zuber's story is accepted by many historians, writers, and Alamo enthusiasts as a "particle" in the Alamo "body of truth."

In 1989 the Daughters of the Republic of Texas, the Alamo overseers, stamped the Rose yarn as the truth with the installation of a brass rod in the flagstone in front of the Alamo chapel to represent Travis's sacrificial line of courage. Also, the story has been incorporated in the history talk that is given to Alamo visitors. The organization's actions demonstrate that attitudes toward Rose and Travis's alleged line in the sand have traveled from disregard to acceptance during the past century. Why the change?[2]

Acceptance of the Rose tale as the truth occurred because of the discovery of documents that seem to verify Zuber's story of Moses Rose. The first evidence came from Nacogdoches land grant records that archivist R. B. Blake discovered in the 1930s. This is the documentation that writer Walter Lord described as "amazing evidence." He wrote: "It showed convincingly that there was indeed a Louis Rose, that he had been in the Alamo during the siege, and that his testimony was accepted by the local Board of Land Commissioners in deciding claims filed on behalf of six Alamo victims."[3]

Robert Bruce Blake, a former printer and small-town newspaper publisher, was a court reporter when he found the documents that he interpreted in a way that suggested Louis Rose, a resident of Nacogdoches, was Moses Rose of the Zuber story. He introduced the new evidence in a paper he delivered at the 1938 meeting of the Texas State Historical Association. The presentation impressed J. Frank Dobie, who convinced Blake to turn the paper into an article for the Texas Folklore Society's publication. Blake, with Dobie's assistance, wrote "A Vindication of Rose and His Story," which appeared in a collection of folklore articles titled *In the Shadow of History* in 1939.[4]

In regard to the Alamo defenders that Louis Rose gave testimony about, Blake wrote: "Taking these applications in the order in which they appear on the docket of that board, in the case of F. H. K. Day, Lewis Rose testified that he 'died with Travis in the Alamo.' In the application of John

Old stone fort at Nacogdoches
Photo courtesy of Texas State Library and Archives Commission

Forbes, administration of M. B. Clark, Rose 'states he saw him a few days before the fall of the Alamo.' In the application of the 'Heirs of John Blair, decd., by J. Lee, administrator,' the testimony of Louis Rose is even more specific, when he states that he 'left him in the Alamo 3 March, 1836.' Again, in the case of Charles Haskell, Rose testified that he 'knew him four years, supposes him killed in the Alamo.' In the application of 'The Heirs of David Wilson,' Rose testified that he 'knew him before the 2nd May 1835, was in the Alamo when taken.' And finally, in the application of 'The Heirs of Marcus Sewell,' Louis Rose stated that he 'knew him in the Alamo and left him there three days before it fell.'"[5]

At first glance, this does indeed seem to be unassailable corroboration of Zuber's escape story. But Blake's article, despite its acceptance by historians and writers, does not reflect the true nature of the evidence. Blake's notes and transcriptions differ in crucial ways from the *primary* source materials of the Louis Rose land grant testimony.

In evaluating the Louis Rose evidence and Blake's presentation of it, two questions must be addressed. Was Rose a creditable and truthful witness? Then, because the world only knows of the Louis Rose evidence through Blake's interpretation, one must ask: Is Blake's study a professional and creditable work?

Blake believed Rose was creditable and presented his evidence in a way that, with a superficial examination, appears to support the conclusion that Louis Rose was Moses Rose, who escaped from the Alamo as reported by William P. Zuber. Walter Lord's faith in the testimony notwithstanding, the evidence does not show "convincingly" that Louis Rose was in the Alamo. On the other hand, Lord and other individuals' acceptance of the Louis Rose statements being proof positive that Louis was Moses demonstrates their extremely low threshold for historical proof and accuracy. Just because Louis Rose made statements that identified a number of men as Alamo defenders does not mean he was in the Alamo and left. He may have lied. He might have been mistaken. He may have had knowledge of the men being in the Alamo for a reason or reasons other than having been in the fort himself.

Nor does the Rose testimony verify Zuber's Moses Rose story. Both sources stand alone. The only elements the two sources have in common are the name "Rose" and the date of "March 3, 1836." Blake and other believers simply assume that because Zuber said Moses Rose left the Alamo on March 3 and Louis Rose reported that he left two men in the

Alamo on March 3 that Moses and Louis were the same man. Moses Rose supporters, knowing that proving a negative is very hard, often argue there is no conclusive evidence that proves a man named Moses Rose did not escape the Alamo on March 3, 1836. The previous Rose chapter, however, addressed that question. Also, there is solid and sufficient evidence that suggests Louis Rose's 1838 statements may not be the truth or they may represent an Alamo situation for Rose that is different from the one described by Blake.

First, Blake's presentation of the Louis Rose evidence is compromised by Blake's failure to include in his article all of the relevant Rose data he had found in the land grant materials. Blake claimed: "In no instance was the testimony of Rose rejected as lacking in credibility." Evidence from Blake's papers, however, reveals that Blake, early in his investigation, found evidence that in one case Rose's testimony appears to have been rejected because it was untrue.[6]

The evidence of a Rose rejection is from the second application in which Louis Rose gave testimony for an alleged Alamo defender. The man was Henry Teal, a longtime and well-known resident of Nacogdoches. An early Blake research list, based on post-revolution land grant testimony, contains an entry that reads: "HENRY TEAL, [1] emigrated in 1835, [2] single man, [3] died with Travis in the Alamo. #140." A second Blake list identified "William S. Blount. A. [Albert] Emanuel and Lewis Rose" as the witnesses for the Teal headright application. It appears that, given the order of the data and the witnesses, Rose furnished the Alamo death statement.[7]

Blake's article made no mention of finding Rose's testimony concerning Teal. Blake had a powerful reason for ignoring the Teal data when he went to press. Teal had been a member of Thomas J. Rusk's company at the siege of Bexar in 1835. Teal was in Nacogdoches from February 18 to March 5, when he left with his company to join the main army. Teal and his men reached Houston's army on March 23, while the army was camped on the Colorado River. Teal remained in the army until the fall of 1837, when he was shot and killed while sleeping in his tent at Camp Independence. Rose's claim that Teal had "died with Travis in the Alamo" probably confused Blake because it appears to be conclusive proof that Rose may have lied or been mistaken in the testimony he gave to the land board. And there is other evidence that supports that conclusion.[8]

A bounty certificate for alleged military service offers additional evidence that Rose was most likely a liar and may have been involved in a land grant fraud scheme when he gave testimony to the land board. The certificate had been issued to Louis Rose by Adjutant General James S. Gillett in February 1854 for service in the Texian army from June 22, 1836, to September 22, 1836. Rose sold the certificate to John H. Primer, who registered it with the General Land Office on June 2, 1858. The certificate was suspended the same day. The Court of Claims, which had been set up in 1858 to detect fraudulent certificates for military service, rejected the certificate on September 28, 1860.[9]

The Court of Claims file for the bounty certificate reads: 'Examd. Genl Ld Office Register – correct in Voucher 2602 *Gillett*. No other evidence. Black List." Gillett appears to have been James S. Gillett, the Texas adjutant general. Governor E. M. Pease fired Gillett on February 4, 1854, because of a fire that destroyed the Adjutant General building and the department's military records. It was and is believed that the fire was an act of arson to destroy the military service records so the documents could not be used to detect fraudulent land grant certificates for military service. In sum, the final words on the Rose certificate, "Black List," suggest that either Rose's name was on a roster of noncredible persons or was placed on such a roll after the submission of the fraudulent certificate.[10]

That Louis Rose's testimony might have been untrue and fraudulent is buttressed by the conditions that existed at the time. Texas land historian Thomas Lloyd Miller wrote:

> The words "land" and "fraud" were almost synonymous in Texas.... It confronted the first land commissioner, John P. Borden, who served from 1837 to 1840....
>
> The members of the county boards were dealing with their friends and neighbors, and they found it hard to reject their claims. One county land board commissioner told Borden about the demands made upon the board in these words: "Now Sir please imagine to yourself a Board crowded with near 200 applicants on the first day of the opening of the land office and on subsequent days from 50 to 100...."
>
> Commissioner Borden in his report of November 7, 1839, stated that only 25 fraudulent claims had been detected but added that this resulted not from search but by accident. He

further wrote: "So great have been the facilities for manu-
facturing them that the individual holding less than 10 for a
league and a labor [a family headright] each is considered a
small operator in this line." There is little doubt that the
local land commissioners were not always told the truth,
for Borden wrote: "That frauds have been practiced in pro-
curing the certificates from the Board of Land
Commissioners must be evident to all." At least one citizen
agreed with this for he declared: "But oh-i-the perjury and
fraud that have been practiced. May God forgive them as
individuals and us as a nation."[11]

Blake did acknowledge that fraudulent claims were submitted to
the land board. He, however, argued that such claims were not approved.
As evidence for his view, he quoted Dr. James H. Starr, the board's
president: "The office was of much responsibility, and the duties of
extremely difficult performance; especially in Nacogdoches County,
which embraced the most populous region of Eastern Texas, including a
large number of native Mexicans. Many citizens, especially Mexicans,
had already received their headright grants from the former government; but it soon became known to the board that numerous persons of
this class were fraudulently presenting claims for certificates. 'Americans' (as citizens of the United States were called) were mainly the
criminal instigators of these attempts, bribing the applicants to give false
testimony, and agreeing to purchase their certificates when issued. By
severe scouting the Nacogdoches Board met with gratifying success in
detecting and defeating the attempted frauds; though on more than one
occasion threatened with violence by men of mob power (some of them
men of prominence) whose applications by the score or more had been
rejected."[12]

Blake failed to understand that Starr's statement only addressed one
kind of land grant fraud; individuals who had already received a Mexican
headright during the colonial period, mostly Mexicans, who were being
exploited by well-to-do Anglos. The second requirement for a Texian
first class grant was that the individual had to have arrived in Texas previous to March 2, 1836. The only proof a person needed to meet that
requirement was the testimony of two or more witnesses. While the
local board could not always check to see if an applicant already owned a
Mexican headright, the General Land Office could check for a previous

headright before the Texian headright was patented at the state level. Thus, anyone obtaining a second headright in a fraudulent manner could be detected by the authorities.[13]

Also, the Nacogdoches land office had on file many character certificates that had been completed for the Mexican government. Such documents included the person's arrival date. Thus, verification of arrival dates for some individuals was within the scope of the land board. A person's death at the Alamo was another thing. Evidence, other than testimony from surviving Alamo couriers and surviving noncombatants, to verify such a death appears to have been limited to a list that had appeared in the March 24, 1836 issue of the *Telegraph and Texas Register.* If a witness was willing to lie about a man's death at the Alamo or lie about having been at the Alamo, a challenge was hard to present. That is, except when the alleged dead man was still among the living. The evidence was only as good as the witness's word. Louis Rose's identification of Henry Teal as an Alamo defender and the rejected 1854 bounty certificate suggest that Rose's word might not have been very good. Clearly, Blake's assumption that the Rose testimony was truthful because it was accepted by the land board is not valid.[14]

The certitude of Louis Rose's testimony is further compromised by other problems. For example, if Louis was "Moses Rose" and had been a member of the Alamo and left on the afternoon of March 3, it seems his testimony would have been the same for all six men, that each man was in the Alamo on March 3 when he left and that he assumed each man was killed in the fall of the Alamo. After all, his final experience with each man would have been the same—all of them would have stood in formation listening to Travis's plea for them to remain—all the men, except Rose, would have crossed Travis's line in the dirt. Then Rose climbed a wall and deserted his comrades. Also, Louis Rose, if he was "Moses Rose," could not have testified with confidence that any man he had left in the Alamo had died there on March 6. According to the Zuber tale, Rose was no longer in the Alamo after dark on March 3. Thus, any number of men could have departed the Alamo after Rose had left and he would not have known about it. The Louis Rose statements, however, are not consistent, when common sense says they should be if he was "Moses Rose." Therefore, let us examine each statement that has been attributed to Louis Rose.

In the case of F. H. K. Day, Blake reported in his article that Rose said: "died with Travis at the Alamo." A transcription of the testimony in Blake's papers identifies the witnesses as (1) William S. Blount, (2) Albert Emanuel, and (3) Louis Rose. The testimony reads: "[1] Emigrated in 1838 [probably a typing error]. (2) Single man dies with Travis in the Alamo March 1836. [3] Order of survey from G. W. Smyth." The order of the witnesses and the data indicates that Emanuel made the Alamo death statement, not Rose, who appears to have furnished the Smyth data. It seems that Blake, because he believed Louis Rose was Moses Rose, assumed the order of the witnesses and their statements had to be an error. Thus, Blake attributed the statement that Day had died at the Alamo to Rose. Otherwise, certain facts about this evidence are important. The testimony does not identify Rose as a member of the Alamo force or put him in the Alamo during the thirteen-day siege. Even if Rose had been in the Alamo on March 3 and had testified that Day died with Travis in the Alamo, he could not have stated with any certainty that Day had died with Travis. If the escape tale is true, Rose could not have seen Day killed. Nor could Rose have seen Day's dead body. Thus Blake and others have taken a great leap of faith in assuming Louis Rose had to have been "Moses Rose" in order to have known that F. H. K. Day and the other men Louis Rose testified about died at the Alamo.[15]

Moreover, given the difference in what Blake reported in the article and what is found in his transcript, there is a question of what original document Blake used as his source. The only original document from the Nacogdoches land board hearings still in existence that pertains to Day reports: "106 [certificate number] M. Patton & Teal heirs of F. H. K. Day – Should be Moses L. Patton and heirs of Henry Teal ass [assignees] of F. H. K. Day (given name unknown)." It is possible that whatever Blake saw, the original document or documents may have been lost over the years as there is now no original document detailing the Day statements or the Louis Rose testimony about Henry Teal. The Day evidence, however, does not end at Nacogdoches.[16]

A first class headright certificate, number 117, for Day was also issued by the Gonzales County land board. This certificate and other Gonzales probate affidavits identify Day as Freeman H. K. Day, who immigrated to Texas in 1832. W. W. Smith reported: "... Day did not make his home in any one particular municipality.... Day joined the army and fell in the Alamo...." Thomas L. Grubbs said Day came to San Antonio as a member of Hayden Edwards's company and remained at Bexar after Edwards had returned home in December 1835. Gonzales resident Horace Eggleston swore that "he knew and was acquainted with F. H. K. Day and that . . . Day left Gonzales with the Gonzales Company of volunteer rangers and . . . by the order of Col. Williamson proceeded to San Antonio and that the said Eggleston believes and has good reason to believe that the said Day fell in the Alamo." Both the Nacogdoches certificate and the Gonzales one were approved and patented by the General Land Office.[17]

If Louis Rose and the other Nacogdoches witnesses were lying about having known Day, they could have obtained their information from other sources. Day's Alamo death could have been an assumption based on the list of Alamo defenders that appeared in the March 24, 1836 *Telegraph and Texas Register.* There was some kind of Alamo victims list available in Nacogdoches. In the case of Alamo defender William Charles M. Baker's first class application, J. M. White said: "Knew him in the fall of 1835 was a soldier in the army at the battle of San Antonio, was killed in the Alamo (says report.)." All the data contained in the Nacogdoches testimony, except for the statement that Day died with Travis, could have been obtained from Day's Mexican land grant application. The fact that Day remained in Bexar could have been obtained from Edwards, a Nacogdoches resident. In sum, Louis Rose would not have had to be in the Alamo to have known that Day had died with Travis. But then Rose never said such a thing. As previously stated, in the case of F. H. K. Day, it appears that Albert Emanuel claimed that Day had died at the Alamo. And there is no evidence that Emanuel was at the Alamo or escaped over the wall with Moses Rose.[18]

The second Alamo victim application in which Rose gave testimony was the Henry Teal submission. As previously shown, Teal was not an Alamo soldier and did not die at the fall of the Alamo. Rose might have been mistaken about Teal. Still, such a mistake is hard to understand as Teal was nowhere near the Alamo during the siege and storming of the fortress. Teal was in Nacogdoches until March 5, 1836, the day before the Alamo fell and did not join Houston's army until March 23. Therefore, it appears that Rose gave false testimony in that case.

The third case in which Blake claimed Rose testified was the application submitted by "John Forbes Admr. [administrator] of M. B. Clark, decd."[19] Blake's transcription reads:

> M. B. CLARK – I. W. Burton knew applicant the sum-
> mer of 1835. Left this place for San Antonio, thinks he is
> since dead. Absalom Gibson states [Clark] left here for the
> army, in the Alamo. Stephen Rose states he saw him a few
> days before the fall of the Alamo, a single man.[20]

Part of the original document that contained the Rose testimony appears to have been lost. One page of that original record survives, and it reports Burton's statement about Clark to read: "I. W. Burton states that he knew of [Clark] during the summer of 1835 that he left for San Antonio has never [been] heard of since is of [the] opinion that he died." The differences between Blake's version and the original show that Blake's transcription is not an exact copy, which shows that Blake was not very attentive in transcribing documents.[21]

There are other problems with the Blake transcription of the Clark application. First, the "Rose" witness was Stephen Rose, not Louis Rose. Second, the Stephen Rose testimony does not locate Clark, Louis Rose, or Stephen Rose in the Alamo. Nor does Stephen identify himself or Louis Rose as a member of the Alamo garrison. This testimony is a good example of how the Moses Rose story completely biased Blake's analysis of the evidence. Blake, because he appears to have believed the Zuber story about Moses Rose, made two assumptions. He assumed, without any evidence to prove it, that Stephen Rose was Louis Rose, and that Louis Rose was Moses Rose. Therefore, the only way Stephen Rose could have seen Clark "a few days before the fall of the Alamo" was if Clark and Moses/Louis/Stephen Rose were in the Alamo on March 3, 1836. Nice theory, but where is the evidence to support it?

Blake, without proof, said that "Moses" was a nickname. Also, he offered no explanation as to why the land board would have known Louis Rose as Stephen Rose. A mistaken board identification of Louis Rose does not make sense. There were other Rose families in the Nacogdoches area of which Stephen could have been a member. In fact, he may have been Louis Rose's son. Blake never mentioned it, but Louis Rose had a family when he entered Texas. Also, each witness that appeared before the land board had to take an oath before giving testimony. The oath procedure probably required that the witness state his or her name. Therefore, in the absence of valid evidence, one cannot assume that Stephen Rose and Louis Rose were the same person.[22]

Then there is the problem of the current identification of Clark as an Alamo defender. Yes, the land board issued a certificate for Clark, and the name is on the official roster of Alamo defenders. Yet, the Nacogdoches headright testimony furnishes no clear proof that shows Clark died at the Alamo. The belief that Clark was at the fall of the Alamo is based on Blake's string of suppositions, which have no supporting evidence. Moreover, there is no other evidence that identifies M. B. Clark as an Alamo defender. No, this does not make Stephen Rose a liar, but it does raise suspicions.[23]

The next Alamo application for which Louis Rose gave a statement was: "254 The heirs of John Blair, decd. By I. [Isaac] Lee, administrator." Blake's transcription of the application data identifies the witnesses as "Elisha Roberts & James Carter & Lewis Rose." Blake claimed the men said: "1st [Roberts] knew him as a resident 8 or 11 years ago. 2nd [Carter] states he knew him 8 years – left him at San Antonio. 3rd [Rose] left him in the Alamo 3 March 1836."[24]

The actual record, however, in imperfect language, reads: "Elisha Roberts Know him for 8 or 10 years before May 1835 Killed in the Alimo James Carter Known him for 8 years and allway Left him at San Antonio Knew him to reside Hear [Nacogdoches] Before May 1835 Lewis Rose Knew Mr. Blair Left him in the Alimo 3 March 1836 Single man." While the core element of the Rose statement has not changed, the comparison shows that once again Blake's transcriptions cannot be trusted to be accurate.[25]

While Rose's statement about Blair is the most definitive one yet examined, it does not identify Rose as a member of the Alamo garrison. Blake and others have assumed that because Rose claimed he had left Blair in the Alamo on March 3 that Rose had to have been in the Alamo on March 3 to have preformed such an act. Nevertheless, Isaac Lee, Blair's estate administrator and cousin, was not so sure about Blair's death. In April 1837 Lee reported that Blair had "died while absent in the service of Texas on or about fifth of March 1836." Then, in 1846, Lee reported that Blair had "departed this life sometime during the year A.D. 1835."[26]

While Rose's February 7, 1838 statement about Blair appears to be more definitive than the statements given previously, the following day in his testimony for the Charles Haskell application, Rose was far from certain about Haskell. According to Blake's transcription, Rose said:

"Knew him 4 years supposes him killed in the Alamo." Unfortunately, it appears the original record of the Haskell application has been lost. Nevertheless, Blake's transcription does not identify Rose as a member of the Alamo garrison or place him in the Alamo during the siege. Nor is Rose's testimony by itself conclusive proof that one Charles Haskell was an Alamo soldier or that he died with Travis.[27]

The next application containing a Louis Rose statement offers additional damage to Blake's thesis. The alleged defender was one David Wilson. Blake's transcription identifies the witnesses as "Wm. R. Luce, David Cook & Lewis Rose." Blake reported that the men testified: "1st knew him before 2nd May 1835, lived in this county, went to the Army, knew him on his way to the Army. 3rd Knew him before 2nd May 1835, was in the Alamo when taken."[28]

The actual holographic record reads somewhat different from Blake's typescript. The witnesses were David Luce, David Cook, Lewis Rose, and Juan Mousolla. Luce said: "Known him from [unclear] & living in this country think he died in the Alimo." Cook reported: "Knew before heard he was killed in the Alamo." Rose claimed: "knew him for 6 years 3 Day of March 1836 then he was in the Alimo." Mousolla said: "known him before 3 May 1835." Again, the actual record shows that Blake's transcriptions cannot be trusted.[29]

Also, it is important to understand that the witnesses did not furnish conclusive evidence that Wilson had been killed in the Alamo. Luce said he *thought* Wilson had been killed in the Alamo. Cook *heard* that Wilson had been killed in the Alamo. Nor did Rose claim he was a member of the Alamo garrison or that he was in the Alamo and departed on March 3, 1836. Luce and Cook only believed that Wilson had died at the Alamo, and they could have based their statements on a newspaper report. The *Telegraph and Texas Register* list of Alamo victims included "David Wilson, Nacogdoches." The roll included three other men that Rose testified about: "_____ Blair, _____ Day, and _____ Heiskill [Haskell]."[30]

Rose's testimony in the cases of Heiskill, Blair, and Day was critical evidence. For example, consider the Blair application. Elisha Roberts identified Blair as a resident of Texas previous to March 2, 1836. James Carter put Blair in San Antonio. Rose furnished the final piece. He said *John* Blair was in the Alamo on March 3, 1836. While Rose may or may not have been telling the truth about Blair, one conclusion is clear. Lee, Blair's cousin and administrator, could not have claimed that John Blair, his cousin, was the Blair on the *Telegraph and Texas Register* list without the Louis Rose statement. The same can be said for the F. H. K. Day and Charles Haskell applications for headright certificates. Perhaps Rose's statement was necessary to prove that a "Nacogdoches" David Wilson died at the Alamo, even though he might not have been from that settlement. The newspaper list might have been wrong about Wilson's origin.

One thing, however, is certain. If a man named David Wilson died at the Alamo, he was not the husband of Ophelia P. Wilson, who received the bounty and donation land grants for her husband's death at the Alamo. David Wilson and Ophelia P. Morrell married in Vincennes, Indiana, in 1830. They arrived in Texas in 1835. David appeared before the Harris County land board on February 2, 1838, and received a league and labor headright certificate. He died sometime before July 3, 1847.[31]

The Harris County David Wilson is clearly not the Wilson who was killed at the Alamo. Who was the David Wilson reported to have been killed at the Alamo? A David Wilson signed the Goliad Declaration of Independence on December 20, 1835. At that time Captain Philip Dimmitt was in command at Goliad. Dimmitt's morning reports for the period show that Wilson was not in Dimmitt's unit. The name "D. Wilson" is on the February 1, 1836 Alamo voting list, but is not on Lt. Colonel James C. Neill's return of about December 30, 1835. If D. Wilson was David Wilson, he most likely entered the Alamo with James Bowie on January 18, 1836. Thus, if Louis Rose had been Moses Rose and had been a member of Bowie's company, one would think that Rose would have identified Wilson as one of Bowie's men and would have known more about him. As it is, it appears that Rose identified a man as having been at the Alamo who was not at the Alamo.[32]

The only sources that unequivocally identify one "David Wilson" as an Alamo defender are the *Telegraph and Texas Register* roster and the Rose statement that Wilson was in the Alamo. Wilson was not identified as a single man in the land grant application, but his estate was granted one third of a league, the allotment for a single man. The David Wilson that can be identified as being in Nacogdoches in 1835, however, was David Willson, a married man with family, who had arrived in Texas in 1829. Thus, it appears that the David Wilson, a single man, who was identified by Rose, David Luce, David Cook, and Juan Mousolla, was not the true Nacogdoches Wilson.[33]

The last headright application that Blake claimed Louis Rose had been a witness for was "579 The Heirs of Marcus Sewell by John McDonald Administrator." Blake identified the witnesses as "John Dorset, Adolphus Sterne & L. Rose." Blake reported that Dorset had said he "knew him 3 years ago [and] understood he fell in the battle of the Alamo." Sterne reported: "knew him before the 2 May 1835 [and] understood he fell in the battle of the Alamo." Lastly, Blake wrote that Rose said: "Knew him in the Alamo and left him there 3 days before it fell."[34]

Dorset and Sterne only believed Sewell had died at the Alamo. Dorset and Sterne could have obtained that belief from the *Telegraph and Texas Register* list of Alamo victims, which also included the name "_____ Sewell." Once again it appears Rose furnished the needed proof to put Marcus Sewell in the Alamo. In this case, however, that is not correct. The actual record of the testimony given for the Sewell application shows only two witnesses: Dorset and Sterne. Is this the same document Blake examined? Who knows? But it is the record he claimed he saw.[35]

The examination of the Sewell application concludes the critical analysis of the Louis Rose land grant testimony and Blake's presentation of that evidence. Thus, a number of conclusions can be drawn at this point.

Louis Rose appears to have testified for the estates of five alleged Alamo defenders: F. H. K. Day, Henry Teal, John Blair, Charles Haskell, and David Wilson. W. P. Zuber claimed that Moses Rose had been a member of the Alamo garrison. Yet, in no instance did Louis Rose, who Blake assumed was Moses Rose, testify that he had been a member of the Alamo garrison. In no instance did Louis Rose report that he had been inside the Alamo fortress during the thirteen-day siege. In no instance did Louis Rose claim that he had escaped the Alamo on March 3, 1836. The Rose statement in the John Blair application, "left him in the Alimo 3 March 1836," and the Rose statement in regard to David Wilson (the wrong Wilson), "3 Day of March 1836 then he was in the Alimo" are the only reports that can be interpreted to claim that Rose was in the Alamo on March 3, 1836. The validity of the Rose statements, however, is compromised by Rose's claim that Henry Teal died at the Alamo, and the 1854 fraudulent bounty certificate in Rose's name. Isaac Lee's (Blair's cousin and estate administrator) confusion about when Blair died damages the credibility of Rose's statement about Blair. Lastly, in regard to

David Wilson, it appears that the man Rose identified did not die at the Alamo.

In regard to the application of alleged Alamo defender M. B. Clark, Stephen Rose was the witness, not Louis Rose. Blake furnished no evidence to prove Stephen was Louis or that Stephen was Moses Rose, who Zuber claimed had escaped on March 3, 1836. Nor does the Stephen Rose statement put Clark or Stephen in the Alamo, or prove that Clark died at the Alamo.

Blake's presentation of the Louis and Stephen Rose evidence shows that Blake's research and writing were dominated by his belief that Zuber's story of Moses Rose was true. Blake appears to have abandoned objectivity and perhaps honesty to achieve fame as the person who proved that Moses Rose's tale was true. Blake's Rose article lacks credibility for three reasons: (1) Blake's failure to include Louis Rose's Henry Teal testimony in his article, (2) Blake's incorrect transcriptions of the primary documents, (3) Blake's inclusion of a Louis Rose statement about Marcus Sewell that does not exist in the primary document.

In total, the Louis Rose statements do not appear to be very "amazing," reliable, or creditable. Most certainly, the evidence is not corroboration of William P. Zuber's Moses Rose tale. Still, there are two nagging problems with the Rose land grant evidence that require additional examination.

First, there is the situation of the man Stephen Rose knew as "M. B. Clark," who Rose had seen a few days before the fall of the Alamo. The Clark name does not appear on any of the early Alamo muster rolls or victim lists. The February 1, 1836 Alamo voting list does not include the Clark name or a similar name. The name "B. M. Clark," however, does appear on the roll of Captain John Chenoweth's company of United States Invincibles, one of the units that reinforced the Alamo on March 4, 1836. Chenoweth's list shows Clark as being "killed." Therefore, if Stephen Rose was lying, how did he know to lie about Clark? Or was Stephen telling the truth and simply got the initials reversed?[36]

B. M. Clark appears to have come to Texas as a member of Peyton S. Wyatt's Huntsville (Alabama) Volunteers in late December 1835. On January 27, 1836, Clark, while Wyatt's company was at Goliad, joined the U.S. Invincibles. Nacogdoches County probate records report that Clark "died while absent in the service of Texas on or about" March 5, 1836, a date estimate that includes the March 4 Alamo relief. It may be that Clark was killed outside the Alamo while attempting to enter with the March 4 force, instead of in the final attack on March 6. The date of the fall of the Alamo was well known. The March 4 reinforcement was not that well known. So there may have been some confusion as to the exact date, thus the estimate of "on or about." Therefore, it may be that Stephen Rose knew Clark because he (Rose) was a member of the combined force that reinforced the Alamo on March 4, 1836. Such a situation also explains the nature of Stephen Rose's testimony, which does not place Clark in the Alamo or claim that he was killed in the Alamo. Rose could have known that Clark rode to the Alamo with the group, but did not know for sure that he had entered the Alamo.[37]

Second, there is the Alamo victim list that appeared in the March 24, 1836 *Telegraph and Texas Register.* That list, in addition to identifying a "_____ Blair and David Wilson" from Nacogdoches, identifies a "_____ Rose, of Nacogdoches." Because the other Alamo Rose, James M. Rose, was from Tennessee, the *Register* listing might have been Louis Rose. Louis Rose, however, did not die at the Alamo. If the identification was for Louis Rose, it was a mistake.[38]

Furthermore, the three names are listed as _____ Rose, _____ Blair, and David Wilson, which might mean that whatever their role in the Alamo siege, they were together, or at least whoever identified them as Alamo victims may have based the identification on having seen Blair, Wilson, and Rose together. It may just be there was a second David Wilson in Nacogdoches, who was a single man. That possibility is supported by the fact that Louis Rose's most definitive statements were made about Blair and Wilson. Rose said he had left Blair in the Alamo on March 3. In regard to Wilson, Rose said: "knew him for 6 years 3 Day of March 1836 then he was in the Alimo." The Wilson statement is not clear. It might mean: Knew him for six years and knew him March 3, 1836, when he was in the Alamo. Or it could mean: Knew him for six years and knew him on March 3, 1836, outside the Alamo and then he entered the Alamo. Still, it is clear that whatever Rose knew about the Alamo defenders, he knew the most about Blair and Wilson, whose names followed the name Rose on the *Register* victim list.[39]

The *Register* list had been compiled by John W. Smith and Gerald Navan. Smith was the Alamo's storekeeper who guided the March 1 reinforcement into the Alamo and had departed the Alamo twice as a courier to Gonzales. Navan had been a clerk in the Bexar garrison, working under Green B. Jameson, the Alamo engineer. They created the roll over a three-week period after the fall of the Alamo. The roster was probably based on their own knowledge and interviews with other individuals who had knowledge of who was in the Alamo or who had attempted to enter the Alamo during the thirteen-day siege. If Louis Rose was not in the Alamo on March 3, how is it that Smith and Navan could have believed he had died at the Alamo? If the name of Rose on the *Register* list does represent Louis Rose, how can one explain the mistake, other than Rose having escaped the Alamo as claimed by Zuber?[40]

One explanation is, as with Stephen Rose and B. M. Clark, that Louis Rose participated in the March 4 reinforcement. The *Register* roster has one other identification error, "F. Desauque, of Philadelphia." De Sauque was not a member of the Alamo garrison. He, however, participated in the March 4 reinforcement of the Alamo. After the fall of the Alamo, De Sauque rejoined Fannin's command and was later executed with the Goliad men.[41]

Also, Louis Rose being a member of the March 4 relief force explains the inconsistent character of his testimony in the cases of David Wilson ("3 Day of March 1836 then he was in the Alimo"), Charles Haskell ("supposes him killed in the Alimo"), John Blair ("left him in the Alimo 3 March 1836"), and F. H. K. Day ("died with Travis at the Alimo"). If Rose and the men had been members of the March 4 relief force, Rose's final experience with each man could have been different. Perhaps he actually saw Blair, Day, and Wilson enter the Alamo but did not see Haskell make it into the fort. Thus, in regard to the Blair statement, if Louis had participated in the March 4 reinforcement, he could have left John Blair and David Wilson "in the Alamo" and still not have been in the Alamo himself. Also, such a circumstance explains why Isaac Lee would have believed that John Blair had "died while absent in the service of Texas on or about fifth of March 1836." An estimate that is identical to the estimate found in Nacogdoches County probate records for M. B. [B. M.] Clark's Alamo death.[42]

Moreover, another fact worthy of note is that F. H. K. Day entered with the Gonzales ranger company. Blair, Haskell, and Wilson may have also been part of the March 4 Alamo reinforcement. The three men appear to have been in the Alamo on February 1, 1836, which suggests they did not enter with a reinforcement. A number of men, however, were discharged by Lt. Colonel James C. Neill on February 14, 1836. At least three of the men, John Harris, Robert White, and John Ballard, returned to the Alamo as reinforcements. White and Harris made it into the Alamo and died. Ballard was separated from the group and survived. Thus, it is possible that Louis and Stephen Rose knew of the men they testified for because Louis, Stephen, and the men were among the sixty men from Gonzales and Mina who reinforced the Alamo.[43]

While the evidence for this Rose/reinforcement interpretation will be less than conclusive for many "Moses Rose" true believers, the interpretation also suggests an explanation for another puzzling element of the Alamo story. That being the two men (one badly wounded) who appear to have survived the fall of the Alamo and rode to Nacogdoches to report the tragic event. Perhaps the two men were Louis and Stephen Rose, and they were father and son. Maybe Stephen later died from his severe wounds or for some other reason. Thus he disappeared from the historical record after his testimony for the M. B. Clark estate.[44]

Chapter Six Notes

1   R. B. Blake, "A Vindication of Rose and His Story," in J. Frank Dobie, Mody C. Boatright, and Harry H. Ransom, eds., *In the Shadow of History* (reprint; 1939, Dallas: Southern Methodist University Press, 1980), 32.

2   Author unknown, "Tour Guide History Talk," The Alamo, San Antonio. Thanks to Bruce Winders, the Alamo historian and curator, who obtained a copy of the history talk script for this writer. The Zuber/Rose part reads: "Unsheathing his sword during a lull in the virtually incessant bombardment on March 5, Colonel Travis drew a line on the ground before his battle-weary men. In a voice trembling with emotion he described the hopelessness of their plight and said, 'Those prepared to give their lives in freedom's cause, come over to me.' Without hesitation, every man, save one, crossed the line. Colonel James Bowie, stricken with pneumonia, asked that his cot be carried over."

   Alamo tour guides, however, have been known to alter the story. Writer Stephen Harrigan informed me that when he visited the Alamo in March 1997, the tour guide, who gave the history talk, claimed that Moses Rose's departure from the Alamo so enraged General Santa Anna that he decided to immediately storm the fort.

3   Lord, *A Time,* 202.

4   Tyler, Barnett, Barkley, Anderson, Odintz, eds., *The New Handbook of Texas,* I: 579-580; R. B. Blake to Dr. E. W. Winkler, April 3, 1936, Nacogdoches, J. Frank Dobie to R. B. Blake, May 10, 1938, Austin, R. B. Blake to J. Frank Dobie, May 13, 1938, Nacogdoches, R. B. Blake Papers, CAH.

5   Dobie, Boatright, and Ransom, eds., *In the Shadow of History*, 33-34.

6   Ibid., Zuber, "An Escape From the Alamo"; Dobie, Boatright, and Ransom, eds., *In the Shadow of History*, 32.

7   R. B. Blake Transcriptions, LXI: 204-205, CAH. The Center for American History at the University of Texas, Austin, Texas has two Blake collections: R. B. Blake's Papers and ninety-three bound volumes of Blake's typewritten transcriptions. The Blake Transcriptions, LXIV: 1-3, contain a second reference to Teal having died at the Alamo. Blake wrote: "The official records of Nacogdoches County give the following as those from Nacogdoches who died on that occasion [fall of the Alamo]: Capt. William Blazely of the New Orleans Greys, Dr. Edward F. Mitchueson, Charles Haskel, John Blair, David Wilson, F. H. K. Day, Marcus Sewell, John Harris, Micaijah Autry, Henry Teal, M. B. Clark, Bluford Mitchell, and James Taylor." The names are correct, except for Henry Teal and Bluford Mitchell. Application number 732 for William Baker found in Blake Transcriptions, LXI: 225 identifies Mitchell as the administrator of Baker's estate. Just how Blake came to believe Mitchell died at the Alamo is unknown and hard to understand.

8 Webb, Carroll, and Branda, eds., *Handbook,* II: 718; A. Huston to Sam Houston, March 5, 1836, Nacogdoches, Jenkins, ed., *Papers,* IV: 517; G. W. Hockley to Thomas J. Rusk, March 23, 1836, Camp near Beeson's on the Colorado River, Jenkins, ed., *Papers,* V: 167.

9 Lewis Rose file, Number 7117, Court of Claims records, Archives, GLO.

10 Ibid.

11 Thomas Lloyd Miller, *The Public Lands of Texas 1519-1970* (Norman: University of Oklahoma Press, 1972), 32-33.

12 Dobie, Boatright, and Ransom, eds., *In the Shadow of History,* 31.

13 Miller, *The Public Lands,* 29-30.

14 Character Certificate Collection, Archives, GLO; Character Certificate Collection, Nacogdoches Archives, TSL.

15 Dobie, Boatright, and Ransom, eds., *In the Shadow of History,* 34; Blake Transcriptions, LXI: 156.

16 Ibid.; Number 106, "Proceeding of Land Commissioners," RHRD #114, Nacogdoches County Records, East Texas Research Center, Stephen F. Austin University, Nacogdoches, Texas, hereafter referred to as ETRC. This collection is one of two collections that contain the original holographic records of testimony given to the land commissioners. The other collection is the "Rough Minutes" of the board. Both collections, despite different titles, appear to be the same kind of record—the original notes made in regard to testimony given by individuals before the board. Often it is hard to determine just what Blake saw and used as his sources. Blake, however, cited the "Proceedings of Nacogdoches County Board of Land Commissioners" as his source for the Louis Rose statements. One assumes that Blake's sources were the original handwritten documents. The one original Nacogdoches board document pertaining to F. H. K. Day that this writer located identifies the Day headright application as number 106. Yet Blake claimed he saw a record of the testimony that identified the application as number 125. This writer could not find an original record of the testimony for the Day application as reflected in Blake's transcript of the alleged document.

17 F. H. K. Day first class headright grant – Fannin I-973, GLO; W. W. J. Smith affidavit, June Session, 1839, and Thomas S. Grubbs affidavit, July 7, 1840, Horce Eggleston affidavit, January 3, 1841, found in probate Number 21, Gonzales County Probate records, Archives, Gonzales County Courthouse, Gonzales, Texas.

18 F. H. K. Day unfinished Spanish land grant, number 83:5, GLO; *Telegraph and Texas Register,* March 24, 1836; Blake Transcriptions, LXI: 225.

19 Blake Transcriptions, LXI: 158.

20 Ibid.

21 Number 203, "Proceeding of Land Commissioners," RHRD #114, ETRC.

22 Dobie, Boatright, and Ransom, eds., *In the Shadow of History*, 29; John E. Rose character certificate, number 91:16, Character Certificate collection, GLO; James H. Starr to John P. Borden, Land Commissioner, February 14, 1838, Nacogdoches, General Land Office Correspondence Collection, Archives Division, TSL; Louis Rose character certificate, 1835.

23 The Daughters of the Republic of Texas, "The Story of The Alamo, Thirteen Fateful Days in 1836," a small information sheet given out at the Alamo that contains the official list of Alamo defenders.

24 Blake Transcriptions, LXI: 162.

25 Number 259, "Rough Minutes – Board of Land Commissioners," RHRD #112, ETRC.

26 Isaac Lee petition for letters of administration of the John Blair estate, April 11, 1837, and Isaac Lee petition for letters of administration of the John Blair estate, April 2, 1846, transcriptions found in John Blair folder, Box 3G299, Blake Papers, CAH. Given that these documents are Blake's typewritten transcriptions, the 1835 date might be a typing error.

27 Blake Transcriptions, LXI: 163.

28 Ibid., 165.

29 Number 427, "Proceeding of Land Commissioners," RHRD, #114, ETRC.

30 *Telegraph and Texas Register*, March 24, 1836.

31 David Wilson bounty land grant, Milam B-788, GLO; David Wilson donation land grant, Nacogdoches D-662, Milam, D-781, Duplicate Certificate Voucher 1927, GLO; David Wilson first class headright grant, Travis 1-60, Duplicate Certificate voucher 292, GLO; Henning et al. v. Wren et al., Court of Civil Appeals of Texas, May 27, 1903, *Southwestern Reporter*, Vol. 75, 905-911.

32 Goliad Declaration of Independence, December 20, 1835, Goliad, Jenkins, ed., *Papers*, III: 269; Alamo voting list, February 1, 1836; J. C. Neill Alamo Return, Muster Roll book, 20.

33 *Telegraph and Texas Register,* March 24, 1836; David Willson Character Certificate, number 542, Nacogdoches Archives, TSL.
    As to the true identity of the Alamo David Wilson, Ms. Bette Whitley of Seguin, Texas (Whitley to Lindley, June 20, 1989, Seguin, author's Alamo files) furnished this writer the following information from J. S. Powell, "A Biographical Sketch of Mr. and Mrs. J. H. Powell." Mr. Powell wrote that his grandfather, James Powell, born 1774, "came to Tennessee and married a Widow Allen, who had one child, a son.... The Widow Allen was of a family by the name of Spence. A sister, another of the Spence family, married a Mr. Wilson. A son, David Wilson, was one of those killed in the Alamo." Perhaps, Mrs. _____ Spence Wilson's son was the true Wilson at the Alamo.

34 Blake Transcriptions, LXI: 166.

35 Number 579, "Proceedings of the Land Commissioners," RHRD, #114, ETRC.

A second record of the Sewell testimony is found in a large ledger book titled *A Book Containing the applicant's name and the evidence of his or her residence in the county, Nacogdoches, Texas June, 1835* in the archives of the Nacogdoches County Courthouse, Nacogdoches, Texas. Those records were published in Carolyn Reeves Ericson, *Nacogdoches Headrights,* 22. The entries in both the ledger book and the Ericson book show that the Sewell witnesses were John Dorsett and Adolphus Sterne. No Louis Rose is identified as a witness for the Sewell estate. Either Blake made a huge mistake in his note taking or he misrepresented the Sewell application to include Rose as a witness.

36 *Telegraph and Texas Register,* March 24, 1836; Muster Roll book, 20-28, 104; Alamo voting list, February 1, 1836; John Chenoweth's Muster Roll, February 1836. See Chapters Three and Four for the story of the March 4, 1836 reinforcement of the Alamo.

37 B. M. Clark to Jesse Burnam, January 2, 1836, AMC-TSL; Sam Houston to P. S. Wyatt, December 28, 1835, Washington-on-the-Brazos, Jenkins, ed., *Papers,* III: 351; Webb, Carroll, and Branda, eds., *Handbook,* II: 940; John Chenoweth muster roll, February 1836. The Burnam document reads: "B. M. Clark a volunteer attached to Col. Wyatts command owes Jesse Burnam three dollars to be taken out of his monthly pay."

38 *Telegraph and Texas Register,* March 24, 1836; Groneman, *Alamo Defenders,* 94.

39 Number 259, "Rough Minutes"; Number 427, "Proceedings of the Land Commissioners"; Probate Minutes, Nacogdoches, Vol. B, 61-62. The probate record shows that George Pollett was appointed administrator of the estates of David Wilson and Charles Haskell and obtained an order to sell their real estate. Thomas J. Rusk, Isaac Lee, and Charles S. Taylor testified that Haskell had been a citizen of Nacogdoches previous to March 2, 1836. Adolphus Sterne claimed that Wilson owed him $15.00. Pollett said Wilson or his estate owed him $30.00.

40 *Telegraph and Texas Register,* March 24, 1836; Green B. Jameson to Sam Houston, January 18, 1836, Jenkins, ed., *Papers,* IV: 59.

41 *Telegraph and Texas Register,* March 24, 1836; Yoakum, *History,* II: 87.

42 Number 427, "Proceedings of the Land Commissioners"; Number 259, "Rough Minutes"; Blake Transcriptions, LXI: 156 and 163.

43 Horce Eggleston affidavit, January 3, 1841; J. C. Neill discharge affidavits, February 14, 1836, Bexar, Robert White file, John T. Ballard file, AMC-TSL; "Byrd Lockhart's Muster Roll – February 23, 1836."

44 *Arkansas Gazette*, March 29, 1836, Little Rock.

Chapter Seven

A Rose Is a Rose:
Moses, Louis, and James M.

Of course, she did say "Ross," not "Rose." But letters and spelling meant nothing to Mrs. Dickinson, who couldn't read or write. At this distance, her statement looks good enough – especially since there was no "Ross" in the Alamo.

Walter Lord[1]

Writer Walter Lord discovered the third piece of evidence that seems to verify William P. Zuber's tale of Moses Rose. Lord, because of the Louis Rose land grant statements, had already concluded that Louis Rose was Moses Rose and that he had been a member of the Alamo garrison. Never mind that there was no solid evidence that proved Louis was Moses or that specifically identified Louis as a member of the Alamo command. Lord, like R. B. Blake, assumed that Louis Rose had to have been Moses Rose. Lord wrote: "But did he [Moses] leave under the dramatic circumstances described by Zuber? Freshly uncovered information suggests that he did. This consists of a formal statement, never published, given by Mrs. Dickinson to the State Adjutant General, who was trying to develop a more definitive list of Alamo defenders."[2]

The alleged formal statement, however, is compromised by a major problem that Lord failed to report to his readers. There is no original holographic document that reports this Dickinson data. The piece Lord found is a typed statement, of which there are two different typed versions. The statement has a number of details that compromise its credibility. Also, Lord was wrong about the source of the alleged Dickinson statement. The statement is not part of the holographic record of the September 23, 1876 Dickinson interview document prepared for the Texas Adjutant General's office.[3]

233

Susanna (Dickinson) Hannig, ca. 1880
Photo courtesy of the Daughters of the Republic of Texas Library

The typewritten versions are part of a small collection in the Archives Division of the Texas State Library labeled "Alamo Strays." The assemblage contains typed transcripts of letters to the adjutant general, old newspaper clippings about the Alamo, loose pages from Dr. Amelia W. Williams's master thesis on the Alamo, and other papers pertaining to the Alamo. This box of documents, which is stored in an administrative office, has no finding aid.[4]

The first version of the alleged Dickinson statement reads:

> On the evening previous to the massacre, Col Travis asked the command that if any desired to escape, now was the time, to let it be known, & to step out of the ranks. But one stepped out. His name to the best of my recollection was Ross. The next morning he was missing – During the

final engagement our Milton, jumped over the ramparts & was killed –

Col. Almente [*sic*] (Mexican) told me that the man who had deserted the evening before had also been killed & that if I wished to satisfy myself of the fact that I could see the body, still lying there, which I declined.

[Note made by typist]
Source: Adjutant General's Letters concerning the Alamo, 1875-1878. Texas State Archives.[5]

Version two, with the differences in italics, reads:

On the evening previous to the massacre, Col Travis asked the command that if any desired to escape, now was the time, to let it be known, & to step out of ranks. But one stepped out. His name to the best of my recollection was Ross. The next morning he was missing – During the final engagement *one* Milton, jumped over the ramparts & was killed –

Col *Almonte* (Mexican) told me that the man who had deserted the evening before had also been killed & that if I wished to satisfy myself of the fact that I could see the body, still lying there, which I declined.

Mrs. S. A. Hannig
[Note made by typist]
Mrs. S A Hannig Wife of Almaron Dicenson [sic] (or Dickerson) Source: Adjutant General's Miscellaneous Papers, Archives, Texas State Library.[6]

The differences (misspelling of Almonte in the first document and "our Milton" versus "one Milton") in the two versions seem to suggest that the typescripts were completed at different times by different individuals who had seen an actual holographic document; a document that had been moved from the "Adjutant General's Letters concerning the Alamo" collection to the "Adjutant General's Miscellaneous Papers" collection.

Nevertheless, two questions must be considered in evaluating the Ross documents. First, since no original holographic document can be found, one must ask: Is there a possibility that the documents are forgeries? Second, is the information found in the two typescripts reliable?

On the surface, the Ross data appears to be a godsend to those who want to believe the Moses Rose story. The document eliminates three major flaws in Zuber's tale and a serious problem with the Louis Rose land grant statements. First, the Moses Rose story and the Louis Rose testimony place the event in question on March 3, 1836. The Dickinson documents place the event on the "evening previous to the massacre," which would have been March 5. Thus, this Dickinson evidence counters recent evidence that Travis's alleged speech to his command and Rose's escape could not have taken place on March 3. Second, the Dickinson statements offer verification of the Moses Rose tale from a known eyewitness to the siege and storming of the Alamo. Previous to Lord's discovery of the Dickinson's documents, there was no independent evidence to support the Zuber story and the Louis Rose testimony. Third, the identification of "Rose" as "Ross" solved the problem of authentic Dickinson statements about defender James M. Rose that conflict with Zuber's identification of Moses Rose as an Alamo defender. Years earlier Dickinson had claimed that James M. Rose was the only man named Rose in the Alamo. Lastly, the Ross statement declares that Ross was in the Alamo and that Travis called his men together in a formation and offered them the opportunity to escape. Whereas, the Louis Rose testimony does neither. The 1838 Louis Rose statements only infer that he was in the Alamo and departed on March 3. The 1838 documents offer no evidence that Travis called his men together and offered them a chance to leave the Alamo.[7]

In 1853 and 1857 Dickinson (as Susanna Bellows) furnished affidavits to the heirs of James M. Rose that put him in the Alamo with David Crockett. In 1853 she said that she "knew no other man by that name [at the Alamo]." In 1857 she testified that James M. Rose "was the only man in the army by the name of Rose." Also, she testified: "I saw Rose often, and upon one occasion heard my husband Capt. Dickinson speak to Rose of a narrow escape he (Rose) had made from a Mexican officer upon their first attack."[8]

On the other hand, one can argue that if Dickinson only knew Rose by the name of Ross, then she would not have remembered him by his right name. Lord argued: "Of course, she did say 'Ross,' not 'Rose.' But letters and spelling meant nothing to Mrs. Dickinson, who couldn't read or write. At this distance, her statement looks good enough—especially since there was no 'Ross' in the Alamo. Nor does it seem damaging that her statement postdated the Zuber story by three years. It doesn't have the ring of a coached remark; and Mrs. Dickinson, who was exasperatingly uninterested in her historic role, didn't have it in her to take off all alone on a flight of fancy."[9]

Yes, Mrs. Dickinson was illiterate, but she was not deaf or hard of hearing. Thus, the claim that she would not have known the difference between "Ross" and "Rose" is a weak theory to explain why she would have identified Rose as Ross. Especially, since she had no problem understanding and remembering the name of James M. Rose. Also, Dickinson, being unable to read and write, may have been more attentive to speech sounds than a literate person. After all, her only means of communication was talking and listening to the people in her world.

Unlike the Ross report, the holographic original of Susanna (Dickinson) Hannig's 1876 interview does exist. The holographic document reads:

[page one]

Austin, Tex. Sept. 23, [18]76

Called on Mrs. Susanna Hannig, whose husband Joseph Hannig is living with her. She was at the sacking of the Alamo in 1836, 6th Mch; was then in her 15th year; was then named Susannah Dickinson wife of Lieut. [Captain] Dickinson, and her maiden name was Susanna Wilkerson. Her parents were in Williamson Co. Tenn. Her husband was one of the killed. They had one child, a daughter, who, then an infant, was with them in The Alamo; This daughter married John Menard Griffith, a native of Montgomery Co. Texas, by whom she had 4 children, all of whom are living; She died in Montgomery Co. Tex about the year 1871.

The Mexicans came unexpectedly into San Antonio & witness & her husband & child retreated into the fort. Enemy began throwing bombs into Fort, but no one hurt till

[page two]

the last day, i.e. The assault, except one horse killed. Had provisions enough to last the besieged 30 days. Among the besieged were 50 or 60 wounded men from Cos's fight [siege and storming of Bexar, October 20 to December 11, 1835] About 18 cannon (she believes) were mounted on parapet & in service all the time. The enemy gradually approached by means of earth-works thrown up. Besieged were looking for reinforcements which never arrived. The only outsiders who succeeded in coming into Fort were 3 of our spies who entered 3 days before the assault –

On morning of 6th Mch. about daylight enemy threw up signal rocket &

[page three]

advanced & were repulsed. They rallied & made a 2nd assault with scaling ladders, first thrown up on E. side of Fort. Terrible fight ensued. Witness retired into a room of the old church & saw no part of fight – Though she could distinctly hear it. After the fall she was approached by a Col.(?) Black (an Englishman and officer in the Mexican service) who sheltered her from Mexican injury & took her in a buggy to Mr. Musquiz, a merchant in town, where she staid till the next day, when she was conducted before Santa Anna who threatened to take her to Mexico with her child; when Almonte, his nephew, addressing his English, pleaded for witness, saying he had been educated in N. O. & had experienced great kindness from Americans. Witness was thus permitted to depart to her home in Gonzales. Col. Travis commanded the Fort.

[page four]

The only man, Witness saw killed was a man named Walker from Nacogdoches, who was bayoneted & shot. She knew John Garnet from Gonzales, who she is certain was killed though she did not see it. After her removal to Musquiz's she expressed a wish to visit the scene of carnage, but was informed by the people of the house that it would not be permitted as the enemy was then burning the dead bodies – and in conformation thereof, she was shown a smoke in the direction of the Alamo. She knew Col. Bowie & saw him in the Fort, both before & after his death. He was sick before & during the fight, and had even been expected to die. – Col. Crockett was one of the 3 men who came into Fort during the siege & before the assault. He was killed, she believes.

[page five]

A Negro man named Joe, was in the Fort, & was the slave & body servant of Col. Travis. After the fall of the

Alamo, Joe was forced by the Mexicans at the point of the bayonet to point out to them the bodies of Col. Travis & Col. Crockett among the heaps of dead. Joe was the only negro in Fort. The witness's infant was the only child in the fort. The witness & the two Mexican women already mentioned were the only women in the fort.

The witness has had no children in her present marriage.[10]

D. Juan N. Almonte, Santa Anna's aide-de-camp
Photo courtesy Jack Jackson, Austin, Texas

There are two major problems with the Ross typescript documents when they are compared with the authentic Hannig interview document. First the Ross data is not part of the 1876 interview. Second, the typescript documents are written in first person as if the interviewer had recorded it exactly as Hannig had said it. Whereas, the authentic Hannig document is in third person and in a style that suggests the interviewer listened to Susanna and then recorded the data in pretty much his or her own words, not necessarily in Susanna's language. And there are other problems with the Ross typescripts.

Additional evidence and content analysis of the Ross report reveals that the Almonte and Dickinson dialogue about the deserter most likely could not have occurred in the Alamo on the morning of March 6 or before the defenders' bodies were burned. The Ross documents claim: "Col. Almonte (Mexican) told me that the man who had deserted the evening before had also been killed & that if I wished to satisfy myself of the fact that I could see the body, still lying there...." The statement appears to suggest that Ross was the deserter. Nonetheless, it is important to note that Dickinson did not go out and see that the deserter was Ross. Nor did Almonte identify the deserter as Ross. If the deserter was not Ross, why would Dickinson have mentioned him? After all, was she not being questioned about a man named Rose who had allegedly escaped from the Alamo?[11]

Furthermore, how would Almonte have known that the man was a deserter? If the Ross tale is true, the man could just as easily have appeared to be a departing courier. The only plausible way Almonte could have known the man was a deserter would have been if the Mexican troops captured him, questioned him, and killed him. Moreover, Almonte made no mention of Ross or a deserter in his journal, a daily record in which he reported other Alamo arrivals and departures of which he had knowledge.[12]

Almonte's alleged claim that the deserter's body was "still lying there" indicates that the dialogue would have had to occur between Dickinson's discovery in the chapel and her departure from the Alamo on the morning of March 6 before the collection of the bodies for burning. It is a common belief that Almonte discovered Dickinson and escorted her from the Alamo. That, however, is incorrect; an Englishman named Black found Dickinson, protected her, and transported her in a buggy to the Musquiz home. The available evidence suggests she did not encounter Col. Almonte until the next day, March 7, when she was taken before General Santa Anna.[13]

The defenders' bodies apparently were burned on March 6. Francisco Ruiz, who claimed he supervised the burning of the bodies, said: "About

3 o'clock in the afternoon [March 6] they commenced laying the wood and dry branches, upon which a file of dead bodies was placed; more wood was piled on them, and another file brought, and in this manner they were all arranged in layers. Kindling wood was distributed through the pile, and about 5 o'clock in the evening it was lighted."[14]

The likelihood that Dickinson did not talk with Almonte before the burning of the bodies is reinforced by new evidence, which reveals that Dickinson, soon after seeing David Crockett's body between the chapel and the long barrack, entered a state that made a discussion with Almonte within the Alamo compound unlikely. Dickinson, after her arrival at Gonzales was taken to the George Tumlinson home. Tumlinson's son George W. had died at the Alamo. Dickinson told the family of "the fall of the Alamo and its horrors." Annie White, Tumlinson's eleven-year-old stepdaughter, was an avid listener. In her old age White reported: " Mrs. Dickinson told us . . . that the Mexicans made her go with them through the Alamo and watch them plunge their bayonets into the lifeless bodies of the fallen patriots. They did this in order to be certain that every one was dead. She said she fainted when they came to the body of her husband." Exactly how long Dickinson remained unconscious is unknown, but the condition explains why her Alamo exit reports are limited to the chapel and the battleground in front of the chapel, and why officer Black took her to the Musquiz house in a buggy.[15]

One can argue that Almonte talked with Dickinson after she had been taken to the Musquiz house. There is, however, a conflict between the Ross report and the genuine adjutant general interview that suggests Almonte did not meet with Dickinson at the Musquiz house on March 6. According to the Ross document, Almonte told Dickinson that if she "wished to satisfy" herself that the deserter had been killed, she "could see the body, still lying there," which she declined. Yet, the authentic Dickinson report states: "After her removal to Musquiz's she expressed a wish to visit the scene of carnage, but was informed by the people of the house that it would not be permitted as the enemy was then burning the dead bodies – and in conformation thereof, she was shown a smoke in the direction of the Alamo."[16]

The next problem with the Ross account is Dickinson's alleged claim: "The next morning he [Ross] was missing." That would have been the morning of March 6 when the enemy forces attacked without warning in the darkness. Would Travis have conducted a roll call before his men mounted the walls to fight off a surprise attack? It is highly improbable that Ross's absence would have been discovered during the frantic rush to the ramparts that morning, or that Dickinson or anybody else would have been aware of such a situation. Lastly, the claim that Ross was not discovered missing until the following morning conflicts with Zuber's report of Rose's alleged departure. Zuber claimed that Rose "sprang up, seized his wallet of unwashed clothes, and ascended the wall" in full view of David Crockett and James Bowie during the daylight of late afternoon. Therefore, if the Ross document is authentic and Dickinson was right, Ross could not have been Moses Rose.[17]

In sum, the evidence and its analysis suggest that the typed versions may not have been copied from an original handwritten document. Still, there is evidence that the Adjutant General's Office may have contacted Mrs. Hannig about the veracity of Zuber's Rose story, most likely in August 1877, almost a full year after the date of the authentic interview.[18]

Adjutant General William Steele wrote Zuber on August 29, 1877, concerning the truth of the Rose story. Unfortunately, Steele's copy of the letter is missing from the letter book for that period. We do, however, have Zuber's response, which throws some light on what Steele appears to have written. After his presentation of an obviously untrue story about Lt. Colonel James C. Neill and Mrs. Dickinson, Zuber wrote: "I have made the foregoing digression to explain my reasons for holding that Mrs. Dickinson may be mistaken in the time of Rose's escape. As to General Almonte's remark that Rose was killed & Mrs. Dickinson could see his body if she wished. I presume he would have made the same remark of any other man in the Alamo. I think his meaning was equivalent to this, 'Every man in the Alamo has been killed. Not one has escaped, you can see the bodies of all; or of any one of them, if you wish.'"[19]

Some individuals might argue that Zuber's response is proof that there was an original Ross document. Adjutant General Steele, however, appears to have written Zuber that Dickinson had reported that a man named Rose had been killed in the fall of the Alamo and that Almonte had verified Rose's death. That information clearly conflicts with the Ross document, which does not report that Almonte said Ross was killed. According to the Ross report, Almonte told Dickinson the "deserter" was killed. But by any reasonable interpretation of the Ross document, Ross and the deserter were the same person. Therefore, Ross, Rose, or whoever was killed.[20]

What about Zuber's reference to Dickinson being mistaken about Rose's time of escape? The Ross account reports that Dickinson said Ross escaped on March 5, and Zuber maintained Rose went over the wall on March 3. Does that difference prove there was an original handwritten Ross document? Probably not. Zuber, however, was certainly worried about Dickinson's claim of a different escape time for a defender named Rose. Whatever Dickinson told Steele or his representative about the time of a Rose escape conflicted with Zuber's story that Moses Rose departed the Alamo in late afternoon on March 3. If that is not the case, then why did Zuber respond with a piece of fiction to argue that Dickinson was not in the Alamo during the last three days of the siege and could not have known about Rose's departure. Remember, Zuber claimed that three days before the final assault the local priest had taken Dickinson and her baby out of the Alamo and placed them in cupola of the San Fernando church.[21]

Exactly what Dickinson told the adjutant general or his representative about a defender named Rose will probably never be determined. A written record of the discussion may not have been made. We do, however, know what Dickinson said to a Caldwell County judge about James M. Rose in the summer of 1857. Susanna, when asked to describe Rose, answered: "He was about thirty-five or forty years of age. He was of medium height, heavy set, rather full square face, very quick spoken – he fell with the rest of the defenders of the Alamo – during the siege. I saw Rose often, and upon one occasion heard my husband Capt. Dickinson speak to Rose of a narrow escape he (Rose) had made from a Mexican officer upon the first attack."[22]

First, James M. Rose's escape was from a Mexican officer, not the Alamo. Second, the event most likely occurred during the enemy's arrival and capture of Bexar on the afternoon of February 23. It is highly improbable that James Rose's escape from the Mexican officer occurred in the confusion of the final assault on the morning of March 6, and that Rose stopped to report the incident to Almaron Dickinson, who in turn stopped to tell the story to his wife. The adjutant general or his representative may have simply asked Dickinson: Do you know anything about the escape of a defender named Rose? Dickinson could have answered with her story about James M. Rose's escape. If she was specifically asked about a "Moses Rose," she may have assumed Moses Rose was James M. Rose, the "M" standing for Moses.[23]

Nevertheless, Zuber's answer to General Steele about Dickinson's statements concerning Rose does have one element that is hard to explain. The element is the sentence that reads: "As to General Almonte's remark that Rose was killed & Mrs. Dickinson could see his body if she wished." That statement appears to mirror the third part of the Ross report that reads: "Col[.] Almonte ... told me that the man who had deserted the evening before had also been killed & that if I wished to satisfy myself of the fact that I could see the body, still lying there, which I declined." The similarity of the two statements seems to verify that at one time there was an original Dickinson report about Ross.[24]

There are, however, other explanations for the Almonte "remark." If the Ross document ever existed, Steele or whoever talked with Dickinson may have misunderstood her. For example in the clearly authentic Dickinson document of September 23, 1876, the interviewer wrote that Dickinson was fifteen years old at the fall of the Alamo. That is incorrect. Dickinson married Almaron Dickinson when she was fifteen years old. Her exact age at the time of the Alamo is unknown, but she would have turned twenty-two sometime in 1836. Angelina, Dickinson's infant daughter, would have been fifteen months old on March 14, 1836. Perhaps Susanna said that all the defenders, including Rose (probably meaning James M. Rose), had been killed. Then the interviewer assumed she had obtained that from Almonte because it was a common, though wrong, belief that he had taken her from the Alamo.[25]

Then there is the possibility that Steele made up the Almonte statement about Rose being killed to bluff Zuber to see how he would respond. And Zuber answered with a huge lie about Dickinson not being in the Alamo the last three days of the siege.[26]

Lastly, there is the possibility that there never was a written record of Dickinson's conversation about Rose's escape and that the Ross document is a fraud created by an unknown person to substantiate the Moses Rose tale by furnishing an eyewitness and eliminating the problematic date of March 3 found in the Zuber account and the Louis Rose land grant testimony. If that is the case, the document's creator could have used Zuber's letter to Steele as a springboard for the alleged Almonte statement.

Moreover, the creator of such a forged document would have been confronted with another problem in attributing the statement to Dickinson. The writer, however, would have had no choice as Dickinson was the only Alamo survivor still living in the 1870s who could serve as an acceptable eyewitness to verify the Moses Rose tale. The problem was that Dickinson had given earlier affidavits that identified James M. Rose as the only man in the Alamo with the last name of Rose. The alleged Dickinson statement solves that complication by calling the deserter Ross. In sum, the Ross document seems, at least to this writer, to be almost too perfect in what it says.

In the end there may not be sufficient evidence to prove to most people that the Ross document is fiction. On the other hand, given that there is no original handwritten Ross document; given that Steele's copy of his letter to Zuber is missing; given that Zuber's response to Steele indicates Steele reported that Almonte had told Dickinson Ross had been killed; given the improbable nature of the Ross document's data; given the perfection of the Ross statement in providing answers to the major flaws in the Zuber and Louis Rose evidence, branding the document as highly unreliable and a fraud is a reasonable conclusion.

Nevertheless, if one wants to accept the Ross document as authentic and assume that the typed statements actually refer to Moses Rose/Louis Rose, there are two problems one must do away with in order to make it work. First, the alleged Dickinson statement can be read to mean that Ross had not escaped the Alamo but had been killed in the attempt. Moreover, that interpretation is reinforced by Zuber's response to Steele's missive showing that Dickinson said Rose was killed. Therefore, Ross could not have been Moses Rose, if there ever was such a person.

Additionally, when Walter Lord assumed that the name Ross had to refer to Moses Rose because a man named Ross had never been identified as an Alamo defender, the famed writer made a serious mistake. There was an Alamo defender named "Ross." He was Ross McClelland, a little Irishman from Mina. So, if the alleged Dickinson statement about Ross is authentic, she was most likely talking about McClelland. Still, this investigator believes the Ross document is a forgery.[27]

Chapter Seven Notes

1 Lord, *A Time,* 202-203.

2 Ibid.

3 Ibid.; "Testimony of Mrs. Hannig," September 23, 1876.

4 "Alamo Strays" box, Archives Division, Texas State Library. Former archivist Michael A. Green was kind enough to inform this investigator of the box. The box of documents appears to be the same one that Walter Lord examined in his research on the Alamo.

5 Version number one of the alleged Hannig statement concerning Ross, "Alamo Strays" box, TSL.

6 Version number two of the alleged Hannig statement concerning Ross, "Alamo Strays" box, TSL.

7 Zuber, "An Escape," 81; Dobie, Boatright, and Ransom, eds., *In the Shadow of History,* 36; "Testimony of Mrs. Hannig," September 23, 1876; F. H. K. Day, Number 106, M. B. Clark, Number 203, David Wilson, Number 427, Marcus Sewell, Number 579, "Proceedings of Land Commissioners," John Blair, Number 259, "Rough Minutes."

8 Susanna (Dickinson) Bellows affidavit, November 21, 1853, Harris County, Susanna Bellis affidavit, July 16, 1857, Caldwell County, James M. Rose file, C-7115, Court of Claims collection, GLO.

9 Lord, *A Time,* 202-203.

10 "Testimony of Mrs. Hannig," September 23, 1876.

11 Alleged Hannig statement concerning Ross.

12 Almonte, "Private Journal," 22-23.

13 "Testimony of Mrs. Hannig," September 23, 1876; Annie E. Cardwell interview, "Attended first Texas Presbytery in 1849," *Gonzales Inquirer,* June 7, 1911.

14 Ruiz, "Fall of the Alamo," 80. See Chapter Nine, this book, for the evidence and analysis that explains why Ruiz was not at San Antonio on March 6, 1836.

15 Cardwell, "Attended," June 7, 1911; Morphis, *History of Texas, from its Discovery and Settlement,* 177.

16 Alleged Hannig statement concerning Ross; "Testimony of Mrs. Hannig," September 23, 1876.

17 Alleged Hannig statement concerning Ross; Zuber, "An Escape," 83.

18 Zuber to Steele, September 14, 1877.

19 Ibid.

20 Alleged Hannig statement concerning Ross.

21 Zuber to Steele, September 14, 1877.

22 Susanna (Dickinson) Bellis affidavit, July 16, 1857.

23 Ibid.

24 Zuber to Steele, September 14, 1877; Alleged Hannig statement concerning Ross.

25 Webb, Carrol, and Branda, eds., *Handbook*, I: 500-501.

26 This explanation is pure speculation, but as they say, between heaven and earth anything is possible.

27 Merrett and Saul statement, July 1838; Erath, "Memoirs of Major George Bernard Erath," 230-231.

Chapter Eight

Mexican Casualties at the Alamo: Big and Little

In fact, the plight of our wounded was quite grievous, and one could hardly enter the places erroneously called hospitals without trembling with horror. The wailing of the wounded and their just complaints penetrated the innermost recesses of the heart; there was no one to extract a bullet, no one to perform an amputation, and many unfortunates died whom medical science could have saved.

Jose Enrique de la Pena[1]

The exact number of Mexican soldiers killed and wounded during the siege and storming of the Alamo is one of the minor mysteries of the Alamo story. As almost always with the Alamo, there is little agreement on the issue. The numbers are high and low. Dr. John Sutherland, who said he was Travis's first courier to Gonzales, wrote that Santa Anna told him: "'We brought to San Antonio five thousand men and lost during the siege fifteen hundred and forty-four of the best of them....' The question, however arises, did he mean that 1,544 men were lost to the service, some killed and some permanently wounded, or did he allude to the latter? Mr. [Francisco] Ruiz says 'Santa Anna's loss was estimated at 1,600 men,' which would have left us in the dark, had he not indicated plainly from another remark that he meant the killed only. Speaking of one charge made by the Toluca battalion, he says: 'They commenced to scale the walls and suffered severely. Out of 800 men, 130 only were left alive.' By this remark the former is relieved of mystery, showing that he meant to say that 1,600 was about the number killed; for if 670 men fell out of one battalion in one assault, the number slain during the entire siege must have been fully as great in proportion." Santa Anna, however, on March 6, 1836, wrote that he had lost 70 dead and 300 wounded in the final assault of the Alamo. Other Mexican reports give numbers close to Santa Anna's figures.[2]

General Santa Anna
Photo courtesy of Texas State Library and Archives Commission

Recently, new primary sources have come to hand that add new data to the story of the Mexican dead and wounded at the Alamo and to the medical services available to Santa Anna's troops. The new sources are: (1) a statement, dated August 1, 1836, from Colonel Nicolas Condelle, commander of the Morelos battalion at the siege and storming of Bexar, which reports the activities of Dr. Jose Faustino Moro, the Mexican army's senior doctor at Bexar in 1835 and 1836; (2) a letter, dated December 15, 1835, from General Martin Perfecto de Cos that contains data about the siege and storming of Bexar and his departure from the city; (3) a muster roll for the Morelos battalion, dated October 3, 1835, at Bexar; (4) a Jose F. Moro letter, dated August 5, 1836, which reports medical corp activities in 1835 and 1836; (5) a Martin Perfecto de Cos letter, dated December 3, 1835, which gives details about Mexican activities during the siege and storming of Bexar; (6) a list of the Mexican officers and units that passed through San Antonio in 1836; (7) a summary, dated August 1, 1836, prepared by the physician who treated most of the soldiers, which gives the number of Mexican dead and wounded from the Alamo.

Moreover, when the investigator integrates the new evidence with the old evidence, insights and conclusions arise that go beyond the issues of the number of Mexican dead and wounded at the Alamo and the nature of the Mexican medical services at Bexar in 1835 and 1836. In this case, the investigative process takes the reader in a different direction and reveals evidence about the authenticity of two influential Mexican accounts of the Texas Revolution and one Mexican-Texian account of the fall of the Alamo. Those narratives being *La Guerra de Tejas: Memorias de un Soldado by* Jose Juan Sanchez and *With Santa Anna in Texas: A Personal Narrative of the Revolution*, the Jose Enrique de la Pena narrative. The Sanchez narrative is supposed to be a contemporary diary that he kept during the fall and spring campaigns in Texas. Whereas, the Pena narrative, a manuscript of over four hundred pages, is alleged to be a memoir based on other sources and a second draft of Pena's contemporary campaign diary, a 109-page manuscript that has never been published. The Mexican-Texian chronicle is the much-used Francisco Ruiz report that appeared in the 1860 *Texas Almanac*.[3]

To determine the approximate number of Mexican casualties for the 1836 siege and storming of the Alamo, one must first determine General Martin Perfecto de Cos's number of dead and wounded in the fall

Mexican street scene
Photo courtesy of Joseph Musso collection

campaign of 1835. Cos left a number of wounded men behind when he departed the city on December 12, 1835. Those men were later included in an August 1, 1836 hospital report of the Mexican dead (the men who died from their wounds while being treated) and wounded from the Alamo.

Let us start with the battle of Concepcion in late October 1835, and Lieutenant Colonel Jose Maria Mendoza, General Cos's secretary. Besides Mendoza's main job of taking dictation, he commanded fifty infantrymen from the Morelos battalion at the old mission on October 28. In addition to Mendoza's men, Colonel Domingo de Ugartechea commanded 200 cavalrymen and Lieutenant Francisco de Castaneda commanded two "guerrillas" of sixty horsemen each. The Mexican force had two field pieces, a long bronze six-pounder and a gun of unknown caliber. General Vicente Filisola later observed: "There were more than two hundred of the enemy ambushed at that place, and they were able to fire point blank and with great accuracy. Thus in less than ten minutes almost all fifty brave men of the Morelos group were lying on the ground either dead or wounded, and the artillery piece [the six-pounder] was in the hands of those traitors."[4]

In regard to the Mexican dead and wounded, Rafael Muzquiz, the governor of Coahuila and Texas, reported on November 7, 1835, that after two engagements with the enemy, the Mexican force had suffered forty wounded and fourteen killed. Muzquiz, however, destroyed the credibility of his report by claiming that seventy-five Texians had been killed. When in fact, only one Texian, Richard Andrews, had been killed.[5]

Samuel Maverick, who at the time was a prisoner in the city, reported: "Oct. 28th. Fifteen Mexican infantry out of the 42 wounded brought in are, this morning, dead; besides this havoc of the infantry, artillery-men, etc. there were some of the cavalry killed. It is probable that more than 42 were brought off wounded for they [Mexicans] reported 8 (only) left dead [on the field], whereas the Padre (who went with 10 men at the request of Austin to Gen'l Cos) reports 23 dead [on the field] and some dying in the American Camp. There must be at least 80 put past duty [dead and wounded]. The old Padre reports but one [Richard Andrews of Bastrop] man as being touched, and he only wounded in a tender part [grapeshot in the gut]." Then on October 29 Maverick reported there had been "Several [Mexican] deaths" in the city.[6] Using the Maverick numbers, it appears that as of October 29, the Mexican dead were 15, 23, and 2 for a total of 40 men. The wounded stood at twenty-five or more. Of course, that number would change over time. Men would die, other soldiers would recover, and additional men would be wounded.

The Concepcion wounded forced General Cos to do something about his failure to bring surgeons to San Antonio. To solve the problem, Cos appointed Alejandro Vidal, a local resident, to treat the men. Jose Faustino Moro, who became the first surgeon of the military hospital of Bexar, finally arrived in that city at 9:00 a.m. on December 9. Don Mariano Arroyo, the second surgeon, chief intern G. Guadalupe La Madrid, first interns Nazario Gil and Victor Samarroni, second intern Eduardo Banegas, and at least two unnamed interns (probably second class interns Jose Maria Ylisariturri and Jose Cardenas) came with Moro. They found 54 wounded men in the city.[7]

Moro and his team may have traveled a day or less behind Sanchez and the relief force. The fact that the medical personnel were with the reinforcement group is not included in Sanchez's journal. It is hard to understand why Sanchez, if he wrote the journal, would not have mentioned the much-needed medical personnel, who appear to have ridden to San Antonio with him. Otherwise the Sanchez account goes to great lengths to identify the units and individuals who are alleged to have reinforced General Cos in December 1835. Apparently, whoever wrote the Sanchez chronicle was not aware that the medical staff traveled to Bexar with Sanchez and entered the city a day later than Sanchez.[8]

At about 6:30 a.m., previous to the arrival of the medical corp, Cos had Sanchez halt the combat by approaching the Texians under a white flag to discuss a conditional surrender. A surrender agreement was completed at 2:00 a.m. on December 10, and a final draft written agreement was signed on the eleventh. The Mexican force departed the city the next day, taking forty-some wounded soldiers in the care of Dr. Moro, chief intern G. Guadalupe La Madrid, and interns Eduardo Banegas, Victor Samarroni, and Nazario Gil. About fourteen wounded men were left behind in the Alamo. Dr. Mariano Arroyo and two interns (probably Jose Maria Ylisariturri and Jose Cardenas) remained with the wounded. About those wounded, Filisola reported: "In Bexar they had to leave some officers and soldiers who were wounded and that were in no shape to take the road. Among the former were First Assistant Don Jose Maria Mendoza, Captain of the second [Active] Nuevo Leon company, Don Francisco Rada, and Second Lieutenant Don Ignacio Solio [Solis], who volunteered to remain to take care of them. Of the soldiers we have no knowledge either as to who they were or how many."[9]

It appears that most of the Mexican dead and wounded came from the Morelos battalion. Cos, on December 15, writing from the "Ranch of Salinas at 15 leagues from the city of Bexar," reported that on the morning of December 9 the Morelos battalion only had 120 "faithful soldiers" left, the others having been killed or wounded. The October 3, 1835 muster roll for the Morelos battalion shows that as of that date the command had 246 men present for duty. Thus, it appears that the number of dead and wounded men for that unit may have been as high as 126. The other Mexican casualties appear to have come from the Alamo de Parras company and the other presidial companies. The forty-plus wounded who left with Cos were probably men from the Morelos command. The number of wounded who recovered before December 9 is unknown. Since Cos took forty-some men with him, the Morelos battalion may have had as many as eighty men killed during the siege and storming of Bexar.[10]

Now, let us look at what the Sanchez account reports about the wounded soldiers left in Bexar. The account claims: "The wounded stayed in Bejar in the plaza. Lt. Col. Mendoza, Captain Zenea, 2nd Lt. Solis and more than 30 troops. The first Lt. of the Second Company (Active) of New Leon, don Francisco Rada, remained behind voluntarily while pretending ordered to do so by Commanding General Cos.... Of the Military Sanitation Corps which went from Matamoros to Bejar there remained in Bejar don Fulano Arroyo and 2 assistants to attend the wounded and sick. By orders of Commanding General Cos their Director don N. Moro and 2 more assistants withdrew with us from Bejar. In tribute to these men the 30 and more wounded who marched with us from Bejar were all alive except one who died today [December 30]."[11]

There are several notable differences between the Sanchez description and the data that comes from the Colonel Nicolas Condelle's letter of August 1, 1836, and other sources. First, Sanchez claims the wounded were left in "Bejar in the plaza," which appears to refer to the city's main plaza in front of the San Fernando church. The Condelle document claims the men were left in the Alamo, which makes sense. Why go to the trouble of moving the wounded across the river when their wounds were so severe that they could not travel with the retreating army? Second, Sanchez reports the number of wounded taken from the city as more than thirty. Whereas, the Condelle missive reports that "forty-some" wounded left with Cos. Third, Sanchez incorrectly reports the doctors' names as: "Fulano Arroyo" and "N. Moro." Moreover, Fulano is a Mexican term that means the same as "what's his name" does in English. Sanchez did not know Arroyo's first name. Fourth, Sanchez claims at least thirty-one men were left in Bexar. The Condelle letter indicates that at least fourteen men were left in San Antonio.[12]

Also, there are differences between what the Sanchez account claims about the left-behind wounded and what General Filisola wrote about them. According to the general one of the men was "Second Lieutenant Don Ignacio Solio, who volunteered to remain to take care of them."

Sanchez claimed a "Lt. Solis" was one of the wounded and that First Lieutenant Francisco Rada remained behind to care for the wounded. Filisola, however, identified Rada as one of the wounded, which appears to be wrong. Lastly, Sanchez identified a "Captain Zenea" as one of the wounded. Filisola does not include Zenea.[13]

Additional conflict examples can be found in Filisola's history. First, the Sanchez account claims that at 2:00 a.m. on the morning of January 12, on the Salado River, Sanchez stopped at Filisola's tent. Allegedly, the two men smoked cigars and talked about their dreams. Second, the Sanchez narrative claims that on January 13, as the unit marched toward the village of Lampazos, Filisola had requested more aid for their division. Whereas, Filisola wrote that he had left the Salado River on January 11 to "push ahead" for Lampazos. After conducting his business at that location, Filisola left for Monclova and arrived there on January 14. On that date, Sanchez claimed he was still marching toward Lampazos. Also, Sanchez did not reach Monclova until January 20, six days after Filisola.[14]

Another Sanchez conflict is exposed by a General Cos document. On February 1, 1836, Cos wrote that he had arrived in Leona Vicario (Saltillo) on January 30, 1836. The Sanchez account reports that Cos, his staff, including Sanchez, and a small escort reached that city on January 28.[15]

Archaeologist Jake Ivey is convinced that Filisola used the Sanchez account in writing his memoirs. Ivey wrote: "Independent confirmation that Sanchez actually took part in the events he describes in his journals is readily available. In 1848-1849, General Vicente Filisola published an account of the siege of Bexar that contains frequent mention of Sanchez, leaving no doubt of his presence at San Antonio in 1835; in fact, in his *Memorias,* Filisola used Sanchez's diary as his primary source for his description of the defeat of General Martin Perfecto de Cos, though without giving him credit."[16]

Why would Filisola have failed to credit Sanchez for allowing him to use his diary? Filisola acknowledged his use of Colonel Juan N. Almonte's diary, an "unedited anonymous diary" from a soldier in Antonio Gaona's command, an account by Colonel Francisco Garay, and documents from a Senor Arrillage. The numerous interviews that were obviously conducted for Filisola's book, however, are not cited. Thus, it is more likely that Filisola or Agustin Escudero, Filisola's ghostwriter, interviewed Sanchez.[17]

Sanchez believers, however, claim that the Sanchez journal was written contemporary to the events described in the narrative and that Filisola copied directly from the journal. If Filisola used the Sanchez "diary" in writing his history of the war with Texas, one would think that Filisola's data about the Mexican wounded left behind in Bexar would be the same as the information found in the Sanchez account. But the information is not the same. Nor are other elements in both accounts that deal with the same subject the same. Would these differences in regard to the same events exist in the two accounts if a forger wrote the Sanchez account and used the Filisola history as a source? Probably; a forger can't afford to copy every passage word for word. Otherwise, the act of plagiarism might be obvious to a competent historian. If a forger makes minor changes in what he or she is stealing, then historians accept the differences as reasonable mistakes because of the author's faulty memory or other unexplained reasons.[18]

Moreover, the Sanchez account details a strange and unbelievable story about the circumstances under which Colonel Mendoza was wounded. A story that is not found in Filisola's history. The account claims that after the Mexicans and Texians had agreed to the terms of the Mexican surrender, General Edward Burleson, the Texian commander, asked Sanchez about the Mexican wounded and offered medical help from the Texian doctors. Such an action was within Burleson's character. Still, Burleson's correspondence concerning the defeat of Cos's force reports no such offer of help. Sanchez, instead of accepting Burleson's offer of medical assistance or saying he would forward the offer to General Cos, brought up the "bad luck" of Colonel Mendoza. The account claims that eight days earlier (December 2) Mendoza's equipment, dispatches, clothes, jewels, and money had been taken. Then the narrative reports that Captain Robert Morris, one of the New Orleans Greys's commanders, spoke up with great interest and offered Sanchez a bag of gold coins. Morris is alleged to have said: "This and all the baggage of senor Mendoza I took by force. It gives me great pleasure and satisfaction to return it to the agent of Senor Mendoza."[19]

A footnote furnished by Carlos Sanchez Peon, who edited and self-published the Sanchez account in 1938, reports that Mendoza was "gravely" wounded at the battle of Concepcion on October 28. Sanchez Peon, however, gave no source for his claim about Mendoza. Also, the account and the footnote fail to explain the nature of Mendoza's "grave" wound.[20]

There are a number of problems with the Sanchez's Mendoza/Morris allegation. Problems that suggest the account was not written by Sanchez, who appears to have been a competent and intelligent soldier. First, Morris and his company of Greys did not join the Texian army until November 21. Therefore, Morris could not have taken Mendoza's property from him at Concepcion. Second, Morris was not the kind of man who would have returned captured Mexican property. On November 29 Morris expressed his sentiments to Sam Houston: "There are now here 225 men, nearly all from the U.S. who on no consideration will enter into any service connected with the Regular Army, the name of which is a perfect Bugbear to them, & to them I promised to be one of those who lead them on the road to Matamoros & who declare in the most positive manner that should this not be undertaken they will return home direct from hence." Would Morris, who wanted to take Texas—all the way to Matamoros—have willingly given back a bag of gold to Mendoza? Doubtful; spoils of war were part of the reward for coming to Texas.[21]

Moreover, Mendoza was not wounded at Concepcion. He was wounded on the morning of December 2. General Cos, writing on the third, described the event with these words: "Yesterday, from the sounding of reveille onward, there was resisted for almost the whole day a live cannon fire that resulted in several damages to the buildings and fortifications, because of the nearness of the pieces and the superiority of their caliber [probably the 12-lb gunade and the Mexican long 6-lb captured at Concepcion] – there having been wounded gravely my useful and honorable secretary, the very valiant and estimable Lieutenant Colonel Don Jose Maria Mendoza." Cos failed to note the nature of Mendoza's wound. Sam Maverick, however, on December 2, wrote in his journal: "Great cannonading this day. Col. Mendoza has the calf of his leg shot off." A bouncing round shot probably hit Mendoza.[22]

The evidence strongly suggests that Mendoza lost part of a leg. What Mendoza was doing and where he was doing it when he was wounded is unknown. Still, whatever Mendoza was engaged in, it was most likely behind a street barricade in the main plaza. Cos's description of the damage to the buildings and fortifications suggests that the Texians were firing on the Mexican troops who were defending the city's main plaza. Mendoza, despite the nature of his wound, could have remained unattended for a short time. Still, one thing appears certain: Morris could not have taken Mendoza's property after the colonel was wounded. First, all of the property mentioned by the Sanchez account would not have been on Mendoza's person. Yes, he could have had a bag of gold coins and jewelry. And of course he was dressed in a uniform. The mention of "clothes," however, is not clear in its meaning. His "equipment and dispatches" would have been in his quarters, which were probably the same as General's Cos's or very near Cos's quarters, as Mendoza was Cos's secretary. The same would have been true for any spare uniforms and civilian clothing. Cos's quarters were in La Villita. Then Cos moved into the Alamo on December 8 after the arrival of Ugartechea's reinforcements. Mendoza would have been in the Alamo hospital on that date. Second, the Texians did not storm the Mexican positions until December 5 and most likely did not enter the Alamo until after the surrender agreement had been completed on December 11.[23]

One could argue that the artillery fire on December 2 was in support of a Texian infantry attack on the north side of the city, and that Morris took the property from Mendoza's person as he lay wounded on a San Antonio street. There is, however, no evidence of such a Texian assault in the Texian and Mexican documents. At that time, except for the cannon fire, the Texians were in disarray, about to depart the city for winter quarters in Gonzales or Goliad.[24]

There was a Mexican assault against the Texian cannon after Mendoza had been wounded. Cos wrote: "In the afternoon the silencing of the enemy batteries was achieved by two attacks and 40 men who, with great labor and evident risk, were able to find themselves advancing on the left flank; but at night was necessary to fall back because of the scant force of the garrison of the plaza, and in order not to expose the detachments. The Alamo sustained the artillery fire to advantage, there having been noticed in the field much disorder and uneasiness, and the abandonment of a trench occupied by about 100 [Texian] marksmen."[25]

Given that Sanchez's Mendoza/Morris story appears to be fiction, what does it mean? Why would Sanchez, a competent and professional officer, have invented such a story? Was the tale written to enliven the narrative? If so, why create fiction that shows the enemy in a good light? Why would a forger, who would be concerned with the appearance of authenticity, include such an obvious piece of fiction? Was the pro-Texian incident created to appeal to Texans? In the end, a motive for the story is hard to determine, but clearly the tale is squirrelly, which makes it a suspicious element.

The alleged Jose Enrique de la Pena memoir also has what appears to be a fictional report about Colonel Mendoza that speaks to the authenticity of the Pena narrative. According to Pena: "After the capitulation [December 11, 1836], Lieutenant Colonel Jose Maria Mendoza, who was later to lose a limb from a cannonball wound received defending the Alamo, was saved, together with other officers, thanks to the diligence and assistance given them by Dr. James Grant. Certainly this conduct is in contrast to that followed by our commander in chief: 'I neither ask for nor give quarter,' he used to say at Bejar, and he was known to have said once to one of his aides that he would authorize him to strike him with a pistol were he to deviate from his resolution."[26]

The story is suggestive but does not identify exactly what Grant did to save Mendoza and the other officers. Still, one can assume three things about the Pena description. First, it appears to be constructed on the Sanchez claim that Edward Burleson offered Texian medical help to Cos's wounded soldiers. Second, the incident is used to contrast Texian goodness to Santa Anna's cruelty. Third, Mendoza appears to have been wounded while defending the main plaza of San Antonio, not the Alamo. Fourth, the Pena element does not claim that Grant actually treated Mendoza and the other officers in some kind of medical manner. The chronicle only suggests that Grant, a physician, did something medically to save Mendoza and the other, unnamed Mexican officers. That conclusion, however, is extremely unlikely for two reasons. Grant did not participate in the siege and storming of Bexar as a physician. His was a combat commander. Also, he was seriously wounded on December 5, the first day of the storming of the city. On December 17 Dr. Amos Pollard and Dr. Samuel Stivers, the Texian surgeons, downgraded Grant's condition to "slightly wounded." Moreover, Mendoza's wound, the loss of a lower leg, was one that would have required immediate medical attention. Grant would not have treated Mendoza for the same reason Morris could not have taken Mendoza's property. Grant would not have had access to Mendoza immediately after he was wounded. Alejandro Vidal probably treated Mendoza at the time of his injury. Dr. Moro and Dr. Arroyo would have treated Mendoza after their arrival in San Antonio.[27]

If the Pena account is authentic, why would Pena have created the story about Grant saving Mendoza—a report that portrays Pena's enemies in a positive way? Again, as with Sanchez's Mendoza/Morris story, the answer is hard to determine. One can assume Pena would not have created the tale for he had no admiration for his enemy. In an authentic letter, he wrote: "He [Filisola] has been very ignominious because he retired the whole army from a handful of armed civilians [Texians] who are ignoramuses in the art of war, without union, without tactics, without discipline, and without any of those things that give strength to the masses." Of course, as the story is presented in the Pena document, the tale is not attributed to Pena, but to "Officers who were present when Bejar was besieged in 1835...." But is that the truth? Still, the story appears to be designed to picture the Texians in a positive light and to paint Santa Anna in evil black—a view that was held by most Texas historians and Texana collectors of the 1950s.[28]

In the end, what became of Mendoza and the other officers who had been left behind by Cos? Filisola does not say. Neither do the Pena and Sanchez narratives. Those two accounts give no more information about the men left behind than is found in Filisola's history and an August 11, 1836 letter written by Jose F. Moro that appeared in the September 30, 1836 issue of *El Mosquito Mexicano*, a Mexican newspaper. This letter appears in the appendix of the Jesus Sanchez Garza Spanish language edition of the memoir draft Pena account. If the Pena and Sanchez accounts are authentic, why do they fail to report the fate of the wounded men? Soldiers left in the hands of the enemy was an important event. No soldier wants to be left wounded on the field, and no soldier wants to leave a brother on a battleground. On the other hand, if the two accounts are forgeries, why would the forgers have failed to explain the fate of the wounded men? The answer is simple when one thinks about it. If the forgers did not have a reliable source that answered the question, then they could not afford to create a fictional explanation that might later prove to be incorrect. Better to leave the question of what happened to the wounded men unanswered.[29]

Previous to the storming of Bexar, the last serious engagement was the "Grass Fight" on November 26, 1835. Edward Burleson reported that fifteen Mexican soldiers were found dead on the field and seven wounded men were carried from the field for a total of twenty-two. Whereas, Cos reported one wounded official, three dead soldiers, thirteen wounded soldiers, and thirty-nine horses lost (probably captured) in the action. Either Burleson inflated the number or Cos did not report the true numbers.[30]

In total, Cos appears to have suffered about 170 dead and wounded during the siege and storming of Bexar. He retreated from the city with over forty wounded men and left about fourteen men behind in the Alamo, including Lt. Col. Jose Maria Mendoza and Second Lieutenant Ignacio Solis. Cos's number of dead was probably around 116 men. Doctor Mariano Arroyo and interns Jose Maria Ylisariturri and Jose Cardenas remained in San Antonio to care for the wounded men. Captain Francisco de Rada remained behind to help the wounded, probably with nonmedical activities. Therefore, when Santa Anna and his army marched into San Antonio on February 23, 1836, one surgeon and two interns were there to greet their commander-in-chief.[31]

Nevertheless, in regard to the medical staff available during the February and March 1836 siege of the Alamo, the published Pena account makes this unbelievable claim: "None of these commanders [Cos, Castrillon, Almonte, Duque, Amat, Romero, and Salas] was aware that there were no field hospitals or surgeons to save the wounded, and that for some it would be easier to die than to be wounded, as we shall see after the assault." Pena, speaking to the medical aid available after the attack, quoted an alleged letter from an unknown person: "...it is true that few among us are sick, but we have 257 wounded with no surgeons to treat them, no medicines, no bandages, no gauze, and very meager food."[32]

Then the Pena memoir seems to vacillate about the question of surgeons being available for the Alamo wounded. Pena claims: "Among the victims who perished because of General Santa Anna's faults and lack of resources, one finds the name of Don Jose Maria Heredia, a sapper officer.... Urging on the platoon he commanded, at times scolding with sword in hand the soldier who showed little courage as the Sapper Battalion advanced, he received a mortal wound two inches above the right nipple in one of the last enemy barrages; this courageous officer could have been saved by the services of a good surgeon, but the lack of such and of medicine took him to his grave after thirteen days, during which, with admirable courage, he suffered intense pain." Does the lack of a "good surgeon" mean the army had a surgeon, but he was incompetent, or does it mean there was no surgeon to treat Heredia?[33]

Mexican infantryman
Photo courtesy of Joseph Musso collection

There was an officer named Jose Maria Heredia. He was the lowest ranking lieutenant in the third Zapadore company. At the time of Heredia's death, judging from what Pena actually wrote, the event did not make much of an impression on Pena. According to the Pena memoir Heredia died on March 19. The 109-page Pena second draft campaign diary does not mention Heredia being wounded or his death. The campaign diary manuscript has no entries for March 18, 19, and 20.[34]

Whatever, one surgeon and two interns does not equal Pena's claim of "no" surgeons. There was one surgeon, Dr. Mariano Arroyo, who, with the assistance of the interns, could have handled the amputations. Whereas, the two interns were probably capable of performing minor surgery, such as removing lead balls from soft tissue, cleaning wounds, and stitching up wounds. Second, if there had been no medical personal, it is unbelievable that the commanders mentioned would have been unaware of the situation. Cos, given that he had left Arroyo and his two interns behind, most certainly would have known about them.

Third, as the Pena memoir often does, it reads just like Filisola, who wrote: "By taking the rather insignificant fortification of the Alamo, a large number of the best soldiers, including 26 leaders and officers, were sacrificed for no plausible reason. Santa Anna could have left a guard of the cavalry that could go no further because of the bad condition of the horses, or he could have knocked the adobe walls down with the 20 artillery pieces at his disposal. But he [Santa Anna] wanted blood, and blood was what he got. Those killed suffered no more, but the wounded were left to lie without any attention and with no shelter." Both Filisola and Pena claim it was better for a soldier to have been killed than to have been wounded.[35]

In regard to the previous Filisola quote, there are passages in the Pena memoir that echo Filisola's content. First, Pena reports: "We were in a position to advance, leaving a small force on watch at the Alamo, the holding of which was unimportant either politically or militarily, whereas its acquisition was both costly and very bitter in the end." Second, the account claims: "In fact, it was necessary only to await the artillery's arrival at Bejar for these [rebels] to surrender; undoubtedly they could not have resisted for many hours the destruction and imposing fire from twenty cannon." Then, in regard to Santa Anna having desired a "bloody" battle, Pena alleges: "...because he [Santa Anna] wanted to cause a sensation and would have regretted taking the Alamo without clamor and without bloodshed, for some believed that without these there is no glory." Both Filisola and the Pena memoir express the opinion that the capture of the Alamo by infantry assault was not worth the dead and wounded it cost. Rather, Santa Anna should have left a guard around the Alamo and continued east with the campaign. Or, Santa Anna should have destroyed the Alamo's walls with their twenty cannon, forcing the Texians to surrender. Never mind that regardless of the state of the walls, the Texians were not going to surrender without an agreement that would have allowed them to live, conditions which Santa Anna was not going to give them. Both Filisola and the Pena memoir claim Santa Anna wanted a battle with unneeded bloodshed.[36]

In total, the Pena memoir reports that the casualties for the March 6 attack were 257 wounded and more than 300 dead, for a total of over 557 dead and wounded. Also, the Pena memoir claims that Colonel Esteban Mora, a cavalry officer, was appointed as the hospital director. According to a manuscript in the Pena papers, the order that made Mora the "inspector-general" of the hospital was issued as a general order on March 20, 1836. Dr. Arroyo, however, was most likely the hospital's administrator until the arrival of Dr. Jose F. Moro.[37]

The earliest summary of the Alamo Mexican dead and wounded comes from Colonel Juan Andrade.[38] It reads:

	Officers		Troops		
Corps	Dead	Wounded	Dead	Wounded	Total
Sappers	1	3	2	21	27
Jimenez	1	3	8	22	34
Matamoros	-	2	7	35	44
Aldama	2	5	9	46	62
San Luis	2	-	7	37	46
Toluca	2	5	18	69	94
Dolores	-	-	1	3	4
Totals	8	18	52	233	311

Andrade reported 60 dead and 251 wounded, for a total of 311. Santa Anna reported that he had 70 killed and 300 wounded. Colonel Juan N. Almonte reported "60 soldiers and 5 officers killed, and 198 soldiers and 25 officers wounded." The alleged San Luis battalion journal (a manuscript in the Jose Enrique de la Pena papers) lists the dead and wounded as 21 officers, 295 soldiers, for a total of 316 men. Sergeant Santiago Rabia, of the Tampico lancers, reported the dead and wounded as 500. Jose Juan Sanchez claimed that 11 officers were killed, 19 were wounded and 247 soldiers were wounded and 110 were killed, for a total of 121 dead and 266 wounded men. Caro, Santa Anna's private secretary, claimed: "Though the bravery and intrepidity of the troops was general, we shall always deplore the costly sacrifice of the 400 men who fell in the attack. Three hundred were left dead on the field and more than a hundred of the wounded died afterwards as a result of the lack of proper

Mexican infantryman
Photo courtesy of Joseph Musso collection

medical attention and medical facilities in spite of the fact that the injuries were not serious." Caro's number of immediate dead from the attack appears to match the Pena memoir's number.[39]

Arroyo and his interns worked alone until help from the interior arrived in San Antonio. Previously, on Cos's December 1835 retreat, Dr. Moro and interns Eduardo Banegas, Victor Samarroni, and Narciso Gil had remained at Monclova. Santa Anna and his army arrived in that city on February 5. Soon afterward Moro informed Santa Anna of the medical staff and supplies that were available for the army. Moro wrote: "I notified him that [of] the medical supplies that I took out of that capital, the greater part of it was running out (since requesting it from that city could not be done, because of the distance at which we were located and the continuation of the march of the army). At the same time he commanded me that, with intern Eduardo Banegas [interns Victor Samarroni and Narciso Gil also remained with Moro], I should remain in Monclova for the care of about ninety-some sick [from Santa Anna's force] whom the army had brought." At that city, Santa Anna continued to upgrade the medical department. He appointed a number of interns to serve under Jose Reyes, a "skilled surgeon" who had joined the force at Saltillo on January 8. Strangely, when Santa Anna departed Monclova on February 8, he left Reyes and the medical staff behind. That section departed the city on February 23 with General Vincente Filisola's command. By that time surgeon Andres Urtado and two more interns had joined the force. Moro later wrote that these much-needed people arrived in San Antonio "many days after the battle," which appears to have been on March 9.[40]

By March 9 the Mexican Military Health Brigade at San Antonio contained the following individuals: Second surgeon Mariano Arroyo, third surgeon Jose Maria Reyes, provisional surgeons Andres Urtado and N. Vidal, second class interns Jose Maria Ylisariturri, Jose Maria Rodriguez, Jose Cardenas, Ygnacio Romero, Jose Maria Rojas, and intern Francisco Martinez for a total of four surgeons and six interns. First surgeon Jose Faustino Moro, first intern Nazario Gil, and second intern Eduardo Banegas finally arrived in Bexar on May 15. A short time before Moro and his interns arrived, Dr. Urtado and his interns (Ygnacio Romero and Jose Maria Rojas) had been sent to Goliad with the corp's medical chest. Moro wrote that when he arrived in Bexar, he found all of the above individuals, except Urtado and his interns, in the Hospital of Bejar.[41]

According to the Pena memoir, he was aware of Dr. Moro being in San Antonio. The Pena account reads: "Among the few in the medical corps that finally found themselves in Texas, perhaps only Don Jose F. Moro is entitled to the name of surgeon."[42]

It is strange that Pena would think so highly of Dr. Moro. First, Moro appears to have performed no surgery on the Alamo wounded. Second, Moro did not join the army at Bexar until May 15, 1836. Whereas, Pena departed the city at the end of March 1836 and would most likely not have been aware of Moro until early June 1836, when Colonel Juan

Andrade's force joined Filisola's retreating army south of Goliad. Dr. Arroyo appears to have continued to be the working surgeon at Matamoros. He completed the hospital report on the dead and wounded, not Moro. The fact that the Pena memoir credits Moro as a good surgeon suggests that the writer of the Pena memoir did not have sufficient source material dealing with the medical situation at the Alamo to be able to write about it with authority.[43]

Regardless, the evidence shows that the Mexican army had a surgeon and two interns in Bexar on March 6 and that three additional doctors and four interns arrived on March 9. Therefore, why does the Pena memoir report there were no surgeons to treat the wounded? The reason seems to be that the medical data found in the four-hundred-plus-page manuscript is based on other written sources, rather than on Pena's personal experience at Bexar or Pena's 109-page campaign diary. The Pena memoir has Pena quoting data about the medical situation at Bexar from two letters. The first alleged letter, for which there is no source citation and no author identification, was dated March 18, 1836, and perhaps was written at San Antonio. The writer claimed: "It is true that few among us are sick, but we have 257 wounded with no surgeons to treat them, no medicines, no bandages, no gauze, and very meager food." The medicines were limited, but there were four surgeons at Bexar on March 18. Also, cotton gauze was on hand. The second missive quoted by the Pena memoir is Dr. Jose F. Moro's August 11, 1836 letter that appears in the appendix of the Spanish language edition of the Pena memoir.[44]

Then Pena is alleged to have written: "In fact, the plight of our wounded was quite grievous, and one could hardly enter the places erroneously called hospitals without trembling with horror. The wailing of the wounded and their just complaints penetrated the innermost recesses of the heart; [italics added] *there was no one to extract a bullet, no one to perform an amputation, and many unfortunates died whom medical science could have saved.*" It is true there was not an adequate building for a hospital in the city. The army, however, did have qualified medical people to extract bullets and cut limbs off when needed. So, why would Pena have made such untrue claims? Pena would not have made such allegations. He was in San Antonio, and he was one of the wounded soldiers. He made no such claims in the smaller campaign diary manuscript. More importantly, he would not have needed to use written sources to write about the army's medical services.[45]

The source for the previous Pena statement in the memoir appears to have been *Dr. J. H. Barnard's Journal*, first published in the *Goliad Guard* in 1883, over forty years after Pena's death. Barnard was one of the surgeons who had been with Colonel James W. Fannin's command at Goliad. He and several other doctors were spared so that they could treat the Mexican wounded. Barnard and Dr. Jack Shackelford were sent to San Antonio on April 16 to assist the Mexican surgeons. Barnard reported there were surgeons at San Antonio. Otherwise, he wrote the same thing about amputations, bullet wounds, and soldier deaths from the lack of surgical care that the Pena memoir reports.

According to Barnard on April 21, 1836: "Yesterday and today we have been around with the surgeons of the place [San Antonio] to visit the wounded, and a pretty piece of work 'Travis, and his faithful few' have made of them. There are now about a hundred here of the wounded. The surgeon tells us that there were four hundred of them brought into the hospital the morning they stormed the Alamo, but I should think from [the] appearance that there must have been more. I see many around the town, who were crippled there, apparently, two or three hundred and the citizens tell me that three or four hundred have died of their wounds.

"We have two colonels and a major and eight captains under our charge, who were wounded in the assault. We have taken one ward of the hospital under our charge. Their surgical department is shockingly conducted, *not an amputation performed before we arrived* [italics added], although there are several cases even now, that should have been operated upon at the first, and *how many have died from the want of operation is impossible to tell, though it is a fair inference that there has not been a few* [italics added].

"*There had been scarcely a ball cut out as yet* [italics added], and almost every patient carrying the lead he received that morning."[46]

In regard to the personal experience of a combat soldier, David H. Hackworth, a highly decorated combat soldier observed: "In battle, your perception is often only as wide as your battle sights. Five participants in the same action, fighting side by side, will often tell entirely different stories of what happened, even within hours of the fight. The story each man tells might be virtually unrecognizable to the others." Then Napoleon wrote: "A soldier seldom looks beyond his own company and an officer can, at most, give account of the position or movements of the division to which his regiment belongs." Therefore, if the Pena memoir is authentic, one would think it would be limited to what he experienced and witnessed himself.[47]

Yet, the Alamo chapters in the Pena memoir are totally based on other written sources. One can argue that Pena, like other soldiers who have written memoirs, decided to pad and embellish his story with research. That is a possibility, but it conflicts with what Pena said about his diary in an authentic letter. He claimed that his diary alone was sufficiently detailed to serve as a history and that he planned to publish his campaign diary, not a political and military history of the war based on other written sources from participants, both Mexican and Texian. Granted there is an alleged Pena document that claims Pena used other written sources in writing the memoir. However, that missive is not in Pena's handwriting and is among the documents that are suspected of being forgeries. In other words, the letter appears to have been created to explain why the Pena account is so obviously based on other accounts. Which also happens to be the only way a forger could have created the Pena final draft narrative.[48]

The Pena memoir information about the Mexican dead and wounded at the Alamo supports a forgery explanation for the creation of the Pena memoir manuscript. The Pena data about the Mexican dead and wounded and the army's medical services appears to be a compilation of data found in Filisola's *Memoirs*, Ramon Caro's account of the Texas campaign, Barnard's diary, Dr. Moro's letter of August 11, 1836, and an alleged letter from an unknown person.

Today historians recognize that the Pena memoir is based on other sources. Randy Roberts and James S. Olson: "It [the fact that the Pena narrative was not published in 1836] meant that his [Pena's] story was not constructed immediately after the war but rather written and rewritten over a period of years, during a time when other Mexican officers were publishing their accounts and de la Pena was languishing in prison for opposing the centralist regime. Although the diary is almost certainly not a forgery, it is a highly charged political document, aimed at discrediting the centralist and defending the federalists. As a whole, de la Pena's description of the look, smell, and feel of the campaign is unsurpassed; his grasp of grand strategy, his description of leaders, and his sympathy for the plight of the soldiers is outstanding. But in many cases he clearly drew from a deep pool of rumors, details, and stories that suited his overarching interpretation of the campaign and Mexican politics." Thus, Pena supporters can argue that Pena might have seen Caro's account and Moro's letter. That is true. Pena, however, could not have seen Filisola's *Memoirs* and Barnard's journal.[49]

Pena true believers may argue that Pena did not need to see the Barnard diary. They will say that both Pena and Barnard were correct in their assessment of the medical situation at San Antonio and that Barnard verifies the Pena claim. Thus, the Pena memoir is authentic. An authentic primary account, however, shows that the Pena and Barnard accounts are wrong in their claims about the Mexican surgical care at San Antonio in the days following the fall of the Alamo. The document is Dr. Mariano Arroyo's report on the medical corp's activities at San Antonio and Matamoros between December 12, 1835, and August 1, 1836. It reads:

Ranks Rec'd	Surgery Rec'd	Medication	Totals	Released	Deaths	Remaining
Generals		1	1	1		
Jefes	3		3	3		
Officers	25		25	21	4	
Troops	380	47	427	288	71	68

[total wounded = 427+1+3+25 = 456]
[total released, dead, and remaining = 288 +1+3+21+4+71+68 = 456]

Notes:

First. The number of sick which is on record in this report are those from the attack on the Alamo and those which resulted from the taking of the Plaza of Bexar by the enemies, with the one who subscribes to the care of them remaining with a scant stock of medicines and without more aid for the maintenance of them than that which the enemies themselves provided them, due to Senor General Don Martin Perfecto Cos not having asked to take them when he undertook his withdrawal.

Second. The wounded coming from the Alamo, in spite of not having received more than a scant stock of medicines, which were commanded to be turned over by order of the General in Chief, were attended with all meticulousness and efficiency by him who signs and [by] three aides, as is attested by the discharges and casualties of the foregoing report.

> Third. The amputations that it was necessary to carry
> out were two, one with good success and the other unfortu-
> nate.[50]

The Barnard journal and the Pena memoir are almost identical in what they report about amputations and the removal of rifle and musket balls from the Mexican wounded after the fall of the Alamo. Also, both accounts claim that many Mexican soldiers died because of that lack of surgical care. Pena said there was no surgical care because there were no surgeons. Thus, no amputations were conducted and no balls were removed. Barnard said there were surgeons, but they were incompetent and that amputations were only performed after his arrival. Barnard, however, did not claim that he performed any surgery. Seventy-five men did die, but their wounds may have been beyond the surgical care of the day, not because of the lack of care. Also, Arroyo's report of two amputations and 408 incidents of surgery refutes both Barnard and Pena. One of the amputations may have been performed on Colonel Francisco Duque, who suffered a grave wound in one of his legs. He almost bled to dead and was abandoned on the field. The wound would have required immediate attention and surgery, and it appears to have disabled him. He remained in San Antonio and departed with General Andrade in May 1836. On September 3, 1836, he requested that he be separated from the army because of his wounds.[51]

The fact that the Pena memoir and the Barnard journal make the same wrong claims about the Mexican surgical care is strong evidence that the writer of the Pena memoir copied from the Barnard journal. But then Pena and Barnard could have used the same source for their claims about the lack of surgical care for the Mexican wounded from the Alamo. Sure, it is obvious that the published Pena memoir was created from other written sources. The Barnard journal, however, is a contemporary diary. There is no evidence that Barnard's journal is not an authentic eyewitness narrative. There is no evidence that Barnard used other sources to pad his account. That, however, does not mean every word Barnard wrote is true. His claim about the Mexican surgeons appears to be a misrepresentation to enhance his role in the events and portray his enemy in a negative light. Dr. Jack Shackelford, Barnard's companion, made no such remarks about the skills of the Mexican doctors.[52]

On the other hand, Pena supporters might argue that the surgical care of the Mexican wounded did not start until after the arrival of Dr.

Moro, when Pena had been long gone from Bexar, and that would explain why Pena did not know about the doctors. In Moro's letter of August 11, 1836, which in part is quoted in the Pena account, Moro wrote: "Hurtado, Reyes, and the practitioners [interns] with them did not arrive at Bejar until many days after the events, and Arroyo, who was there at the time, had exhausted the little I had left him during the month of December of the previous year.

"He [Arroyo] had neither bandages nor material for making them, no gauze for the initial dressings, and nothing had been ordered or prepared for him; lacking everything, he made repeated requests, to no avail. The bandages finally given to him were of cotton material which, as your Excellency well knows, is noxious to wounds. Many had been admitted, among them two superior officers and some twenty others, to whom not a single surgeon could attend."[53]

Nevertheless, it appears that Arroyo and his interns, despite their lack of sufficient medical supplies and medicines began cutting on the wounded on March 6 or soon afterward because the number of wounded men being treated decreased as time passed. More likely they started extracting lead balls on February 23 when the army suffered its first casualties: two men killed and eight wounded. While the Francisco Ruiz account is not always reliable, it reports that a "temporary fortification" had been erected "in Potrero Street with the object of attending the wounded, etc." Of course a number of the wounded men died while being treated. Andrade's early report of the Alamo dead and wounded reported there were 251 wounded men. On April 10 Andrade reported he had 150 wounded men and 40 sick men. On April 22 Barnard reported the Mexican wounded at 100 men, down from a start of 400 on March 6. On May 16, the day after Moro arrived in Bexar, Andrade wrote that, after two months, the wounded men were dying because of the lack of medicines. Then, on the way out of Texas, Andrade reported he had more than 150 sick and wounded soldiers.[54]

Again, it appears that Pena's incorrect claims about the medical care of the Mexican wounded at the Alamo indicates that the published Pena manuscript is a forgery. The Pena narrative, however, is not the only account that claims there were no surgeons to treat the Mexican soldiers at the siege and storming of the Alamo. The Sanchez chronicle reports: "There are no hospitals, medicines, or surgeons; and the condition of the wounded is such as to cause pity. They have no mattresses on which to lie or blankets with which to cover themselves, in spite of the fact that on entering Bexar, we took from the enemy the remnants of three or four stores and that one has been set up and called the Government Store, where everything is sold at a high price and for cash."[55]

True, there was no established hospital at Bexar similar to what might have been found in Mexico City or any major city in the United States or Europe. There was, however, a facility of some kind in which Dr. Mariano Arroyo and his two interns worked on the Alamo wounded. The medicines were severely limited, but Arroyo did have some medicine.

Like the Pena memoir, if the Sanchez account is authentic and he was in San Antonio at the fall of the Alamo, why does the account also incorrectly claim there were no surgeons at San Antonio to treat the Alamo wounded? While there is no evidence, independent of the Sanchez account, that puts Sanchez at the storming of the Alamo, he probably was in Bexar sometime during the spring campaign. So it is not logical that Sanchez would have claimed there were no surgeons to treat the Mexican army's Alamo wounded. Moreover, the account reports that Arroyo and two interns were left behind in San Antonio by General Cos. Then the chronicle reports that there were no Mexican surgeons in the city in March—a claim that is refuted by the Arroyo report about the Alamo wounded. Like the case with the Pena memoir, the incorrect data about the Mexican medical care at the Alamo indicates that the Sanchez account is most likely a forgery.

In total, the medical-care data in the Sanchez account apes the incomplete data found in Filisola's *Memoirs* and Ramon Martinez Caro's account. First, Filisola reports: "Those killed suffered no more, but the wounded were left to lie without any attention and with no shelter." Second, he wrote: "No troops carried a medicine chest, and much less surgeons." Third, the old general reports: "A large number of the wounded died because of poor care and lack of beds, surgical instruments, etc." Then Caro wrote: "...the wounded died afterwards as a result of the lack of proper medical attention and medical facilities in spite of the fact that their injuries were not serious." In regard to the sale of captured items, Caro wrote: "In the meantime, the public sale of the goods and supplies taken from the enemy, who had hurriedly taken refuge in the Alamo the moment we entered Bexar, continued."[56]

Lastly, one thing about Andrade's figures has to be explained for his numbers to make sense. Andrade's first report of the Alamo dead and wounded reported a total of 251 wounded men. Yet, Arroyo's report indicates that he treated 408 men with surgery and 48 with medicine for a total of 456 wounded men. That gives us a difference of 205 wounded men. The explanation is simple. Historians and writers have assumed all these years that the Andrade report represented the dead and wounded of March 6. That appears to be wrong. Andrade did not reach Bexar until March 10. More likely, his report shows the status of the hospital soon after March 31 when he assumed command at Bexar because Santa Anna had left for the Colorado River. Thus, it appears that around April 1, Arroyo and his two interns had treated and released at least 205 men who had been wounded on or before March 6. Thus Andrade's report of 70 dead appears to be the number of wounded who had died between March 6 and April 1.[57]

Therefore, using Arroyo's numbers, the Mexican wounded for the siege and storming of the Alamo would have been 456 men. Of that number, 14 came from the siege and storming of Bexar in 1835. So the actual Alamo wounded number would have been 442 men. Of that number 75 died while under the care of Arroyo and his interns. Add the 70 dead reported by Santa Anna, and the total dead for the March 6 attack was 145. Santa Anna reported that 300 men were wounded on March 6. If that is correct, then the Mexican army suffered 142 wounded during the twelve days previous to the final assault. Adding Santa Anna's 70 dead for March 6 to 442 wounded for siege and storming of the Alamo results in 512 dead and wounded. Add the two men killed on February 23 and the two killed on February 25, and we have 516 dead and wounded for the entire siege. The total known dead would be 149. The total of 149, however, is most likely not the total number of Mexican soldiers killed during the thirteen days. There is no evidence that indicates the total number of men killed during the twelve days previous to the March 6 attack. Thus, the number may have been higher than four soldiers.[58]

But what of the Sutherland's claim of over 1,600 Mexican dead? What of the Ruiz claim of a similar number? The explanation for both claims is simple. The Sutherland and Ruiz accounts are not what they appear to be, and because of that, the accounts are not totally trustworthy.

John Sutherland wrote the original manuscript about the fall of the Alamo in 1860 as a reply to Reuben M. Potter's Alamo account. He submitted the manuscript to James P. Newcomb for inclusion in the *Alamo Express*, a pro-union newspaper in San Antonio. Secession sympathizers, however, destroyed the press in May 1861, before Newcomb could publish Sutherland's narrative. After the Civil War and Sutherland's death (1867), Newcomb returned the manuscript to one of Sutherland's sons. That manuscript is not the narrative published in 1936 by Annie B. Sutherland, Dr. John's granddaughter. The 1936 version is the work of John S. Ford. Ford obtained (probably in the 1880s) a copy of Sutherland's disjointed manuscript and reworked it into what today is known as the Sutherland account. He did that by cutting certain elements and adding new material to the narrative.[59]

In the original manuscript, Sutherland wrote that Ramon Caro, not Santa Anna, made the claim of 1,544 Mexican dead, and that Susanna Dickinson and Joe, Travis's slave, verified Caro's number. Sounds good, but other false allegations in the narrative discredit most of what Sutherland wrote about the Alamo. Sutherland was not Travis's courier to Gonzales on the afternoon of February 23. Sutherland was not even in San Antonio on that date. His expense record for his trip to San Antonio with Captain William H. Patton indicates that Sutherland and Patton departed Bexar for Gonzales on February 19. They probably rode with Jesse Badgett, Samuel Maverick, and other individuals, who were headed to the convention at Washington-on-the-Brazos.[60]

Sutherland first made the courier claim in January 1854 in a petition to the Texas legislature. The doctor wanted the government to grant him bounty and donation grants for his alleged military service. First, Sutherland, instead of having his representative, Samuel Maverick, submit the petition, had a relative, who was a member of the legislature, submit the request. Second, Sutherland failed to furnish that body any witness statements to support his claim. The request was forwarded to the land committee, where it was rejected for the lack of evidence. If Sutherland had been telling the truth, there were numerous individuals such as Susanna Dickinson, Samuel Maverick, Juan Seguin, Antonio Menchaca, and R. M. Williamson, who were still living and could have probably furnished Sutherland statements to verify his claim.[61]

Moreover, as for Sutherland being a medical doctor, the title was self-conferred. He was of the "Thomsonian System." The method was not the model of treatment practiced by Dr. Amos Pollard, the garrison physician at San Antonio. In Pat Ireland Nixon's *The Medical Story of*

Early Texas, the Thomsonian System is discussed in the section titled: "Quackery and Medical Ethics." Nixon explained: "Steam treatment, based on the absurd ideas of one Samuel Thomson, a New Hampshire blacksmith, was quite the vogue in Texas. It was the accepted plan of the charlatans of the day." It may upset many individuals, but little of what charlatan Sutherland wrote about the Alamo can be trusted.[62]

The Francisco Ruiz Alamo account, like the Sutherland narrative, is a report that has been accepted by historians and writers without sufficient examination. Most recently, historian William C. Davis and illustrator Gary Zaboly used the Ruiz report to claim that David Crockett's body might have been found near the Alamo's west wall or just outside the west wall.[63]

The report was translated into English by Jose Agustin Quintero, a Cuban, who later wrote for the New Orleans *Daily Picayune*. Quintero's translation was published in the 1860 *Texas Almanac*. Did Ruiz approach Quintero or did Quintero seek out Ruiz for the *Almanac*? We don't know the circumstances of how the account was created. Nevertheless, Quintero was clearly a competent translator. New evidence shows that the problem with the report is not the translation, but the author, Francisco Ruiz.[64]

Even without the new data, the credibility of the Ruiz narrative is compromised by a number of factors. First, incorrect statements such as: "At the third charge the Toluca battalion commenced to scale the walls and suffered severely. Out of 800 men, 130 were only left." The Toluca men did get hit hard but not that hard. The unit only contained 364 to start with and suffered about 20 dead and 74 wounded in the March 6 attack. The battalion went on to fight at San Jacinto on April 21, 1836. Just why Ruiz made such an outrageous claim is hard to understand, unless it was done to appease the racist Texans of 1860.[65]

Second, unbelievable claims such as: "The dead [1,600] Mexicans of Santa Anna were taken to the graveyard, but not having sufficient room for them, I ordered some of them to be thrown in the river, which was done on the same day." This Ruiz claim is refuted by a statement Sam Houston made on March 13, 1836: "...all killed in the fort were burned: The Mexicans killed in the assault were buried."[66]

Nevertheless, the figure of 1,600 Mexican dead appears to have been a rumor that started soon after the Mexican defeat at San Jacinto. On May 18, 1836, Samuel T. Allen wrote his brother: "Santa Anna says he lost a thousand men in Storming the Alamo and about as many more at Goliad, but all the rest of the prisoners say that their loss at the Alamo was upwards of 1600 so that his victory there was worse than an ordinary defeat." Thus, the myth of the tragic defeat as a victory was born. More likely, Santa Anna and the prisoners appear to have been trying to convince the Texians that enough enemy blood had been shed. Because the Texians were consumed with the belief that they were far superior soldiers to the soldiers of Mexico, they seem to have accepted the unbelievable figures.[67]

Also, would Ruiz, who already had at least one strike against him because his father was a delegate to the independence convention, have thrown the bodies of the Mexican soldiers into the San Antonio River, rather than giving them proper Catholic burials? Had he been caught doing such a thing, Santa Anna might have had him executed. Moreover, given the family's pro-Texian role in events, would Ruiz have remained in San Antonio?[68]

Third, Ruiz claimed he was the *alcalde* (mayor) of San Antonio during the siege and storming of the Alamo in February and March 1836. On February 28 Santa Anna wrote that there was no political authority in San Antonio, which indicates that the city fathers had departed the town for a safer situation. If Ruiz was the *alcalde* at the time and was in town, why does Santa Anna say there was no political authority in San Antonio? Given that the *ayuntamiento* had previously given Colonel J. C. Neill and the Alamo garrison a five-hundred-peso loan, it certainly makes sense that they had hit the road. The actual *alcalde*, however, was Francisco Flores, not Ruiz. Historians have assumed, without independent evidence, that Santa Anna appointed Ruiz *alcalde* to replace the absent Flores. On April 6, 1836, an election was conducted to fill the Flores vacancy. At that time, Ruiz was elected *regidor* (alderman). What happened to Francisco Flores? Other than being a pro-Texian mayor, why was Flores out of town? Was Ruiz also out of town during the Alamo siege and storming?[69]

Flores's Republic of Texas pension application indicates that he was on a mission for Alamo commanders Travis and Bowie. Flores was one of over twenty *Tejano* cart drivers who were attempting to transport ammunition, clothing, and provisions to the Alamo. The Tejanos were chosen for the job because they were the only individuals available who knew the route to Dimitt's Point on Lavaca Bay.[70]

The cart train also included Miguel Benites, whose pension application reads: "Miguel Benites, a resident citizen of this country, who being duly sworn, under oath, attests and affirms that at the declaration of independence, he took the Texian side, and volunteered his services, that soon after the taking of San Antonio (December 10, 1835) he was sent by Colonels B. Travis and James Bowie, with several others, to Port La Vaca [Dimitt's Point] in order to bring up with their carts and oxen, ammunition and stores for the troops garrisoning the city of San Ant. – *that the train was under the immediate command of Francisco Ruiz*; That, when they arrived at Camp Preston, near the La Vaca, which was commanded by Genl Th.[omas] Rusk, all the men of the train, together with their teams, were detained at said camp, by express order of said General, and employed to carry provisions and stores, for the use of the troops, that they were detained at said place till the month of February, when on returning to San Antonio, they were dismissed by the military authority." The application includes a statement from Antonio Menchaca, Ygnacio Espinosa, and Juan Ximenes that gives the same data as Benites's statement. Menchaca, Espinosa, and Ximenes put the return arrival at San Antonio at "about the middle of February."[71]

The story, taken at face value, does not make sense. The conditions described in the Benites petition do not fit the time frame of late December 1835. First, Travis and Bowie were not Colonels or in command at San Antonio "soon after the taking of San Antonio." F. W. Johnson was in command of the Volunteer force, and J. C. Neill commanded the Regular army in San Antonio. The only time Travis and Bowie were both colonels and in command at Bexar was between February 14 and about February 24.[72]

Second, if the cart train had departed Bexar in late December, why did J. C. Neill write on January 28: "I have respectfully to advise that the efforts of the government be all concentrated and directed to the support and preservation of this town, that supplies of Beef, port, hogs, salt & c be forthwith forwarded, and if wagons cannot be procured let as much as possible come by hand, men, money, rifles, and cannon powder are also necessary. I shall consult with some of the influential Mexicans known to be attached to our cause, about obtaining the effectual assistance of these citizens of whom I judge that 4/5 would join us if they entertained reasonable expectations of reinforcements." Neill does not write like he was expecting twenty or more carts loaded with supplies and ammunition to arrive at any moment. One would think if over twenty local citizens had been sent to the coast to obtain supplies for the Alamo, Neill would have mentioned it.[73]

Then, on February 2, James Bowie continued the complaint about the lack of supplies: "*Relief* at this post, in men, money, & provisions is of *vital* importance & is wanted instantly." On February 14 Bowie and Travis (in joint command) wrote the council: "We had detained Mr. [Samuel] Williams [a government contractor] for the purpose of saying that the Garrison is in a very destitute situation we have but a small supply of provisions and are without a dollar." Clearly, Bowie and Travis were not expecting a supply train's arrival.[74]

Third, ammunition, clothing, and other provisions from New Orleans did not reach Dimitt's Point until early February 1836. On February 2, R. R. Royall wrote the governor and council: "I herewith send you a copy of a bill of lading, of supplies for the Texas Army, which arrived in our Port [Matagorda] on the day before yesterday. I have no orders from the Government, and no discretionary powers, but will take the liberty to order the supplies, to Dimit's Landing on the La Baca (well knowing that our troops at Goliad and Bexar are much in want of Provisions) and shall instruct Capt. Dimmit to furnish the proper officers of the Government, such Provisions as they may require . . . . " On February 16, acting governor James W. Robinson wrote Philip Dimmitt: "I have sent you a commission as public store keeper at your own residence . . . . I have given order to Cols. [J. C.] Neill & [James W.] Fannin, [at Goliad] & Lt. [Francis W.] Thornton [at Goliad] to draw on you for supplies, out of the said stores."[75]

Third, Thomas J. Rusk, though he was inspector general of the army, was in East Texas in January and February 1836. Rusk was brigadier general of the Texian army between May 4 and October 31, 1836. When General Rusk reached Victoria at the end of May 1836, he was for the first time about 30 miles northwest of Dimitt's Point, and the one thing he did not have was over twenty cartloads of supplies.[76]

Lastly, five other pieces of evidence show that Francisco Ruiz's cart train must have left San Antonio shortly before the arrival of Santa Anna's force, probably around February 20 or 21, instead of late December 1835, as the pension claims. First, on February 16, Travis sent G. B. Jameson's "Plan or Demonstration of the Alamo & its present state of defense" to Henry Smith. The ending of Travis's note is supposed to have read: "Men, money, and provisions are needed – with them this post can & shall be maintained & Texas [that is] the colonies, will be saved from the fatal effects of an Invasion." At that point it appears the Alamo was still in need of supplies and there was no plan in effect to send a cart train to Dimitt's Point. Second, soon afterward, Travis and Philip Dimmitt, who was in Bexar, probably received Robinson's February 16 missive that ordered the Alamo and Goliad troops to obtain their supplies from Dimitt's Point. Third, in late February, Fannin pressed a number of *Tejano* carts into service to transport supplies from Dimitt's Point to Goliad. Travis or Bowie made no statement about a cart train having been sent from Bexar in February. Nevertheless, Fannin's cart activity is evidence that such an event could have also been taking place at the Alamo.[77]

The fourth piece of evidence is from Santa Anna. On the evening of March 3, the general wrote General Jose Urrea. Among other things, he ordered Urrea to "detach a body of troops with a chance of intercepting the provisions that the enemy is going to receive by the La Vaca river, according to the information that I have received."[78] This appears to refer to the Ruiz cart train that might have been returning to San Antonio by way of a road that ran from Lavaca Bay north to intersect the Gonzales/Columbus road. Almonte described the route with these words: "At La Baca, coming from Gonzales, and about a mile from the farm [an abandoned farm on the Lavaca River], the road goes to the mouth of the La Baca, a small harbor where the articles destined to Gonzales arrived. All along the La Baca, (below) there are small farms about two leagues apart, with cattle, hogs, good pasture, and wood." In 1837 Camp Preston appears to have been located near the Gonzales/Lavaca Bay road.[79]

Lastly, James W. Fannin offers evidence that the Lavaca effort to supply the Alamo took place in February 1836. On March 1, 1836, he wrote: "I have some quantity of beef cattle and hope soon to have more, and flour, clothing & e. I immediately forwarded an express to Washington, Dimitts Landing & c. And one after any provisions that might be on the way to Bexar and inform them of our movements also the committee of safety of Gonzales – I will soon bring to bear this place – which I think can be defended some time by 200 men and am informed by persons from Victoria that Col. [John A.] Wharton crossed the Guadalupe on Saturday with 270 men and 9 carts with about 70 barrels of flour and proceeded toward Bejar." Wharton was at that time a public contractor for the Texas army. Thomas J. Rusk had also been a contractor for a short time in December 1835. Thus, Benites, Flores, and their witnesses probably mistakenly identified Wharton as General Rusk.[80]

Given that the cart train appears to have departed San Antonio four or five days past mid-February 1836, why did Flores, Benites, and their witnesses claim the train departed the city in late December 1835 and returned in mid-February? The claims were made almost forty years after the event; it could have been a memory problem. Also, the claims were not the first time Antonio Menchaca and other Seguin men placed an 1836 incident in 1835. In November 1839 Antonio Menchaca, Manuel Flores, Ambrosio Rodriguez, and Nepomuceno Flores claimed: "Certify that we know that Don Erasmo Seguin furnished to and for Col. [James W.] Fannin's Division one hundred and twenty beeves, twenty five fanegas of corn, two yoke of oxen, one cart, seven horses and five mules, in the year 1835. We were present and saw the same in possession of Capt. [Francis] Desaque who was sent by Col. Fannin to receive the same." The event actually took place in late February 1836 or during the first days of March.[81]

If Francisco Ruiz was not in San Antonio on March 6, and the evidence strongly suggests that was the case, his absence would explain the many problems with his account of the fall of the Alamo. In other words, Ruiz told a story of what he *may have heard* about the Alamo from other individuals—truth, hearsay, rumor, and fiction.[82]

Chapter Eight Notes

1 Jose Enrique de la Pena, *With Santa Anna in Texas: A Personal Narrative of the Revolution*, Carmen Perry, ed. and trans. (College Station: Texas A&M University Press, 1975), 61.

2 Sutherland, *The Fall of the Alamo*, 43-44; Ruiz, "Fall of the Alamo," *80-81*.

3 *La Guerra de Tejas: Memorias de un Soldado* was self-published at Mexico City in 1938 by Carlos Sanchez-Navarro. The Pena memoir manuscript was also self-published at Mexico City in 1955 by J. Sanchez Garza under the title of *La Rebelion de Texas: Manuscrito inedito de 1836 Por Un Oficial de Santa Anna*. *With Santa Anna in Texas*, the English translation of the Pena manuscript, was published in Texas in 1975. The Sanchez and Pena accounts have been accepted by many historians as authentic without any critical examination of those narratives.

4 Filisola, *Memoirs*, II: 68; Rafael Ugartechea to General Cos, October 28, 1835, Bexar, Jenkins, ed., *Papers*, II: 254-255.

According to Filisola the second gun was an iron 16-pounder, and Texians captured both cannon. Texian sources report that the Mexican force had two guns, but that a long bronze 6-pounder was the only one captured. Also, Filisola's identification of the second gun as a 16-pounder appears to be wrong. The cannon was probably a long 12-pounder; the same long iron gun that is on display on the Alamo grounds today.

The meaning of "*guerrillas*" is not clear from the content of the document. The two sections may have been irregular units made up of local horsemen, or the term may refer to the manner in which the troops were operating on the field of battle.

5 Rafael Ecay Muzquiz to Minister of State and Relations, November 12, 1835, page 48, L-E-1060, *Tomo 6, Secretaria de Relaciones Exteriares,* Mexico City, Jack Jackson research notes, July 2000, copy furnished to this investigator.

The other combat actions in which Cos had some dead and wounded were two skirmishes near Stephen F. Austin's army at the Cibolo Creek ford on the Gonzales road, twenty miles east of San Antonio. Austin reported that on October 22 the Mexican army had "one or two wounded, one mortally." The second encounter was on October 24 for which Austin reported: "... they had 4 or 5 killed and many wounded."

6 Maverick, *Samuel Maverick*, 33.

7 Samuel Augustus Maverick, *Notes on The Storming of Bexar: In the Close of 1835*, Frederick C. Chabot, ed. (San Antonio: Frederick C. Chabot, 1942), 28, n. 37; General Nicolas Condelle statement in regard to Faustino Moro's service at Bexar, August 1, 1836, Matamoros, Box 2Q174, Center for American History, University of Texas at Austin; Filisola, *Memoirs*, II: 90; C. D. Huneycutt, ed., *At The Alamo: The Memoirs of Capt. Navarro* (New London, NC: Gold Star Press, 1988), 1-6; Maverick, *Samuel Maverick*, 38-39; Filisola,

Memoirs, II: 156.

Maverick reported that on November 15 a Mexican soldier had his "shin bone" broken and that "Vidal" cut the man's leg off using John W. Smith's carpenter saw. Maverick wrote: "His operation was singular and savage; he (the man) died at sunset, killed by Vidal." Vidal came to Texas from Louisiana and was married to the daughter of Joseph de La Baume, eventual heiress to one-fifth of the estate of Baron de Bastrop.

Based on the time of their arrival at San Antonio, the Mexican medical troops appear to have traveled with Colonel Domingo de Ugartechea and Sanchez, but the medical corps did not enter with the cavalry reinforcement for some unknown reason—perhaps safety. Doctors and interns would not have been able to help anyone if they had been killed attempting to ride into Bexar during the night.

8   Condelle statement, August 1, 1836.

9   Ibid.; Filisola, *Memoirs,* II: 96-97. According to the *Batalon Perm. Morelos. Rexista de Comissanio parado en Bejar on 3 October de 1835,* Bexar Archives, CAH, second Lieutenant Don Ignacio Solio appears to have been sublieutenant "D. Ignacio Solis" of the Third Company of Morelos.

10   Martin Perfecto de Cos to Santa Anna, December 15, 1835, Box 2Q174, CAH; *Batalon Perm. Morelos,* October 3, 1835; Erasmo Seguin affidavit, October 3, 1835, Bexar Archives, CAH. This document shows that 200 Bexar citizens, probably members of the militia company of San Antonio, were serving with General Cos. Their names, however, were not listed. The Moroles battalion document also shows that Cos had 13 men from the Permanent battalion of Abasolo, 21 men from the Permanent battalion of Ximienes. The roll even lists the Moroles battalion's mules (6) and gave their colors. The presidial cavalry companies of San Antonio de Bejar, Agua Verde, Tamaulipas, Nuevo Leon, and Rio Grande were also with Cos.

The Campo Santo burial records indicate two soldiers from the Morelos battalion were buried in that graveyard in 1835; Captain Jose Maria Escalante, buried October 23, and Sergeant Felipe Salazar, buried December 5. Both are alleged to have died from wounds suffered at the battle of Concepcion. The record, however, shows that Escalante was put under five days before the battle. The date may be a transcription error. Salazar was third sergeant in the Morelos Cazadore company. The Morelos battalion muster roll does not include the name of a Captain Jose Maria Escalante. Captain Felipe Gomez Escalante, however, was the commanding officer of the fourth company of Morelos.

11   Huneycutt, ed., *At The Alamo,* 34 and 36. The *Batalon Perm. Morelos,* October 3, 1835, shows that the commanding officer of the Morelos Cazadores company was one Captain "D. Benito Zenea." One could argue that because the Sanchez account includes the name Zenea that is proof the narrative is authentic. Any person doing a little research in the Bexar archives could have found (just as this investigator did) the Morelos battalion muster roll and learned of the name in that manner.

12 Juan Jose Andrade, *DOCUMENTOS QUE EL GENERAL ANDRADE Publica sobre la evacucion de la ciudad de San Antonio de Bejar, de Departamento de Tejas, A SUS COMPATRIOTAS,* 1836, Monterey, Mexico. This document gives Moro's first name. Jack Jackson furnished this investigator a copy of the Andrade document.
       History professor Jesus F. de la Teja of Southwest Texas State University informed this investigator of the meaning of the Spanish word *fulano.*

13 Huneycutt, ed., *At The Alamo,* 34; Filsola, *Memoirs,* II: 96-97; Capitulation Entered into by General Martin Perfecto De Cos, of the Permanent Troops, and General Edward Burleson, of the Colonial Troops of Texas, December 11, 1835, Bexar, Jenkins, ed., *Papers,* III: 158. De Rada was one of the Mexican commissioners who negotiated the surrender agreement. Thus, it is unlikely that he was wounded.

14 Huneycutt, ed., *At The Alamo,* 39-40, 42, 46; Filsola, *Memoirs,* II: 137-138. If a forger used the Filisola history to create the Sanchez account, why would he or she have made such an obvious mistake? Simple; forgers, like all humans, make mistakes.

15 Filsola, *Memoirs,* II: 95-96; Huneycutt, ed., *At The Alamo,* 29 and 48; Martin Perfecto de Cos to Secretary of War and Marine, February 1, 1836, Leona Vicario, Box 2Q174, CAH.

16 Jake Ivey, "Mystery Artist of the Alamo: Jose Juan Sanchez," a paper read at The Daughters of the Republic of Texas Ninth Texas History Forum, February 16, 2001. Jack Jackson furnished this investigator a copy of this paper.
       A complete analysis of the Sanchez account has not been conducted for this chapter. The basic argument about the authenticity of Sanchez boils down to one major question. Did Filisola copy from the Sanchez ledger or did the creator of the Sanchez diary copy from Filisola's history and other written sources of the period? Ivey and Jackson believe that Filisola used the Sanchez ledger as a primary source, which explains the identical data in the two accounts in a way that lets the alleged diary remain authentic. I believe whoever wrote the Sanchez narrative copied from Filisola and other sources, which, coupled with other forgery characteristics of the Sanchez book, indicate that the journal is a forgery. See Bill Groneman, *Defense of a Legend: Crockett and the de la Pena Diary* (Plano, Texas: Republic of Texas Press, 1994), 95-106, for more information on the belief that the Sanchez account is a modern forgery.

17 Filsola, *Memoirs,* II: 212; Jake Ivey, "Another Look At Storming the Alamo Walls," *The Alamo Journal,* number 120, p. 10. Filisola, like everybody who has used it, probably obtained his Almonte diary data from the New York *Herald* version that was published in the summer of 1836.

18 One of the historians who oppose me on the authenticity of the Pena and Sanchez accounts said this argument "stacked the deck" against Sanchez because I claim it would be a forgery either way, that I leave no way out for the question of authenticity. That historian appears to be confused about a

self-evident axiom of logic, known as the Law of Non-Contradiction, which says something cannot be both A and non-A. I, however, said that Sanchez could be a forgery if it was either A or non-A. I do not claim it was both A and non-A.

19 Huneycutt, ed., *At The Alamo*, 23-24.

20 Ibid.

21 Stephen F. Austin order, November 22, 1835, Jenkins, ed., *Papers*, II: 489; Robert Morris to Sam Houston, Nov. 29, 1835, Jenkins, ed., *Papers*, III: 31-32; "Sundry Individuals to Republic of Texas of amounts of goods purchased by them of the public property taken from the [Mexican] army at the Battle of San Jacinto," February 1, 1839, Audited Military Claims, Texas State Library, Austin. General Sam Houston bought the most captured property at $426. Santa Anna's army did the same with the Texian property they obtained at the fall of the Alamo. It was part of the game.

22 Cos to Minister of War, December 3, 1835, Box 2Q174, CAH; Maverick, *Samuel Maverick*, 43.

23 Cos to Santa Anna, December 15, 1836.

24 Alwyn Barr, *Texans In Revolt: The Battle for San Antonio, 1835* (Austin: University of Texas Press, 1990), 41; Hardin, *Texian Iliad*, 67-68.

25 Cos to Minister, Dec. 3, 1835.

26 Pena, *With Santa Anna*, 83.

27 F. W. Johnson to Edward Burleson, December 11, 1835, Bexar, Jenkins, ed., *Papers*, III: 164; F. W. Johnson to Government, December 17, 1835, Bexar, Jenkins, ed., *Papers*, III: 226.

28 De la Pena to Editors of *El Mosquito Mexicano*, February 3, 1837, translation in Roger Borroel, *The Papers of Lieutenant Colonel Jose Enrique de la Pena, Selected Appendixes from His Diary, 1836-1839* (East Chicago: La Villita Publications, 1997), 10. The Pena memoir's pro-Texian and anti-Mexican passages certainly worked their magic on historian Llerena Friend, who wrote the introduction for the first Texas A&M University Press edition of the narrative. She wrote: "Perhaps this book will provoke further writing: a character analysis of Santa Anna based on descriptions of him by de la Pena, an essay on the potential of Texas as seen by a man sensitive alike to pain and beauty and possessed also of a sense of history, or an essay on de la Pena as a writer."

29 *Relacion de los senores Gefes Y Oficiales perteneciente al Ejercito de Operaciones sobre Tejas, Operaciones*, 17, XI/481.3/1713, tomo 2, ff. 375-384v, *Archivo Historico of the Secretaria de la Defensa Nacional*; phone interview with Dr. "Red" Duke, University of Texas Medical School, Houston, January 5, 2001; Jose F. Moro letter, August 11, 1836, in Roger Borroel, ed. and trans., *The Papers of Lieutenant Colonel Jose Enrique de la Pena, The Last of His Appendixes* (2 vols., East Chicago: La Villita Publications, 1997), II: 33.

The roll of the officers and units in San Antonio in 1836 shows Mendoza alive and lists him under Permanent Infantry, General Command of Coahuila y Texas. Captain Pedro Saliega, Captain Juan Cortina, and Lieutenant Gregorio Berdejar are listed with Mendoza.

Dr. Duke stated that Mendoza's total loss of the lower leg in question probably saved his life. When a limb is lost, the artery closes at the damage point and the blood starts to clot. Whereas, a partial injury or cut of an artery will cause an individual to bleed out because the artery does not collapse at the wound site.

30 Edward Burleson to Government, Nov. 27, 1835, Jenkins, ed., *Papers,* III: 6; Cos to Tornel, Nov. 27, 1835, Jenkins, ed., *Papers,* III: 8.

31 Pena, *With Santa Anna,* 43, 59, 63; Filisola, *Memoirs,* II: xii, 178; Caro, "A True Account of the First Texas Campaign" in Castaneda, trans. and ed., *The Mexican Side,* 105. Caro and Filisola did not report that there were no surgeons or other medical staff at the Alamo. They only claimed that the medical response was far from adequate for the situation. Perhaps that was the case, but the Texians were no better off.

Susanna Dickinson in "Testimony of Mrs. Hannig," September 23, 1876, reported that during the Alamo siege: "Among the besieged were 50 or 60 wounded men from Cos's fight." The number does not appear to refer to the Mexican wounded left behind by General Cos, but to the Texian wounded from the siege and storming of Bexar.

32 Pena, *With Santa Anna,* 43-44, 59. There is no way to know if the letter quoted in the account is authentic. The writer of the account failed to give a citation for the alleged missive.

33 Ibid., 62-63.

34 Pena, Campaign Diary, 17-18, Jose Enrique de la Pena Papers, folder 8, 2J146, Center for American History, University of Texas, Austin, Texas.

35 Borroel, *The Papers,* II: 33; Filisola, *Memoirs,* II: xii.

36 Pena, *With Santa Anna,* 42-44.

37 Pena, *With Santa Anna,* 45, 62; "Extract of General Orders of The Army of Operations in Texas," Borroel, *The Papers,* II: 27. The Pena memoir also claims that Mora was soon replaced by Lieutenant Trinidad Santos Esteban of the Guerrero battalion. This investigator has not been able to locate any other source that verifies the Pena claims about Mora and Esteban being directors of the hospital at Bexar after the fall of the Alamo. Esteban is not listed as an officer in the Guerrero battalion on the *Relacion de los Senores* master list of officers and units that passed through Bexar in the Texas campaign in 1836.

38 Filisola, *Memoirs,* II: 178.

39 Ibid.; Santa Anna to Tornel, March 6, 1836, Bexar, Jenkins, ed., *Papers,* V: 11-12; Almonte, "Private Journal," 23; Roger Borroel, ed. and trans., *The Itineraries of the Zapadores and San Luis Battalions During the Texas War of 1836* (East Chicago: La Villita Publications, 1999), 20; Santiago Rabia

diary, Santiago Rabia Papers, DRT Library, Alamo; Honeycutt, ed., *At The Alamo*, 66; Caro, "A True Account of the First Texas Campaign" in Castaneda, trans. and ed., *The Mexican Side*, 105.

This investigator's use off the alleged San Luis daybook does not mean that this writer believes it is an authentic document. The manuscript is extremely suspect because it is part of the Jose Enrique de la Pena collection and is not in Pena's handwriting.

40   Condelle statement, August 1, 1836; Jose Faustino Moro to Pedro del Villar, August 27, 1836, Mexico [City], Box 2Q174, CAH; *Relacion de los senores, 17,* Filisola, *Memoirs*, II: 140 and 155; Almonte, "Private Journal," 23-24.

About Doctor Reyes, Filisola wrote: "The commander in chief was attacked at that time by an inflammation of the stomach that was very serious. Since the troops had neither physicians nor surgeons there was contracted in that capacity a certain Don N. Reyes, who was scarcely a bad country quack doctor...."

In Santa Anna to V. Filisola, February 6, 1836, Monclova, in Jenkins, ed., *Papers*, IV: 276-277, we find these orders: (1) "you will take the ox-carts to carry the sick, that the corps might have on the march [to Bexar], and to replace any disabled ox-carts." (2) "Those which might be sick in the army, of this city, and who may not be able to follow the army, shall remain in charge of a doctor [Moro] who shall have a house placed at his disposal to establish a hospital, and the necessary funds for medicines and utensils; at the same time commissioning an officer of trust to remain and take care of the arms, equipment, and uniforms of each patient, until the end of the month, and also of the pay which they will receive from the commanders of their respective corps." (3) "The aforesaid officer shall be instructed, beforehand, to join the army with the sick men as soon as they are well enough to continue the march to Bejar, providing themselves, first, with the necessary items." These orders certainly indicate that Santa Anna was concerned about taking care of his sick and wounded men.

41   Jose F. Moro letter, August 11, 1836; Condelle statement, August 1, 1836; Moro to Villar, August 27, 1836; *Relacion de los senores,* 17; Mariano Arroyo medical report on Alamo wounded, August 1, 1836, Matamoros, Exp. XI/481. 3/1150, *Secretaria de la Defensa Nacional,* Mexico City. Arroyo claimed that only three interns and he treated the Mexican wounded after the assault of the Alamo.

Dr. J. H. Barnard, who was in San Antonio on May 15, 1836, appears to acknowledge the arrival of the Mexican medical staff. He wrote in *Dr. J. H. Barnard's Journal* (Goliad, Texas: *The Goliad Advance*, 1912), 32: "*Sunday* [May] *15 - Nothing more of* news. A Mexican surgeon from Nondova [Monclova?] arrived. His name is Nioran [Narciso Gil?] and he seems something more respectable for a surgeon than the others I have seen. Yesterday I strolled over to the Alamo with our hospital captain (Martinez [intern Francisco Martinez?])...." Remember, Barnard did not speak Spanish, which may explain the error of his names and titles. At Goliad, Joseph H. Spohn, who had been saved from the massacre of Fannin's men, acted as an interpreter for Barnard and the other Texian doctors, who had been saved to treat the Mexican wounded.

42 Pena, *With Santa Anna,* 60.

43 Jose F. Moro letter, August 11, 1836; Arroyo statement, August 1, 1836.

44 Pena, *With Santa Anna,* 58-59; Moro letter, August 11, 1836.

45 Pena, *With Santa Anna,* 61; Miguel A. Sanchez Lamego, *Apuntes Para la Historia Del Arma De Ingenieros En Mexico: Historia De Batallon De Zapadore* (Mexico City: *Secretaria de la Defensa Nacional,* 1943), I: 172. Lamego reported Pena suffered a *"golpe contuso"* in the storming of the Alamo. This appears to refer to a severe blow to the head or a concussion. Salvatore Ramondino, ed., *The New World Spanish/English English/Spanish Dictionary* (New York: Penguin Reference, 1996), 533, reports: "concussion n. concusion; golpe." A number of my South Texas Mexican friends also report that a *"golpe contuso"* could mean a blow to the head that caused a concussion.

46 Barnard, *Dr. J. H. Barnard's Journal,* 29-30; Jack Shackelford, "Some Few Notes Upon a Part of the Texan War," in Foote, *Texas and The Texians,* 45-46; Andrade, *Documentos Que El General,* #2, April 10, 1836, #5, May 16, 1836, and #8, June 13, 1836.

   Barnard claimed that Dr. Jack Shackelford and he arrived in San Antonio on April 22, 1836. Shackelford reported they had been requested to go to San Antonio because the Mexicans did not have a person with the skill to amputate a leg, and many of the wounded had died because of that reason. Whereas, Barnard said they found about a hundred wounded at Bexar, Shackelford reported they found 400 wounded. Shackelford, however, other than saying they practiced medicine at San Antonio, gave no specific information about their work. Barnard does not say they performed any amputations; he only suggests they did so, saying no amputations took place until Shackelford and he arrived in San Antonio.

   My special thanks to Alamo historian Rod Timanus for pointing out to me the extreme similarity of the Pena account and the Barnard account.

47 David H. Hackworth, *About Face: The Odyssey of an American Warrior* (New York, London, Toronto, Sydney, Tokyo: Simon and Schuster, 1989), 21; Phillips, ed., *Roots of Strategy,* 426; Jose Enrique de la Pena to Editors of *El Mosquito Mexicano,* Mexico City, February 13, 1837, English translation in Borroel, *The Papers,* II: 10.

48 Pena to Editors, February 13, 1837; Ivey, "Another Look," 10; Adrian Woll interview of Alijo Perez Garcia, witnessed and recorded by Jose Enrique de la Pena, June 27, 1836, XI/481.3/1151, *Archivo Historico of Secretaria de la Defensa Nacional;* Lillian I. Hutchison & Assoc. October 21, 2001, Georgetown, Texas, to Thomas Ricks Lindley.

   The Adrain Woll document was written by Pena. The document is the first independent example of Pena's handwriting and his signature that has been located, and one does not have to be a professional document examiner to see that the handwriting does not match the handwriting found in the alleged Pena letter of September 15, 1836, that has been used as a prologue in *With Santa Anna in Texas*. That missive makes the claim that he was going to use other written sources in publishing his campaign diary. Nor does the handwriting match the handwriting found in the Pena manuscript published as *With Santa Anna in Texas*.

Ms. Lillian I. Hutchison, a professional document examiner, examined the Woll/Pena document, the Pena prologue letter, a number of pages from the Pena Campaign Diary manuscript, and a number of pages from the Pena memoir manuscript. Her opinion was that the Woll/Pena document and the Campaign Diary manuscript were written by the same person. Her opinion in regard to the Pena prologue letter and the Pena memoir manuscript was that they were not written by the person who had written the Woll/Pena document. Her opinion was based on the numerous differences in the documents.

Even Ivey understands that the Pena account is research based. He wrote: "For that matter, it [Filisola's history] is the same as that of Pena, who although present at the battle, knew little other than what he immediately witnessed, and had to fill out his narrative with other sources.... Accepting such a document as authentic does not mean you accept all its statements (like Crockett being executed) as true."

49 David Uhler, "'Sand' sifts through myth and reality," *San Antonio Express*, February 6, 2001; Randy Roberts and James S. Olson, *A Line in the Sand: The Alamo in Blood and Memory* (New York, London, Toronto, Sidney, Singapore: The Free Press, 2001), 289.

There is another document reflected in the Pena final draft narrative. That being data about David Crockett. In a letter to a Charles Jeffries, dated August 17, 1904, William P. Zuber wrote of the tale of Crockett being executed. Zuber believed the execution story was pure Texas "bull." Zuber wrote of the tale of Crockett's execution that he had heard. Zuber claimed he got the tale from Dr. George M. Patrick, who heard it from General Cos, who claimed he had found Crockett, unhurt, locked up alone in an Alamo room. Crockett is alleged to have told Cos: "I am David Crockett, a citizen of the State of Tennessee and representative of a district of that State in the United States Congress. I have come to Texas on a visit of exploration; purposing, if permitted, to become a loyal citizen of the Republic of Mexico. I extended my visit to San Antonio, and called in the Alamo to become acquainted with the officers, and learn of them what I could of the condition of affairs. Soon after my arrival, the fort was invested by government troops, whereby I have been prevented from leaving it. And here I am yet, a noncombatant and foreigner, having taken no part in the fighting." Crockett had been a citizen of Tennessee. He did explore northeast Texas. Otherwise, the story is false. The Zuber letter was not available to the public until 1939 when it was published in *In the Shadow of History*.

The Pena account (*With Santa Anna*, 53) has a very similar passage in its description of Crockett's execution. It reads: "He was the naturalist David

Crockett, well known in North America for his unusual adventures, who had undertaken to explore the country, and who, finding himself in Bejar at the very moment of surprise, had taken refuge in the Alamo, fearing that his status as a foreigner might not be respected." Crockett was "well known in North America for his unusual adventures." Otherwise, the Pena claims are not true.

Roberts and Olson, in their understanding and description of how the Pena memoir narrative was constructed, have jumped the next to last hurdle in understanding why the alleged memoir appears to be a modern forgery. The last hurdle is being able to see and understand that a number of the written sources reflected in the Pena account *did not exist when Pena is alleged to have written the final draft*. Also, the final draft is *not in Pena's known handwriting style*. Therefore, Pena could not have written the final draft account

50   Arroyo statement, August 1, 1836, Matamoros. Arroyo claimed that four out of twenty-five officers died after having received treatment. The *Camposanto* burial records (typed transcript, DRT Library, Alamo) show that four Mexican officers were buried on March 6, 1836. The men were: #1563, Captain Joaquin Guillen, #1564 - Lt. Jose Maria Torres, Zapadore, #1565 - Lt. Irineo Guerrero, San Luis battalion, and #1566 - Lt. Jose Maria Alcala. All four are listed as having "died of wounds from the battle of the Alamo." This would seem to indicate they were not killed in the assault, but later died in the makeshift hospital. This investigator, however, has not seen the original documents. The transcript identifies #1563 as Gregorio Esparza, an Alamo defender. Number 1563 is also identified as Joaquin Guillen. Kevin Young informed me that the Esparza name is not on the actual record; that it was added to the typed document. If the names of the Mexican officers are on the original and appear to be authentic entries, then it would seem the Pena account is correct when it claims that Jose Maria Torres was killed. On the other hand, it would appear that the Pena description is wrong in claiming: "...young Torres, died within the fort at the very moment of taking a flag. He died at one blow without uttering a word." Also, it is of interest that the death of Torres is not mentioned in Pena's Campaign Diary manuscript.

The San Antonio burial records and evidence about the arrival of Dr. Moro and his interns in Bexar have forced this writer to take a second look at the *Relacion de los senores* document. Dr. Moro and interns Narciso Gil and Eduardo Banegas did not reach San Antonio until May 15, 1836, yet they are on the *Relacion de los senores* list, which is identified as being compiled in March 1836. I now believe the list was probably made in 1841, compiled from contemporary muster rolls and other documents. Thus, the roll probably lists people as living after the fall of the Alamo who had been killed in the battle.

Also, just because a name appears on the list, for example, the name Jose Julian Sanchez as the adjutant inspector, one cannot assume that is proof the person participated in the March 6 attack on the Alamo. First,

Sanchez, like Dr. Moro, could have arrived after March 6. Second, the Sanchez name is not listed as Jose Juan Sanchez, which is probably a mistake. But the name may be correct and the identification of Sanchez as the adjutant inspector may be wrong. Until somebody checks to see if there is a service record for a Jose Julian Sanchez who served at the Alamo in 1836, we will not know for sure which element is wrong—the middle name or the title.

Jake Ivey, in "Another Look At Storming the Alamo Walls," *The Alamo Journal*, March 2001, claims that a letter in the Mexican archives shows that Sanchez was a member of the 1836 campaign. Ivey cites: "Cancelados, XI/2-357, ff. 1-2." The missive is a June 13, 1836, letter that Francisco V. Fernandez wrote, in which, according to Jack Jackson's research notes: "says auydante inspector writes me on 4th of present month. Refers [to the] defeat on margins of Rio San Jacinto on 21 April. If possible [he] wants to return to Texas on new campaign; 15 pesos out of [his] pay [is] volunteered." If this is the evidence Ivey is referring to, it is not proof that Sanchez was at the Alamo or on the 1836 campaign. When Sanchez wrote of returning to Texas, it may refer to his service at the storming of Bexar in December 1835, which is not being questioned by this investigator. Also, according to Jackson's notes on Sanchez, he found no evidence in those documents (military service records) that indicates Jose Juan Sanchez served at the Alamo in 1836.

51 Jack Jackson research notes on Francisco Duque service record, Book 2, p. 261-267, *Secretaria de la Defensa Nacional,* Mexico City. Duque's request was either refused or he later rejoined the army.

52 Shackelford, "Some Few Notes," in Foote, *Texas and The Texians*, 45-46.

53 Pena, *With Santa Anna*, 61.

54 Barnard, *Dr. J. H. Barnard's Journal,* 29-30; Andrade, *Documento Que El General,* April 10, 1836, May 16, 1836, and June 13, 1836; Santa Anna to Filisola, February 27, 1836, Jenkins, ed., *Papers*, IV: 448; Ruiz, "Fall of the Alamo," 81.

55 Helen Hunnicutt, "A Mexican View of the Texas War," *The Library Chronicle of The University of Texas*, IV: 64.

56 Filisola, *Memoirs*, II: xii, 153, and 178; Caro, "A True Account of the First Texas Campaign" in Castaneda, trans. and ed., *The Mexican Side*, 105 and 109.

57 Almonte, "Private Journal," 23; Filisola, *Memoirs*, II: 211. According to Filisola, Santa Anna departed Bexar on March 31, 1836.

58 Almonte, "Private Journal," 18. The wounded men Almonte reported were not added into the total wounded number because they would have been included in Dr. Arroyo's total for the number of wounded during the entire siege.

59 James P. Newcomb, "How the Alamo Looked Nine Years After Its Fall," *San Antonio Express,* April 9, 1905; Dr. John Sutherland, "The Fall of the

Alamo," 1860, typescript copy, Dr. Amelia W. Williams Papers, CAH; Dr. John Sutherland, Annie B. Sutherland, ed., *The Fall of the Alamo* (1936), vii. In her foreword, Annie B. reported that she worked from John S. Ford's copy, which she had obtained from his papers at the University of Texas. Location of the original Sutherland manuscript is unknown. Also, how Dr. Williams obtained her transcript is unknown, but it appears she obtained it many years after the publication of her study in the 1930s. This investigator has been searching for the original but so far has not found it. Sutherland may have written his article to make his story about being Travis's first courier seem creditable and establish the tale in the source material in order to obtain the bounty and donation land grants he had been denied in 1854. Sutherland probably understood that once something appeared in a newspaper it was accepted as the truth by most people. Even today, the number of writers and historians who are willing to accept anything written in an old newspaper or magazine as the truth is amazing. The William P. Zuber Moses Rose story is a good example of such uncritical acceptance.

In Jacques Barzun, *From Dawn to Decadence* (New York: Harper Collins Publishers, 2000), 203-204, we find a great observation about uncritical acceptance. Barzun, in discussing the influence of Francis Bacon, wrote: "The ancients, he [Bacon] pointed out, can no longer be invoked as authority, because we know more than they did.... Besides, authority is worthless. The notion that something is true because a wise man said it is a bad principle. Is the thing true in fact, tested by observation?" If to accept, without examination, something that a wise man said as the truth is a bad principle, then it would seem that to accept, without examination, anything that was said by any man as the truth is an even worse principle.

60 1860 Sutherland account; John Sutherland account record, January 25, 1836 to April 6, 1836, John Sutherland file, Audited Military Claims collection, Archives Division, Texas State Library, Austin, Texas. None of the Joe accounts report the Mexican dead. The only evidence that verifies Sutherland's claim that Mrs. Dickinson verified Caro's claim of 1,544 Mexican dead is found in the 1875 Dickinson account found in Morphis's *History of Texas, from its Discovery and Settlement*, 174-177. Morphis reported that Dickinson claimed 1,600 Mexicans were killed. Given that Sutherland died in 1867, he could not have taken his Dickinson number from Morphis's book.

61 John Sutherland petition, January 18, 1854, John Sutherland file, Memorials and Petitions collection, TSL. Sutherland furnished the government two statements from friends, who pretty much just claimed he was a fine fellow. Those who wish to know more of the evidence that Sutherland was not at the Alamo on February 23, 1836, can read: Thomas Ricks Lindley, "The Revealing of Dr. John Sutherland." The work is unpublished and needs a rewrite as I now have more evidence on the subject. The DRT Library at the Alamo has a copy of my analysis.

62 Pat Ireland Nixon, *The Medical Story of Early Texas* (Lancaster: Mollie Bennett Lupe Memorial Fund, 1946), 402.

63 William C. Davis, "How Davy Probably Didn't Die," *Journal of the Alamo Battlefield Association*, Fall 1997; Huffines, *Blood of Noble Men*, 185. Davis acknowledged that the Ruiz account is probably compromised by the fact that the account is not what Ruiz said, but rather it is what the translator said Ruiz reported.

64 Webb, Carroll, and Branda, eds. *The Handbook of Texas*, II: 424.

65 Ruiz, "Fall of the Alamo," 80-81; Filisola, *Memoirs*, II: 150 and 178.

66 Ruiz, "Fall of the Alamo," 81; Houston to Raguet, March 13, 1836.

67 Samuel T. Allen to Thomas J. Allen, San Augustine, May 18, 1836, Jenkins, ed., *Papers*, VI: 319; Susanna Dickinson account, *Telegraph and Texas Register*, March 24, 1836, in Bill Groneman, *Eyewitness to the Alamo* (Revised Edition) (Plano: Republic of Texas Press, 2001), 20. Dickinson is alleged to have claimed: "It is stated that about fifteen hundred of the enemy were killed and wounded in the last and previous attacks."

68 Charles Merritt Barnes, "Aged Citizen [Pablo Diaz] Describes Alamo Fight and Fire," *San Antonio Express*, July 1, 1906. According to Barnes, Diaz claimed: "As I reached the ford of the river my gaze encountered a terrible sight. The stream was congested with the corpses that had been thrown into it. The *alcalde* had vainly endeavored to bury the bodies of the soldiers of Santa Anna who had been slain by the defenders of the Alamo. Nearly six thousand of Santa Anna's ten thousand had fallen before they annihilated their adversaries and captured their fortress. Then involuntarily I put my hands before my eyes and turned away from the river, which I hesitated to cross. Hurriedly I turned aside and up La Villita and went to south Alamo. I could not help seeing the corpses which congested the river all around the bend from Garden to way above Commerce Street and as far as Crockett Street is now." Clearly, the Diaz story repeats and embellishes Ruiz's claim of having thrown dead Mexican soldiers into the San Antonio River.

Historian Richard G. Santos, in *Santa Anna's Campaign Against Texas*, 84, wrote: "This author has unsuccessfully attempted for several years to locate the original Ruiz account translated by Quintero due to some obvious errors or misconceptions. It is highly unlikely that the Alcalde of San Antonio would order the Mexican dead to be thrown in the river not only because of the possible consequences from the insult, but also because the stream furnished the community's drinking water."

69 Ruiz, "Fall of the Alamo," 80-81; Francisco Antonio Ruiz statement (identifying the body Toribio Losoya as an Alamo defender), April 16, 1861 in Matovina, *The Alamo Remembered*, 37; Santos, *Santa Anna's Campaign*, 83, n. 50; Ruiz, "Fall of the Alamo," 80-81; Rachel Bluntzer Hebert, *The Forgotten Colony: San Patricio de Hibernia* (Burnet, Texas: Eakin Press, 1965), 57.

70 Francisco Flores pension file, Republic of Texas Pension collection, TSL.

71 Miguel Benites statement, December 5, 1874, Antonio Menchaca, Ygnacio Espinosa, and Juan Ximenes statement, December 5, 1874, Miguel Benites

file, Republic of Texas Pension collection, TSL. In 1836 there was no location known as Camp Preston. That site was established in 1837 and was on the east side of the Navidad River about two or three miles from the confluence of that river and the Lavaca River. Dimitt's Point was on the east side of Lavaca Bay. Thus, the site that became Camp Preston was a few miles north of Dimitt's Point. There was a road that ran parallel (west side) to the Lavaca River and ran north to intersect the Gonzales to Columbus road. Camp Preston appears to have been placed in the vicinity of that road.

72 F. W. Johnson to James W. Robinson, December 25, 1835, Jenkins, ed., *Papers*, III: 325-327; Sam Houston to J. C. Neill, December 21, 1835, Jenkins, ed., *Papers*, III: 278-279; William B. Travis and James Bowie to Henry Smith, February 14, 1836, Jenkins, ed., *Papers*, IV: 339.

73 J. C. Neill to Government, January 28, 1836, Jenkins, ed., *Papers*, IV: 174-175.

74 James Bowie to Henry Smith, February 2, 1836, Jenkins, ed., *Papers*, IV: 238. Mr. Williams should not be confused with Samuel May Williams, Stephen F. Austin's secretary and close friend.

75 R. R. Royall to Henry Smith, February 2, 1836, Jenkins, ed., *Papers*, IV: 243; James W. Robinson to Philip Dimmitt, February 16, 1836, Jenkins, ed., *Papers*, IV: 353; Schooner *Caroline* Invoice of goods shipped to Texas, January 19, 1836, New Orleans, Schooner *Tramaulipas* Invoice of Goods shipped to Texas, January 20, 1836, New Orleans, consigned to R. R. Royal and John H. Wharton, Box 2-9/17, TSL; John S. Brooks to Mother, March 2, 1836, Goliad, Jenkins, ed., *Papers*, IV: 486; J. G. Ferguson to A. J. Ferguson, March 2, Goliad, Jenkins, ed., *Papers*, IV: 488.

The two invoices total seven pages. A sample of the items shows: 389 barrels of flour, 50 barrels of pork, 20 sacks coffee, 20 barrels cider vinegar, 10 boxes sperm candles at 325 each, 40 barrels beans, 15 barrels ship bread, 6 barrels brown sugar, carpenter tools, blacksmith tools, 4 dozen spades, 10 corn mills, 52 and ½ dozen butcher knives, 7 and ½ dozen coffee pots, 5 dozen boilers, 4 dozen broad head hatchets, 59 bags of musket balls at 312 each, 2 Letts Scots Infantry Tactics, 150 kegs gunpowder, 3 field drums with eagles, 4 field drums plain, 4 field bugles, 2 Octave bugles, 20 fifes, 1 case of 50 iron pistols, 400 pair thick boots, 800 pair Russet Brogans, 1200 Mens Kip Brogans, 16 infantry and artillery tactics, 1 standard staff and the making, 30½ dozen jackets, 30½ dozen pantaloons, 49½ dozen socks, 62 dozen shirts, 22 cases of U.S. muskets at 20 each, 200 cartridge boxes and belts, 30½ dozen canteens, 1 large telescope, 75 sabers, 50 pistols, 6 iron ladles, 81 bags of corn, 2 bales of blankets at 200 each, and 10 boxes of tobacco. This listing is about 2/3 of the items found on the two invoices.

76 Webb, Carroll, and Branda, eds., *The Handbook of Texas*, II: 516-517; Thomas J. Rusk to M. B. Lamar, May 17, 1836, Jenkins, ed., *Papers,*VI: 314-315; Thomas J. Rusk to M. B. Lamar, May 29, 1836, Victoria, Jenkins,

ed., *Papers*, VI: 410. In both letters Rusk complains of his lack of supplies and provisions. At Victoria, Rusk was about 35 miles from Dimitt's Point.

77 James W. Fannin to James W. Robinson, February 27, 1836; Victor Lopez statement, August 14, 1837, Thomas G. Western file, Audited Military Claims, TSL. Fannin wrote: "All our provisions are at Matagorda, Dimitt's Landing, Coxes Point & and on the way here." Lopez reported that Fannin had hired carts at Victoria to transport the goods.

78 Santa Anna to Jose Urrea, March 3, 1836, in Roger Borroel, ed. and trans., *The Papers of Lieutenant Colonel Jose Enrique de la Pena: The Last of His Appendixes*, II: 44,

79 Almonte, "Private Journal," 26: James W. Fannin to Francis De Sauque and John Chenoweth, March 1, 1836, Goliad, Jenkins, ed., *Papers*, IV: 477.

80 Fannin to De Sauque and Chenoweth, March 1, 1836.

81 Antonio Menchaca, Manuel Flores, Ambrosio Rodriguez, Nepomuceno Flores statement, November 7, 1839, San Antonio, Erasmo Seguin statement, November 8, 1839, San Antonio, Erasmo Seguin file, Audited Military Claims file, TSL; Fannin to De Sauque and Chenoweth, March 1, 1836. Seguin did not give a date when the property was taken, but he did say it was taken to Fannin at Goliad, and Fannin did not arrive at Goliad until about February 2, 1836.

82 After the fall of the Alamo, the *Tejanos* outside of Bexar had three choices. They could join the Texians, hide in the countryside, or return to San Antonio and accept Santa Anna's pardon offer. Given that Ruiz was elected as *regidor* on April 6, 1836, he must have returned to Bexar and accepted the pardon.

Chapter Nine

Alamo Strays:
Question and Answer

It is worth remembering that in life, as in other mysteries, there are no answers, but part of the pleasure of intellection is to refine the question, or discover a new one. It is analogous to the fact, that there are no facts—only the mode of our approach to what we call facts.

Norman Mailer[1]

No other event in American history is as clouded with myth and historical error as the siege and storming of the Texian Alamo of February and March 1836. Some of the reasons for that situation were examined in the previous chapters. Still many questions remain. As Walter Lord said: "The answers come hard, even when someone wants to know the facts." This work does not provide an answer to every possible Alamo question, and other Alamo puzzles will be addressed in future works. Nevertheless, here are explanations for a few of the clouded elements of the Alamo story.[2]

The Alamo Flag

As this book was being written, President George W. Bush, then governor of Texas, and state senator Carlos Truan were attempting to bring the New Orleans Greys flag back to Texas from Mexico. The Greys were two companies of United States volunteers that were organized in New Orleans in September and October 1835. Both companies participated in the storming of Bexar in December 1835. The Greys' flag was captured at the fall of the Alamo. Santa Anna quickly sent the war trophy home to the Mexican minister of war. In regard to Bush and Truan's actions, *The*

Dallas Morning News reported: "In June [1996], Mr. Bush signed into law a bill authorizing the Texas State Library and Archives Commission to negotiate an agreement with Mexican authorities to help return a flag Mexican forces took during the famous 1836 fight at the Alamo. In return, Texas would offer three Mexican flags captured at the Battle of San Jacinto." Bush and Truan, like many historians and Alamo partisans,

John S. "Rip" Ford, early Alamo historian

believe the Greys flag was the banner flown at the Alamo.[3] The belief appears to come from Walter Lord, who wrote:

> Traditionally the Alamo flew a modified Mexican flag, but the best evidence indicates that was not the case.
>
> The early Texan sources mention no specific flag, but in 1860 Captain R. M. Potter remedied the omission. In the first of several [two] accounts he did on the subject, Captain Potter declared that the Alamo flag was the regular Mexican tricolor, but with the date 1824 substituted for the usual golden eagle. This was based on no evidence but on Potter's theory that the Texans were fighting for the Mexican Constitution of 1824, until the Declaration of Independence was formally passed on March 2, 1836. Since the Alamo defenders knew nothing of this event, the theory ran, they went down still fighting for a liberal Mexico. The irony of Potter's theory was appealing; others backed it up and it lingers on.
>
> But the theory does not jibe with the facts. Actually, Texas had stopped fighting for the Constitution of 1824 long before the Alamo.[4]

Lord concluded that the Alamo defenders, all supporters of independence, would not have maintained a banner that represented Mexican federalism. Therefore, since Colonel Juan N. Almonte's journal only mentions the capture of one flag, which appears to have been the New Orleans Greys banner, Lord decided that the Greys' azure blue standard was the Alamo flag.[5]

Lord was right about the Alamo defenders' feelings on independence. He was wrong about the Alamo flag. The Greys banner was nothing more than "a flag captured at the fall of the Alamo." At that point the blue cloth only represented proof of the involvement of United States volunteers in the Texian struggle against the Mexican government. Therefore, about an hour and a half after the dawn attack, Santa Anna wrote his government: "The bearer takes with him one of the flags of the enemy's Battalions, captured today. The inspection of it will show plainly the true intentions of the treacherous colonist, and of their abettors, who came from parts of the United States of the North." Santa Anna's statement proves that the Greys banner was a unit standard, not *the* Alamo flag. The story of the true Alamo flag starts with the siege and storming of Bexar in 1835.[6]

Francis W. Johnson, co-commander of the storming of Bexar, in answering a letter from writer Julia Lee Sinks, wrote: "Your note of the 6th inquiring 'what kind of flag was used by the Texans, if any, at San Antonio.' I have to inform you that it was the Mexican flag – *Red, White and Green.* We at that time were contending for our rights as citizens of Mexico." That flag was the Mexican tricolor that contained a golden eagle, with rattlesnake in mouth, perched on a cactus on the flag's middle white band. This was the Mexican national standard of the federal government of the constitution of 1824. After the surrender of the Mexican army on December 11, 1835, Herman Ehrenberg, a Greys private, confirmed Johnson's statement: "We still considered Texas and Mexico as one...three colors floated over the church."[7]

The Mexican federalist flag has ever since been confused with a flag created by Philip Dimmitt at Goliad. On October 27, 1835, Dimmitt wrote Stephen F. Austin: "I have had a flag made – the colors, and their arrangement the same as the old one – with the words and figures, 'Constitution of 1824,' displayed on the white, in the center." Did Dimmitt's flag make it to San Antonio? Many believe it did, but there is little reliable evidence to indicate the flag joined Austin's army. On October 15, 1835, Dimmitt sent a company of Tejanos, under the command of Placido Benavides, to join Austin's force, which was on the road to San Antonio. Dimmitt, however, at that time, had yet to create his flag.[8]

If Dimmitt's flag had made it to Bexar, it would have joined the national federalist flag, the Gonzales "Come and Take It" cannon flag, the Greys banner, and Sarah Dodson's single starred red, white, and blue banner in the army's color guard that was commanded by Captain William Scott. After Scott's discharge on November 18, the color guard detail was assigned to Captain Peter J. Duncan's company. Future Alamo assistant quartermaster A. Anderson was a member of that unit.[9]

During the last days of December 1835, the forces at Bexar abandoned the federalist cause and the Mexican national flag. On December 30 Horatio H. Alsbury, translator for the garrison and future Alamo courier, wrote Sam Houston of the garrison's attitude toward independence and requested his opinion on the subject:

> I take the privilege of addressing you this note flattering
> myself that you will be pleased to know our operations at
> this place, but I am actuated more by the uneasiness I feel
> about our Country from the declaration [of independence]

of Dimitt's party at La Bahia [Goliad], & the disposition of the troops remaining at this place to a second [of] that declaration. You will excuse me therefore when I beg of you to inform me by letter the disposition of the Council & Texas in general relative to a premature declaration of independence or an immediate declaration to that purport.

I will be truly grateful to you to give me *candidly* your own ideas on the subject of Independence. The army will leave this evening to the number of 300 men for Matamoros where from authentic information they will meet the enemy fifteen hundred in number.[10]

Houston's opinion was important to the American volunteers who planned to capture the Mexican port of Matamoros on the Rio Grande. On November 29, 1835, Robert C. Morris, a Greys captain, wrote Houston to reject an appointment in the Texian regular army: "There was no one [who] more ardently wished you as a leader in the Camp & your appearance there at any period previous to the taking of Bexar, would have given you the command of the army by eleven twelfths of the votes.... There are now here 225 men, nearly all from the U.S. Who on no consideration will enter into any service connected with the Regular Army, the name of which is a perfect Bugbear to them, & to them I promised to be one of those who lead them on the road to Matamoros & who declare in the most positive manner that should this not be undertaken they will return home direct from hence."[11]

During December's last days or the first week of January 1836, a flag appeared at Bexar that seems to have been designed to take advantage of Houston's popularity with the American filibusters. On January 6, 1836, Texas governor Henry Smith wrote: "I have anticipated them and ordered the commander-in-Chief forthwith to proceed to the frontier, take charge of the army, establish his headquarters at the most eligible point, and to immediately concentrate his troops, at the different points, so as to be in readiness for active operations, at the earliest possible day. A descent will be made on Matamoros, as soon as it can possibly be fitted out.... They have hoisted a flag at Bexar for independence, with Gen. Houston's name upon it! This I have learned to be the fact. I find it necessary, in order to circumvent them, to order Gen. Houston to immediately take charge."[12]

Why would Smith, who supported independence and separation from Mexico, have been upset about a "Sam Houston for Independence" flag flying at San Antonio? After all, such a banner suggests loyalty and support for Houston as the commander-in-chief. The problem was that the flag did not represent the kind of separation from Mexico that Smith, Houston, and James Bowie were working to achieve. F. W. Johnson and James Grant appear to have created the Houston flag as a way to convince the U.S. volunteers that Houston supported the Johnson and Grant version of the Matamoros expedition.[13]

On January 7, in a letter to John Forbes of Nacogdoches, Houston answered Alsbury's question about independence and identified the problem with the Houston flag that Smith wanted him to solve.

> You are aware that I have been opposed to a Declaration of Independence up to this time. I was so, because I thought it premature and that some policy demanded of us a fair experiment – I now feel confident that no further experiment need be made, to convince us that there is but one course left for Texas to pursue, and that is, an unequivocal Declaration of Independence, and the formation of a constitution, to be submitted to the people for their rejection or ratification.

> It is the project of some interested in land matters, very largely, for Texas to unite with some three or four of the Eastern States of Mexico, and form a Republic – This I regard as worse, than our present, or even our former situation.

> Their [the Mexican people of those states] wars would be our wars, and their revolutions: While our Revenues, our lands, and our lives would be expended to maintain their cause, and we could expect nothing in return; but prejudice, and if we relied on them disappointment. Let Texas now Declare her independence, and it will cost her less blood, and treasure to maintain it; than it would cost her to maintain her integral interest in such a confederacy; the preponderance, would be so decidedly against her, that she would have less influence if possible, than she has heretofore enjoyed in the Congress of Coahuila and Texas.

> The citizens of Texas can never be happy, until they are confident in the certainty of their rights – so long as they

are subject to Mexican policy they never can be confident;
Then if these are truths sanctioned by experience – Texas
must be free, that her citizens may be happy.[14]

In early February 1836, Governor Smith stated his and Houston's
political and military goals in a private letter. He wrote:
    ... The first of March will give the death blow to their
    main project, as I have no doubt the independence of Texas
    will be proclaimed to the world, and then a long farewell to all
    Mexican policy....
    "This country can never prosper until a few of that bane-
    ful faction are immolated on the alter of their own perfidy.
    The convention will, I hope, afford the grand corrective.
    "Owing to their [James Grant and F. W. Johnson] base
    management, much confusion prevails among our volunteer
    troops on the frontier, but, by using much vigilance, I have
    now got Bexar secure. On the last advices the enemy were
    concentrating on our border in considerable numbers and
    every exertion used, and everything put in requisition for a
    formidable campaign against the colonies in the spring.
    Flying rumors have been sent in to delude us, by saying
    many of the Eastern States have declared in opposition to
    the dictator. In this, however, I have no confidence, believing
    it is intended to delude us.
    "Copano has been assigned as our headquarters for the
    present, until we make a declaration and have a sufficient
    number of men and means to operate on, when we will
    immediately remove to the west, of which you will be
    informed from this department.[15]

Then on January 7 Houston responded to Smith's concern about the
flag at Bexar and the political position it represented by departing for
Goliad to seize control of the Matamoros expedition to stop Johnson and
Grant from using it as their opening engagement in a campaign to create
a new Mexican/Texian republic.[16]

In opposition to the Johnson and Grant design for a new nation, Bowie
was already on the road to Goliad with orders from Houston to organize a
volunteer force that could take Matamoros in the name of independence
and secure the land all the way up the Rio Grande, which Smith and

Houston erroneously believed was Texas's southwestern border. On January 10, probably unaware that Houston was on the road, Bowie wrote the general: "Some dark scheme has been set on foot to disgrace our noble cause. I shall leave with Captain Blount in an hour, and shall reach Goliad by daylight, and put a stop to Grant's movements." The Bowie, Houston, and Smith "noble cause" was simple. They wanted a Texas that was free of Mexican political dominance and influence that could be quickly annexed to the Untied States. Any successful Anglo-Celtic alliance with Mexican federalists, be it the Johnson and Grant project or the one advocated by Lt. Governor James W. Robinson and the Council, that defeated Santa Anna's centralist government would have prevented a union of Texas and the United States.[17]

Houston, after arriving at Goliad, received news from Lt. Colonel James C. Neill, the commander at San Antonio, reporting an expected attack on that city and the reinforcement of the Mexican garrison at Matamoros. A part of the letter, which has been overlooked by historians, mentions the Bexar flag: "You [Houston] will learn what sneaking and Gambling has been done, to operate against you by J [Johnson] & G [Grant]. You will hear all about the Houston flag, and the Houston House in Bexar, for fear you would be elected Commander of the Volunteer army, they never would let it come near an election, but shuffled it off, and threw all the army into confusion several times, and the responsibility on the heads of the several Captains."[18]

In the end, Houston, Bowie, and Smith's attempted invasion of Matamoros was postponed until after the convention. Santa Anna's arrival at Bexar, however, prevented the move to the west until the Mexican War in 1846. Still, the evidence suggests that in January 1836, the Bexar troops were flying a flag for independence with Sam Houston's name on it, which appears to have represented the Johnson and Grant proposed new republic made up of Texas and three or four Eastern Mexican states. Was that flag the Alamo flag?[19]

Other evidence strongly suggests that the Houston flag was most likely the Alamo banner. When Santa Anna's army approached San Antonio sometime after 2:00 p.m. on February 23, the Alamo defenders welcomed them with a flag that appears to have flown from the San Fernando church tower. Colonel Juan N. Almonte described the standard with these words: "The enemy, as soon as the march of the division was seen, hoisted the tri-colored flag with two stars, designed to represent

Coahuila and Texas. The President with all his staff advanced to Camp Santo (burying ground.) The enemy lowered the flag and fled, and possession was taken of Bexar without firing a shot."[20]

In spite of Almonte's belief, it is extremely unlikely that the standard represented Texas and Coahuila. Texians had been working to separate Texas from Coahuila since the early 1830s. At this time there is no other evidence that clearly defines the two-star tricolor. Speculation, however, suggests that the banner was probably the Sam Houston flag for independence. The stars, a United States design attribute, most likely represented the Anglo-Celtic American and Mexican partnership in the proposed Grant and Johnson confederacy. The Mexican tricolor element probably symbolized the proposed nation's genesis from Mexican soil. The use of Sam Houston's name, probably on the reverse of the two-star panel, was an attempt to convince the volunteers from the United States that Houston supported the confederacy. Even if this explanation for the design is off base, the two-star tricolor appears to have been the Alamo standard.[21]

Almonte's words and two other eyewitness reports indicated that the two-star tricolor was the flag flown from the Alamo fortress during the thirteen-day siege. Pablo Diaz, a young man in 1836, reported in 1906: "…From the mission [Concepcion] I could see also the flag of the Constitutionalists [federalists] floating from the Alamo. The later flag was not the flag that was afterward adopted by the Texas Republic, with its blue field and single star and a stripe of white and one of red, but the flag of Mexico under the Constitution and prior to the usurpation and assumption of the dictatorship by Santa Anna."[22]

Antono Chavez, who was nine years old in 1836, reported in 1907: "I was born under the Mexican dominion. Its constitutional flag of A.D. 1821, against which Santa Anna contended and prevailed, was floating over the Alamo when he came here in 1836. He captured it together with the Alamo and annihilated its brave defenders."[23]

Diaz and Chavez are wrong about the Alamo flag having been the national federalist Mexican flag. As Walter Lord said, the Alamo defenders were supporters of independence. They would not have flown a federalist flag. Diaz, however, seeing the flag from the Mission Concepcion would not have been able to tell the difference between the two-star tricolor and the federalist tricolor. As for Chavez, it is possible that as a young boy, he did not realize there was a difference in the two flags. He may have assumed the two-star tricolor was another version of the federalist banner.

The important element in the Diaz and Chavez evidence is that both reported the Alamo banner appeared to be a Mexican tricolor, which coupled with Almonte's report and the Houston independence banner evidence, suggests the flag that was flying over the Alamo was the two-star flag. That flag was also most likely captured by the Mexican army. Still, Mexican historians, like Lord, mistakenly believe that the banner captured during the dawn attack was the New Orleans Greys flag.[24]

Several reasons strongly indicate that the Greys flag was not the emblem the Mexican troops captured on March 6. Given that the captured flag was most likely ripped from its pole, it would have probably been torn. The Greys flag does not appear to have been damaged in such a manner. Also, the banner had no eyelets or cords to attach it to a pole.[25]

Moreover, the Greys flag includes the motto "God and Liberty," a Mexican saying that dates to Mexico's first attempts at independence. General Santa Anna and other Mexicans officers closed their correspondence with the dictum. The flag and its adage were appropriated during the siege and storming of Bexar when the Texian forces were fighting under the Mexican national flag of federalism. During the Alamo siege, however, it is extremely hard to believe that when Travis wrote on February 24, "... our flag still waves proudly from the walls," he was writing about the Greys banner.[26]

Nevertheless, Mexicans appear to accept the Greys flag as the Alamo standard because it was the one Santa Anna sent to Mexico City with his March 6 report of the final assault. The Mexican narrative detailing the capture of the Alamo flag, however, is probably close to the truth. It reads:

> Three officers formerly of the old 70th [Infantry Regiment] (at that time in the Jimenez Battalion) lively carried the tri-colored flag [Mexican national *pabellon* that represented the centralist government], they fell dead in succession before reaching the height in order to replace the flag, the names of these heroic soldiers, as important as they were, were carelessly lost to our military history.
>
> In order to reinforce the column of attack that was progressing slowly, and in order to spare more bloodshed, they

rushed in the reserve formed by the battalion of Sappers under the command of the then Lieutenant Colonel Romulo Diaz of the five companies Grenadiers of the permanent battalions of Matamoros, Jimenez, and Aldama and the active of Toluca and San Luis, unorganized at that time.

A Lieutenant of Sappers, Jose Maria Torres was one that planted the three colors on the flagstaff. According to official data, that lieutenant lost his life after finishing his epic exploit. It is another name to unite to the heroic saviors of the Flag and among those who have surrendered the due honor dying for her![27]

It is appropriate that Mexican historians honor the brave Mexican soldiers who fought and died at the Alamo *for their government.* On the other hand, it is important to note that it would be a disgrace and insult to the memory of the Alamo defenders to trade the Mexican unit flags captured at the Battle of San Jacinto for the Greys flag. The United States banner did not represent the Alamo unit because the Greys were disbanded after the fall of Bexar. A few men remained in San Antonio and joined the garrison under Lt. Colonel James C. Neill as the San Antonio Greys. The other members were either discharged or joined the Johnson and Grant expedition that moved down the road to Goliad.[28]

Besides, in reality, the Greys flag no longer truly exists. In 1961 Lord reported: "The flag remains in Mexico City today...it is not on exhibit but buried in the files...crumbling to pieces in brown wrapping paper. Thanks to the courtesy of the Mexican government, it was recently brought out once again, and enough of it pieced together to identify it beyond any doubt." The banner that former governor Bush and Truan wanted to return to Texas is essentially a replica that contains an unknown number of scraps of the original material. The two politicians might as well purchase a replica of the Greys flag from the IMAX Theater in San Antonio.[29]

In sum, any Texan politician who exchanges the San Jacinto flags for the Greys banner will be giving back to Mexico the flags that truly symbolize the victory that Travis, Bowie, Crockett, and the men, women, and children of the Alamo were fighting for and died for; a triumph to create an independent and prosperous Texas based on North American political principles. The captured Mexican banners represent the San Jacinto victory that gave birth to Texas, and the Alamo defenders' deaths were its down payment. That fact should not be forgotten or dishonored by modern political ambitions.

Alamo Independence

Were the Alamo defenders fighting for independence or for the federalist constitution of 1824?

On this question, there is no doubt. The defenders were for independence. As previously stated, Alsbury said on December 30, 1835, the troops at Bexar were disposed to second the Goliad Declaration of Independence. On January 12 William R. Cary wrote: "The Colo. [James C. Neill] and myself has twice called a general parade and addressed them in such a manner that they would get satisfied for a while, but we are now discouraged ourselves.... We have sent and made known our situation to them, and as the safety of Texas depends mostly upon the keeping of this place they certainly will soon as possible do some thing for us especially when we expect to declare *independence* as soon as the convention meets."[30]

Later in January, Joseph M. Hawkins wrote Governor Henry Smith a letter of support. Hawkins closed with: "May God bless you and prosper you is the sincere wish of an honest son of Erin and a friend of Texian Independence."[31]

Then, at the end of January, Amos Pollard, the Alamo's surgeon, also sent a supportive missive to Smith. He said: "I hope that the provisional government would continue till we could establish another and a more firm one – This we shall endeavor to do in March and God grant that we may create an independent government."[32]

On February 1, 1836, the citizens of Bexar elected Jose A. Navarro, Jose F. Ruiz, and Gaspar Flores to represent them at the convention to be held in Washington-on-the-Brazos on March 1, 1836. On February 13 Pollard again wrote Governor Smith. Pollard made it clear as to what was expected of the three Tejanos at the convention. He wrote: "However, I intend that those representatives shall distinctly understand, previous to their leaving, that if they vote against independence, they will have to be very careful on returning here."[33]

Likewise, Green B. Jameson, the garrison's engineer, wrote Governor Smith on February 11: "I have been in the field on actual duty more than four months and have not lost one hour from duty on account of sickness nor pleasure. But have served my country in every capacity I possibly could. When I left home it was with a determination to see Texas free & Independent sink or swim die or perish."[34]

Finally, on March 3, Travis wrote his friend Jesse Grimes, a member of the convention: "If independence is not declared, I shall lay down my arms, and so will the men under my command. But under the flag of independence, we are ready to peril our lives a hundred times a day, and to drive away the monster who is fighting us under a blood-red flag, threatening to murder all prisoners and make Texas a waste desert."[35]

James C. Neill's Departure From Bexar

When did Bexar garrison commander Lieutenant Colonel James C. Neill leave Bexar and turn the command over to Travis?

Neill first left Bexar sometime, probably in the morning, February 11, 1836. Green B. Jameson, on that date, wrote Governor Smith: "Col. Neill left today for home on account of an express from his family informing him of their ill health." The following day Travis wrote Smith: "In consequence of the sickness of his family, Lt. Col. Neill has left this post, to visit home for a short time, and has requested me to take Command of the Post."[36]

After Neill's departure a bitter argument erupted between James Bowie and Travis over who would command the troops at Bexar. Neill had commanded both regulars and volunteers. The volunteers had voted to serve under Neill on December 31, 1835. Bowie appears to have believed that because he had declared himself a full colonel of volunteers he had rank over Travis, a regular army lieutenant colonel. Thus the fractious knife-fighter felt that he should have been left in command of the garrison.[37]

J. J. Baugh and Travis wrote Smith of the disagreement that took place on February 12 and 13. Baugh wrote: "An Election was consequently ordered by Col. Travis and Bowie was Elected. – without opposition none but the volunteers voted & in fact not all of them – The consequence was, a split in the Garrison, Col. Travis, as a matter of course, would not submit to the control of Bowie and he (Bowie) availing himself of his popularity among the volunteers seems anxious to arrogate to himself the entire control." Travis wrote that Bowie was "roaring drunk all the time" and had taken total command of the garrison. Travis then added: "I do not solicit the command of this post but as Col. Neill has applied to the Commander in Chief to be relieved.... I will do it if it be your order for a time until an artillery officer can be sent here."[38]

Travis's statement about Neill's request for a release from command at San Antonio suggests that Neill, in addition to visiting his family, was probably going to confront Governor Smith and Sam Houston about the lack of support for the Bexar garrison. On January 27 Neill had written Smith: "In my communication to the Executive I did not ask for pledges and resolves, but for money, provisions and clothing. There has been money given or loaned by private individuals expressly for the use of the army, and none has been received.... We can not be fed and clothed on paper pledges. My men cannot, nor will not, stand this state of things much longer...."[39]

Whatever the reason for Neill's departure, he was in Gonzales on February 13. The Alamo courier that carried the Baugh and Travis letters to San Felipe appears to have encountered Neill at Gonzales and informed him of Bowie's behavior. Thus Neill was forced to return to the Alamo to settle the clash over command at San Antonio.[40]

There is no doubt that Neill returned to San Antonio. The audited military claims collection at the Texas State Library contains seven army discharge documents for Bexar troops that were signed by Neill on February 14, 1836, at Bexar. Also, on February 2, 1838, Neill gave the heirs of I. L. K. Harrison an affidavit placing Harrison at the fall of the Alamo. The document reports: "Col. Neill being called upon states that he knows of I. L. K. Harrison – states that he distinctly knows he was on the Roll of Capt. Harrison's company – when he relinquished the command to Col. Travis on 14 Feby 1836 and that Capt. Harrison's Company was enlisted for six months."[41]

That Neill returned to Bexar to settle the fight between Travis and Bowie is reinforced by a Bowie and Travis letter dated February 14, 1836, which closed with: "By an understanding of today Col. J. Bowie has the command of the volunteers of the garrison, and Col. W. B. Travis of the regulars and volunteer cavalry. All general orders and corrispondence [*sic*] will henceforth be signed by both until Col. Neill's return."[42]

February 28 found Neill in San Felipe where he obtained six hundred dollars from Governor Smith for the support of the garrison. Then, Neill, anxious to assist his men at the Alamo, hurried to Gonzales and assumed command of the Alamo reinforcement effort until March 11, when he turned the command over to Sam Houston.[43]

Chapter Nine Notes

1   Norman Mailer, *Oswald's Tale: An American Mystery* (New York: Random House, 1995), 515-516. This book is an excellent piece of research and writing. Mr. Mailer makes a convincing presentation that Lee Harvey Oswald most likely acted alone in the killing of John F. Kennedy. Still, I don't believe it.

2   Lord, *A Time*, 198.

3   *The Dallas Morning News*, November 12, 1996.

4   Lord, *A Time*, 210-211; Tyler, Barnett, Barkley, Anderson, and Odintz, eds., *The New Handbook*, IV: 998-999. The New Orleans Greys flag was made by a group of Texas women who greeted the Greys between San Augustine and the Sabine River in November 1835 and presented the flag to the volunteers from the U.S.

5   Ibid; Almonte, "Private Journal," 16-17.

6   Antonio Lopez de Santa Anna to Jose Marto Tornel, March 6, 1836, Bexar, Jenkins, ed., *Papers*, V: 11-12; Michael P. Costeloe, "The Mexican Press of 1836 and the Battle of the Alamo," *Southwestern Historical Quarterly*, XCI: 539. When Mexico's minister of war presented the Greys flag to the Mexican Congress, some of the members showed "their patriotic bravery" by throwing it on the floor and trampling it.

7   Francis W. Johnson to Julia Lee Sinks, June 2, 1874, Round Rock, Julia Lee Sinks Papers, CAH; Edgar William Bartholomae, "A Translation of H. Ehrenberg's *Fahrten und Schicksale eines Deutschen in Texas,* with Introduction and Notes" (M.A. thesis, University of Texas at Austin, 1925), 95.

8   Philip Dimmitt to Stephen F. Austin, October 27, 1835, Goliad, Jenkins, ed., *Papers,* II: 234; Philip Dimmitt to Stephen F. Austin, October 15, 1835, Goliad, Jenkins, ed., *Papers,* II: 134-135.

9   Stephen F. Austin affidavit (William Scott discharge), November 18, 1835, Bexar, William Scott file, AMC-TSL; Peter Duncan, Captain of the Color Guard, affidavit, September 1836, Luke Moore file, AMC-TSL; "List of the names of those who fell in the Alamo at San Antonio De Bexar," Muster Roll book, 2; Edward Gritten to Alcalde, Ayuntamiento and People of Gonzales, October 4, 1835, Bexar, Jenkins, ed., *Papers*, II: 38; Edward Gritten claim for expenses for A. Anderson as express rider to Gonzales, Edward Gritten file, AMC-TSL; Alamo voting list, February 1, 1836; "List of men who have this day volunteered to remain before Bexar, November 24, 1835," Austin Papers, CAH.

10 Horatio A. Alsbury to Sam Houston, December 30, 1835, Bexar, Jenkins, ed., *Papers,* III: 367-368.

11 Robert Morris to Sam Houston, November 29, 1835, Bexar, Jenkins, ed., *Papers,* III: 31-32.

12 Henry Smith to William Ward, January 6, 1836, San Felipe, Jenkins, ed., *Papers*, III: 427-428.

13 James C. Neill to Sam Houston, January 14, 1836, Bexar, William C. Brinkley, ed., *Official Correspondence of the Texian Revolution, 1835-1836* (2 vols.; New York and London: D. Appleton-Century Company Incorporated, 1936), I: 294-295. Jenkins failed to include the complete text of this letter in *The Papers of the Texas Revolution, 1835-1836.*

14 Sam Houston to John Forbes, January 7, 1836, Washington-on-the-Brazos, Jenkins, ed., *Papers*, III: 436-437.

Ironically, Stephen F. Austin on the same date, Austin to Houston, January 7, 1836, New Orleans, Jenkins, ed., *Papers*, III: 432-433, informed Houston: "I now think the time has come for Texas to assert her natural rights; and were I in the convention I would urge an immediate declaration of independence."

Previously, Austin had supported James W. Robinson and the Council's political goal of uniting with northern Mexican federalists through the Matamoros expedition. In sum, Austin appears to have been the driving force behind the Council's plans for Matamoros.

On December 22 Austin had written: Austin to Provisional Government, December 22, 1835, Quintana, Jenkins, ed., *Papers*, III: 315-317, the government: "The best interests of Texas, I think require that the war should be kept out of this country and beyond the Rio Grande.... There are about 200 volunteers here, and probably will be a 1000 or more in a month.... I think that head quarters should be fixed at Goliad, and that a federal auxiliary army should be collected there, and offered to the federal party should it be needed by them.... I give my opinions frankly and refer you to Col. Fannin for a further explanation of them, I believe that this meritorious officer and myself do not differ materially on these subjects."

Austin, Robinson, Fannin, and the Council represented the third political view behind the conquest of Matamoros: Texas's continued participation in the Mexican nation as a state independent from Coahuila in a federalist country versus Houston, Bowie, and Smith's goal of an independent nation that could be taken to the U.S., and the Johnson and Grant proposal of a new nation composed of Texas and northern Mexican states. Clearly, the Texas insurrection was a continuation of the centralist/federalist civil war until March 2, 1836, when Texas representatives voted for independence.

15 Henry to William Bryan, February 5, 1836, San Felipe, Jenkins, ed., *Papers*, IV: 268-269. Smith had commenced his campaign against the Mexican federalists with his rejection of assistance from federalists Jose Antonio Mexia and Augustin Viesca in December 1835.

16 Sam Houston to Henry Smith, January 8, 1836, Washington-on-the-Brazos, Jenkins, ed., *Papers*, III: 446.

17 Henry Smith to Sam Houston, December 17, 1835, San Felipe, Jenkins, ed., *Papers*, III: 239; Sam Houston to James Bowie, December 17, 1835, San Felipe, Jenkins, ed., *Papers*, III: 222-223; James Bowie to Sam Houston,

January 10, 1836, North of Goliad, found in Yoakum, *History*, II: 57-58. The actual southwestern boundary of Texas was the Nueces River, not the Rio Grande.

18 Neill to Houston, January 14, 1836, Bexar, Brinkley, ed., *Official Correspondence*, 295.

19 Robert Maberry Jr., *Texas Flags* (College Station: Texas A&M University Press, 2001), 31-32; David Crockett, *The Life of David Crockett: The Original Humorist and Irrepressible Backwoodsman* (New York: A. L. Burt Company, 1902), 393. This book includes *Col. Crockett's Exploits and Adventures in Texas, Written by Himself.*

Maberry believes the Alamo flag might have been one that was described in *Col. Crockett's Exploits and Adventures* published in the summer of 1836. The book was supposed to be based on Crockett's Alamo diary that had survived the fall of the Alamo. For many years the alleged diary was believed to be authentic. Today it is known to be spurious. The fake diary reports: "We have had a large national flag made; it is composed of thirteen stripes, red and white, alternately, on a blue ground with a large white star, of five points, in the center, and between the points the letters Texas."

The "Crockett" flag appears to have been a cross between the 1836 United States flag and the Lorenzo de Zavala Republic of Texas flag that was adopted by the Convention of 1836. The de Zavala flag is reported to have been a blue field with a white five-pointed star in the center, with the letters T-E-X-A-S, one letter between each star point.

The "Crockett" flag would have made a great Alamo flag. There is, however, no evidence that such a flag was ever at the Alamo.

20 Almonte, "Private Journal," 16-17. Ultimately, we do not know why Almonte believed that the flag represented Texas and Coahuila. However, if he asked Bexar citizens what the banner stood for, it is doubtful they would have said "independence." The safer course for Tejanos would have been to claim that it represented the Mexican state of Coahuila y Tejas, be that entity centralist or federalist. For an excellent review of Tejanos' attitudes toward the Mexican state of Coahuila y Tejas see Chapters VI and VIII in Andres Tijerina's *Tejanos & Texas Under the Mexican Flag, 1821-1836* (College Station: Texas A&M University Press, 1994).

21 Webb, Carroll, and Branda, eds., *Handbook*, I: 607. Previous to the fall of Bexar in December 1835, the "star" as a symbol of independence had already been used in one Texas flag. The banner was William Scott's flag, which represented the desire for a complete break with Mexico and probable annexation to the United States. The standard was made of blue silk with a white star in the center and the word Independence under the star. Charles Lanco, an Italian who later died at the Alamo, painted the star. The flag was most likely at the siege of Bexar, but it is extremely doubtful that Austin would have included it in the color guard because of its promotion of an independent Texas at a time when Austin was supporting federalism and continued participation in the Mexican nation. Of course after the

revolution when Texas stood alone as an independent nation, a single star was used to represent that status.

22 Matovina, *The Alamo Remembered*, 74. Matovina deserves credit for pulling all of these accounts together, but as he indicated in his introduction the evidence cries for "critical assessment."

23 Ibid., 96.

24 Lord, *A Time*, 212; Anexo No. 32, "La Bandera De Alamo," Jose Enrique de la Pena, *La Rebelion De Texas: Manuscrito inedito de 1836 Por Un Oficial de Santa Anna. With Santa Anna in Texas*, J. Sanchez Garza, ed, (Mexico City: A. Frank de Sanchez, 1955), 299-300. An English translation of this document was furnished to this investigator by Alamo scholar Bill Groneman.

25 Lord, *A Time,* photograph section between pages 112 and 113. The excellent black and white photo of the Greys flag before restoration fails to show any damage, tie strings, or eyelets. Long, *Duel*, 171, also has a supreme photograph of the flag.

26 Ibid., Interview with Jesus F. de la Teja, professor of history at Southwest Texas State University, San Marcos, Texas, May 11, 1996, for the origin of the motto "God and Liberty"; Travis to the People of Texas and All Americans, February 24, 1836.

   In Lord, *A Time*, photograph section, we see that in Bowie's short note to the enemy on February 23, he first wrote, *"Dios y Federacion Mexicano"* indicating loyalty to God and the Constitution of 1824, then he crossed that out and wrote, *"Dios y Texas"* meaning God and Texas. In Jose Batres to Bowie, February 23, 1836, we see Santa Anna's answer to Bowie. Batres signed off with "God and Liberty!" The two documents show that a motto supporting Mexico or Mexican federalism was not valid during the siege of the Texian Alamo.

27 De la Pena, *La Rebelion*, 299-300.

28 Tyler, Barnett, Barkley, Anderson, and Odintz, eds., *New Handbook*, IV: 998-999.

29 Lord, *A Time*, 212. The IMAX Theater is a special motion picture house that presents short historical or special interest films, using an extremely large film format.

30 Alsbury to Houston, December 30, 1835; William R. Carey to Brother and Sister, January 12, 1836, Bexar, Jenkins, ed., *Papers*, III: 493-494.

31 M. Hawkins to Henry Smith, January 20, 1836, Bexar, Jenkins, ed., *Papers*, IV: 88.

32 Amos Pollard to Henry Smith, January 27, 1836, Bexar, Jenkins, ed., *Papers*, IV: 160.

33 Amos Pollard to Henry Smith, February 13, 1836, Bexar, Jenkins, ed., *Papers*, IV: 324-325.

34 G. B. Jameson to Henry Smith, February 11, 1836, Bexar, Jenkins, ed., *Papers*, IV: 303.

35 Travis to Grimes, March 3, 1836, Jenkins, ed., *Papers*, IV: 504-505.

36 Jameson to Smith, February 11, 1836; W. Barret Travis to Henry Smith, February 12, 1836, Bexar, Jenkins, ed., *Papers*, IV: 318.

37 "Meeting of the troops of the Bexar Garrison: December 31, 1835, *Telegraph and Texas Register*, January 23, 1836, San Felipe; Edward Burleson affidavit, November 9, 1836, Columbia, James Bowie file, AMC-TSL. At the December meeting the volunteer soldiers resolved: "That we approve and recognize colonel Neill as commander-in-chief. . . ." Burleson listed Bowie's service as a colonel in the volunteer army as being from October 20 to December 15, 1835.

Ordinarily, a full colonel would have commanded a regiment, not a small company like Bowie took to the Alamo. Because Bowie was not in the regular army and had been discharged from the volunteer force at Bexar on December 15, it appears his Alamo rank of full colonel was some kind of unofficial rank that was contingent on him raising a volunteer force to attack Matamoros.

Bowie, after his arrival at Bexar on January 18, appears to have commanded the troops that came with him, but otherwise he seems to have functioned as an advisor to Lt. Colonel Neill. Bowie, in Bowie to Smith, February 2, 1836, referred to Neill as the "Col. Comdt." Thus, it appears that Bowie did not consider himself as in command of Bexar while Neill was in San Antonio. Therefore, Bowie could not have had any authority over Travis, who like Neill was a regular army officer.

38 J. J. Baugh to Henry Smith, February 13, 1836, Bexar, Jenkins, ed., *Papers*, IV: 320-321; W. Barret Travis to Henry Smith, February 13, 1836, Bexar, Jenkins, ed., *Papers*, IV: 328. Travis wrote Smith that two small companies had voted to serve under Bowie. One of the companies Bowie commanded was a detachment of Captain John Chenoweth's United States Invincibles that traveled to San Antonio with Bowie under the command of William C. M. Baker of Clinton, Mississippi. Bowie's second company was most likely William H. Patton's Columbia company, which as of February 12 had only five or six men.

39 J. C. Neill to Henry Smith, January 27, 1836, Bexar, Jenkins, ed., *Papers*, IV: 160.

40 Entry for February 13, 1836, Audited Military Claims ledger, 77; Nancy Timmons Samuels and Barbara Roach Knox, compilers, *Old Northwest Texas: Historical – Statistical – Biographical* (Fort Worth: Fort Worth Genealogical Society, 1980), I-B: 547-548.

The AMC ledger shows that on February 13, 1836, Neill purchased $333 worth of military supplies from "Horton & Clements." The identity of Horton is unknown, but the only "Clements" residing within a two-day ride of Bexar who sold supplies to the military was Joseph D. Clements at Gonzales. Also, Neill's action of obtaining the supplies and the amount of the purchase indicates that he was returning to his command.

Samuels and Knox reported that Neill's wife, Margaret Harriett, probably died in February 1836, in Gonzales County. Their source for that data appears to have been obtained from a Mrs. C. L. Neill of Pharr, Texas. The two researchers also reported that Neill departed San Antonio on February 14, 1836, and rode to Gonzales. John Alexander Neill, a cousin to James C. Neill, lived in Gonzales. Thus, Neill's sick wife may have been staying with the John A. Neill family while she was ill. That way she would have been closer to her husband than she would have been in Bastrop, where they had a home.

41   J. C. Neill discharge affidavits, February 14, 1836, Bexar, John T. Ballard file, Robert White file, David Davis file, Thomas Hendrick file, Jesse B. Badgett file, Chester S. Corbit file, William A. Irwin file, AMC-TSL; J. C. Neill affidavit, February 20, 1838, I. L. K. Harrison file, M & P-TSL.

42   W. Barret Travis, Comd. of Cavalry, and James Bowie, Comd. of volunteers, to Henry Smith, February 14, 1836, Bexar, Jenkins, ed., *Papers*, IV: 339. The Alamo's volunteer cavalry was most likely composed of Captain William B. Harrison's company and David Crockett's small spy unit. James L. Vaughan, one of Travis's recruiting officers, assisted Harrison's unit in obtaining provisions (see chapter two) at San Felipe and Mina.

43   J. C. Neill to Henry Smith, February 28, 1836, San Felipe, James C. Neill Papers, Daughters of the Republic of Texas Library, Alamo, San Antonio, Texas; Sam Houston affidavit, December 9, 1839, Austin, Samuel Williams file, AMC-TSL. Houston wrote: "I certify that Col. Jas C. Neill was commander of the Troops until I arrived at Gonzales."

Conclusion

Last Word:
"The Truth Shall Set You Free"

Walter Lord, in regard to the source material he used to write *A Time To Stand* (p. 227), wrote: "The Alamo has intrigued writers for more than 125 years, but the contradictions and gaps in the story remain as exasperating as ever. In the end, the only solution was to go back to the original sources and start all over again."

Lord, by starting over, believed he had solved many of the Alamo's contradictions and filled some of the gaps. He did carry the Alamo story to a new level of knowledge. However, he also created a number of new problems with his uncritical acceptance of certain old sources and some of the new evidence he discovered. Lord's incorrect and negative depiction of Alamo commander James C. Neill in order to make William B. Travis, the Alamo's temporary commander, look more competent and heroic is especially galling. Neill was one hell of a fighting man, and Lord most likely knew it.

Still, what Lord said about the Alamo story being "exasperating" and full of contradictions and gaps is almost as true today as it was in 1961 when his book went on sale. Not only is that the case for the Alamo, but the most recent military and political histories of the Texas Revolution still have their contradictions and holes. The Alamo and the Revolution are areas ripe for a new look. Many explosive primary sources are still out there—some unknown to historians—others sources have been ignored because they did not dovetail with the historian or writer's bias.

Hopefully, this study has done away with some of the Alamo contradictions and bridged many of the gaps in the Alamo story. Moreover, I hope this work is a new beginning that other investigators and historians can build upon with new sources and valid interpretations. Perhaps historians will agree with my conclusions. Perhaps not. I make no claim that *Alamo Traces* is the best or the most correct study of the Texian Alamo and its role in the Texas Revolution; it is only, as of its publication date, the new kid on the block.

Alleged execution of David Crockett

Appendices

This section examines a number of new documents that speak to the Alamo and the Texas Revolution. Each document is presented with a short analysis of its importance to history.

[1]

[Alamo Voting List]

Bejar Feb. 1st. 1836	Mavrick	Hays	Badgett	Bon[ham]
Jn. James	1		1	
G. B. Jameson	1		1	
Richard Storr	1		1	
R. Perry	1		1	
J. B. McManemy	1		1	
H. Johnson	1		1	
Wm. Smith	1		1	
R. M. Russell	1		1	
Jn. Harris	1		1	
James Lewis	1		1	
James Dickins	1		1	
M. Shidal	1		1	
Jn. Burns	1		1	
G. Evans	1		1	
T. Mussulman	1		1	
J. H. Nash		1		1
Saml Holaway	1		1	
Thos Ryan	1		1	
M. Hawkins	1		1	
James Ingraham	1		1	
C. Grimes	1		1	
Square Dayman	1		1	
Jonathan Lindley	1		1	
H. G. Nelson	1		1	
M. R. Wood	1		1	

C. C. Hieskell	1	1
C. C. Wyatt	1	1
James J. Valentine	1	1
M. Heter	1	1
P. Pevyhouse	1	1
J. Duff	1	1
C. Lanco	1	1
J. M. Hays	1	
J. Jackson	1	
G. Gemmys	1	1
I. Fitch	1	1
N. D. Mitchell	1	1
Wm. Hearsy	1	1
Wm Bell	1	1
Jno. Mc Gregor	1	1
Jesse B. Badgett	1	
Asa Walker	1	1
Char. Asner	1	1
James Bowie	1	1
Geo. Washington	1	1
C. Parker	1	1
Milton Atkinson	1	1
Wm T. Malon	1	1
J. C. Neill	1	1
Jacob Roth	1	1
Gregoine	1	1
Jn. Pevyhouse	1	1
Wm. Lightfoot	1	1
Jn. Ballard	1	1
Lewis Duel	1	1
Cap Flowers ?	1	1
Henry Warnell	1	1
Jn. E. Garven	1	1
James T. Garner	1	1
Jno. Blair	1	1
A. Dickenson	1	1
S. A. Maverick		1
P. H. Herndon	1	1
W. C. M. Baker	1	1

T. Holland	1	1
Lewis Johnson	1	1
L. Bateright	1	1
E. Melton	1	1
L. M. Smith	1	1
Wm. Marshall	1	1
Wm. Spratt	1	1
A. Wolf	1	1
E. Nelson	1	1
A. Hilegor	1	1
Geo. M. Fagam	1	1
J. Rutherford	1	1
Wm. Blazely	1	1
Wm. Lynn	1	1
H. Johnson	1	1
J. Baugh	1	1
S. B. Evans	1	1
D. Wilson	1	1
Jno. Johnson	1	1
H. Lebarb	1	1
W. R. Cary	1	1
James McGee	1	1
Robt Grossen	1	1
Jn. Gerrand ?	1	1
Jno. Morcan	1	1
Hasey Mana Garcia	1	1
R. M. Cunningham	1	1
Thos Walters	1	1
Wm. Heagl	1	1
Wm. Thomas	1	1
Mills Andrews	1	1
Robt Moon	1	1
M. Rusk	1	1
H. Noland	1	1
G. W. Maine	1	1
A. Anderson	1	

Bonham 1 Badgett   Maverick 103
Hays 1   100

Vote

Maverick 103	Badgett 100
Bonham 1	Hays 1

Certificate

We certify that in pursuance of an order from the Senior officer in command here & influenced by an urgent general request, we proceeded by order of Lt. Col. J. C. Neil to an election of two persons as members of the convention to represent the citizens of Texas now here on duty, in the convention ordered by the late General Consultation, and to sit at Washington. The election was held in the Alamo fort on the first day of February, in strict conformity with the law and with general usage the within we certify to be a correct return of the polls as kept principally by our clerk, whose name is herewith appended: the return exhibits one hundred and four votes; one hundred and three votes were given to Samuel A. Maverick, one hundred to Jesse B. Badgett and one vote given to each of two other persons: we therefore return Maverick and Badgett, as elected. Given under our hands at Bejar this 2d of Feby 1836.

J Melton	W. C. M. Baker Capt.
Clerk of the Election	Samuel C. Blair Capt.
	Wm. Blazeley, Capt.[1]

Analysis

Alamo historians, in their identification of the Texians who died at the Alamo, have always been hampered by the lack of contemporary muster rolls for the Alamo garrison. The rolls that do exist were compiled days, months, or years after the fall of the Alamo. The names came from non-combatant survivors, couriers, and other veterans of the revolution. In the absence of a February and March 1836 Alamo roster, the February 1, 1836 voting list probably identifies all of the defenders in San Antonio at that time who were old enough to vote. Thus, it will be extremely useful in creating a new and more accurate list of the Texians and Americans who died at the Alamo while fighting under Travis, Bowie, and Crockett.

[2]

Bexar Meeting

At a meeting of the troops now in the garrison of Bejar, on the 31st of December 1835, the following resolutions were adopted.

Resolved, That this be a meeting to ascertain the rights of the volunteers.

Resolved, That we approve and recognize colonel [James C.] Neill as commander-in-chief, and unanimously agree in the sentiments expressed by that gentleman in his letter to us.

Resolved, That we consider it highly essential that the existing army remain in Bejar.

Resolved, That we have at all times the privilege of electing our own company officers, and for the commander-in-chief to recognize the same.

Resolved, That we consider the above highly essential for the unity and interest of the existing volunteer army in Bejar.

Resolved, That the thanks of this meeting be given to major [Green B.] Jameson, for his prompt, communicative, and kind attention to this meeting.

Resolved, That a copy of the proceedings of this meeting to be addressed to the Convention at San Felipe.

Wm. Blazeby
Chairman[2]

Analysis

This document furnishes an explanation as to why the Alamo's volunteer soldiers refused to serve under Lt. Colonel William B. Travis after Colonel James C. Neill left the Alamo in mid-February 1836. All Texian volunteer units had the right to elect their commanding officers. As the document shows, the Alamo volunteers voted to serve under Lt. Colonel James C. Neill, despite the fact he was a regular army officer. Neill, however, did not have the right to transfer his control over the volunteers to Travis. Thus, they rebelled against Travis and demanded the right to elect a new commanding officer, who turned out to be James Bowie.

[3]

Communication from Fernando De Leon and Charles Laso

The Citizens Fernando de Leon & Charles Laso also citizen of the village of Guadalupe Victoria advises the commandancy of this place – that on the 18th of the past month [November 1835] they were made prisoners [and] taken by the Schn Montezuma from on board the Schn Anna Elizabeth in company with six Mexicans and Nine foreigners, at the Port of Matagorda – and was confined in Irons until they arrived at the Brassos de Santiago, treating them without any respect but as common prisoners, that there they received intelligence that they were to be sent to Vera Cruz under the same security, but the two undersigned persons have found means to make their escape and have escaped and presented themselves in this village [Goliad], that on their departure they were informed by a friend that there was in circulation a Decree of the general Government That all Mexicans, foreigners, or Americans, without any distinction whatever taken as prisoners on this side of the Rio Grande should be immediately put to death.

That on their march they met with a friend that provided them with horses to facilitate their escape advising them to avoid the main road and cross the country that there were five foreigners found dead on the road in pursuance of the above said Decree so circulated. That Sadly the command out of the Port of the Brassos de Santingo had informed them that the Mexican government had issued a Decree that all vessels from N. Orleans bound to any port of Texas should be taken into vera cruz as a Lawful Prize – All the foregoing intelligence we thought proper to communicate to the commandant of this village Citizen Filipe Dimitt, in order that it would be generally circulated and communicated to the Army and people of Texas.

We were also informed by the same command of Brassos de Santiago that there was in the Harbor of Vera

Cruz five schooners Ready for sea under orders to cruise along the coast of the Department of Texas. We also were informed that information was received by a courier Extra ordinary that there were three thousand troops under command of general Sesma to start from Saltillo destined for Texas, with three pieces of heavy artillery.

God & Liberty Goliad 18 of December 1835
Fernando de Leon
Carlos Laso[3]

Analysis

On December 20, two days after Captain Philip Dimmitt's Goliad troops learned of the execution decree aimed at North Americans, they issued a declaration of independence. A section of that document, which appears to have been influenced by the De Leon and Laso report, reads: "The [federalist] counter-revolution in the interior once smothered, the whole fury of the contest will be poured on Texas. She is principally populated with North-Americans. To expel these from its territory, and parcel it out among the instruments of its wrath, will combine the motive and the means for consummating the scheme of the President Dictator [Santa Anna]. Already, we are denounced, proscribed, outlawed, and exiled from the country. Our lands, peaceably and lawfully acquired, are solemnly pronounced the proper subject of indiscriminate forfeiture, and our estates of confiscation. The laws and guarantees under which we entered the country as colonists, tempted the unbroken silence, sought the dangers of the wilderness, braved the prowling Indian, erected our numerous improvements, and opened and subdued the earth to cultivation, are either abrogated or repealed, and now trampled under the hoofs of the usurper's cavalry.

"Why, then, should we longer contend for charters, which, we are again and again told in the annals of the past, were never intended for our benefit? Even a willingness on our part to defend them, has provoked the *calamities of exterminating warfare* [italics added]. Why contend for the shadow, when the substance courts our acceptance? War – exterminating war is waged; and we have either to fight or flee."[4]

Prior to the declaration, Dimmitt was a determined supporter of Mexican federalism and had strong ties to the Mexican community in

Texas. Thus, historians have speculated about why Dimmitt became such a strong supporter of independence in an almost overnight fashion.

Hobart Huson, author of *Captain Philip Dimmitt's Commandancy of Goliad, 1835-1836*, believed that Dimmitt had commanded a Tejano company at the storming of Bexar and that the experience caused him to change his view about the political goal of the struggle.

Huson wrote: "During his brief absence from his post [Goliad], Dimmitt's political opinions appear to have undergone almost complete reversal. Whereas, on December 2d, when he wrote his much publicized letter of that date, urging upon the General council the advisability of an expedition of Matamoros, he yet adhered to the Austinian orthodoxy of *Loyalty to Mexico; separate statehood for Texas within the framework of the Mexican Confederacy, under restored Federal Constitution of 1834 [sic]*; he had now come to the conviction of its impracticability or, more rather the utter impossibility of its realization."[5]

Huson was wrong about Dimmitt. The Goliad commander sent a Tejano company to San Antonio that participated in the siege and storming of Bexar. Dimmitt, however, did not go to San Antonio himself. Thus, he could not have changed his mind about federalism because he had taken part in the siege and storming of Bexar.[6]

Historian Paul D. Lack, who was either unaware of Huson's excellent study of Dimmitt's command or ignored it, claims that the garrison issued their declaration because of their anti-Mexican posture. Lack wrote: "The Goliad declaration of December 22, provided the most complete statement of the independence ideology. It emphasized council ineptitude, *hatred of Mexicans* [italics added] (including Texas 'creoles'), the evils of deceitful, office-seeking speculators, and a kind of class rhetoric not uncommon in the Jacksonian era."[7]

Lack not only paints the Goliad soldiers as racists, he stained all Texians who supported independence when he wrote that the Goliad declaration was "the most complete statement of the independence ideology." Lack's interpretation is contaminated by his agenda—political correctness, an intellectual illness that infected academic historians in the late twentieth century, very much in the same way racism compromised many historians' objectivity previous to the civil rights movement of the 1960s.

The Goliad Declaration states:

We have indulged sympathy, too, for the condition of many whom, we vainly flattered ourselves, were opposed, in common with their adopted brethren, to the extension of military domination over the domain of Texas. But the siege of Bexar has dissolved the illusion. Nearly all their physical force was in the line of the enemy and armed with rifles. Seventy days' occupation of the fortress of Goliad, has also abundantly demonstrated the general diffusion among the Creole population of a like attachment to the institutions of their ancient tyrants. Intellectually enthralled, and strangers to the blessings of regulated liberty, the only philanthropic service which we can ever force on their acceptance, is that of example. In doing this, we need not expect or even hope for their cooperation. When made the reluctant, but greatly benefited recipients of a new, invigorating, and cherishing policy – a policy tendering equal, impartial, and indiscriminate protection to all; to the low and the high, the humble and the well-born, the poor and the rich, the ignorant and the educated, the simple and the shrewd – then, and not before, will [Texas Mexicans] become even useful in the work of political or moral renovation.[8]

Lack sees anti-Mexican attitudes in documents that are just not there. Simply pointing out that Northern Mexican federalists and the majority of the Tejano population did not understand the freedoms found in the United States and did not support the Texians is not, by any reasonable standard, "hatred of Mexicans."

In defense of Huson and Lack, they were not aware of the De Leon and Laso report. Huson would have most likely understood its significance in regard to the Goliad declaration of independence. Whereas, Lack would probably have ignored the document because it does not fit with his thesis that the Texians were nothing more than racists, who hated all Mexicans. Also, Lack and other pro-Mexican historians of today would not want to acknowledge the ethnic cleansing aspect of Santa Anna's campaign against the North Americans of Northern Mexico and Texas. Nevertheless, it is reasonable to believe the De Leon and Laso data influenced Dimmitt and his soldiers in their decision to make their declaration of independence.

[4]

Pioneer Says Bones Were Texas Heroes

Slain Men Beheaded After Battle of the Alamo, Spared Funeral Pyre by Foes

---

There is no rest for the numerous skeletons unearthed at the site of the old post office!

Now comes Charles A. Herff of Seguin, a resident of San Antonio for 81 years, who, from conversation with men who lived in the last century, claims the bones belong to Texans which the Mexicans decapitated following the Battle of the Alamo.[9]

Mr. Herff declares:

"On Alamo Plaza in 1870 I had a conversation with a Mr. [Antonio] Menchaca and a Mr. [Juan] Losoya [younger brother of Alamo defender Toribio Losoya], a Mr. Castanola and a Peter Gallagher, whose residence, by the way, was immediately back of the Alamo facing Nacogdoches street.[10]

Place of Slaughter

"All of these men, who lived in the beginning of the last century, declared that the Texans, to a man, were slaughtered in front of the church, in a space between the Alamo proper and a building known as the powder house, which extended east and west in the center of Alamo plaza. This building was constructed of stone with very thick walls and was about 70 feet long, 20 feet wide and approximately 15 feet high at the highest point and stood exactly on the space where now [1935] stands a hollow imitation cypress stump on the plaza.

"The building was connected with the church proper by high cedar palisades and I can remember well some of these still standing. They were gradually whittled down by campers who spent the night in the open space of the plaza.

Used as Barracks

"My informants told me that not a single Texan fell on top or inside of the building where the long wall has been reconstructed running north and south from Houston street to the Alamo chapel. The building which stood on the garden site was occupied by a Spanish garrison when Texas still belonged to Spain and the few dismal chambers which were connected with the building were not used as places for either nuns or priests to do penance but were used entirely as prisons for refractory soldiers.

"They further stated that after the Battle of the Alamo Mexican soldiers began cutting off the heads of the Texans, but they were soon stopped by Mexican officers.

Bodies Cremated

"It became imperative by reason of the already existing unsanitary conditions to bury the dead as quickly as possible, but to do this was slow proceeding by reason of the rock bottom which is all around the Alamo. It was thereupon decided to cremate the bodies and a great funeral pyre served this gruesome purpose, which took place on ground located from Blum street south across the block to the Alameda, now East Commerce street, including the site where now stands the Halff building on the corner of Commerce and Rusk streets.

"I was told by Menchaca, Losoya and a noted Mexican woman by the name of [Madam] Candelaria that the Mexican officers felt remorse for the soldiers having mutilated the dead bodies of the Texans and those were buried where the post office now stands.

"Those particular bodies were not burned. They were not buried where they fell, but were buried at the post office where there is a gravel formation which made the burials much easier. I can recall when the basement of the post

office was excavated over 50 years ago, that 13 or 14 head-
less bodies were found at that time, which would confirm
the statements made to me."[11]

Analysis

First, this Alamo account from a 1935 *San Antonio Express* article
contains data not found in other accounts. Second, Herff's informants
appear to have been Antonio Menchaca, a member of James Bowie's
Alamo unit; Juan Loysoa, an Alamo noncombatant; and Louis Castanon, a
member of Juan N. Seguin's siege of Bexar company. Peter Gallagher, the
fourth informant, served in the Texian army in the spring and summer of
1836. In addition, he was a member of the Santa Fe expedition and a
member of Jack Hays's San Antonio ranger company. Thus, given their
backgrounds, the informants were probably reliable.[12]

Most historians and writers place the Alamo's storage place for powder in the chapel, rather than the low barrack. It makes sense that the
powder would have been stored in several places so it would be near the
guns that were spread out on the walls. Also, no other account claims
that a number of the defenders were buried. Nor are the decapitations
mentioned in any other Alamo account. The account also has a good
description of the size of the low barrack and identifies the wood that was
used to build the palisades between the chapel and the low barrack.

[5]

Jon Winfield Scott Dancy Diary

March 29, 1837

Mr. Smith walked with us to the Alamo which is on the
eastern side of the river and explained to us Santa Anna's
plan of attack. He showed where Bowie & where Travis
fell; and where the Americans made the last bold stand
after they were driven from the walls. It was in a room near
the old church. The Alamo is now in ruins. Much of the wall
is still standing, but a portion is entirely torn down. It looks
like the tomb of those brave men who were sacrificed for
the liberty of Texas. He also pointed out the spot where
they were burned. A few fragments of bones mixed with

ashes are all that remains. Crockett sleeps with the heroes of the Alamo.

Mr. Smith also showed where and how the Americans entered the town in 1835. The stone houses which they occupied are still marked by musket and cannon balls. Under the command of the brave Col. Milam and after his death continued the attack they advanced until the town was taken. He showed where Milam fell and was buried. It is a little strange that San Antonio and its vicinity, one of the most beautiful and delightful places upon earth, a place where a man might so easily enjoy as many of the blessings of life as this world can yield; it is strange that this place so lovely, should be the scene of more bloodshed, than any other perhaps on the American continent.

March 30, 1837

Here you behold the fertile valley of the San Antonio – spread out before you like a map surrounded by a range of beautiful eminences, which the river comes leaping by the Alamo and the town over a succession of rapids and flowing on to the south where the hills seem to have left an opening for it to escape and make its way to the great reservoir of waters.[13]

Analysis

This account is interesting because it allows us, in a small way, to see San Antonio in the same way the Alamo defenders might have seen the city. Also, the Dancy visit to San Antonio occurred a little over a month after Colonel Juan N. Seguin had collected ashes from two of the three burn sites and had buried the ashes with military honors at the third burn location.[14] It would have been nice, however, if Dancy had given more exact detail about what Smith had told him.

[6]

Jesse Burnam Claim

State of Texas

County of Lavaca

Before me the undersigned personally came Jesse Burnam who states upon oath – That during the war between Texas & Mexico his home & outhouses situated in the County of Fayette were burned by order of Genl Sam Houston – by Col [George W.] Hockley & Capt [William H.] Patton. Affiant being absent at the time – And his house on the Navadad [*sic*] [River] was also burnt during his absence by order of Gen. Houston, by Capt [Benjamin F.] Smith.

That subsequently he had this following conversation with the parties who had set fire to his premises –

Question by affiant to Capt Patton –

I was told you burned my possessions on the Colorado River in Fayette County – I shall come to know the truth of it.

Answer – I did.

Question – By what authority?

Answer – I considered it direct from Gen. Houston – Col. Hawkly [*sic*] second in command came galloping up and told me to put every thing in flames and he assisted me in lighting the fires.

Question – Will you give me a certificate to that effect?

Answer – I will.

A certificate embodying the foregoing statement was made by Capt Patton and given to me.

Questions by Affiant to Capt Smith.

I am told you burnt my possessions on the Navadad – Colorado Co.

Answer – I did.

Question – By what authority?

Answer – I had a direct order from Genl Houston – He told me to keep before [General Martin Perfecto de] Cos's division and lay the country in waste.

Question – Will you give me a certificate to that effect?

Answer – I will.

And thereupon Genl [Edward] Burleson at my request wrote the certificate which was signed by Capt Smith.

I made claim under this certificate to the Texas Congress of 1840 for relief and the certificates were filed – The action taken upon my claim will appear by reference to the congressional journals of 1840. The claim went over with unfinished business and the certificates were lost.

After the destruction of my property, I had two men to value the same and go before a justice of peace & make oath to evaluation. This certificate was also filed with my claim & was lost with other certificates. The amount of my claim appears upon Journal of Congress of 1840.

Sworn and subscribed before me this 26th day of March 1874, witness my hand and seal, March 1874, Edward Thomas Notary Public, Travis

Jesse X Burnam
Mark[15]

Analysis

Jesse Burnam operated a ferry on the Colorado River between La Grange and Columbus. His claim is further evidence that General Sam Houston did give orders to burn all the property of the Texas colonists between Gonzales and San Jacinto.

[7]

Gonzales Letter from 1835 Ayuntamiento Minutes

To Col. [Domingo de] Ugartechea explaining a transaction or affair which occurred in Gonzales between a citizen of this Municipality [and] a party of soldiers passing through sd town.

Excellent Sir

The Ayuntamiento of the Municipality of Gonzales in order to preserve a good understanding between the Authorities of the country and the citizens of their Municipality have taken upon themselves the task of informing your Excellency of a circumstance which occurred here a few days ago. The facts alluded to are as follows – A party of soldiers amounting to perhaps twenty five men (including officers) arrived in this place on Thursday [September 9, 1835] last and remained until the succeeding day, during which time they took up their residence or quarters in a building in which Mr. [Adam] Zumwalt keeps a store. A citizen Jesse McCoy [Second lieutenant of the Gonzales militia company] without any intention of interfering or interrupting those Soldiers, not knowing anything of their regulations or not thinking of their presence attempted to pass them on his way into the Store room, a Soldier met him and attempted to push him aside without as he says and thinks speaking to him; he still without noticing the movement of the cause attempted to move forward when he received a violent blow from the Soldier with his gun giving him a severe wound on the head and causing the blood to flow profusely. Desperate consequences would have followed but for the interference of some peaceable and well disposed citizens who were conscious that a small matter might produce great evil in these excited times, and they thought that an individual had better suffer injustice and outrage than that a whole community should involve themselves by the acts which the excitation of the moment might occasion. This representation is not made to your Excellency for the purpose of obtaining satisfaction or revenge for the outrage and insult this offered to one of our citizens but to prevent misrepresentation and consequently a misunderstanding which might arise between the authorities and the people of this Municipality. For your further information we would remark that [the] house spoke of was occupied by the soldiers without any permission from the owner or any other person interested in it.

With sentiments of the highest consideration

We have the honor to be Yours etc.

Andrew Ponton [Alcalde][16]

Analysis

The Texas Revolution started on October 2, 1835, at Gonzales. Colonel Ugartechea had sent a small Mexican force to that settlement to obtain a bronze cannon. The six-pounder had been loaned to the colony in 1831 for protection against Indians who often raided the colony. The Texians refused to give the gun to the soldiers, advising them that the colonists were at war with the centralist government. The centralist troops were given the choice of joining the federalist force at Gonzales or they could "Come and Take It [the cannon]" and suffer the consequences. The Mexican force decided to remain centralist and started back to San Antonio. The Texians attacked the centralists the following morning.

Prior to that incident, the Green De Witt colonists had been very loyal Mexican citizens and were not part of the War Party of Texas. On July 7, 1835, Edward Gritten had written Colonel Ugartechea and reported that he thought the colonists desired peace, but advised that no soldiers be sent to Texas. On the same date the Gonzales citizens passed a set of resolutions demonstrating their loyalty to the Mexican government. The Gonzales relations with Ugartechea were so good that on August 29 he had asked them to assist the Mexican soldiers in pursuing Tahuacana Indians who had been committing depredations in the area.[17] What made the Gonzales colonists go from peaceful and loyal Mexican citizens to revolutionists?

It appears that the Mexican soldier's attack on Jesse McCoy and Ugartechea's response to the colony's report of the incident is what changed the attitude of the Gonzales citizens. Soon after receiving Andrew Ponton's letter detailing the attack on McCoy, Ugartechea answered the concerns of De Witt colonists by sending soldiers to pick up the Gonzales cannon. At that point it became clear that the Mexican army was up to no good.

[8]

Jose Enrique de la Pena's Authentic Handwriting and Signature — Sample A[18]

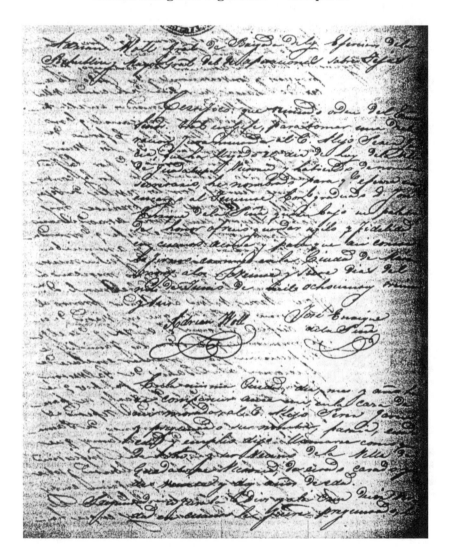

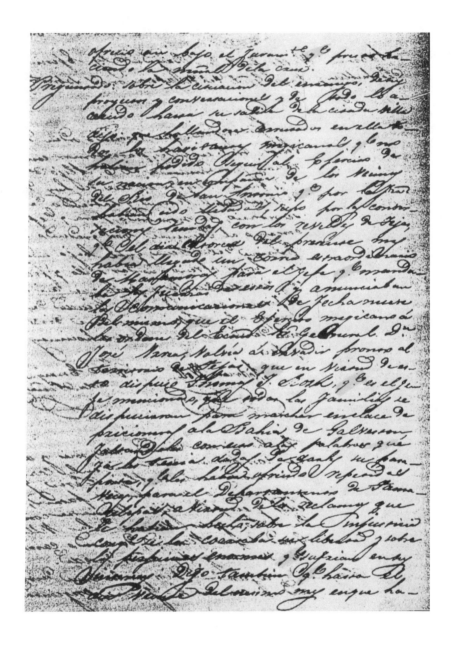

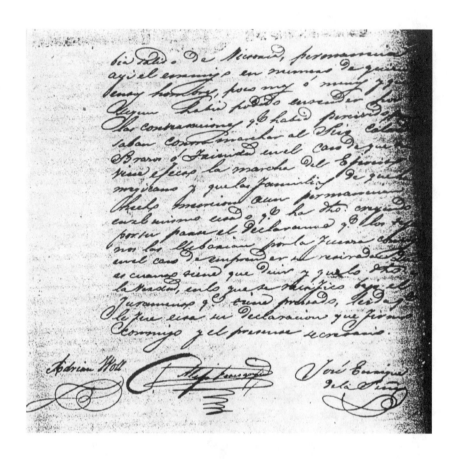

[9]

Pena's Campaign Diary — Sample A[19]

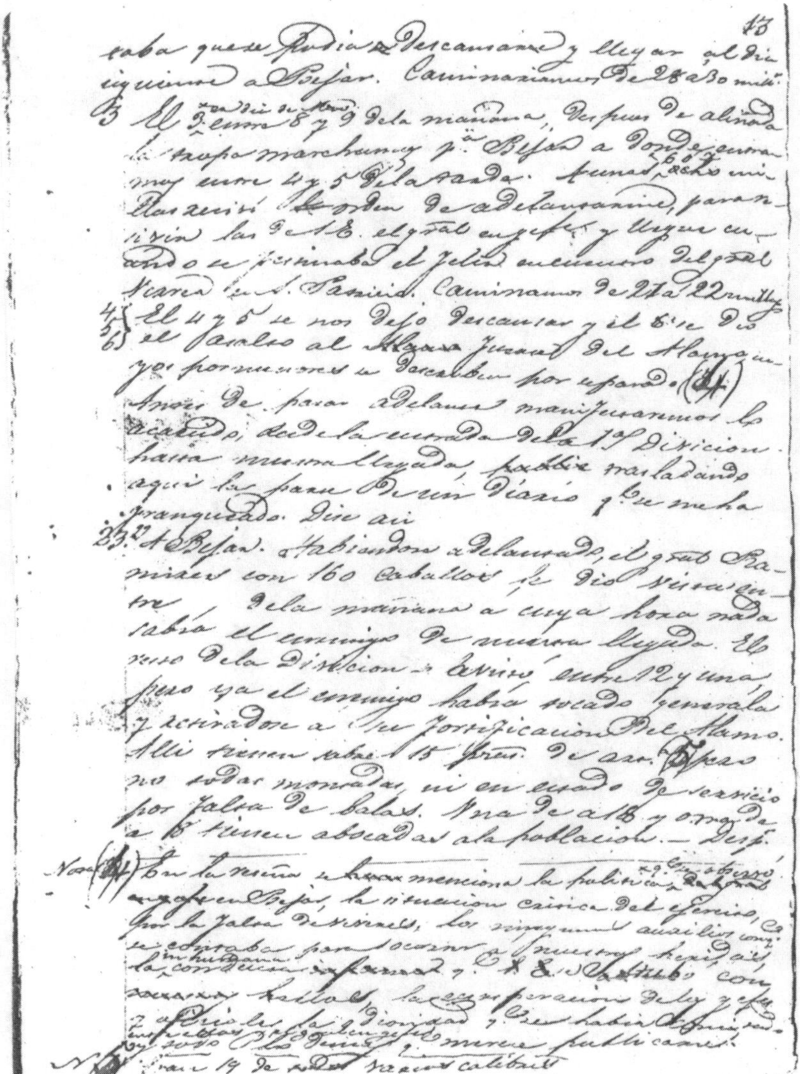
taba que se podía descansar y llegar al día
siguiente a Béxar. Caminaríamos de 28 a 30 millas.
3 El 3 [illegible] entre 8 y 9 de la mañana, después de alineada
la tropa marchamos p.a Béxar a donde entramos
muy entre 4 y 5 de la tarde. Apenas [illegible] millas recibí la orden de adelantarme, para reu-
nir [illegible] el gral en gefe y llegué cuando se terminaba el [illegible] del gral
[illegible] Caminamos de 21 a 22 millas.
4 5 El 4 y 5 se nos dejó descansar y el 6 se dió
6 el asalto al [illegible] del Alamo cu-
yos pormenores se describen por separado. (24)
Antes de pasar adelante manifestaremos lo
ocurrido desde la entrada de la 1.a División
hasta nuestra llegada, [illegible] trasladando
aquí lo que [illegible] de un diario q.e se me ha
franqueado. Dice así
23 [illegible] a Béxar. Habiéndose adelantado, el gral Ra-
mírez con 160 caballos se dió vista en-
tre [illegible] de la mañana a cuya hora nada
sabía el enemigo de nuestra llegada. El
resto de la División arribó entre 12 y una
pues ya el enemigo había tocado generala
y retirádose a su fortificación del Alamo.
Allí tienen sobre 15 piezas de art.a [illegible]
no todas montadas, ni en estado de servicio
por falta de balas. Una de a 18 y otra de
a 12 tienen abocadas a la población. — Desp.
[illegible]

Pena's Campaign Diary — Sample B[20]

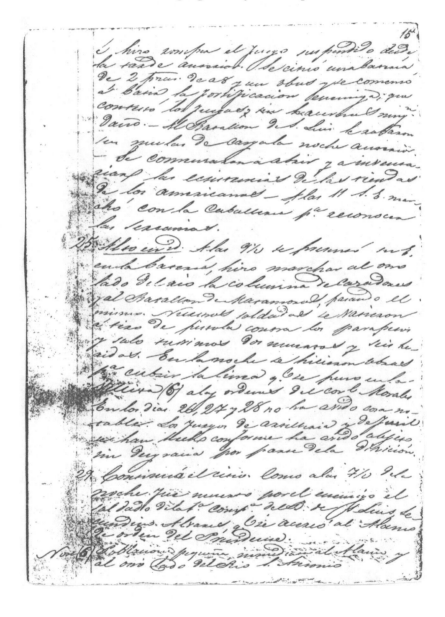

Pena's Campaign Diary — Sample C[21]

21

marcha. Me adelanté al arroyo del
Cíbolo p[a] reconocer el terreno y en dos
horas de la tarde ví la sierra del camino,
atajos de Béxar os. q[e] ascendían reunidos
á Cuernavaca. Llegué al cíbolo ya de noche
y la acción lo hizo a las ocho de ella
después de haber andado de 21 á 22 millas.
La guerrilla derecha de Zapad[or] hizo
presa á un hermoso tigre.

31. El día 31, jueves Santo, salimos del cíbolo
y campamos en un paraje sin nombre
donde había corros charcos de agua, después de haber caminado de 16 á 18 millas.
Aquí suprime el autor del diario la causa
que puso en toda en peligro, pesar del diez
de la noche.

1[o]. de Abril. Ese día salimos y campamos en
otro paraje igualm[te] desconocido, pero
ambos comprendidos entre el Srún[nal]
y el Carrizal. Llegamos entre 5 y 6 de
la tarde y antes de venir la jornada
encontramos cuatro paisanos q[e] conducían m[as] de 300 reses, q[e] habían recogido en el camino, siendo la mayor parte
de ellas hermosas vacas preñadas de cría.
Tomamos nosotros p[a] calmar la hambre del nuestros soldados, q[e] no habían
tomado comer, desde el día anterior
en que salimos de Béjar.

2. El día 2 sábado de gloria amaneció lloviendo y salimos del paraje cuando
la lluvia había cesado. Habíamos
andado unas 8 o 9 millas cuando otros

[10]

Pena's Alleged Memoir — Sample A[22]

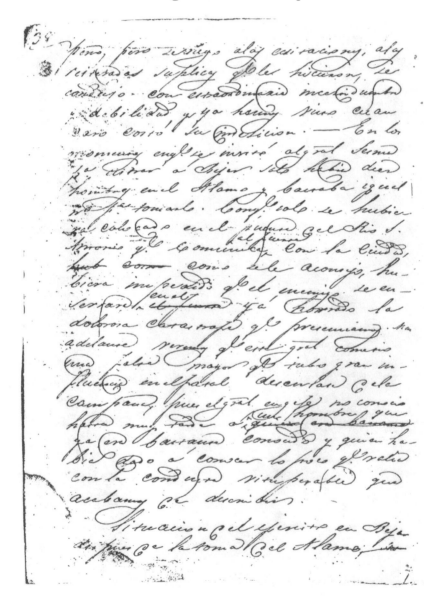

Pena's Alleged Memoir — Sample B[23]

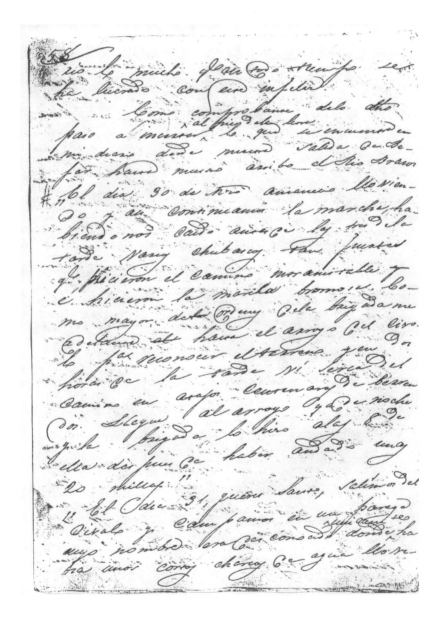

Pena's Alleged Memoir — Sample C[24]

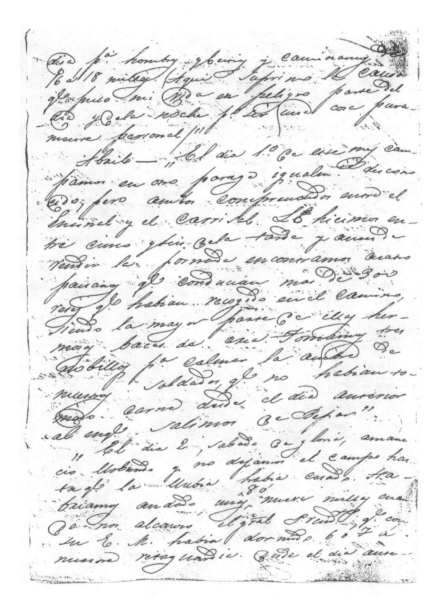

Signature Page from the Alleged Memoir's Prologue — Sample D[25]

Analysis

Soon after the University of Texas at Austin library officials obtained the Jose Enrique de la Pena manuscripts, they selected Dr. David Gracy, the Governor Bill Daniel Professor in the university's Graduate School of Library and Information Sciences, to defend their belief that the Pena documents were not forgeries. Gracy, who is not a certified document examiner, ruled that the handwriting similarities he found in the questioned documents (the Pena memoir manuscript and its prologue letter) and the one known authentic Pena document (Adrian Woll/Pena report, dated June 27, 1836) were sufficient to declare the alleged Pena documents and their Pena signature authentic.[26] Dr. Gracy, however, ignored the fact that if a forger had created the Pena memoir manuscript and its prologue letter, there were bound to be handwriting similarities between the authentic handwriting and the alleged handwriting. After all, a forger would have been attempting to replicate the authentic handwriting of Pena. Therefore, it is reasonable that the alleged Pena documents can share handwriting characteristics with Pena's bona fide handwriting (the Woll/Pena report, dated June 27, 1836, and the Campaign Diary) and still be a forgery.[27]

In examining the alleged Pena handwriting and signature, Gracy should have not only looked at the similarities that the authentic document and the alleged documents share, but he should have looked at the differences between the authentic Pena handwriting and signature and the alleged Pena handwriting and signature to determine the truth about the alleged Pena documents. He did not do this. He did, however, admit that such an examination was the best approach to proving the authenticity of the alleged Pena documents. Gracy wrote: "...the better strategy for demonstrating falsity is to establish the differences between the suspect document and genuine writing of the purported author of the suspect document." Therefore, let us look at some of the differences found in the authentic document and the alleged Pena documents.[28]

First, let us examine the authentic writing of Jose Enrique de la Pena found in the three samples in appendix number eight, the report of an interview conducted by General Adrian Woll on June 27, 1836, at Matamoros. Pena served as Woll's secretary in recording the interview and is so identified in the document. The spacing of the words in Pena's writing is constricted, with a jammed up appearance. A *few* words end with loops below the sentence lines and a *few other* words end with flourishes or swirls above the lines. These loops, swirls, and flourishes, however, do not visually dominate the writing. This description of the authentic Pena handwriting is also true of the three handwriting samples (appendix nine) from Pena's 109-page Campaign Diary.

Whereas, in the alleged Pena memoir sample pages and the alleged Pena signature page (appendix ten), the word spacing is more spread out and does not appear constricted. Second, the actual length of the words appear to be longer than in the authentic sample and the campaign diary samples. Third, the vertical spacing between the sentences is also greater than in the authentic samples and in the campaign diary samples. Fourth, the loops, swirls, and flourishes that appear below and above the sentence lines dominate the alleged Pena writing. Visually, these writing characteristics practically jump up from the page.

These observations are supported by the number of words that appear on the page samples. The three pages from Pena's Campaign Diary average 258 and 2/3 words per page. Whereas, the three pages taken from Pena's alleged memoir average 165 and 1/3 words per page. Despite the page size being the same in both manuscripts, the authentic Pena averages 93 and 1/3 more words to the page. This comparison appears to hold true for all the pages of the Campaign Diary and the memoir manuscript.[29]

Ironically, the constricted handwriting found in the authentic Pena documents is more characteristic of handwriting that is forged. Forgery expert Joe Nickell observed: "The forger often unconsciously shrinks the writing of his subject; according to [Charles] Hamilton this is 'probably because of a psychological desire to conceal his fraud by making it less easy to read.'"[30]

When this situation was pointed out to Dr. James Crisp, the most vocal of the Pena authenticity supporters, he stated that Pena was probably stressed out when he wrote the documents that contain the Woll interview report and the Campaign Diary manuscript. Thus, also suggesting that Pena was not under any stress when he wrote the memoir manuscript. Such a case seems unlikely as Crisp and other Pena supporters believe Pena wrote the memoir manuscript while he was in prison. Whereas, he wrote the diary manuscript while the Mexican army and he were at rest in Matamoros in the summer of 1836.[31]

Pena, who joined a federalist rebellion in support of the Mexican constitution of 1824, was captured in May 1838 by centralist forces after he surrendered his force at Mazatlan, Mexico. Seeing that he and his men were in an Alamo situation, he decided he was not *that* committed to Mexican federalism. He was first imprisoned at Guadalajara on May 27, 1838. From that confinement he had a fellow prisoner write a letter for him. Pena's reason for not writing himself was: "I consider how much our friends must have felt the event at Mazatlan – I am unable to give you even an idea of it, because so much thinking has affected my nervous system, my brain is not well, and I must rely on a friend to write...."[32]

In regard to the conditions under which he was imprisoned, he wrote: "...they treat me with such care that soldiers look after my existence even when I must tend to my most pressing needs. The air reaches me only at times and the sun never.... You, my good friend, know my sensibility and can guess what my soul is suffering seeing myself slandered, in a prison, without friends, without relations, after having lost everything that a man and a soldier can lose. My implacable fate, not content with what it had made me suffer, willed that a servant who had given me many evidences of his faithfulness should leave me the day after I arrived here, leaving me almost naked and without the few monetary resources I had with me, and among other things he took a small box with a few mementos, the picture of my beautiful one, that of a good friend, and that of Malibran that you might have seen on my chest sometimes, the loss of which I will not be consoled of in a long time."[33] Clearly, Pena was up the proverbial creek without a paddle, which undoubtedly was plenty stressful.

Pena's prison conditions did not improve. On December 6, 1838, he wrote that he and the other prisoners from Mazatlan were in "solitary confinement." He continued to complain: "...today it makes seven months that I have been reduced to imprisonment, ...and it is going on three [months] that I am held incommunicado, deprived of every recourse.... The sentiment which causes injustice, the ill will that produces excessive oppression, the torments that make me suffer my physical ills which grow every day, have pulled out from me a new outcry and this digression, and servile souls will not be lacking who may look on the frankness of my language as a crime, because their blindness reaches such a gloomy level; but fortunately the power of tyrants does not extend to consciences, nor to volitions, and mine is invariable in order to tell the truth; the truth embitters him who provokes it; my suffering will even be refined by it still more, but I shall not be the one to kiss the hand of my executioner.... Moreover, because General Paredes has subjected me to a salary less than that which a second infantry sergeant enjoys, I cannot pay the board that in that hospital is required from the prisoners of Mazatlan...." [34]

Ironically, on March 6, 1839, the three-year anniversary of the fall of the Alamo, Pena again wrote of his prison conditions in a petition to the powers that controlled his situation. He wrote:

A Mexican official [Pena] who today has been deprived for ten months of his liberty, submerged in a dirty and unhealthy jail, oppressed and mistreated by a power as unjust as it is arbitrary, which has not respected in his person any of the social guarantees, is finally deciding to raise his complaints to Your Excellency....

It is eight months ago that they took the declarations of my companions and me with charges [being brought]; in conformity with the laws we were afterward put in full communication, but it is now more than five months that we are held incommunicado, depriving us thereby of the resources that our debtors could have provided us, of the consolations with which friendship could have sweetened the bitterness of our misfortune, and of consulting a lawyer to promote the appeals most in conformity with our rights....

My demands against a solitary confinement so contrary to the laws, to humanity, and to the spirit of the century in which we live have been useless, and it will not have an end, I believe, if Your Excellency does not put the justification thereof to the test. The injuries that they have caused us with this proceeding, besides those which are consequences of an imprisonment, are unspeakable. In consequence of the first solitary confinement, a servant marched off carrying the few pecuniary resources which I relied on, and everything that had any value in my luggage; another followed after this bad example, absconding with the few resources that some good friends had provided me. A lady who was taking care of the scant clothing that remained to me, a month and a half ago disappeared with it, and this very day, sympathizing with my [bad] luck, the official of the guard has had to employ his authority so that another woman did not keep the only change of clothing that I possess....

Although since the 10th of July of last year, four reales are provided to us daily, with the punctuality that the notorious scarcities of the public treasury permit, this quantity is not Sufficient to attend [even] to the most urgent necessities, because those that we have contracted by our upbringing and our respective classes in the army, far exceed those that a common soldier has, and therefore a law provided that every accused official should enjoy thirty pesos, and besides, of one-third of the amount by which his pay should [have] exceeded this, if I do not remember incorrectly....

The moral ills that I have mentioned and that affect my soul infinitely, contribute to making my physical sufferings more cruel. I have seen myself in the bed of grave illness, without any effort being sufficient for them to permit me to go to the hospital, and although it is true that I was allowed to have a doctor prescribe for me in the presence of a sentry, it also is [true] that afterward I was deprived of this aid so necessary to my preservation.... Because of the unhealthfulness of the jail in which I have found myself since a month ago, my illnesses have been considerably aggravated, but I have resolved to die in silence, and not breathe here a single complaint, because I am personally convinced that pity will not be taken on my sorrows by those who can and should mitigate them – even on behalf of their good name, seeing that they do not want to do it in deference to humanity.[35]

Pena did not die at that time. In May 1839 he escaped his prison cell and hit the road for Culiacan. However, after a chance encounter with a General Alcorta, he changed plans and traveled to Durango. Soon after his arrival, he was betrayed by a "false and vile female accuser" and thrown back into jail.[36]

Sometime later Pena was transferred to Inquisition prison in Mexico City. From there he wrote on October 7, 1839: "In the calamitous age in which we live, in which inconsequentiality, denunciation, villainy and the most immoral actions are rewarded, it seems to be in the order [of things] that the one who detests infamy and speaks the truth is punished.

Because of this, undoubtedly, I am still being oppressed after sixteen months of imprisonment and of suffering all classes of mistreatment....

"Only if I die soon will I leave unpublished the infamies that the commander in chief has done to the prisoners of Durango and to me, and the base actions of his vile minions Don Miguel Gomez, Don Jose Maria Aldana, Don Augustin Cevallos, and Don Rafael Andrade, so that they may receive at least the indignation of sensible men of all parties – although they are men so lacking in modesty that public contempt will have scant effect on them, since they still have the audacity to live in a settlement where because their evils are known, they are generally detested even by the prostitutes."[37]

Clearly, Pena's own words show that his prison time was stressful. Also, given the conditions under which he was imprisoned, it seems extremely doubtful he would have had the resources to obtain the books and documents that contain the additional source material reflected in the memoir manuscript.

[11]

A Comparison of Entries from the Campaign Diary and the Pena Memoir[38]

31. El dia 31, jueves santo, salimos del cibolo y campamos en un parage sin nombre donde habia corro chaves de agua, despues de haber caminado de 16 a 18 millas. Aqui suprime el autor del diario la causa que puso su vida en peligro, parte del dia y de la noche.

20 millas."

El dia 31, jueves santo, salimos del cibolo y campamos en un parage . . . cuyo nombre era . . . conocido donde había unos corros chaves de agua llovediza p[ar]a hombres y bestias y caminamos 16 a 18 millas. (Aqui suprimo el autor q[ue] puso mi vida en peligro parte del dia y de la noche . . . una cosa puramente personal).

Analysis

Appendix number eleven contains two handwriting samples. The first comes from the Campaign Diary, Sample B., appendix nine. The second sample is from the memoir manuscript, Samples B and C, appendix ten. Both samples are entries for March 31, 1836, and both report essentially the same information in about the same language. Thus, we have almost a word for word comparison in the examination of the two handwriting samples. In transcription and translation, the two samples read:

Campaign Diary

31. El dia 31, Jueves Santo, salimos del Cibolo y campamos en un paraje sin nombre donde habia cortos charcos de agua, despues de haber caminado de 16 a 18 millas. (Aqui suprime el autor del diario la causa que puso su vida en peligro, parte del dia y de la noche).[39]

31. The thirty-first day, Holy Thursday, we set out from the Cibolo and camped at a spot with no name, where there were scarce ponds of water, after having traveled 16 to 18 miles. (Here the author of the diary omits the cause that put his life in danger for part of the day and of the night.)

Memoir Manuscript

El dia, 31, Jueves Santo, salimos del Civolo y campamos en un parage cuyo nombre era des conocido [desconocido] donde unicam. te habia unos cortos charcos de agua llove disa p. a hombres y bestias y caminamos de 16 a 18 millas. (Aqui suprimo la causa q. e puso mi vida en peligro parte del dia y de la noche p.r ser una cosa pura-Mente personal.)[40]

The 31st, Holy Thursday, we set out from the Cibolo and camped in a spot whose name was unknown, where there were only some ponds of rainwater for men and beasts, and we walked 16 to 18 miles. (Here I omit the cause that put my life in danger part of the day and of the night, because it was a purely personal matter.)

In comparing individual words from the two March 31 entries, we find a number of words that were clearly not written by the same person.

First, is the creek name Cibolo.

Campaign Diary   Memoir Manuscript

The authentic Campaign Diary uses "Cibolo" three times. The name is spelled once with a "b" and twice with a "v," which is normal for Spanish. Two examples of Cibolo come from the Memoir manuscript. Both are spelled with a "v." The ending "o" in Cibolo in the Campaign Diary was formed by having the pen stroke turn downward to the right and turn up and connect with line to form the "o." Whereas, in the two examples from the Memoir manuscript, the pen stroke for the ending "o" in Cibolo turns upward to the left and travels down to cross the line forming an "o" that looks like a lowercase "e." Also, the capital "C" is different. In the Memoir manuscript the pen stroke closes to form an egg shaped figure. In the authentic diary, one example of the "C" is closed, but it is not as pronounced as in the Memoir manuscript.

The second example is the manner in which *Dela noche* is written.

Campaign Diary   Memoir Manuscript

The beginning "D" in "*Dela*" found in the Memoir manuscript looks more like a capital "C." The Memoir manuscript "D" looks nothing like the starting "D" in the Campaign Diary example of *Dela noche*.

The same difference in the writing of "D" is also found in formation of "*Del.*"

Campaign Diary   Memoir Manuscript

The third word that shows difference in its formation is *millas* or in English, miles. The majority of time Pena spells the word by ending with a modern Spanish "s." Whereas, in the Memoir manuscript the word is ended with an old fashioned "s" that looks more like a "y." An occasional y-like "s" can be found in the Campaign Diary, but its bottom loop looks nothing like the loops found in the two Memoir manuscript examples of *millas* that end with the old style "s."

Campaign Diary   Memoir Manuscript

Another handwriting characteristics of note is the whip-like flourish shown below. The element is common in the Memoir manuscript, but nowhere is it found in the authentic 109-page diary.

Lastly, is the manner in which *que* and the abbreviation for *que* is written. Pena almost always lifted his pen from the paper in writing *que* and its abbreviation. Thus, writing *que* with a break in the stroke, and the abbreviation is written with two parts. Whereas, the writer of the Memoir manuscript almost always kept the pen down on the paper, with no break in the stroke.

Campaign Diary   Memoir Manuscript

[12]

Comparison of Pena's Authentic Signature and His Alleged Signature[41]

A.   June 1836 Authentic

B.   June 1836 Authentic

C.   September 1836 Alleged

D.   December 1836 Authentic

Point by Point Comparison of Signatures B and C

Point One

The manner in which the top of the capital "J" is formed in the name *Jose*. The authentic signature shows the top of the "J" with a v-like indentation that points downward. The top of the capital "J" in the alleged signature does not have this v-like indentation. This difference is also found in the manner in which the word June is written.

Authentic   Alleged

The v-like indentation is also found in the way Pena wrote a capital "T" in the authentic manuscript.

Authentic   Alleged

Point Two

The manner in which the loop at the bottom of the capital "J" is formed in the name *Jose*. The real signature shows a loop that is flat on the right side and the left side is curved—a shape somewhat like one would get if they dropped a ball of clay to the floor. This loop is almost parallel to the letter stem, which connects the v-like top to the loop.

Whereas, the bottom loop in the capital "J" in the alleged signature is an elongated leaf-like shape that juts from the stem at almost a ninety degree angle.

Point Three

In the authentic signature, the ending small "a" in *dela* runs into the capital "P" of *Pena,* thus linking *dela* and the "P" together. This does not occur in the alleged Pena signature. Also, *dela* is incorrect. It should be written as two words: *de la*. Both examples, however, make the same mistake. Still, in the previous example of *dela noche*, we find that the authentic example runs the ending "a" of *dela* into *noche*. Whereas, the alleged handwriting does not do so.

Authentic   Alleged

Point Four

The capital "P" in *Pena* in the authentic signature is shaped differently from the "P" in the alleged signature. The authentic signature has an egg-shape loop at bottom left of the letter. The alleged signature does not have this oval loop in the capital "P" in Pena. This oval shaped loop can also be seen in the way Pena wrote the name *Portilla* and the manner in which he formed a capital "B."

Authentic   Alleged

Point Five

The ending small "e" of *Enrique* in the authentic signature crooks back to the left with a sharp bend shaped like a hook. Whereas, in the alleged signature, the pen stroke in the "e" turns back to the left with a wide curve.

Point Six

The *tilde* that appears over the "n" in *Pena* in the authentic signature is shaped like a curve. Whereas, in the alleged signature it is written like a straight line.

Summary

The differences in the authentic signature and the alleged signature are obvious. This investigator is not a certified document examiner, but one does not have to be so trained and qualified to see them. The alleged Pena signature does not appear to be an attempt to copy the true Pena signature. Rather, the alleged signature appears to be an attempt to simulate Pena's signature.

Moreover, bona fide signatures, A and B, which were written in June 1836, pretty much match genuine signature D, which was penned in December 1836. Thus, signatures A, B, and D are fairly consistent in their characteristics. Also, the rubrics for signatures A, B, and D appear to have been written by the same hand. Whereas, signature C, the alleged Pena signature, which was written in September 1836, and by date, appears between the authentic signatures, looks to be in a different hand. It makes no sense that Pena would have written his signature one way in June, changed the manner of the signature in September, then returned to the June form in December. In sum, the September 1836 signature does not appear to be Pena's true signature.

Conclusion

When historian and illustrator Jack Jackson reviewed the handwriting comparisons presented in this section, he exclaimed, "It's obvious they're different handwriting!" Then he offered an explanation for the memoir manuscript not being in Pena's handwriting. He said Pena could have dictated the memoir manuscript to someone while in prison. Yes, that is a possibility. On the other hand, given the conditions (sick and without money and property in solitary confinement) under which Pena was imprisoned, how probable is it that he could have created the manuscript and dictated it to a fellow prisoner? Also, how likely is it that the document could have been created without Pena writing a single page of the memoir? On top of that, Pena's alleged secretary often formed his letters and words almost exactly as Pena did. What are the odds of that happening?[42]

Then, look at the conditions under which Pena wrote the "clean" copy of the Campaign Diary. The diary was written in the summer of 1836 when Pena, a lieutenant colonel, was at rest in Matamoros, awaiting a decision from the Mexican government about a second Texas campaign. This was a time when Pena had the resources to dictate the chronicle to a military aide or a hired secretary. Instead, Pena penned the rewrite himself. The "clean" manuscript is totally in Pena's handwriting. Moreover, the 109 pages of the manuscript are all of the same paper, with only one watermark. Thread holes along the left sides of the pages show that at one time the manuscript was bound.[43]

The memoir manuscript, however, is written on various types of paper. In total, fourteen different graphic watermarks and eleven different name watermarks can be found in the document. Yes, the paper appears to be the right age and for the most part is paper that could have been obtained in Mexico in the 1830s. Still, the numerous watermarks feature is a forgery characteristic.[44]

Pena supporters argue that many different types of paper found in the memoir manuscript simply reflect Pena's prison situation. That he had to "beg, borrow, and steal" to obtain paper while in prison. Yes, that is an explanation. Pena did write a number of letters to Mexican officials and newspapers while he was imprisoned. So he obviously had a source for a small amount of writing paper when in prison. However, Pena's petition to the government demanding his release from prison was rejected because of the disrespect for military officials that was exhibited in the document. Thus, is it not logical that prison officials would have given Pena a large amount of paper to write a personal and unofficial chronicle of the campaign against Texas that also was disrespectful of military and government officials?[45]

In summary, the Pena memoir manuscript has a number of elements that indicate it was not written by Pena. First, there is the lack of a satisfactory provenance. Jesus Sanchez Garza, the Mexico City coin collector and dealer who discovered the Pena collection and first published the memoir manuscript in Spanish, never reported how and where he obtained the Pena documents.[46] If this were the only problem for the memoir manuscript, it would not be sufficient to declare the document a forgery. There are, however, other problems. Second, there are at least fourteen different kinds of paper in the manuscript. Forgers often have to collect period paper from many different sources to obtain enough paper for a forgery project. Third, the memoir manuscript is clearly not in Pena's handwriting. Fourth, a great deal of the information in the memoir manuscript is not found in the Campaign Diary. This data appears to come from other sources. In some cases the material came from sources that were not available to Pena because they were written after his death. Thus, these derivative sections in the memoir manuscript are best described as source anachronisms.

The source anachronisms that deal with David Crockett as a noncombatant and the lack of Mexican surgeons at the Alamo were covered in chapter eight. There are other such anachronisms in the memoir document. For example, look at what the chronicle says about the burning of the bodies of the Alamo defenders. That account reports: "... within a few hours a funeral pyre rendered into ashes those men who moments before had been so brave that in a blind fury they had unselfishly offered their lives and had met their ends in combat."[47]

Any fireman or crime scene investigator will tell you that a complete burning of that many bodies in a "few hours" is impossible. A wood fire does not produce the high and constant heat necessary to completely burn a body. Even in a modern cremation a body's large bones are not destroyed. Also, the burning of a human body does not produce ashes. That belief is a misnomer. The "ashes" that come from cremation are machine-crushed bone, not true ashes.[48]

Another questionable Mexican account, however, makes the same claims about the burning of the Alamo defenders' bodies. Francisco Becerra, a Mexican sergeant, in 1882 allegedly furnished a description of the body burning that is identical in meaning to Pena's report. Becerra claimed: "The bodies of those brave men, who fell fighting that morning, as men have seldom fought, were reduced to ashes before the sun had set."[49]

The words used in the Pena and Becerra accounts are different, but they convey the same meaning: (1) the defenders were brave; (2) they died in combat; (3) the way they fought was unique; (4) their bodies were burned to ashes in a few hours.

More likely, the burning of the Alamo bodies continued into the night and perhaps the morning of March 7, 1836. Undoubtedly, the bodies' large bones were not destroyed. Also, a large number of charred hunks of flesh probably survived the fires. That was certainly the case with the Texian bodies that were burned after the executions at Goliad.[50]

Pena was at the Alamo and would not have reported such an inaccurate story about the burning of the Alamo dead. Pena supporters, however, might argue that Becerra was at the Alamo, and his statement about the disposal of the Texian bodies verifies Pena's account.

That would be a superficial view of the source materials. There is no doubt Pena participated in the storming of the Alamo. Becerra appears to have claimed he was at the Alamo. There is, however, no independent evidence that proves Becerra participated in the famous fight. Moreover, the Becerra report is extremely unreliable. Walter Lord described the chronicle as: "Probably the least reliable of all the Mexican accounts." The late Dan Kilgore, though he used the account in his book *How Did Davy Die?*, viewed the Becerra story as unreliable. Also, he wrote: "The early accounts by Urissa and Becerra have a ring of folklore instead of history...." The Becerra description of the burning of the Texian bodies more likely came from the mind and pen of John S. Ford, the old Texas Ranger and newspaperman, who allegedly interviewed Becerra while he was in Ford's military unit during the Civil War and published the account in 1882 in the Texas School for the Deaf magazine, *Texas Mute Ranger.*[51]

The alleged Pena memoir manuscript has other characteristics that indicate it was not written by Pena. Limited time and space, however, make additional analysis impossible. In the end, the debate boils down to Occam's Razor, a rule of logic that states: "...a person should not increase, beyond what is necessary, the number of entities required to explain anything, or that the person should not make more assumptions than the minimum needed."[52] Pena believers can spin all kinds of different theories to explain the many forgery characteristics found in the Pena memoir manuscript and its presentation to the world by Jesus Sanchez Garza, a known counterfeiter of nineteenth-century Mexican coins.[53] There is, however, only one reasonable answer that explains all of the Pena problems: it is a forgery. Lastly, one must remember that old observation about the truth: "if it looks like a duck, if it quacks like a duck, if it walks like a duck, then it is most likely a duck." Think about it. The Campaign Diary manuscript has no forgery characteristics. Yet, the memoir manuscript and the manner in which Sanchez Garza published the document are loaded with forgery characteristics. The memoir manuscript sure looks like a duck to this investigator.

[13]

Crockett at the Alamo

They saw the bloody Spaniard near,
His legions gath'ring thick and fast—
"We fall, but it shall cost you dear,"
Words by each soldier briefly past.

For mortal fight they quick prepared,
Undaunted by the num'roas host,
To heaven each sent his dying prayer,
And hastened to his *fatal* post.

A thought to wife and children dear,
On life's rough sea without a guide,
Drew from each eye the "Soldier's Tear,"
Brushed away quick with soldier's pride.

And 'mong the names that Fame has spread,
For daring deeds to every land;
'Mong heroes who have nobly bled,
Crockett in bold relief shall stand,

Like tiger turning on his foe,
When driven to his last retreat,
His hand dealt many a fearful blow,
And *heaps* lay welt'ring at his feet.

Till covered thick with gashes deep,
Borne down by numbers, Crokett fell,
Calmly as to an evening's sleep,

Lull'd by the tolling curfew bell.

His soul from Nature's quarry wrought,
Own'd not the world's adultering mould—
But rough as by the miner bought,
Remained the virgin gold.

And Texas Phoenix-like shall rise,
Shall freedom's pinions proudly spread,
Hail'd by those spirits of the skies,
That on *her* alters nobly bled.

J. A.[54]

Analysis

None needed. The poem speaks for itself.

Appendices Notes

1   Election Returns Collection, TSL.

2   *Telegraph and Texas Register*, January 23, 1836, San Felipe. This important document does not appear in *The Papers of the Texas Revolution, 1835-1836*. Historian Stephen L. Hardin located the document and shared it with this investigator.

3   Fernando de Leon and Charles Laso to Philip Dimmitt, December 18, 1835, Goliad, Box 2-9-19, Council Papers, TSL. Laso was Dimmitt's father-in-law.

4   Goliad Declaration, December 20, 1835, Goliad, Jenkins, ed., *Papers*, III: 266.

5   Hobart Huson, *Captain Philip Dimmitt's Commandancy of Goliad, 1835-1836* (Austin: Von Boeckman-Jones Co., 1974), 198.

6   "Detailed Report of the Names of those persons who volunteered and formed the first Division in the attack on San Antonio de Bexar and entered the House of La Garza on the morning of the 5th of December 1835 under the command of Col. B. R. Milam assisted by Major Morris," and "Detailed Report of Names of those persons who Volunteered and formed the Second Division in the Attack on San Antonio Bexar and entered the house of Berramander [*sic*] on the night of the 5th of Dec 1835 under Command of Col. F. W. Johnson assisted by Cols J. Grant & WT Austin Adjt N. R. Brister & Jno. Cameron," Texas Revolution Rolls, Box 401-714, Military Rolls Collection, TSL. Dimmitt's name does not appear on either roll.

7   Paul D. Lack, *The Texas Revolutionary Experience: A Political and Social History 1835-1836* (College Station: Texas A&M University Press, 1992), 58.

8   Goliad Declaration, December 20, 1836; Proceedings of General Council, January 3, 1836, Gammel, *The Laws of Texas*, I: 735-736. The federalist Council of Texas became quite disturbed over the Goliad declaration. They refused to allow it to be published in the Texas newspapers and declared that it had been "inconsiderately adopted – without designing to produce the consequence to the country inevitable upon its execution."

9   Chabot, *With The Makers*, 387. Charles A. Herff appears to have been the third son of Dr. Ferdinand von Herff, a German doctor who settled in San Antonio in 1850.

10 Ibid., 300. Peter Gallagher was a builder who was in San Antonio as early as 1841.

11 *San Antonio Express*, September 1, 1935.

12 Thomas Lloyd Miller, *Bounty and Donation Land Grants of Texas 1835-1888* (Austin and London: University of Texas Press, 1967), 163, 281, 742; Luis Castanon file and Peter Gallagher file, PC-TSL.

13 Jon Winfield Scott Dancy Diary, p. 29 and 31, Box 3N186, CAH. Mr. Smith appears to have been John W. Smith, who served as a guide for the Texians during the storming of Bexar in December 1835.

14 *Telegraph and Texas Register*, March 28, 1837. The ceremony took place on February 25, 1837.

15 Jesse Burnam file, OS Box 7, M&P- TSL; William B. Dewees & Benjamin Beeson Claim, August 23, 1848, M&P-TSL. The Dewees and Beeson properties at Columbus were also burned on orders from Sam Houston.

16 "Minutes of the Gonzales Ayuntamiento of 1835," found in a ledger titled "Deed Records," Box 2N242, Julia Lee Sinks Papers, CAH.

17 Gonzales Meeting, July 7, 1835, Jenkins, ed., *Papers*, I: 214-216; Edward Gritten to Domingo de Ugartechea, Gonzales, July 7, 1835, Jenkins, ed., *Papers*, I: 216; Domingo de Ugartechea to Alcalde, August 29, 1835, Bexar, Jenkins, ed., *Papers*, I: 376.

18 Alejo Perez Garcia statement, June 27, 1836, Matamoros, original in Operaciones, XL/481.3/1150, f. 33-34, *Archivo Historico of the Secretaria de la Defensa Nacional,* Mexico City. The photocopy used came from the Palo Alto Battlefield National Historic site in Brownsville. Special thanks to the staff at the location for their help in obtaining the photocopy.

19 Jose Enrique de la Pena, Campaign Diary, 13, Jose Enrique de la Pena Collection, CAH.

20 Pena, Campaign Diary, 15.

21 Pena, Campaign Diary, 21.

22 Memoir Manuscript, Quarto 38, Pena Collection.

23 Memoir Manuscript, Quarto 58.

24 Memoir Manuscript, Quarto 59.

25 Prologue letter, September 15, 2836, Pena Collection.

26 This investigator, Thomas Ricks Lindley, is not a certified document examiner. He, however, hired one—Ms. Lillian I. Hutchison, a court qualified professional, who examined the Woll/Pena document, the alleged Pena prologue letter, a number of pages from the Campaign Diary manuscript, and a number of pages from the memoir manuscript. Based on the differences in the handwriting, she concluded that the Woll/Pena letter and the Campaign Diary were written by the same person. She concluded that the prologue letter and the memoir manuscript were written by the same person, but that person was not the individual who wrote the Woll/Pena missive and the Campaign Diary. Thanks to Joe Musso, Bill Groneman, and Steve Harrigan for their contributions that helped me pay for Ms. Hutchison's professional handwriting analysis.

27 David B. Gracy II, "'Just As I Have Written It': A Study of the Authenticity of the Manuscript of Jose Enrique de la Pena's Account of the Texas Campaign," *Southwestern Historical Quarterly,* CV: 280-291.

28   Gracy, "'Just As I have Written It,'" 277.

29   The word count for each page was complied by professional Spanish translator Ned Brierly of Austin.

30   Joe Nickell, *Pen, Ink, & Evidence: A Study of Writing and Writing Materials for the Penman, Collector, and Document Detective* (Lexington: The University Press of Kentucky, 1990), 188-189.

31   Phone conversation with Dr. James Crisp, June 10, 2001.

32   Jose Enrique de la Pena to the President of Mexico, June 11, 1838, Item 487, Valentin Gomez Farias Collection, Nattie Lee Benson Latin American Collection, University of Texas, Austin, Texas.

33   Ibid.

34   Jose Enrique de la Pena to Editors, December 6, 1838, Guadalajara, *El Cosmopolita,* Mexico City, January 2, 1839.

35   Jose Enrique de la Pena Petition, March 6, 1839, Hospice of Guadalajara, Mexico, *El Cosmopolita*, Mexico City, October 12, 1839. Based on a second petition, dated June 6, 1839, from Durango, it appears the two petitions were sent to a district judge.

36   Jose Enrique de la Pena Petition, June 6, 1839, Durango, Mexico, *El Cosmopolita*, Mexico City, October 19, 1839.

37   Jose Enrique de la Pena to the Editors, October 7, 1839, House of the Holy Office, *El Cosmopolita,* Mexico City, October 12, 1839.

38   Campaign Diary, 21; Memoir Manuscript, Quarto 58.

39   Campaign Diary, 21.

40   Memoir Manuscript, Quarto 58.

41   Signatures A and B, Alejo Perez Garcia statement, June 27, 1836; Signature C, Jose Enrique de la Pena to Mariano Mando, September 15, 1836, Pena Collection, CAH; Signature D, Jose Enrique de la Pena declaration, December 14, 1836, volume 200, f. 210-213v, *Archivo de Guerra Groupo Documental, Archivo General de la Nacion,* Mexico City. Thanks to Jack Jackson for furnishing this investigator with a photocopy of signature D.

42   Meeting with Jack Jackson, August 22, 2002, Austin, Texas.

43   Pena Collection, CAH. The Campaign Diary. This manuscript also includes 38 endnotes. Notes 1-7 are embedded in the text of the Diary. Notes 8-38 were written as endnotes on six separate pages. The six pages of notes, however, are not archived with the Diary manuscript. They are misplaced in the larger Memoir manuscript. The notes are written in the authentic Pena handwriting, thus there is no doubt about their authenticity.

44   Gracy, "'Just As I Have Written It,'" 261.

45   *Lic. Lenero* to Commander-in-Chief, December 17, 1838, *El Cosmopolita,* Mexico City, January 2, 1839.

46 Groneman, *Defense of a Legend*, 36-37; Jose Bravo Ugarte, "La 'Resena y Diario de la Campana de Tejas' por el Teniente Coronel Jose Enrique de la Pena y su Primera Edicion (1955)," *Memorias De la Academia Mexicana De La Historia*, XVI, Mexico City. Groneman furnishes a complete review of the Memoir manuscript's provenance as it was known in 1994. Whereas, Ugarte, in his 1957 review of Sanchez Garza's Spanish language publication of the memoir manuscript, reports that the document came out of *La Lagunilla*, Mexico City's ancient flea market.

47 Pena, *With Santa Anna*, 54-55.

48 Interview with Don Finch, professional mortician, September 8, 2002; Bill Groneman, author of *Defense of a Legend: Crockett and the de la Pena Diary* and *Death of a Legend: The Myth and Mystery Surrounding the Death of Davy Crockett*, is the fireman I talked with about the burning of bodies.

49 Francisco Becerra account in Bill Groneman, *Eyewitness to the Alamo* (Plano: Republic of Texas Press, 1996), 92-93.

50 Moses Austin Bryan to Editors, August 24, 1873, Independence, *Galveston News*, date not given, found in *Texas Scrap-Book*, 169.

51 Dan Kilgore, *How Did Davy Die?* (College Station and London: Texas A&M University Press, 1978), 35; Groneman, *Eyewitness*, 93.

52 The quotation is from *The Academic American Encyclopedia*, on-line edition, Grolier Electronic Publishing, Danbury CT., 1991.

53 Jose Tamborrel interview, *The De La Pena Diary* (film), Brian Huberman, 2000, Brian Huberman interview with author, November 27, 2002

54 *The Morning Star* (Houston), Saturday, May 18, 1839. The poem first appeared in the *Red Lander*, San Augustine, Texas. Thanks to Jack Jackson for sharing this interesting research find with me.

Selected Bibliography

Archival Collections

Archives Division, Texas General Land Office, Austin, Texas
  Bounty and Donation Land Grant Records
  Character Certificate Records
  County Clerk Returns Records
  Court of Claims Records
  First Class Headright Land Grant Records
  Lost Book of Harris County
  GLO Land Grant Indexes
  Muster Rolls Book
  Republic of Texas Veteran Donation Grant Applications Collection
  Spanish Land Grant Index

Archives Division, Texas State Library, Austin, Texas
  Alamo Papers
  Alamo Strays
  Adjutant General Correspondence
  Army Papers
  Audited Military Claims Collection
  Audited Military Claims Ledger
  Department of State Papers
  Election Returns Collection
  General Land Office Correspondence
  Home Papers
  Houston, Andrew Jackson Papers
  Journal of the General Council
  Manuscript Collection
  McArdle's *Alamo Scrapbook*
  Memorials and Petitions Collection
  Military Warrant Ledger
  Miller, Washington D. Papers
  Muster Rolls Collection

Nacogdoches Archives
Ordnance Records
Permanent Council Records
Proceedings of the General Council
Public Debt Claims Collection
Quarter Master Records
Republic of Texas Claims Index
Republic of Texas Pension Collection
State Law Library
Unpaid Claims Collection

Center for American History, University of Texas at Austin
Adriance, John Papers
Austin, Stephen F. Papers
Barrett, Don Carlos Papers
Bexar Archives
Blake, R. B. Papers
Blake, R. B. Transcriptions
Burnet, David Gouverneur Papers
Dancy, John Winfield Scott Diary
De La Pena, Jose Enrique Collection
Dimmitt, Philip Morning Report Papers
Fontaine, W. W. Papers
Ford, John S. Papers
Holley, Mary Austin Papers
Raguet, Henry Papers
Sinks, Julia Lee Papers
Smith, Henry Papers
Texas Veterans Association Papers
Williams, Amelia W. Papers

Daughters of the Republic of Texas Library, Alamo, San Antonio, Texas
Alamo Defenders Files
Ewing, Finley Jr. Papers
Gentilz Collection
Neill, James C. Papers
"The Revealing of Dr. John Sutherland," Unpublished manuscript

East Texas Research Center, Stephen F. Austin University, Nacogdoches
Nacogdoches County Records

Gonzales County Archives
Probate Records

Liberty County Archives
Deed Records

Montgomery County Archives
Deed Records

Nacogdoches County Archives
Final Record Book A

Rosenberg Library, Galveston, Texas
Samuel May Williams Papers

Somervell County Archives
Deed Records

Washington County Archives
Probate Records

Archivo General de la Nacion, Mexico City
Archivo de Guerra Group Documental
Military Reports by Various Officers

Archivo Historico Mexicano Militar, Mexico City
Expediente XI/481.3/1655

Archivo Historico of Secretaria de la Defensa National, Mexico City
Military Service Records
Cancelados (Military Service) Records

Secretaria de Relaciones Exteriares, Mexico City
Tomo 6

Published Primary Materials

Books and Pamphlets

Andrade, Juan Jose. *DOCUMENTO QUE EL GENERAL ANDRADE Publica sobre la evacucion de la ciudad de San Antonio de Bejar, de Departamento de Tejas, A SUS COMPATRIOTAS.* Monterey, Mexico: 1836.

Baker, Clinton De Witt, ed. *A Texas Scrap-Book.* New York and New Orleans: A. S. Barnes & Company, 1875.

Barnard, J. H. *Dr. J. H. Barnard's Journal.* Goliad: *The Goliad Advance,* 1912.

Breeden, James O., ed. *A Long Ride in Texas: The Explorations of John Leonard Riddell.* College Station: Texas A&M University Press, 1994.

Brinkley, William C., ed. *Official Correspondence of the Texian Revolution, 1835-1836.* 2 vols. New York and London: D. Appleton-Century Company Incorporated, 1936.

Burnet, D. G. *Review of the Life of Gen. Sam Houston.* Galveston: News Power Press Print, 1852.

Borroel, Roger, ed. and translator. *The Papers of Lieutenant Colonel Jose Enrique de la Pena, Selected Appendixes from His Diary, 1836-1839.* East Chicago: La Villita Publications, 1997.

_____. *The Papers of Lieutenant Colonel Jose Enrique de la Pena, The Last of His Appendixes.* 2 vols. East Chicago: La Villita Publications, 1997.

_____. *The Itineraries of the Zapadores and San Luis Battalions During the Texas War of 1836.* East Chicago: La Villita Publications, 1999.

Caro, Ramon Martinez. "Verdadera Idea De La Primera Campana De Texas Y Sucesos Ocurridos Despues De La Accion De San Jacinto." In *The Mexican Side of the Texas Revolution.* Carlos E. Castaneda, translator and editor. 1928. Reprint, Austin and Dallas: Graphic Ideas Incorporated, 1970.

Coleman, Robert M. *Houston Displayed, or Who Won the Battle of San Jacinto By a Farmer In the Army.* Velasco: Press of the Velasco Herald, 1837.

Crockett, David. *The Life of David Crockett: The Original Humorist and Irrepressible Backwoodsman.* New York: A. L. Burt Company, 1902.

Day, James M., compiler. *The Texas Almanac 1857-1873: A Compendium of Texas History.* Waco: Texian Press, 1967.

De la Teja, Jesus F., ed. *A Revolution Remembered: The Memoirs and Selected Correspondence of Juan N. Seguin*. Austin: State House Press, 1991.

De la Pena, Jose Enrique. *La Rebelion De Texas: Manuscrito inedito de 1836 Por Un Oficial de Santa Anna*. J. Sanchez Garza, ed. Mexico City: A. Frank de Sanchez, 1955.

_____. *With Santa Anna in Texas: A Personal Narrative of the Revolution*. Carmen Perry, ed. College Station: Texas A&M University Press, 1975.

Erath, Lucy A., ed. *The Battle of San Jacinto*. Houston: The Union National Bank, 1936.

Ericson, Carolyn Reeves. *Nacogdoches Headrights*. New Orleans: Polyanthos, 1977.

Filisola, Vicente. *Memoirs for the History of the War in Texas*. Wallace Woolsey, editor and translator. 2 vols. Austin: Eakin Press, 1986, 1987.

Gammel, H. P. N. *The Laws of Texas 1822-1897*. 10 vols. Austin: The Gammel Book Company, 1898.

General Laws of Texas. Austin: Austin State Printing Company, 1905.

Gray, William Fairfax. *From Virginia to Texas, 1835: Diary of Col. Wm. F. Gray, Giving Details of His Journey to Texas and Return in 1835-1836 and Second Journey to Texas in 1837*. 1909. Reprint, Houston: Fletcher Young Publishing Co., 1965.

Groneman, Bill. *Eyewitness to the Alamo*. Revised Edition. Plano: Republic of Texas Press, 2001.

Hill, George Alfred. *The Centennial Celebration of the Battle of San Jacinto*. Washington D.C.: U.S. Government Printing Office, 1936.

Huffines, Alan C. *Blood of Noble Men: The Alamo Siege & Battle*. Austin: Eakin Press, 1999.

Huneycutt, C. D., ed. *At The Alamo: The Memoirs of Capt. Navarro*. New London, N.C.: Gold Star Press, 1988.

Jenkins, John H., ed. *The Papers of the Texas Revolution, 1835-1836*. 10 vols. Austin: Presidial Press, 1973.

Jones, Dr. Anson. *Memoranda and Official Correspondence Relating to the Republic of Texas, its History and Annexation*. New York: D. Appleton & Co., 1859.

Lamar, Mirabeau Buonaparte. *The Papers of Mirabeau Buonaparte Lamar*. 6 vols. Edited by Charles A. Gulick, Katherine Elliot, Winnie

Allen, and Harriet Smither. Austin and New York: Pemberton Press, 1968.

Linn, John J. *Reminiscences of Fifty Years in Texas*. New York: D. & J. Sadlier & Co., 1886.

Matovina, Timothy M. *The Alamo Remembered: Tejano Accounts and Perspectives*. Austin: University of Texas Press, 1995.

Maverick, Samuel Augustus. *Notes on The Storming of Bexar: In the Close of 1835*. Frederick C. Chabot, ed. San Antonio: Frederick C. Chabot, 1942.

_____. *Samuel Maverick, Texan: 1803-1870*. Rena Maverick Green, ed. San Antonio: Rena Maverick Green, 1952.

Menchaca, Antonio. *Memoirs*. San Antonio: Yanaguana Society Publications, 1937.

Miller, Thomas Lloyd. *Bounty and Donation Land Grants of Texas 1835-1888*. Austin and London: University of Texas Press, 1967.

Sanchez-Navarro, Carlos. *La Guerra de Tejas: Memorias de un Soldado*. Mexico: Editoral Polis, 1938.

Santa Anna, Antonio Lopez de. "Manifesto Relative to His Operations in Texas Campaign and His Capture." In *The Mexican Side of the Texas Revolution*. Carlos E. Castaneda, translator and editor. 1928. Reprint, Austin and Dallas: Graphic Ideas Incorporated, 1970.

Seguin, Juan N. *Personal Memoirs of John N. Seguin, From the Year 1834 to the Retreat of General Woll From the City of San Antonio, 1842*. San Antonio: Ledger Book and Job Office, 1858.

Sherman, Sidney. *Defense of Gen. Sidney Sherman Against the Charges Made by Gen. Sam Houston in His Speech Delivered in the United States Senate, February 28th, 1859*. Galveston: "News" Book and Job Office, 1859.

Smith, Richard Penn. *Col. Crockett's Exploits and Adventures in Texas*. 1836. Reprint, New York: Nafis & Cornish, Philadelphia: John B. Perry, 1845.

Smithwick, Noah. *The Evolution of a State; or, Recollections of Old Texas Days*. Compiled by Nanna Smithwick Donaldson. 1900. Reprint, Austin: University of Texas Press, 1983.

Sowell, Andrew Jackson. *Rangers and Pioneers of Texas*. 1884. Reprint, New York: Argosy-Antiquarian, Ltd., 1964.

_____. *Early Settlers and Indian Fighters of Southwest Texas*. Austin: Ben C. Jones and Company, 1900.

Swisher, John M. *The Swisher Memoirs*. San Antonio: The Sigmond Press, 1932.

Sutherland, John. *The Fall of The Alamo*. Annie B. Sutherland, ed. San Antonio: The Naylor Company, 1936.

Urrea, Jose C. *Diario De Las Operaciones Militares De la Division Que Al Mando Del General Jose Urrea Hizo La Campana De Tejas*. Victoria de Durango, Mexico: Imprenta Del Gobierno & Cargo de Manual Gonzalez, 1838.

Williams, Amelia W. and Eugene C. Barker, eds. *The Writings of Sam Houston, 1813-1863*. 1938-1943. Reprint, 8 vols. Austin and New York: Pemberton Press, 1970.

Zuber, William Physick. *My Eighty Years in Texas*. Janis Boyle Mayfield, ed. Austin and London: University of Texas Press, 1971.

Articles

Alsbury, Samuel E. "The Private Journal of Juan Nepomuceno Almonte February 1-April 16, 1836." *Southwestern Historical Quarterly*, XLVIII.

Austin, Stephen F. "General Austin's Order Book for the Campaign of 1835." *The Quarterly of the Texas State Historical Association*, II.

Austin, William T. "Account of the Campaign of 1835 by William T. Austin, Aide to Gen. Stephen F. Austin & Gen. Ed. Burleson." *Texana*, IV.

Barker, Eugene C. "J. H. Kuykendall's Recollections of the [San Jacinto] Campaign." *The Quarterly of the Texas State Historical Association*, IV.

Beerstecher, Ernest, Jr. "Historical Probate Extracts." *Texana*, VII and VIII.

Erath, Lucy A. "Memoirs of Major George Bernard Erath." *Southwestern Historical Quarterly*, XXVI.

Ford, John S. "The Fall of the Alamo." *Texas Mute Ranger*, April 1882.

Henning et al. v. Wren et al., Court of Civil Appeals of Texas, May 27, 1903. *Southwestern Reporter*, Vol. 75.

Horton, Alexander. "The Life of A. Horton and Early Settlement of San Augustine County." *The Quarterly of the Texas State Historical Association*, XIV.

Miller A. S. et al. v. Mary S. Rogers. *Texas Reporter*, XLIX.

Ruiz, Francisco. "Fall of the Alamo and Massacre of Travis and His Brave Associates." *The Texas Almanac for 1860*. Galveston: The Galveston News, 1860.

Secondary Materials

Books

Barr, Alwyn. *Texans In Revolt: The Battle for San Antonio, 1835*. Austin: University of Texas Press, 1990.

Barzun, Jacques. *From Dawn to Decadence*. New York: Harper Collins Publishers, 2000.

Bowman, Bob and Doris. *The Search for an Alamo Soldier*. Lufkin: Best of East Texas Publishers, 1997.

Brown, John Henry. *Indian Wars and Pioneers of Texas*. Austin: L. E. Daniel, 1896.

Chabot, Frederick C. *The Alamo: Mission, Fortress and Shrine*. San Antonio: Frederick C. Chabot, 1941.

_____. *With The Makers of San Antonio*. San Antonio: Artes Graficas, 1937.

Crook, Elizabeth. *Promised Lands: A Novel of the Texas Rebellion*. New York: Doubleday, 1994.

Davis, William C. *Three Roads to the Alamo: The Lives and Fortunes of David Crockett, James Bowie, and William Barret Travis*. New York: Harper Collins Publishers, 1998.

De Bruhl, Marshall. *Sword of San Jacinto: A Life of Sam Houston*. New York: Random House, 1993.

Derr, Mark. *The Frontiersman: The Real Life and the Many Legends of Davy Crockett*. New York: William Morrow and Company, Inc., 1993.

De Zavala, Adina. *The Alamo: Where the Last Man Died*. San Antonio: The Naylor Company, 1905.

Dobie, J. Frank, Mody C. Boatright, Harry H. Ransom. *In the Shadow of History*. 1939. Reprint, Dallas: Southern Methodist University Press, 1980.

Edmondson, J. R. *The Alamo Story: From Early History to Current Conflicts*. Plano: Republic of Texas Press, 2000.

Foote, Henry Stuart. *Texas and The Texians; or Advance of the Anglo-Americans to the Southwest Including a History of Leading Events in Mexico, From the Conquest of Fernando Cortes to the Termination of the Texas Revolution*. 2 vols. Philadelphia: Thomas, Cowperthwait & Co., 1841.

Goldfield, David R. *Promised Land: The South Since 1945*. Arlington Heights, Ill.: Harlan Davidson, 1987.

Groneman, Bill. *Alamo Defenders A Genealogy: The People and Their Words*. Austin: Eakin Press, 1990.

_____. *Defense of a Legend: Crockett and the de la Pena Diary*. Plano: Republic of Texas Press, 1994.

_____. *Eyewitness to the Alamo*. Revised edition. Plano: Republic of Texas Press, 2001.

Hackworth, David H. *About Face: The Odyssey of an American Warrior*. New York, London, Toronto, Sydney, Tokyo: Simon and Schuster, 1989.

Haley, James L. *Sam Houston*. Norman: University of Oklahoma Press, 2002.

Hardin, Stephen L. *Texian Iliad: A Military History of the Texas Revolution, 1835-1836*. Austin: University of Texas Press, 1994.

Hebert, Rachel Bluntzer. *The Forgotten Colony: San Patricio de Hibernia*. Burnet, Texas: Eakin Press, 1965.

Huson, Hobart. *Captain Philip Dimmitt's Commandancy of Goliad, 1835-1836*. Austin: Von Boeckman-Jones Co., 1974.

James, Marquis. *The Raven: A Biography of Sam Houston*. New York: Book-of-the-Month Club, Inc., 1990.

Jenkins, John H., ed. *Basic Texas Books*. Austin: Texas State Historical, 1988.

Kemp, Louis Wiltz. *The Signers of the Texas Declaration of Independence*. Houston: Anson Jones Press, 1944.

Kerr, Rita. *The Immortal 32*. Austin: Eakin Press, 1986.

Kesselus, Kenneth. *Bastrop County Before Statehood*. Austin: Jenkins Publishing Company, 1986.

Kilgore, Dan. *How Did Davy Die?* College Station: Texas A&M University Press, 1978.

Lack, Paul D. *The Texas Revolutionary Experience: A Political and Social History 1835-1836*. College Station: Texas A&M University Press, 1992.

Lamego, Miguel A. Sanchez. *Apuntes Para la Historia Del Arma De Ingenieros En Mexico: Historia De Batalion De Zapadore*. Mexico City: Secretaria de la Defensa Nacional, 1943.

Lind, Michael. *The Alamo*. New York and Boston: Houghton Mifflin Company, 1997.

Long, Jeff. *Duel of Eagles*. New York: William Morrow and Company, Inc., 1990.

_____. *Empire of Bones.* New York: William Morrow and Company, Inc., 1993.

Lord, Walter. *A Time To Stand.* 1961. Reprint, New York: Bonanza Books, 1987.

Mailer, Norman. *Oswald's Tale: An American Mystery.* New York: Random House, 1995.

Maberry, Robert, Jr. *Texas Flags.* College Station: Texas A&M University Press, 2001.

Miller, Thomas Lloyd. *The Public Lands of Texas 1519-1970.* Norman: University of Oklahoma Press, 1972.

Morphis, J. M. *History of Texas, From its Discovery and Settlement.* New York: United States Publishing Company, 1874.

Myers, Albert Cook. *Immigration of the Irish Quakers into Pennsylvania 1682-1750.* 1902. Reprint, Baltimore: Genealogical Publishing Company, 1985.

Nickell, Joe. *Pen, Ink, & Evidence: A Study of Writing and Writing Materials for the Penman, Collector, and Document Detective.* Lexington: The University Press of Kentucky, 1990.

Nixon, Pat Ireland. *The Medical Story of Early Texas.* Lancaster: Mollie Bennett Lupe Memorial Fund, 1946.

Oates, Stephen B., ed. *The Republic of Texas, by the editors of the American West and the Texas State Historical Association.* Palo Alto, California: American West Publishing Company, 1968.

Pennybacker, Anna M. J. *A New History of Texas for Schools.* Palestine: Percy V. Pennybacker, 1895.

Phillips, General T. R., ed. *Roots of Strategy.* Harrisburg, Penn.: Stackpole Books, 1985.

Ramondino, Salvatore, ed. *The New World Spanish/English English/Spanish Dictionary.* New York: Penguin Reference, 1996.

Roberts, Randy and James S. Olson. *A Line in the Sand: The Alamo in Blood and Memory.* New York, London, Toronto, Sidney, Singapore: The Free Press, 2001.

Samuels, Nancy Timmons and Barbara Roach Knox, compilers. *Old Northwest Texas: Historical–Statistical–Biographical.* For Worth: Fort Worth Genealogical Society, 1980.

Santos, Richard G. *Santa Anna's Campaign Against Texas, 1835-1836.* Waco: Texian Press, 1968.

Schoewer, Susan Prendergast with Tom W. Glaser. Introduction by Paul Hutton. *Alamo Images*. Dallas: DeGolyer Library and Southern Methodist University Press, 1985.

Speer, William S. and John Henry Brown, eds. *The Encyclopedia of the New West*. Marshall, Texas: The United States Biographical Publishing Company, 1881.

Stevens, Walter B. *Through Texas – A Series of Interesting Letters*. St. Louis: St. Louis Globe-Democrat, 1892.

Templeton, Frank. *Margaret Ballentine or The Fall of the Alamo*. Houston: State Printing Company, 1907.

Tinkle, Lon. *13 Days to Glory: The Siege of the Alamo*. New York, Toronto, London: McGraw-Hill Book Company, 1958.

Tijerina, Andres. *Tejanos & Texas Under the Mexican Flag, 1821-1836*. College Station: Texas A&M University Press, 1994.

Tyler, Ron, Douglas E. Barnett, Roy R. Barkley, Penelope C. Anderson, Mark F. Odintz, eds. *The New Handbook of Texas*. 6 vols. Austin: Texas State Historical Association, 1996.

Todish, Tim J. and Terry S. Todish, *Alamo Sourcebook 1836: A Comprehensive Guide to the Alamo and the Texas Revolution*. Austin: Eakin Press, 1998.

Webb, Walter Prescott, H. Bailey Carroll, and Eldon Stephen Branda, eds. *The Handbook of Texas*. 3 vols. Austin: Texas State Historical Association, 1952 and 1976.

Yoakum, Henderson. *History of Texas From its First Settlement in 1655 to its Annexation to the United States in 1846*. 2 vols. New York: Redfield, 1855.

Young, Kevin R. *Texas Forgotten Heroes*. Goliad: Goliad County Historical Commission, 1986.

Articles

Barnes, Charles Merritt, "The Alamo's Only Survivor," *San Antonio Express*, May 12 and 19, 1907.

Bennett, Miles S. "The Battle of Gonzales, the 'Lexington' of the Texas Revolution." *The Quarterly of the Texas State Historical Association*, II.

Brewer, Thomas B. "The 'Old Department' of History at the University of Texas, 1910-1951." *Southwestern Historical Quarterly*, LXX.

Bonham, Milledge, Jr. "James Butler Bonham: A Consistent Rebel." *Southwestern Historical Quarterly*, XXXV.

Crisp, James E. "In Pursuit of Herman Ehrenberg: A Research Adventure." *Southwestern Historical Quarterly*, CII.

Costeloe, Michael P. "The Mexican Press of 1836 and the Battle of the Alamo." *Southwestern Historical Quarterly*, XCI.

Davis, William C. "How Davy Probably Didn't Die." *Journal of the Alamo Battlefield Association*, Fall, 1997.

Elliott, Claude. "Book Reviews." *Southwestern Historical Quarterly*, XLIII.

Green, Michael R. "To The People of Texas & All Americans in The World." *Southwestern Historical Quarterly*, XCI.

Gracy, David B. II. "'Just As I Have Written It': A Study of the Authenticity of the Manuscript of Jose Enrique de la Pena's Account of the Texas Campaign." *Southwestern Historical Quarterly*, CV.

Hunnicutt, Helen. "A Mexican View of the Texas War." *The Library Chronicle of The University of Texas*, IV.

Irvine, Laura J. "Sketch of Guadalupe County." *American Sketch Book*. Austin: Sketch Book Publishing House, 1882.

Ivey, Jake. "Another Look At Storming the Alamo Walls." *The Alamo Journal*, Number 120.

Kellman, Steven G. "The Yellow Rose of Texas." *Journal of American Culture*, Vol. 2.

Lindley, Thomas Ricks. "James Butler Bonham: October 17, 1835-March 6, 1836." *The Alamo Journal*, August 1988.

_____. "Alamo Artillery: Number, Type, Caliber, and Concussion." *The Alamo Journal*, July 1992.

_____. "Drawing Truthful Deductions," *Journal of the Alamo Battlefield Association*, September 1994.

_____. "Storming the Alamo Walls." *The Alamo Journal*, June 2000.

_____. "At the Alamo Walls Again." *The Alamo Journal*, December 2000.

Miller, Thomas Lloyd. "Mexican-Texas at the Alamo." *The Journal of Mexican American History*, II.

Potter, R. M. "The Fall of The Alamo." *Magazine of American History*, January 1878.

Powell, J. S. "A Biographical Sketch Mr. and Mrs. J. H. Powell." Seguin, Texas: Ms. Bette Whitley, 1989. Unpublished.

Rather, Ethel Zively. "De Witt's Colony." *The Quarterly of the Texas State Historical Association*, VIII.

Schoelwer, Susan Prendergast. "The Artist's Alamo: A Reappraisal of Pictorial Evidence, 1836-1850." *Southwestern Historical Quarterly,* LCI.

Ugarte, Jose Bravo. "La 'Resena y Diario de la Campana de Tejas' por el Teniente Coronel Jose Enrique de la Pena y su Primera Edicion." *Memorias de la Academia Mexicana de la Historia,* XVI.

Williams, Amelia W. "A Critical Study of the Siege of the Alamo and of the Personnel of Its Defenders." *Southwestern Historical Quarterly,* XXXVI and XXXVII.

Winston, James E. "Pennsylvania and the Independence of Texas." *Southwestern Historical Quarterly,* XVIII.

Zuber, W. P. "An Escape From the Alamo." *The Texas Almanac for 1873.* Galveston: The Galveston News, 1873.

_____. "The Escape of Rose From the Alamo." *The Quarterly of the Texas State Historical Association,* V.

_____. "Last Messenger from the Alamo." *The Quarterly of the Texas State Historical Association,* V.

_____. "Rose's Escape From the Alamo." *The Quarterly of the Texas State Historical Association,* VI.

Theses and Dissertations

Mixon, Ruby. "William Barret Travis, His Life and Letters." M. A. thesis, University of Texas at Austin, 1930.

Bartholomae, Edgar William. "A Translation of H. Ehrenberg's *Fahrten und Schicksale eines Deutschen in Texas,* with Introduction and Notes." M. A. thesis, University of Texas at Austin, 1925.

Newspapers

Arkansas Gazette (Little Rock)
The Advocate (Little Rock)
Austin-American Statesman
The Dallas Morning News
Dallas News
El Cosmopolita (Mexico City)
El Mosquito Mexicano (Mexico City)

El Nacional (Mexico City)
Frankfort [Kentucky] *Commonwealth*
Gonzales Inquirer
Houston Chronicle
The Morning Star (Houston)
Red River Herald (Clarksville, Texas)
San Antonio Evening News
San Antonio Express-News
San Antonio Light
Telegraph and Texas Register (San Felipe, Texas)
Wichita Times (Wichita Falls)

Films - Video Tapes

Huberman, Brian. *The De La Pena Diary*, Public Broadcasting System, 2000.

Index